LEARNING MAYA
FOUNDATION

LEARNING MAYA | FOUNDATION

Credits:

Roark Andrade, Deion Green, Bob Gundu, David Haapalehto, Alan Harris, Rachael Jackson, Danielle Lamothe, Julio Lopez, Carla Sharkey, Michael Stamler, Marcus Tateishi

Special Thanks:

Tim H. Brown, Don Chong, Steve Christov, Bruce Darrell, Haskell Friedman, Dallas Good, Ronald Halabi, Steve Hinan, Lincoln Holme, Jill Jacob, Lisa Kelly, Robert MacGregor, Robert Magee, Scyalla Magloir, Tim McIlravey, Eli Miller, Cory Mogk, Remko Noteboom, Alan Opler, Matt Payne, Amber Reddin, Aki Ross, Lorna Saunders, Jason Ungerman, Israel Yang

Printed in Canada.

ALIAS | WAVEFRONT
EDUCATION

CONTENTS

CONTENTS

CONTENTS

CONTENTS

INTRODUCTION

Learning Maya I Foundation

Maya is a character animation and visual effects system designed for the professional animator. Built on a procedural architecture called the *Dependency graph*, Maya offers incredible power and flexibility for generating digital images of animated characters and scenes.

This tutorial book gives you hands-on experience with Maya as you complete a series of project-focused lessons. In each project, you will model, animate, texture map, add visual effects and render.

Shown below are the five projects that you will be animating as you complete this book:

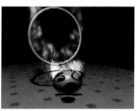

Project One: Bouncing Ball

Project Two: Jack-in-the-box

Project Three: Space Battle

Project Four: Primitive Man

Project Five: Salty the Seal

How to use this book

How you use this book will depend on your experience with computer graphics and 3D animation. This book moves at a fast pace and is designed to help both the novice and the expert as outlined below:

Novice - If this is your first experience with 3D software, we suggest that you glance over each lesson before you complete it. This will give you a better understanding of what is going to happen before you tackle the software directly.

Intermediate - If you are already familiar with the world of 3D animation, you can dive in and complete the lessons as written. You may want to keep the *Using Maya* manual handy to help give you a more complete understanding of each tool.

Expert - Experts can run through the exercises in this book at a quicker pace. The location of Maya's tools and the terminology surrounding its use will be the most helpful aspect of this book for experts.

What you should already know

This book assumes that you have some experience with computers and computer graphics. Basic skills such as how to use a three button mouse and the keyboard are essential. Some familiarity with using a computer to draw, paint or model would help.

IRIX®, Windows, and Macintosh

This book is written to cover IRIX, Windows, and Macintosh platforms. Graphics and text have been modified where applicable. You may notice that your screen varies slightly from the illustrations depending on the platform you are using.

Things to watch for:

Window focus may differ. For example, if you are on Windows, you have to click in the panels with your middle mouse button to make it active.

To select multiple attributes in Windows, use the **Ctrl** key. On Macintosh, use the **Command** key. To modify pivot position in Windows, use the **Insert** key. On Macintosh, use the **Home** key.

Maya packaging

This book can be used with either **Maya Complete™**, **Maya Unlimited™**, or **Maya Personal Learning Edition™**. Its focus is on functionality that is shared between the three packages. These include all the tools necessary for modeling, animating and rendering a scene, as well as particle and dynamic effects.

Learning Maya DVD-ROM

At the back of this book you will find the Learning Maya DVD-ROM containing support files, tutorial movies and 4 hours of instructor-led overviews to guide you through the lessons in this book.

Also included on the DVD-ROM is the Learning Maya | Beginner's Guide - a one hour overview which will allow you to get your feet wet with some easy to follow lessons and provide you with the knowledge you need to start discovering the possibilities Maya can open to you. If you are new to 3D, It is recommended that you watch this DVD before proceeding with the Learning Maya book tutorials.

Installing Tutorial files - To install the tutorial scene files, copy the *support_files* directory from the DVD found at the back of this book.

You can also download these tutorial scene files from the Alias|Wavefront web site at:

www.aliaswavefront.com/maya/learningtools_updates/

Understanding Maya

To understand Maya, it helps to understand how Maya works at a conceptual level. This introduction is designed to give you the *story* about Maya. This means that the focus of this introduction will be on how different Maya concepts are woven together to create an integrated workspace.

While this book teaches you how to model, animate and render in Maya, these concepts are taught with a particular focus on how Maya's underlying architecture supports the creation of animated sequences.

You will soon learn how Maya's architecture can be explained using a single line – *nodes with attributes that are connected.* As you work through this book, the meaning of that statement becomes clearer and you will learn to appreciate how Maya's interface lets you focus on the act of creation, while giving you access to the power inherent in the underlying architecture.

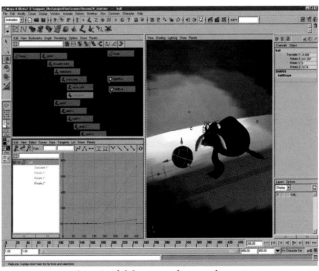

A typical Maya workspace layout

The user interface

The Maya user interface includes a number of tools, editors and controls. You can access these using the main menus or using special context-sensitive marking menus. You can also use *shelves* to store important icons or hotkeys to speed up workflow. Maya is designed to let you configure the user interface as you see fit.

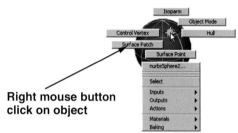

Right mouse button click on object

Marking menu

To work with objects, you can enter values using coordinate entry or you can use more interactive 3D manipulators. Manipulator handles let you edit your objects with a simple click-drag.

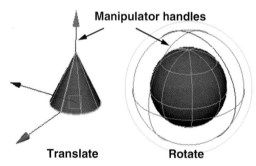

Manipulator handles

Translate   **Rotate**

Maya manipulators

Maya's user interface supports multiple levels of *undo* and *redo* and includes a drag-and-drop paradigm for accessing many parts of the workspace.

Working in 3D

In Maya, you will build and animate objects in three dimensions. These dimensions are defined by the cardinal axes which are labeled as X, Y and Z. These represent the length (X), height (Y) and depth (Z) of your scene. These axes are represented by colors – red for X, green for Y and blue for Z.

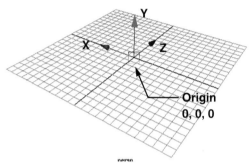

Origin
0, 0, 0

The cardinal axes

In Maya, the Y-axis is pointing up which is also referred to as *Y-up*.

As you position, scale and rotate your objects, these three axes will serve as your main points of reference. The center of this coordinate system is called the origin and has a value of 0, 0, 0.

UV coordinate space

As you build surfaces in Maya, they are created with their own coordinate space that is define by U in one direction and V in another. You can use these coordinates when you are working with *curve on surface* objects or when you are positioning textures on a surface.

One corner of the surface acts as the origin of the system and all coordinates lie directly on the surface.

You can make surfaces *live* in order to work directly in the UV coordinate space. You will also encounter U and V attributes when you place textures onto surfaces.

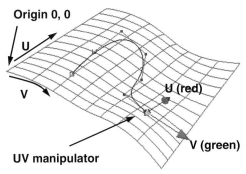

UV coordinates on a live surface

Views

In Maya, you visualize your scenes using view panels that let you see into the 3D world.

Perspective views let you see your scene as if you were looking at it with your own eyes or through the lens of a camera.

Orthographic views are parallel to the scene and offer a more objective view. They focus on two axes at a time and are referred to as the *Top*, *Side* and *Front* views.

In many cases, you will require several views to help you define the proper location of your objects. An object's position that looks good in the Top view may not make sense in a Side view. Maya lets you view multiple views at one time to help coordinate what you see.

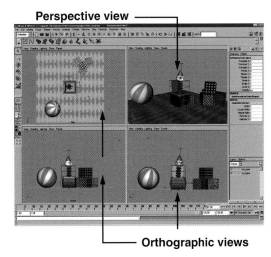

Orthographic and Perspective views

Cameras

To achieve a particular view, you look through a digital camera. An orthographic camera defines the view using a parallel plane and a direction while a perspective camera uses an *eye point*, a *look at point* and a *focal length*.

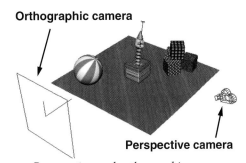

Perspective and orthographic cameras

Image planes

When you work with cameras, it is possible to place special backdrop objects called *image planes* onto the camera. An image plane can be placed onto the camera so that as the camera moves, the plane stays aligned.

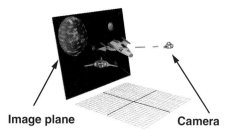

Image plane   **Camera**

Image plane attached to a camera

The image plane has several attributes that allow you to track and scale the image. These attributes can be animated to give the appearance that the plane is moving.

Image plane seen looking through the camera

THE DEPENDENCY GRAPH

Maya's system architecture uses a procedural paradigm that lets you integrate traditional keyframe animation, inverse kinematics, dynamics and scripting on top of a node-based architecture that is called the **Dependency graph**. If you wanted to reduce this graph to its bare essentials, you could describe it as *nodes with attributes that are connected*. This node-based architecture gives Maya its flexible procedural qualities.

Below is a diagram showing a primitive sphere's Dependency graph. A procedural input node

defines the shape of the sphere by connecting attributes on each node.

Node

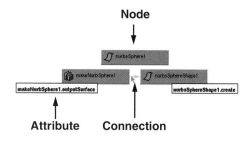

Attribute   **Connection**

The Dependency graph

Nodes

Every element in Maya, whether it is a curve, surface, deformer, light, texture, expression, modeling operation or animation curve, is described by either a single node or a series of connected nodes.

A *node* is a generic object type in Maya. Different nodes are designed with specific attributes so that the node can accomplish a specific task. Nodes define all object types in Maya including geometry, shading, and lighting.

Shown below are three typical node types as they appear on a primitive sphere.

Transform node

Input node   **Shape node**

Node types on a sphere

Transform node - Transform nodes contain positioning information for your objects. When you move, rotate or scale, this is the node you are affecting.

Input node - The input node represents options that drive the creation of your sphere's shape such as radius or endsweep.

Shape node - The shape node contains all the component information that represents the actual look of the sphere.

Maya's user interface presents these nodes to you in many ways. Below is an image of the Channel box where you can edit and animate node attributes.

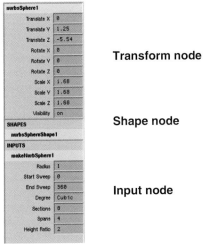

Channel box

Transform node

Shape node

Input node

Attributes

Each node is defined by a series of attributes that relate to what the node is designed to accomplish. In the case of a transform node, *X Translate* is an attribute. In the case of a shader node, *Color Red* is an attribute. It is possible for you to assign values to the attributes. You can work with attributes in a number of user-interface windows including the *Attribute Editor*, the *Channel box* and the *Spread Sheet Editor*.

Node tabs

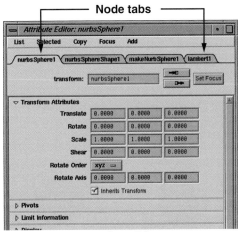

Attribute Editor

One important feature in Maya is that you can animate virtually every attribute on any node. This helps give Maya its animation power. You should note that attributes are also referred to as *channels*.

Connections

Nodes don't exist in isolation. A finished animation results when you begin making connections between attributes on different nodes. These connections are also known as *dependencies*. In modeling, these connections are sometimes referred to as *construction history*.

Most of these connections are created automatically by the Maya user-interface as a result of using commands or tools. If you desire, you can also build and edit these connections explicitly using the *Connection editor*, by entering MEL™ (Maya Embedded Language) commands, or by writing MEL-based expressions.

Pivots

Transform nodes are all built with a special component known as the pivot point. Just like your arm pivots around your elbow, the pivot helps you rotate a transform node. By changing the location of the pivot point, you get different results.

Pivots are basically the stationary point from which you rotate or scale objects. When animating, you sometimes need to build hierarchies where one transform node rotates the object and a second transform node scales. Each node can have its own pivot location to help you get the effect you want.

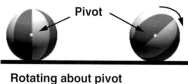

Rotating about pivot

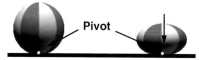

Scaling about pivot

Rotation and scaling pivots

Hierarchies

When you are building scenes in Maya, you have learned that you can build dependency connections to link node attributes. When working with transform nodes or joint nodes, you can also build hierarchies which create a different kind of relationship between your objects.

In a hierarchy, one transform node is *parented* to another. When Maya works with these nodes, Maya looks first at the top node, or *root* node, then down the hierarchy. Therefore, motion from the upper nodes is transferred down into the lower nodes. In the diagram below, if the *group1* node is rotated, then the two lower nodes will rotate with it. If the *nurbsCone* node is rotated, the upper nodes are not affected.

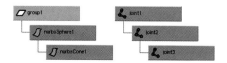

Object and joint hierarchy nodes

Joint hierarchies are used when you are building characters. When you create joints, the joint pivots act as limb joints while bones are drawn between them to help visualize the joint chain. By default, these hierarchies work just like object hierarchies. Rotating one node rotates all of the lower nodes at the same time.

You will learn more about joint hierarchies later in this introduction where you will also learn how *inverse kinematics* can reverse the flow of the hierarchy.

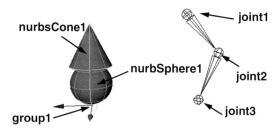

Object and joint hierarchies

MEL scripting

MEL stands for Maya Embedded Language. In Maya, every time you use a tool or open a window, you are using MEL. MEL can be used to execute simple commands, write expressions or build scripts that will extend Maya's existing functionality.

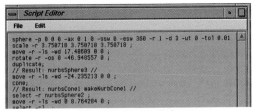

The Irix Script Editor

MEL is the perfect tool for technical directors who are looking for easy access to customizing how Maya works to suit the needs of a particular production environment. Animators can also use MEL to create simple macros that will help speed up more difficult or tedious workflows.

ANIMATING IN MAYA

When you animate, you bring objects to life. In Maya, there are several different ways in which you can animate your scenes and the characters who inhabit them.

Animation in Maya is generally measured using frames that mimic the frames you would find on a film reel. You can play these frames at different speeds to achieve an animated effect. By default, Maya plays at 24 frames for every second.

Keyframe animation

The most familiar method of animating is called *keyframe animation*. Using this technique, you determine how you want the parts of your objects to look at a particular frame, then you save the important attributes as keys. After you set several keys, the animation can be played back with Maya filling motion in between the keys.

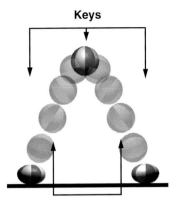

Keys

In-between frames

Keys and in-between frames

When keys are set on a particular attribute, the keyed values are stored in special nodes called *animation curves* nodes.

These curves are defined by the keys which map the value of the attribute against time. The following is an example of several animation curve nodes connected to a transformation node. One node is created for every attribute that is animated.

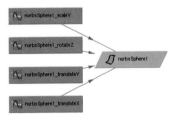

Dependency graph showing curve nodes

Once you have a curve, you can begin to control the tangency at each key to determine the quality of the motion in between the main keys. You can make your objects speed up or slow down by editing the shape of these animation curves.

Generally, the slope of the graph curve tells you the speed of the motion. A steep slope in the curve means fast motion while a flat curve means no motion. Think of a skier going down a hill. Steep slopes increase speed while flatter sections slow things down.

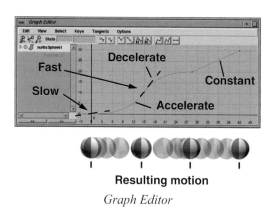

Graph Editor

Path animation

Path animation is already defined by its name. You can assign one or more objects so that they move along a path which has been drawn as a curve in 3D space. You can then use the shape of the curve and special path markers to edit and tweak the resulting motion.

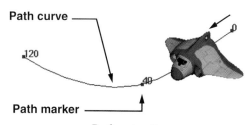

Path animation

Nonlinear Animation

Nonlinear Animation is a way to layer and mix character animation sequences nonlinearly -- independently of time. You can layer and blend any type of keyed animation, including motion

capture and path animation. This is accomplished through the Trax Editor.

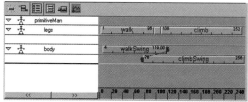

Trax Editor

Reactive animation

Reactive animation is a term used to describe animation in which one object's animation is based on the animation of another object.

An example of this technique would be moving gears where the rotation of one gear is linked to the rotation of other gears. You can then set keys on the first gear and all the others animate automatically. Later, when you want to edit or tweak the keys, only one object needs to be worked on and the others update reactively.

Diagram of animated gears

In Maya, you can set up reactive animation using a number of tools including those outlined below:

Set Driven Key

This tool lets you interactively set up an attribute on one object to drive one or more attributes onto another.

Expressions

Expressions are scripts that let you connect different attributes on different nodes.

Constraints

Constraints let you set up an object to *point at*, *orient to* or *look at* another object.

Connections

Attributes can be directly linked to another attribute using dependency node connections. You can create this kind of direct connection using the Connection Editor.

Dynamics

Another animation technique is *dynamics*. You can set up objects in your Maya scene that animate based on physical effects such as collisions, gravity and wind. You set up the different variables such as *bounciness, friction* or *initial velocity*. When you playback the scene, you run a simulation to see how all the parts react to the variables.

This technique gives you natural motion that would be difficult to keyframe. You can use dynamics with rigid body objects, particles or soft body objects.

Rigid body objects are objects that don't need to be deformed. You set up this kind of simulation by setting objects as either *active* or *passive rigid bodies*. Active bodies react to the dynamics, whereas passive bodies act only as colliding objects for active bodies.

To simulate effects such as wind or gravity, you use dynamic *fields* that are added to the scene then connected to your objects.

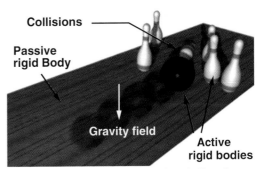

Rigid body simulation of bowling ball and pins

Particles are tiny points that can be used to create effects such as smoke, fire or explosions. These points are emitted into the scene where they are also affected by the dynamic fields.

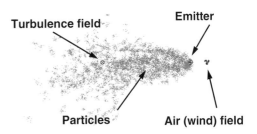

Particles

Soft bodies are surfaces that you want to deform during a simulation. To create a soft body, you will combine a surface with a series of particles. The particles react to the dynamic forces to help make the surface deform.

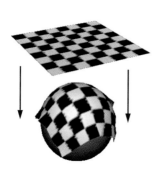

Soft bodies

MODELING IN MAYA

The objects you want to animate in Maya are usually built using either NURBS surfaces or polygonal meshes. Maya offers you both of these geometry types so that you can choose the method best suited for your work.

NURBS curves

NURBS stands for *non-uniform rational b-splines* which is a technical term for a spline curve. By modeling with NURBS curves, you can lay down control points and smooth geometry will be created using the points as guides.

Shown below is a typical NURBS curve with important parts labelled:

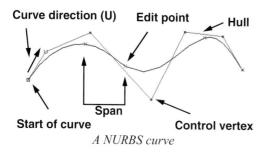

A NURBS curve

These key components define important aspects of how a curve works. The flexibility and power of NURBS geometry comes from your ability to edit the shape of the geometry using these controls.

As your geometry becomes more complex, you get more of these controls. For this reason, it is usually better to build using simpler geometry so that you can more easily control the shape. If you need more complex geometry, then controls can be inserted later.

NURBS surfaces

Surfaces are defined using the same mathematics as curves except now there are in two dimensions – U and V. You learned about this earlier when you learned about UV coordinate space.

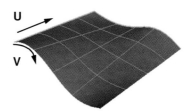

A NURBS surface

Below are some of the component elements of a typical NURBS surface:

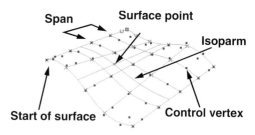

NURBS components

Complex shapes can be, in essence, sculpted using this surface type as you push and pull the controls to shape the surface.

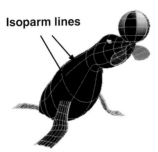

A completed NURBS model

A polygonal model before and after smoothing

Polygons

Polygons are another geometry type available in Maya. Whereas NURBS surfaces interpolate the shape of the geometry interactively, polygonal meshes draw the geometry directly to the control vertices. When a polygonal mesh is rendered, it is then interpolated to see a smoother form.

Below are some of the components found on a polygonal mesh:

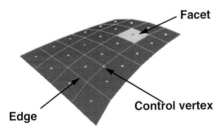

Polygon components

You can build up polymeshes by extruding, scaling and positioning polygonal facets to build shapes. You can then smooth the shape to get a more organic look for your model.

Construction history

When you create models in Maya, the various steps are recorded as dependency nodes that remain connected to your surface.

In the example below, a curve has been used to create a revolved surface. Maya keeps the history by creating dependencies between the curve, a revolve node and the shape node. Edits made to the curve or the revolve node will update the final shape.

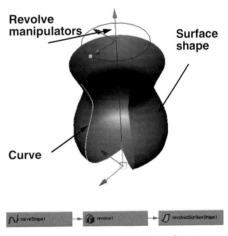

Revolve surface with dependencies

Many of these nodes come with special manipulators that make it easier to update the node attributes. In the case of the revolve, manipulators are available for the axis line and for the revolve's sweep angle.

It is possible to later delete history so that you are only working with the shape node. Don't forget though, that the dependency nodes have attributes that can be animated. Therefore, you lose some power if you delete history.

DEFORMATIONS

Deformers are special object types that can be used to reshape other objects. By using deformers, you can give your animations more of a squash and stretch quality.

A powerful feature of Maya's deformers is that they can be layered for more subtle effects. You can also bind deformers into skeletons or affect them with soft body dynamics.

The following lists some of the key deformer types available in Maya.

Lattices

Lattices are external frames that can be applied to your objects. If you then reshape the frame the object is deformed in response.

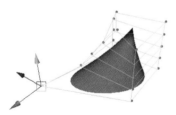

Lattice deformer

Sculpt objects

Sculpt objects let you deform a surface by pushing it with the object. By animating the position of the sculpt object, you can achieve animated surface deformations.

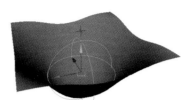

Sculpt object deformer

Clusters

Clusters are groups of CVs or lattice points that are built into a single set. The cluster is given its own pivot point and can be used to manipulate the clustered points. You can weight the CVs in a cluster to get more subtle effects.

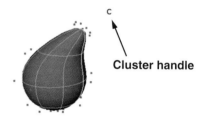

Cluster handle

Cluster deformer

CHARACTER ANIMATION

In Maya, character animation typically involves the animation of surfaces using skeleton joint chains and inverse kinematic handles to help drive the motion. At the same time, the chains can be set up to work with special sculpt objects and lattices known as *flexors*. These let you perform surface deformations that will add realism to your character.

Skeletons and joints

As you have already learned, skeleton joint chains are actually hierarchies. A skeleton is made up of joint nodes that are connected visually by bone icons. These hierarchies let you group or bind in geometry which creates your surface deformations.

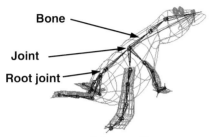

Joints and bones

Inverse kinematics

By default, joint chains work like any other hierarchy. The rotation of one joint is transferred to the lower joint nodes. This is known as *forward kinematics*. While this method is powerful, it makes it hard to plant a character's feet or move a hand to control the arm.

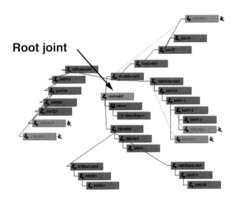

Character joint hierarchy

Inverse kinematics lets you work with the hierarchy in the opposite direction. By placing an IK handle that runs from a start joint to an end joint, you can better control the chain of joints. There are three kinds of solvers in Maya – the IK spline, the IK single chain and the IK rotate plane.

Each of these solvers is designed to help you control the joint rotations using the IK handle as a goal. As the IK handle moves, the IK solver defines the joint rotations that let the end joint move to the IK handle position.

The individual solvers have their own unique controls. Some of these are outlined below:

Single chain solver

The *single chain solver* provides a straight forward mechanism for posing and animating a chain. By moving the IK handle, the chain will update so that the joints lie on a plane.

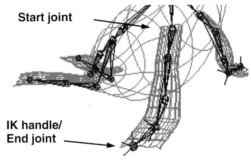

IK single chain solver

Rotate plane solver

The *rotate plane solver* gives you more control. With this solver, the plane that acts as the goal for all the joints can be moved by rotating the plane using a *twist attribute* or by moving the *pole vector handle*.

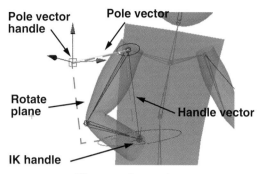

IK rotate plane solver

IK spline solver

The IK spline solver lets you control the chain using a spline curve. You can edit the CVs on the spline to update the rotation of the joints in the chain.

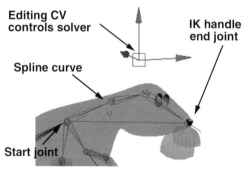

IK spline solver

Skinning your characters

Once you have a skeleton built, you can bind skin the surfaces of your character so that they deform with the rotation of the joints. In Maya you can use either soft skinning or hard skinning. Soft skinning uses weighted clusters while hard skinning does not.

Surface deformations

Flexors

In many cases, skinning a character does not yield realistic deformations in the character's joint areas. You can use *flexors* to add this secondary level of deformations to help with the tucking and bulging of your character.

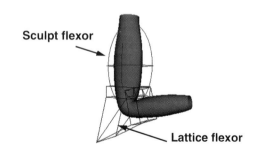

Flexors

RENDERING

Once your characters are set up, you can apply color and texture, then render with realistic lighting.

Shading groups

In Maya, you add texture maps and other rendering effects using *shading groups*. A shading group is a network of dependency nodes that all connect into a shading group node. Even the assigned surfaces and related lights are part of a shading group.

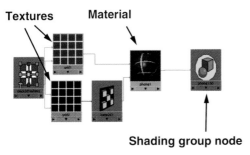

Textures **Material**

Shading group node

Shading group dependencies

You can think of a shading group as a sort of bucket into which you place all the color, texture and material qualities that you want on your surface. You then dip in the surface and throw in a light or two and the final effect is achieved.

Texture maps

To add detail to your shading groups, you can *texture map* different attributes. Some of these include bump, transparency and color.

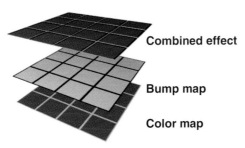

Combined effect

Bump map

Color map

Texture map layers

Lighting

Before you render, you can light your scenes using any number of lights. These lights let you add mood and atmosphere to a scene in much the same way as lighting is used by a photographer. Maya lets you preview your lights interactively as you model, or you can render to see the final effect.

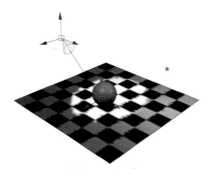

Light manipulator

Motion blur

When a real-life camera takes a shot of a moving object the final image is often blurred. This *motion blur* adds to the animated look of a scene and can be used in Maya. Maya contains two types of motion blur – a 2 1/2 D solution and a 3D solution. You will use both these types of motion blur in this book.

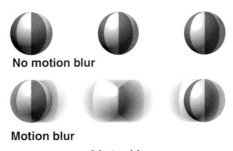

No motion blur

Motion blur

Motion blur

Hardware rendering

Maya includes *hardware rendering* that lets you see rendered images on your screen for previewing your animations. You can also use the hardware renderer to render some particle effects. These effects can later be composited in with software rendered images of your geometry.

Hardware rendering

A-buffer rendering

By default, Maya uses an *A-buffer* renderer for *software rendering*. This render type lets you see shaded scenes with shadows and motion blur. This method of rendering is great for most of your rendering needs. If you want reflections and refractions, then you need to turn on raytracing.

A-buffer rendering

Raytrace rendering

Raytracing lets you include reflections and refractions into your scenes. Maya has a selective raytracer which means that only objects or shading groups that have raytrace capabilities will use this renderer. Raytracing is slower than the default A-buffer and should be used only when it is required to enhance the look of a scene.

Raytrace rendering

How the renderer works

The Maya renderer works by looking through the camera at the scene. It then takes a section or tile, and analyzes whether or not it can render that section. If yes, then it combines the information found in the shading group (geometry, lights and shading network) with the Render Globals information, and the whole tile is rendered.

As the renderer moves on to the next section, it again analyzes the situation. If it hits a tile where there is more information than it wants to handle at one time, it then breaks the tile down into a smaller tile and renders.

Rendering of A-buffer tiles in progress

When you use raytracing, each tile is first rendered with the A-buffer, then the renderer looks for items that require raytracing. If it finds any, then it layers in the raytraced sections. When it finishes, you have your finished image, or if you are rendering an animation, a sequence of images.

IPR

Maya includes an Interactive Photorealistic Renderer that gives you fast feedback for texturing and lighting updates. You will use IPR throughout this book.

Conclusion

Now that you have a basic understanding of what Maya is designed to do, it is time for you to start working with the system directly. The concepts outlined in this introduction will make a lot more sense when you experience them first hand.

Don't forget to place the *learningMaya* directory into your project directory so that you have tutorial support files on hand. If you haven't done this yet, you can still complete the **Getting Started** section which does not require any support files.

Project
One

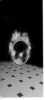

Project One

In Project One, you are going to animate a ball bouncing through a ring of fire. This will give you the chance to work with the Maya workspace while animating a scene.

You will learn about building models, adding textures and light, keyframing your objects and rendering your scene. With the ring of fire, you will also explore Maya's preset particle effects while adding your own particles to create the sparks that are emitted when the ball hits the flames.

After bouncing the ball, you will then take a more in-depth look at Maya's user interface and the dependency graph. These lessons offer you a more complete look at some of the key concepts and workflows that drive how Maya works.

1. The ball begins to bounce towards a flaming ring of fire.

2. Bravely, the ball leaps up into the flames.

3. Sparks fly as the ball brushes past the deadly fire.

4. Everyone is relieved as the ball bounces off safely with barely a scratch.

STORYBOARD

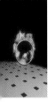

1 Bouncing a Ball

This lesson teaches you how to build and animate a simple bouncing ball that jumps through a hoop. You will explore Maya's user interface as you learn how to build and develop an animated scene.

A bouncing ball

In this lesson you will learn the following:

- How to create primitive objects

- How to move objects in 3D space

- How to use Maya's view tools

- How to change the display of your objects

- How to set keys on your objects

- How to playback animated sequences

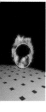

Setting up Maya

Before beginning, install Maya and add the Learning Maya support files to your projects directory. These can be found on the *support_files* directory on the DVD-ROM included with this book.

Note: To avoid the Cannot Save Workspace error, ensure that the support files are not read-only after you copy them from the DVD-ROM.

If you have been working with Maya and have changed any of your user interface settings, you may want to delete your preferences in order to start with the default Maya configuration.

If you are running multiple versions of Maya on the same machine, you should also backup and delete the preference files for those versions. Otherwise, Maya will use these preferences when it first launches and some of the new marking menu and hotkey settings will not be available. You can replace them later when you know that your Maya prefs have been created.

Creating a new project

Maya uses the concept of a project to organize files. You can create project directories that contain sub-directories for storing your files. You will be saving your work into scene files.

1 Launch Maya

- To get started, you need to launch Maya.

2 Set the courseware project

To manage your files, you can set a project directory that contains sub-directories for

different types of files that relate to your project.

- Go to the **File** menu and select **Project → Set...**

  A window opens that points you to the Maya projects directory.

- Open the folder named: *support_files*.

- Click on the folder named *projectOne* to select it.

- Click on the **OK** button.

  This sets the learningMaya directory as your current project.

- Go to the **File** menu and select **Project → Edit Current...**

  Make sure that the project directories are set up as shown below. This ensures that Maya is looking into the proper subdirectories when it opens up scene files.

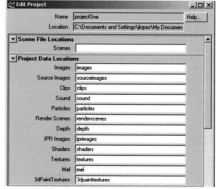

Edit Current Project window

- If any of the entries are incorrect, edit them to match the preceding image shown above.

3 Make a new scene

- Select **File** → **New Scene.**

  This makes sure that your current scene is part of the new project.

BUILDING OBJECTS

Every scene you create in Maya will begin with objects. These objects can include things like surfaces, deformers, skeleton joints or particle emitters. For this scene, you will build a ball and a floor surface.

Creating the ball

To start, you will build a few simple objects that you will animate, texture and render. The first object is a primitive sphere which will act as the ball.

1 Change menu sets

There are four main menu sets in Maya: *Animation, Modeling, Dynamics* and *Rendering*. These menu sets are used to access related tool sets.

- From the pop-up menu at the left edge of the Status line, select **Modeling**.

  As you change menu sets, the first six menus remain the same while the remaining menus change to reflect the chosen menu set.

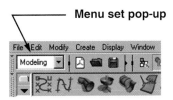

Menu set pop-up

Menu set pop-up menu

2 Create a NURBS sphere

A primitive sphere will be used for the ball. It will be built using *non-uniform rational b-spline* (NURBS) geometry. In later lessons, you will learn more about this geometry type.

- From the **Create** menu, select **NURBS Primitives** → **Sphere.**

  A sphere is placed at the origin.

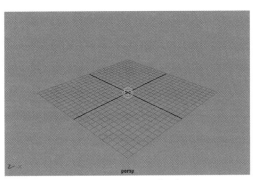

Perspective view of sphere

3 Change the ball's radius

The sphere is a procedural model. This means that it is broken down into parts called *nodes*. One node contains its positioning information, one contains its shape information and another contains input information that defines the sphere's construction history using attributes such as radius, sweep, and degree. You can edit

PROJECT ONE

this input node's attributes in the Channel box in order to edit the sphere's shape.

The Channel box is found at the right side of the screen and lets you make changes to key attributes very easily.

- From the Channel box's Inputs section, click on *makeNurbSphere*.

  This will make several new attributes available for editing.

- Type **2** in the *Radius* entry field then press the **Enter** key.

  Now the sphere is double the size in the perspective view.

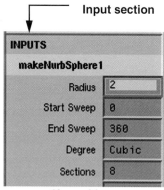

Input section

Channel box

Note:	Another method for increasing the size of the sphere would be to scale it. In Maya, you can often achieve the same visual results using many different methods. Over time, you will begin to choose the techniques that best suit a particular situation.

---

4 Rename the ball node

You should rename the existing transform node to make it easier to find later.

- Click on the *nurbsSphere* name at the top of the Channel box to highlight it.

- Type the name *ball* then press the **Enter** key.

Renaming the node in the Channel box

Moving the ball

You will now use the **Move** tool to reposition the ball. This will involve the use of manipulator handles that let you control where you move your object.

1 Position the ball

You can now use the **Move** tool to reposition the sphere above the working grid.

- Select the **Move** tool.

  A transform manipulator appears centered on the object.

- Click-drag on the green manipulator handle to move the sphere along the Y-axis.

  The manipulator handle turns yellow to indicate that it is active.

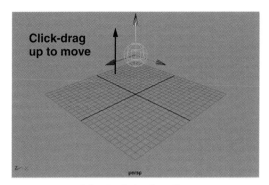

Manipulator handles

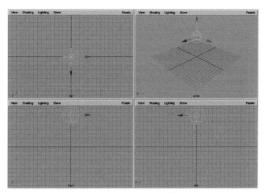

Four view panels

Tip: The transform manipulator has three handles which let you constrain your motion along the X, Y, and Z axes. These are labeled using red for the X-axis, green for the Y-axis and blue for the Z-axis. In Maya, the Y-axis points up by default. This means that Maya is "Y-up" by default.

---

2 Create four view panels

By default, a single perspective window is shown in the workspace. To see other views of the scene, you can change your panel layout.

- At the top of the Perspective view panel, go to the **Panels** menu and select **Saved Layouts → Four View.**

  You can now see the sphere using three orthographic views – Top, Side, and Front – which show you the model from a projected view. You can also see it in a Perspective view that is more like the 3D world we see every day. This multiple view set-up is very useful when positioning objects in 3D space.

3 Reposition the ball

When moving in an orthographic view, you can work in two axes at once by dragging on the center of the manipulator or constraining the motion along a single axis using the handles.

- In the Front view, click-drag on the square center of the manipulator to move the sphere along both the X and the Y axes.

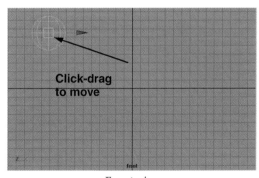

Front view

- Use the manipulator in the various view windows to position the sphere on top of the ground plane as shown below.

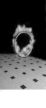

Be sure to refer to all four view windows to verify that the object is positioned properly.

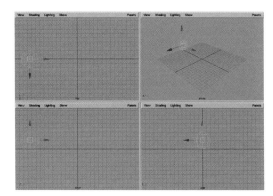

Start position of the ball

Note: If you click-drag on the center of the manipulator in the Perspective view, you will notice that it doesn't move along any particular axis. It is actually moving along the camera's view plane.

Create a floor surface

To create a floor surface, a primitive plane is used. This plane using polygonal geometry which is different from the sphere which uses NURBS geometry. You can use the hotbox as an alternative method for accessing tools.

1 Create a polygonal plane

- In a view panel, press and hold the spacebar to display the hotbox.
- In the hotbox, select **Create →
  Polygon Primitives → Plane.**

  A plane is placed at the origin.

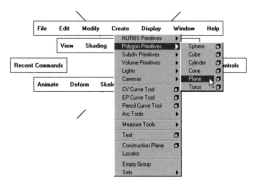

Hotbox access to menu items

Tip: You can access all functions in Maya using either the main menus or the hotbox. As you become more familiar with the hotbox, you can use the user interface options found in the **Display** menu to turn off the panel menus and therefore reduce screen clutter.

2 Change construction history

Just like the sphere, you can edit the plane using its input node. You will increase the size of the plane, then reduce the number of subdivisions to simplify the plane. Since the floor will not be deformed, the extra polygons are not required.

- In the Channel box shown at the right side of your screen, click on the *polyPlane* Input node.

- Set the following:

  Width to **40**;

  Height to **40**;

  Subdivisions Width to **1**;

  Subdivisions Height to **1**.

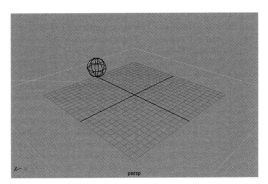

Updated poly plane

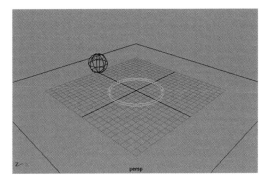

Edited torus

3 Rename the plane node

It is a good idea to rename the existing transform node to make it easier to find later.

- Click on the *polyPlane* node's name in the top of the channel box.

- Enter the name *floor*.

Create a Ring

You are now going to add a NURBS torus to the scene that will act as a hoop for the ball to jump through when you animate it bouncing.

1 Create a NURBS Torus

The torus offers a shape that is perfect for the ring. You will create the torus, and then size and position it to get the ring.

- From the **Create** menu, select **NURBS Primitives → Torus**.

- In the Channel box, click on the *makeNurbsTorus* Input node.

- Set the following attributes:

  Radius to **5**;

  Sections to **16**;

  Height Ratio to **0.05**.

2 Position the Torus

- In the *nurbsTorus* section of the Channel box, set the following attribute:

  Rotate Z to **90**.

- Rename this node to *ring*.

- With your middle mouse button click in the perspective view to make it active then press the **w** key to select the **Move** tool.

- **Move** the ring up so that it sits above the ground plane. Its **Translate Y** attribute should read about **12**.

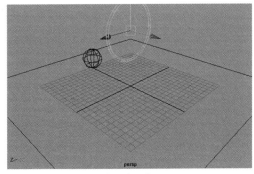

Ring in place

Viewing the scene

When you work in 3D space, it is important to see your work from different angles. The different view panels let you see your work from the Front, Top, Side and Perspective.

You can also use Maya's view tools to change the views to reposition how you see your scene. In some cases, a view change is like panning a camera around a room, while in other cases a view change might be like turning an object around in your hand to see all the sides. These view tools can be accessed using the **Alt** key in combination with various mouse buttons.

1 Edit the Perspective view

You can use the **Alt** key with either your left mouse button (LMB), your middle mouse button (MMB) or the two together to tumble, track and dolly in your Perspective view.

- Change your view using the following key combinations:

  Alt + LMB to tumble;

  Alt + MMB to track;

  Alt + LMB & **MMB** to dolly.

You can also use the **Ctrl** key to create a bounding box dolly, where the view adjusts based on a bounding box:

  Ctrl + Alt + LMB to box dolly.

Click-drag to the right to dolly in and to the left to dolly out.

You can also undo and redo view changes using the following keys:

  [to undo views; and

  ] to redo views.

- Alter your Perspective window until it appears as shown below.

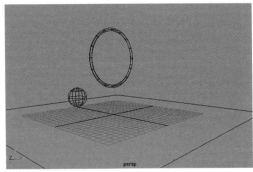

New view

2 Edit the view in the Side view

Orthographic views use similar hot keys – except that you cannot tumble an orthographic view.

- In the Side view, change your view using the following key combinations:

  Alt + MMB to track;

  Alt + LMB & **MMB** to dolly

- Keep working with the orthographic views until they are set up as shown in the following.

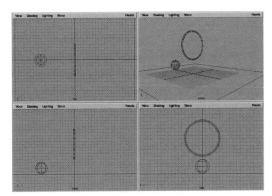

New orthographic views

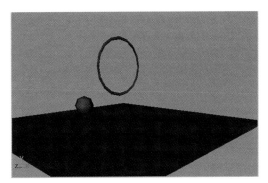

Smooth shaded view

Setting display options

The view panels let you interactively view your scene. By default, this means viewing your scene as a wireframe model. To better evaluate the form of your objects, you can activate hardware shading and increase the sphere's smoothness.

1 Turn on Hardware shading

To help visualize your objects, you can use hardware rendering to display a shaded view within any panel.

- From the Perspective view's **Shading** menu, select **Smooth Shade All.**

This setting affects all of the objects within the current view panel.

Tip: You can also turn on smooth shading by moving your cursor over the desired panel, clicking with your middle mouse button and pressing the **5** key. The **4** key can be used to return the panel to a wireframe view.

2 Hide the grid

You can hide the grid to simplify your view using one of two options:

- From the Perspective view panel's **Show** menu, select **Grid** to hide the grid for that view only.

OR

- From the **Display** menu, deselect **Grid** to hide the grid for all views.

3 Adjust the sphere's smoothness

To better evaluate the sphere's surface qualities, you can increase the smoothness.

- **Select** the *ball*.
- From the main **Display** menu, select **NURBS Smoothness → Fine.**

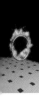

This setting affects how selected NURBS objects are displayed in all view panels.

4 Adjust the ring's smoothness

Maya also includes some hotkeys for setting surface smoothness.

- Select the *ring*.

- Press the **3** key.

  The smoothness setting allows you to see your objects at various degrees of complexity without actually altering the geometry.

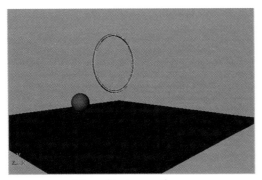

New object smoothness

Tip: A NURBS object can have its smoothness set using the following hotkeys:
   1 - rough
   2 - medium
   3 - fine

ANIMATING THE BALL

You now have your scene set up and ready to animate. Using the *ball* node, you will start by keying the overall translation of the ball.

Next, you will add in the peaks and valleys of the bouncing.

Setting keys

To animate the ball, you must define its position at certain points in time. This is accomplished by setting keys. As you playback the animation, Maya reads these key positions and interpolates the position of the ball in between the keyframes.

1 Position the ball

- Select the *ball*.

- **Move** the ball along the X axis to the edge of the *floor*. Use the Red manipulator handle to constrain along X.

Repositioning the ball

2 Set a start key on the ball

You will use the current position to set a key for frame 1.

- **Select** the *ball*.

- Make sure that the current time is set to 1 in the Time slider.

- Press **F2** to select the animation menu set.

- From the **Animate** menu, select **Set Key.**

  This places a key at frame 1 for all of the ball's transform attributes.

Tip: The menu sets can be changed using the following hotkeys:
F2 - Animation
F3 - Modeling
F4 - Dynamics
F5 - Rendering

---

3 Set end key on the ball

A new position for the ball can be set for frame 60.

- In the Time slider, change the end time and the playback end time to **60** and press **Enter**.

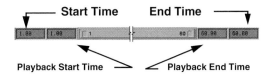

Time slider frame range settings

This changes the range of the animation to 60 frames.

- Move the Time slider to frame **60**.

Current time indicator

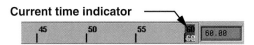

Time slider at frame 60

- Click-drag on the X-axis handle on the sphere to move it forward.

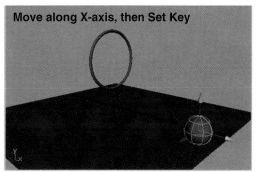

Sphere moved along X-axis

- Press the **s** key to **Set Key** at this position and time.

Tip: The **s** key is a hotkey for the Set key command.

- Playback the results using the Playback controls which are located in the lower right corner.

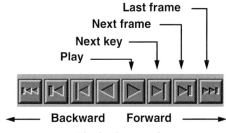

Playback controls

Note: Playback will only be visible in the view panel that is highlighted. If you are not seeing any playback then be sure to click in the perspective panel with your middle mouse button.

4 Add intermediate keys

To make the ball hit the ground four times, you will need two more key positions set at frames 20 and 40.

Any time you want to make sure an object is at a certain place at a certain time, set a key.

- Drag the Time slider to frame **20**.

  The ball is positioned based on existing keys.

- Press the **s** key to **Set Key**.

- Drag the Time slider to frame **40**.

- Press the **s** key to **Set Key**.

  You now have keys set at the following frames:

1   20   40   60

Diagram of initial keys

Tip: Every time you set a key, a red mark is placed in the Time slider to help you identify where your keys are.

---

5 Add more intermediate keys

To create the peaks of the bounce, you need to set new keys at frames 10, 30 and 50. These keys will require that you move the ball into a new position along the Y-axis.

- Move the Time slider to frame 30.

- Click-drag on the green Y-axis manipulator to move the sphere up

along the Y-axis until it sits inside the ring.

- Press the **s** key to **Set Key**.

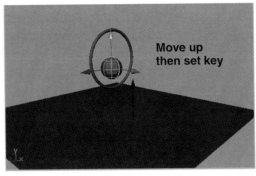

Move up then set key

Y-axis move

- Move the Time slider to frame 10.

- Click-drag on the Y-axis manipulator to move the sphere up along the Y-axis. Don't raise it as high as you did for frame 30.

  This will put emphasis on the bounce at frame 30 where the ball is jumping through the ring.

- Press the **s** key to **Set Key**.

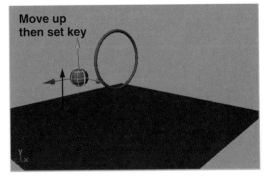

Move up then set key

Y-axis move

- Repeat these steps to create the last bounce at frame 50. Don't forget to set a key after placing the ball.

6 Set the playback speed

- Click the **Animation Preferences** button found at the far right side of the Range slider.

  This opens a window that lets you set various animation and playback options. Currently, the scene is playing back as fast as it can. Since you only have two objects, playback is a little too fast.

- In the **Playback** section, set the following:

  Playback Speed to **Real-time.**

- Click the **Save** button.

- Playback the results using the Time slider controls.

7 Save your work

- From the **File** menu, select **Save Scene As...**

- Enter the name *bounce_01*.

Windows Save As dialog box

- Click the **Save** button or press the **Enter** key.

  Make sure you save this file since you will be continuing with it in the next lesson.

| Note: | Throughout this book, you will be using the final saved file from one lesson as the start file for the next. Save your work at the end of each lesson to make sure that you have the start file ready. |

Conclusion

Congratulations. You have completed your first exercise using Maya. In the next lesson, you will take this simple bouncing ball and refine the motion for more dramatic results.

Adding Character

In the last lesson, you built and animated a bouncing ball. As you playback the bounce, you can see that the ball seems to float and is not bouncing in a convincing manner. In this lesson, you will begin to edit the quality of the original animation to add character to the bounce.

This lesson will begin to layer the animation with secondary motion such as *squash and stretch*. In Maya, you can create these effects using non-linear deformers, that allow you to reshape the ball as it animates.

Adding squash and stretch

In this lesson you will learn the following:

- How to refine animated channels with the Graph Editor

- How to create a Bend and a Squash deformer

- How to set keyable and non-keyable channels

- How to use Set Driven Key

- How to use Auto Key

- How to edit an animation's timing using the Dope sheet

Refining the animated channels

In the last lesson, the bouncing ball does not appear to bounce properly. It seems to float as it touches the ground instead of hitting hard as you would expect. To edit the quality of the bounce, you can use the Graph editor to work with the animation channels.

1 Select the ball

If you are continuing straight from Lesson 1, the *ball* may already be selected. If not, then you must select this object to work with the animated channels.

- If the ball is not selected, then select it in one of the view panels.

2 Create a new panel layout

You can switch the contents of a panel to other panel types such as lists or graphs.

- In the perspective view panel's **Panels** menu, select **Saved Layouts → Persp/Graph**.

   This places a perspective view panel above a Graph editor panel.

- Click-drag down on the bar that separates the two panels to make the new perspective panel larger.

- From the Graph Editor's **View** menu, select **Frame All**.

   Now you can see all of the animation curves for the *ball*.

   Earlier, you set keys for the ball. This set keys for all the *Translate, Rotate* and *Scale* attributes, in all three axes, as well as *Visibility*. Each of the animated attributes creates an animation curve that represents how each channel changes over time.

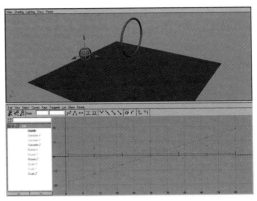

Graph Editor panel

Tip: Remember that you can also access the View menu from the hotbox by pressing and holding the spacebar.

3 Focus on the Translate Y channel

To focus on the up and down motion of the ball, you need to focus on the Translate Y channel.

- Click on the *Translate Y* channel. Now only its curve is shown in the graph.

- Press the **Alt** key and click-drag with the left and middle mouse buttons to dolly into the graph.

- Press the **Shift** and **Alt** keys and click-drag up and down with the left and middle mouse buttons to dolly only along the Y-axis.

- Press the **Shift** and **Alt** keys and click-drag up and down with the middle mouse button to track along the Y-axis.

- Use these tools to position the graph as shown below:

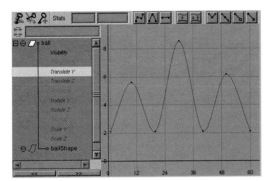

New view of curve

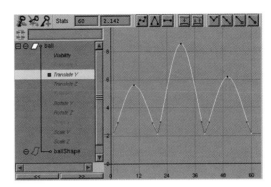

Linear tangents

Tip: The same view tools used in the modeling views apply to other panel types. The **Shift** key constraint works in all view panels and with tumbling and tracking.

4 Edit the shape of the curve

The floating effect as the ball touches the ground is a result of the smoothing of the curve as it approaches a value of 0.

This smoothing is created by the curve tangents. The tangents define the motion in between the keys. By editing the tangents, you will change how the ball moves between the keys.

- Click-drag over all of the points at the bottom of the bounce to select the keys.

- Press the **Linear Tangents** button to make the curve tangents meet at a point.

- Move the pointer over the Perspective view and press the spacebar quickly.

  This pops the panel to a full size panel. Playback is a little faster without the Graph Editor present.

Tip: You can use a quick tap on the spacebar to pop any panel to full size and back. A longer click would reveal the hotbox.

- Playback the results in the Perspective view panel.

  The resulting motion now results in more of a bounce as the ball hits the ground.

- Move your pointer over the Perspective view panel and press the spacebar quickly.

  This returns you to the two view panels you had earlier.

5 Edit the tangents at the keys

To accentuate the bounce even further, you can edit the actual tangents to make the curve steeper as it approaches the ground.

PROJECT ONE

- Press the **Break Tangents** button to break the connection between the opposite tangents at the key.

- Click-drag a selection box around the tangent handle on the first key.

- Make sure that you select only the tangent handle and not the key itself.

- Make sure that the **Move** tool is active.

- Click-drag with your middle mouse button to edit the curve's tangent until it is almost vertical and you don't get a bump at the next key.

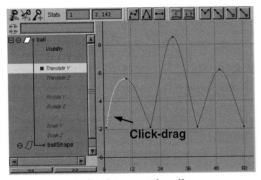

Click-drag

Edited tangent handle

- Click-drag a selection box around the next key on the curve.

  This reveals the tangent handles for that key.

- Click-drag a selection box around one of the tangent handles.

- Edit the tangent using the middle mouse button to make it more vertical.

- Repeat the tangent edit for all of the other tangents until the curves appear as shown:

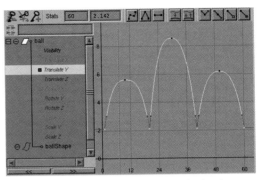

Action curve with keys highlighted

- Playback the results in the Perspective view.

Diagram of edited bounce

The bounce is much more sharp and appears to be affected by gravity.

Cleaning up your curves

Now that the quality of the motion has been set, you can look for ways to clean up your animation curves so that unnecessary information is removed. For this scene, the extra curves will have little influence, but in larger scenes they can add up and affect performance.

1 Remove static channels

If an action curve is flat along its whole length then its value is not changing. This means that it is not being animated.

These curves should be removed to reduce the amount of data in the scene.

- In the name list, press the **Ctrl / Command** key and click on the following channel names:

    Translate Z;

    Rotate X, Y and Z;

    Scale X, Y and Z;

    Visibility.

    The *Translate X* and *Translate Y* should remain unselected.

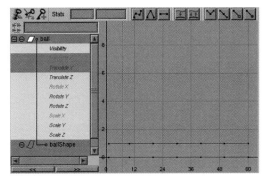

Static channels

- From the Graph Editor's **Edit** menu, select **Delete**.

    This removes the selected curves from your scene.

Note: In the Channel box, you will see that the remaining input fields – *Translate X* and *Translate Y* – use a different background color. This color helps you distinguish channels which have been keyed.

2 Remove extra keys

In some cases, you may have keys on animated channels that don't contribute to the results. These keys are found when a straight line can be drawn from the key before to the key after.

- In the name list, click on the *Translate X* channel.

- Select **View → Frame All**.

- Use the **Alt** key to track and dolly so you can see the whole curve.

    You will see that there are five redundant keys on this curve. Since you want the ball to move along a straight path, these keys are not required.

- Click-drag a selection box around the five middle keys.

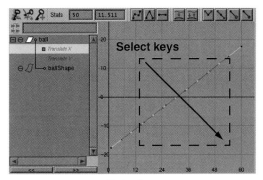

Extra keys

- Press the **Delete** key to remove the keys.

    The resulting curve would now be easier to edit because there are no intermediate keys.

SQUASH AND STRETCH

One of the best methods to infuse your animation with life is to add *squash and stretch*. This traditional animation technique helps you avoid a rigid looking animation as the ball hits the ground with more emphasis and seems to soar as it leaps into the air. In Maya, you can create this effect using a squash deformer.

Adding a squash deformer

A deformer is a special object type that lets you reshape a surface or group of surfaces. By using deformers to change the shape of the object over time, you can create a more visually appealing animation.

1 Set up a front view

- Go to frame 1.

  This will place the ball at its starting point.

- In the perspective view's **Panels** menu, select **Panels → Orthographic → Front**.

  This gives you a view of the ball looking down the Z-axis.

- Dolly and track the view until you are looking at the side of the ball.

2 Add the squash to the ball

- Select the *ball*.

- Press **F2** to go to the **Animation** menu set.

- From the **Deform** menu, select **Create Nonlinear → Squash**.

- This adds the *squashHandle* to the ball. You do not see any

deformation yet since the squash attributes have not been edited.

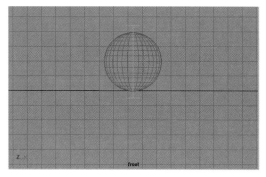

Scale deformer

3 Move and Scale the deformer

- **Move** the *squashHandle* so that the manipulator is at the base of the ball.

- **Scale** the squashHandle until the handle appears at the top of the ball.

  Now the squash will occur from the base of the ball instead of in its middle. This ensures that the bottom of the ball doesn't leave the ground during the squash.

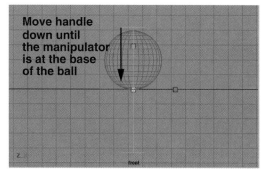

Scale deformer

4 Test the squash's Factor attribute

- In the Channel box, click on the *squash* input node.

- Select the **Show Manipulator** tool.

- Click-drag on the middle manipulator handle to squash and stretch the ball.

- When you are finished check the channel box and make sure that the **Factor** attribute is set to about **0.4** to give the ball a little stretch.

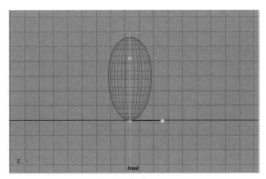

Scale deformer

5 Test the playback of the ball

- Dolly out of the view so that you can watch the whole bouncing motion.

- Playback the animation.

  The ball animates but the deformation of the ball only works properly at frame 1. This is because the deformer is not moving with the ball.

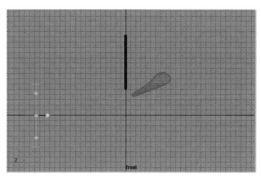

Playing back the animation

6 Parent the deformer

To make the deformer move with the ball, you need to parent the deform handle to the ball.

- Go back to frame 1.

- Select the *squashHandle* then press the shift key and select the *ball*.

- Select **Edit** → **Parent**.

  You could also press the **p** key to parent the handle to the ball.

- Playback the animation.

  Now the deformer moves with the ball.

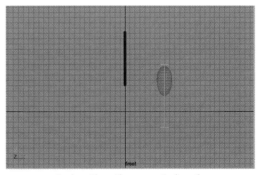

Animating the parented nodes

Animate the squash

To animate the ball's squash and stretch, you could set keys, but if you later edited the timing of the ball's bouncing then these keys would have to be reset. For this reason, you will use a *reactive* animation technique called **Set Driven Key**.

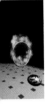

This technique allows you to have one attribute drive another attribute. Since you know that you want the ball to squash when it touches the ground and stretch when it is in the air, you can use the ball's *Y translation* to drive the squash's *factor* attribute. Therefore if you later edit the timing of the ball's bouncing or change its *Y translation*, the squash will *react* appropriately and squash on cue.

1 Load the Set Driven Key window

The Set driven key window lets you choose which attribute will be the driver and which attribute(s) will be driven.

- From the **Animate** menu, select **Set Driven Key** → **Set** - ☐ to open the Set Driven Key window.

Note: When you want to open an option window, you need to select the menu item then move your cursor over the square icon – ☐.

- Select the *ball*.
- Click on the **Load Driver** button in the Set Driven Key window.
- In the right hand column of the **Driver** section, click on **translate Y**.

This sets up *translate Y* as the attribute that will drive the action.

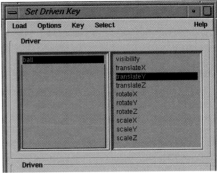

Driver attribute highlighted

- **Select** the *squashhandle*.
- Highlight the **squash** input node in the Channel box.
- Click on the **Load Driven** button in the Set Driven Key window.

Both the *squash* input node and the *squashHandle* node are loaded. You will only be using the *squash* node.

- In the left hand column of the **Driven** section, click on **squash**.
- Click on **factor** in the right hand column to highlight it as the driven attribute.

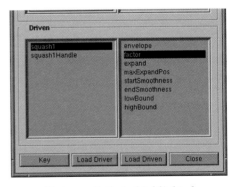

Driven attribute highlighted

2 Key the initial position

- Go to frame 1.
- Again highlight the **squash** input node in the Channel box.
- Set the *squash* node's **factor** attribute to show the ball in a squashed position.

  The image below shows a value of about -0.5.

  You can either use the Channel box or the **Show Manipulator** tool.
- Click on the **Key** button in the Set Driven Key window.

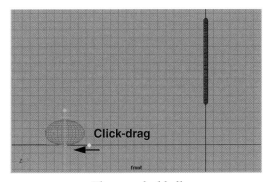

The squashed ball

3 Key the second position

- Go to frame 30.
- Set the *squash* node's **factor** attribute to show the ball in a stretched position.
- Click on the **Key** button in the Set Driven Key window.

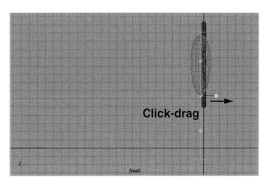

The stretched ball

- Playback the animation

  Now the ball stretches at the peak of each bounce and squashes as the ball hits the ground. Set Driven key is using the height of the ball to decide whether to use squash or stretch.

4 Edit the Animation curve

- Select the *squashHandle*.
- From the editor's **View** menu, select **Frame all**.

  The smaller of the two curves on the graph maps the ball's translate Y attribute to the squash's factor attribute.

  Select this curve and select **View → Frame Selection**.
- Edit the curve as shown in the following image.

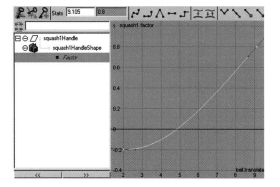

Edited animation curve

- Playback the animation

  You can see that there is a little more emphasis on the point where the ball hits the ground.

Bending the ball

As the ball goes into and out of a bounce, it might be helpful to have it lean forward as it bounces up and lean back as it falls. You can do this with a second deformer. This time you will use a bend deformer.

This will help give the appearance that the ball is propelling itself forward each time it hits the ground. This will give the ball a life of its own as it bounces along.

1 Add a Bend deformer

- Go to frame 1.
- Select the *ball*.
- From the **Deform** menu, select **Create Nonlinear → Bend**.

  Just like the Squash deformer, the Bend adds a *bendHandle* and a *bend* node to the ball. The *bendHandle* node is currently highlighted.

2 Parent the deformer

To make the deformer move with the ball, you need to parent the deform handle to the ball.

- From the **Window** menu, select **Outliner**.

  This window offers you a listing of all the objects in the scene.

  With your middle mouse button drag the *bendHandle* onto the ball node.

Parenting the bendHandle

- Click on the plus sign next to the ball node to open up the hierarchy.

  Now you can see that the ball is the parent of the two deformer handles.

Viewing the hierarchy

- Close the outliner window.

3 Key the bend node's curvature

The bend node has an attribute called curvature that is used to control how much bending will occur. This is the attribute that you will set keys on in order to animate the bending of the ball.

- In the Channel box, click on the *bend* Input node to open it up.
- Click on the **Curvature** attribute's name to highlight it.
- From the Channel box's **Channels** menu, select **Key Selected**.

   This sets a start key for the curvature attribute.

4 Turn on Auto Keying

To set more keys for the curvature, you will use Auto key. This method of keying lets you set keys by simply changing the attribute value.

- Turn on Auto Key.

   Now when you update an attribute that has existing keys, a key will be set automatically.

5 Edit the bend's boundary

- Go to frame **5**.
- Make sure that the **bend** input node's name is highlighted in the channel box.

- Select the **Show Manipulator** tool.

   This tool displays some handles that let you edit the attributes of the bend deformer. This gives you interactive control over the deformer's attributes.

- Click drag on the top manipulator to extend the **high bound** of the deformer.

   This will ensure that the bending works properly when the ball is fully stretched.

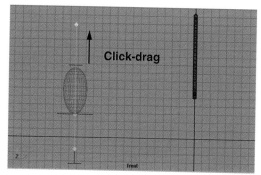
Updated high bound

6 Edit the curvature

- Click-drag to the right on the center manipulator handle to edit the bend node's **curvature**. Stop when the ball is bending forward. The value in the Channel box should read about 0.5.

   A new key has been set. Auto Key creates the new key when you adjust the curvature attribute.

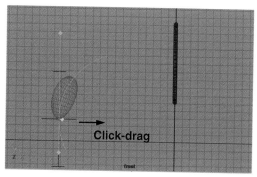
Bending forward

7 Set another key

- Go to frame **15**.
- Drag to the left on the center manipulator handle to bend the ball back. This will set the node's **curvature** to about -0.6.

  Another key is set by Auto Key.

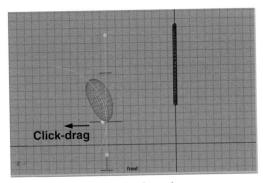

Shear backward

8 Continue animating the bending

- Use the Auto key method to set new keys for the bend node's **curvature** so that the ball bends forward at frames 25 and 45 and back at frames 35 and 55.
- Go to frame 60 and change your **curvature** to **0**.
- Change the front view panel back to a perspective panel.
- Playback the results.

Editing timing

To give the impression that the ball is pushing off as it bounces, you will have to edit the timing of the bend action. The goal is to move the bend action closer to the bounce of the ball to make it appear more immediate.

You can edit the timing of your keys in the Graph editor.

Earlier, you edited the quality of the animation using the Graph editor. To edit the timing of the bouncing, you can also use the *Dope sheet*. The Dope sheet lets you focus on timing without having to look at all of the curve information.

1 Select keys in the Dope sheet

- Make sure the *bendHandle* node is selected and the *bend* node is not highlighted in the Channel box.
- In the Graph editor panel's **Panels** menu, select **Panel → Dope Sheet**.

  This window shows each channel as a series of ticks on a long bar which represent frames. Some of these are highlighted with color bars that show you where keys have been set. The top bar shows a summary of the keys while each channel of the selected nodes has its own bar.

- Click on the plus sign next to the *bendHandle* node that is in the square.
- Click on the second plus sign next to the *bendHandleShape* node that is in the circle.
- With the left mouse button, click on the key at frame **15**.

  It will be the only key highlighted in yellow.

- Press the **Shift** key and click with the left mouse button on the keys at frames **35** and **55**.

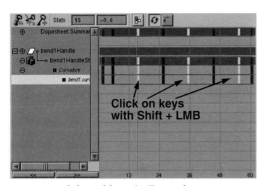

Selected keys in Dope sheet

2   Move the bend handle keys

- Select the **Move** tool.
- With the middle mouse button, click-drag to the right in the Dope sheet until the first key is at about frame 19.

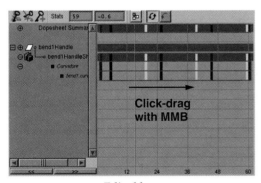

Edited keys

- Playback the results.

3   Edit the shape of the curve

While editing the timing of the bending in the dope sheet helps a bit, you may not be getting the look that you want. To edit how the curve reacts between the keys, you can edit the shape of the curve in the Graph editor.

- In the Dope Sheet's **Panels** menu, select **Panel → Graph Editor**
- Use the techniques learned earlier in the lesson to reshape the curve as shown below:

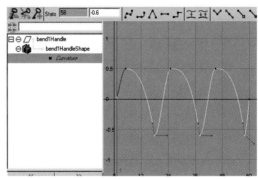

Reshaped curve

The key is that when the ball hits the ground, the bending changes sharply to emphasize the bounce.

- Playback the results.

4   Save your work

- From the **File** menu, select **Save Scene As...**
- Enter the name *bounce_2* next to the file's path.
- Press the **Save** button or press the **Enter** key.

Tip: It is a good idea to give your file a new name after significant changes have been made. The different files give you a record of past stages in case you want to go back. Once you have saved a few versions, you can clear earlier files to help conserve disk space.

PROJECT ONE

Conclusion

You have now added some character to the bouncing ball. In the next lesson, you will learn how to texture and light your scene in order to begin creating rendered animations.

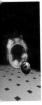

If desired, you could now use the Dope sheet or the Graph editor to further refine the quality and timing of the various channels to achieve a bounce with different kinds of character. You might want the ball to bounce higher or the bending to be more subtle.

This refinement is ultimately your role as an animator. While the actual work of setting keys is finished, you will find that the refinement stage could become the most time-consuming, and yet the most rewarding. Since this book is focused on technique, the refinement will be left up to you to add at the end of each lesson.

3 Rendering

Now that you have animated the ball, you are ready to render the scene. The rendering process involves the preparation of shaders and textures for your objects and the manipulation of cameras and lights. You can also add effects such as *motion blur* to accentuate the motion during playback of the rendered frames.

Software rendering of the ball

In this lesson you will learn the following:

- How to work with a menu-less user interface
- How to work with the Hypershade panel
- How to create a shading group
- How to texture map an object
- How to add lighting to your scene
- How to test render a single frame
- How to set up motion blur
- How to software render an animation

Hiding the general UI

In the last two lessons, you used menus, numeric input fields and other user interface elements to work with your scene. In this lesson, you will hide most of the user interface and rely more on the hotbox and other hotkeys that let you access the UI without actually seeing it on screen.

1 Turn off all of the menus

- Move your cursor over the Perspective view panel, then press the spacebar quickly to pop this panel to full screen.

- Press and hold on the spacebar to evoke the hotbox.

Tip: Tapping and holding down the spacebar, respectively, can be used to both toggle between window panes and to bring up the hotbox.

- Click on the **Hotbox Controls**.
- From the marking menu, go down to **Window Options** and set the following:

  (Windows only) **Show Main Menubar** to **Off**;

  Show Pane Menubars to **Off**.

Marking menu

Now the various menus are hidden and you must rely on the hotbox to access tools.

2 Turn off all of the workspace options

- From the hotbox, select **Display** → **UI Elements** → **Hide UI Elements**.

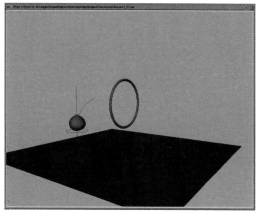

Simplified user interface

You now have a much larger working area which will let you focus more on your work.

3 Change the panel organization

- Press and hold on the spacebar to evoke the hotbox.

- Click in the area above the menus to invoke a marking menu.

- Select **Hypershade/Render/Persp** from this marking menu.

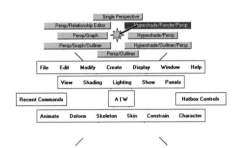

Marking menu

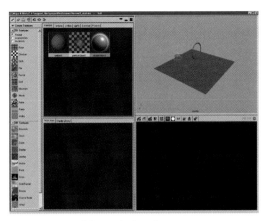

New window layout

Tip: Each of the four quadrants surrounding the hotbox and the hotbox's center all contain their own marking menu set. You can edit the contents of these menus using **Window → Settings/ Preferences → Marking Menus**...

This saved layout puts a Hypershade panel above a Perspective panel and a Render view panel.

The Hypershade is where you will build shading networks and the Render view is where you will test the results in your scene.

4 Open the Attribute Editor

- From the hotbox, select **Display → UI Elements → Attribute Editor**.

Now you also have an Attribute editor panel on the right side of the workspace. This will make it easy to update shading group attributes.

Hotkeys

When working with a minimal UI, you will rely on the hotbox and hotkeys for your work. The following is a list of relevant hotkeys that you may need to use as you work:

spacebar	hotbox/window popping
Alt v	Start/stop playback
Alt + Shift v	Go to first frame
Alt .	Move one frame forward
Alt ,	Move one frame back
k	Click-drag to scrub animation

If you have selected an animated node such as the ball, then you can also use the following hotkeys:

.	Go to next key
,	Go to last key

For a complete listing of available hotkeys, go to **Window → Settings/Preferences → Hotkeys...**

SHADING GROUPS

To prepare the ball and the floor for rendering, you need to add color and texture. In Maya, this is accomplished using *shading groups* that bring together material qualities, textures, lights and geometry to define the desired look.

The Hypershade panel

The Hypershade panel is made up of three sections –the Create bar, the Hypershade tabs and the Work area. The Create bar allows you to create any rendering nodes you require for your scene. The Hypershade tabs list all nodes that make up the current scene while the Work area allows you to look more closely and alter any part of the shading network that is used to create a shading group.

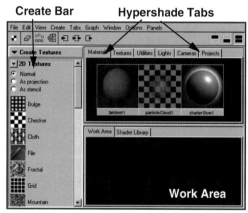

Create Bar   Hypershade Tabs

Closeup of Hypershade

Creating a shading group

A shading group is made up of a series of nodes which input into a *shading group and material nodes*. In the following examples, you will create several nodes that define the material qualities of the ring and the floor.

1 Create a material for the ring

To build a material for the ring, you will use the Hypershade and the Attribute editor.

- Click with your right mouse button in the work area and select **Graph** → **Clear Graph**.

  This clears the workspace so that you can begin working on a new shading network.

- In the create bar section, click on the Create menu bar at the top of the create bar window. From the pop-up select **Create Materials**

  This offers you a series of icons that represent new materials.

- Click on **Blinn**.

  This adds a new blinn material under the materials hypershade tab and in the work area. You will also see the Attribute editor update to show the new nodes information.

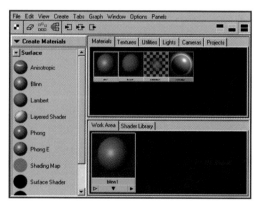

New node in Hypershade

Blinn is a particular type of shading model that defines how the material will look. The Blinn model gives you control over the look of the materials highlights using special attributes.

2   Rename the material node

- In the Attribute editor, change the name of the material node to *ringM*.

  The *M* designation is to remind you that this node is a material node.

3   Edit the material's color

To define how the material will render, you will need to set several key material attributes such as color.

- In the Attribute editor, click on the color swatch next to the **Color** attribute.

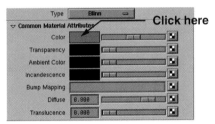

Color swatch in the Attribute Editor

This opens the Color Chooser. This window lets you set color by clicking in a color wheel and editing HSV (Hue, Saturation, Value) or RGB (Red, Green, Blue) values.

Color Choosers

- Choose any color you want then click the **Accept** button.

4   Assign the material

- With your middle mouse button, click-drag on the *ringM* node and drag it from the Hypershade panel into the perspective view and drop it on the ring.

  This assigns the material to the object.

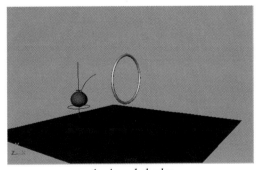

Assigned shader

Creating a texture map

To give the floor a pattern, a grid texture will be added to the *floor* material's color. This will be accomplished using the drag and drop capabilities of the Hypershade.

1 Create a material for the floor

To build a textured material for the floor, you will use the Hypershade panel to build up the material using a grid texture.

- In the Hypershade clear the work area by holding down the right mouse button and selecting **Graph → Clear Graph**.

- In the create bar section, click on the **Phong**.

- In the Attribute editor, change the name of the material node to *floorM*.

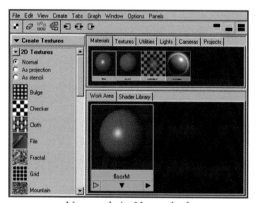

New node in Hypershade

2 Create a checker texture

- In the create bar section, click on the Create Materials bar and from the pop-up menu select **Create Textures**.

  This offers you a series of icons that can be used to create new textures.

- Select **Grid** from the menu.

- From the Work area, click with your **MMB** on the **Grid** icon and drag it

onto the **floorM** material node in the work area of the Hypershade.

- Release the mouse button.

  A pop-up menu appears offering you a number of attributes that can be mapped by the checker texture.

- Select **color** from the menu to map the grid to the material node's color attribute.

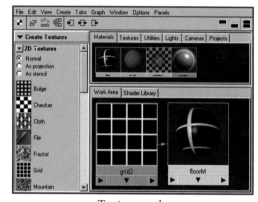

Texture node

3 Assigning the material

You will assign the texture map to the floor and then use hardware shading to preview it.

- With your middle mouse button, click on the *floorM* material node and drag it onto the floor surface in the perspective view.

- Move your cursor over the Perspective window and click with your middle mouse button to make it the active window.

- Evoke the hotbox and select **Shading → Hardware Texturing**.

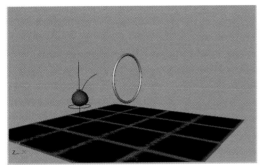

Hardware texturing

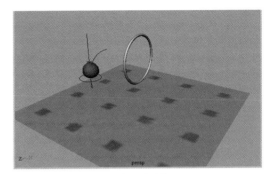

New Grid

Tip: You can also turn on hardware texturing by making the desired panel active and pressing the **6** key.

4 Edit the grid attributes

- In Hypershade, click on the *grid* node.

- In the Attribute Editor, click on the color swatch next to the **Line Color** attribute.

- Choose any color you want then click the **Accept** button.

- Click on the color swatch next to the **Filler Color** attribute.

- Choose any color you want then click the **Accept** button.

- Change the grid's width attributes as shown below:

    U Width to **0.75**;

    V Width to **0.75**.

The Attribute editor allows you to easily update the look of a procedural texture.

5 Display the whole shading group

- With the *grid* texture highlighted in the Hypershade, go to the second last button of the window and click on the **Input and Output Connections** button.

    This displays some other nodes that help define this shading group.

- Press the **Alt** key then click-drag with your left and middle mouse button to zoom out.

Input and Output Connections

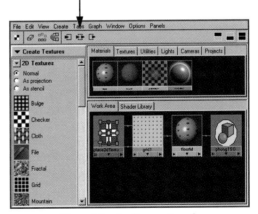

Complete shading network

6 Edit the texture's positioning

The placement of a texture on a surface is defined by the *place2DTexture* node.

- Click on the *place2dTexture* node to highlight it.

- In the Attribute editor, change the following attributes:

  Repeat U to **8**;

  Repeat V to **8**.

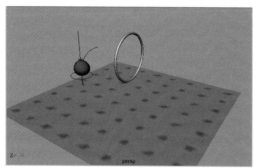

Updated texture placement

Creating a ball material

You will create a material for the ball that uses a file texture instead of a procedural texture. Many digital artists like to create textures in a 2D paint package. For the ball, you will use a painted texture of a face.

Face texture

1 Create a material for the ball

- From the Hypershade panel's work area right-click with the mouse and select **Graph** → **Clear Graph**.

- Re-select the Create Material menu and select **Phong**.

- Rename this node *ballM*.

2 Create a file texture node

To load an external texture, you need to start with a file texture node.

- In the Attribute editor, click on the **Map** button next to **Color**. The map button is shown with a small checker icon.

  This opens the Create Render node window.

- Click on the **Textures** tab in the **2D Textures** section, then click on **File**.

  A file node is added to the phong material. All the appropriate connections have already been made.

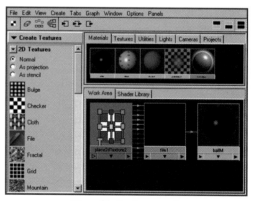

New file texture node

3 Import the file texture

- In the Attribute editor, click on the **File folder** button next to **Image name**.

- Select the file names *face.iff* then click on the **Open** button.

  The file texture is now loaded into the shading network.

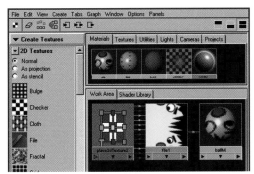

Imported file texture

Note: This file will be available only if you set up your project as indicated at the beginning of lesson 1.

---

4 Apply the material to the ball

- **Select** the ball in the perspective view.

- In the Hypershade, click on the *ballM* node with your right mouse button and choose **Assign Material to Selection** from the pop-up menu.

  The texture is assigned to the ball but it doesn't seem to be positioned correctly. You will correct this using the placement node.

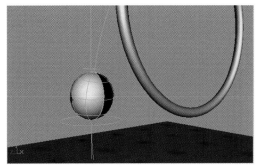

Ball with texture

Tip: This method of assigning materials works better than the click-drag method when you want to assign a material to multiple objects.

Positioning the texture

When the file texture was assigned to the ball, it was mapped to the actual surface of the ball based on the surface's topology. In this case, this results in the texture being rotated on the surface of the ball. You can rotate the texture's placement to correct the problem.

1 Change the texture's rotation

- Click on the file texture node's *place2DTexture*. This will activate it in the Attribute Editor.

- In the Attribute Editor, set the following attribute:

  Rotate UV to **90**.

  If you are using hardware texturing, you can see the file texture is now oriented properly on the ball's surface but it is facing the wrong

way. This is because the ball's seam is facing forward. You need to offset the texture.

Backward ball texture

- In the Attribute Editor, set the following attribute:

  Offset V to **0.5**.

  This will place the file texture so that it is facing the front of the ball.

Rotated ball texture

2 Test Render the scene

Now that you have the textures ready, it would be a good time to do a test rendering.

- In the Render view panel, click with your right mouse button and select

Render → Render → persp from the pop-up menu.

You can now see a rendered image of your scene. However because you have not created any lights the image renders using a default light.

LIGHTING

In the real world, it is light which allows us to see the surfaces and objects around us. In computer graphics, digital lights play the same role. They help define the space within a scene, and in many cases help to set the mood or atmosphere.

Placing a spot light

To create the primary light source in the scene, you will use a spot light. This light type lets you define important attributes such as the light's cone angle and its intensity.

1 Create a spot light

- Press **F5** to go to the rendering menu set.

- Click on the perspective view panel with your middle mouse button then press the **spacebar** quickly to pop to a full view.

- From the hotbox, select **Create → Lights → Spot Light.**

  This places a spot light at the origin.

2 Edit the spot light's position

This tool gives you a manipulator for the light's *look at point* and *eye point*. You can edit these using the same method as you would with a typical transform manipulator.

- Press the **t** key to access the **Show Manipulator** tool.

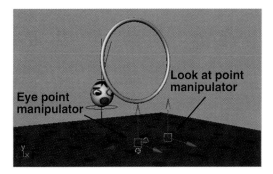

Show manip tool

- Click-drag on the manipulator handles to reposition the light.
- Move the manipulators until they appear as shown below.

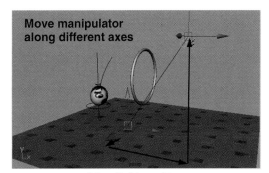

New light position

3 Turn on hardware lighting (if possible)

One step beyond hardware texturing is *hardware lighting*. This lets you see how the light is affecting the surface that it is shining on.

- From the hotbox, select **Lighting → Use All Lights.** You could also use the **7** key.

At first you may not see much lighting on the surface. You need to update the floor's subdivisions.

- In the Perspective window, click and hold with the right mouse button on the floor object.
- From the marking menu, select **Inputs → PolyPlane - ❑.**

This node now displays in the Attribute editor.

- Set the following attributes:

   Subdivisions Width to **20**;

   Subdivisions Height to **20**.

The spot light's cone of illumination can now be seen on the surface of the floor.

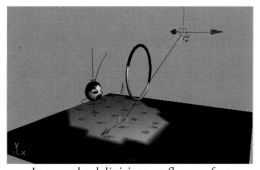

Increased subdivisions on floor surface

Note: You only need to increase the subdivisions for a hardware texturing preview of the scene. If you are software rendering, then one subdivision in each direction should work fine.

4 Edit the spot light's cone angle

You can now edit some of the light's attributes to control its effect. You will

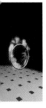

reveal other light manipulators to let you edit this attribute interactively.

- **Select** the spotlight.
- Press **t** to select the **Show Manipulator** tool.

Next to the light is a small icon that displays a circle with a small line pointing up and to the right. This icon is the cycling index and is used to cycle between different types of light manipulators.

- Click two times on the manipulator's cycle index.

  The cycling index rotates to show that you are accessing new manipulators. The chosen manipulator consists of a little blue dot just outside of the light cone. The new manipulator lets you edit the cone angle of the spot light.

- Click-drag on the cone angle manipulator to illuminate more of the scene.

  In the Attribute editor, you can watch the **Cone Angle** attribute update as you click-drag.

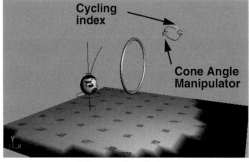

New angle of view

5 View through the light

It is sometimes difficult to position a light when standing beside the scene. In Maya, you can also look *through* the light to aid in positioning.

- Click with your middle mouse button over the perspective view panel to make it active.
- Using the hotbox, select **Panels →️ Look Through Selected**.

  You are now looking at the scene from the light's point of view. The Cone Angle manipulator is still available for you to click-drag.

- Click-drag on the manipulator to set the **Cone Angle** to about **60** degrees.

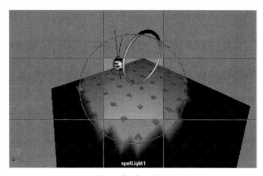

Spot light view

6 Reposition the light

You can now use the view change tools to edit the position of the light.

- Press the **Alt** key to tumble, pan and dolly into the view.

  Work with these tools until you see a view similar to the view shown below:

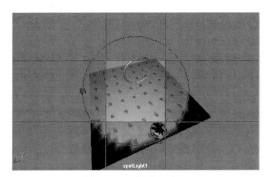

New spot light view

Tip: You may want to playback the animation to make sure that the ball is illuminated throughout its bouncing.

7 Adjust the Penumbra angle

To get some softness at the edge of the spotlight, you can adjust the light's penumbra.

- In the Attribute editor, set the **Penumbra Angle** to **5**.

- You can now see a second circular line outside the cone angle icon that indicates the area where the light will be soft.

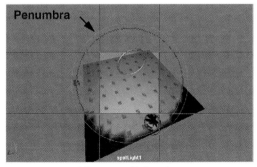

New spot light view

8 Return to Perspective view

- Middle mouse click in the perspective view panel to make it active.

- Using the hotbox, select **Panels** → **Perspective** → **persp.**

You are now looking at the scene from your old point of view.

Tip: You can click-drag lights and cameras from the Outliner to any view panel.

9 Playback the animation

- Use the view tools to center the action within the view panel.

- Playback the animation using the necessary hotkeys to see how it looks with hardware lighting.

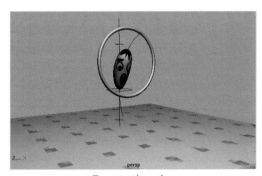

Perspective view

Rendering the scene

Now that you have a light in your scene, you can turn on shadow casting then create a test render. This will let you see a higher quality image of a still frame.

1 Turn on depth map shadows

In Maya, shadows are turned off by default for each light. This allows you to turn shadows on for only those lights that require shadows.

- Select the *spotLight*.

- In the Attribute Editor, open the **Shadows** section and click on **Use Depth Map Shadows**.

  Leave the default settings. They will be explained in more depth in a later lesson.

2 Set Render Globals

The Render Globals are a set of global attributes that you can set to define how your scene will render. To set up the quality of the test rendering, you need to set the Render Globals.

- Quick tap with the space bar in the perspective window to go back your original Persp/Hypershade/ Render View layout. In the Render View panel, click with your right mouse button and choose **Options → Render Globals...**

- Select the **Maya Software** tab.

- Open up the **Anti-aliasing Quality** section.

- Set the presets to **Intermediate Quality**.

  Anti-aliasing is a visual smoothing of edge lines in the final rendered image. Because bitmaps are made up of square pixels, a diagonal line would appear jagged unless it was somehow anti-aliased.

- Close the Render Globals window

3 Display resolution gate

Your current view panel may not be displaying the actual proportions that will be rendered. You can display the camera's resolution gate to see how the scene will actually render.

- Make the Perspective view the active panel.

- Use the hotbox to select **View → Camera Settings → Resolution Gate**.

  The view is adjusted to show a bounding box that defines how the default render resolution of 320 x 240 pixels relates to the current view.

- Dolly into the view so that it is well composed within the resolution gate. Try to set up a view where the ball starts in the back of the scene then animates to the front.

  Keep in mind that only objects within the box will be rendered.

- Playback the animation to confirm that the scene works for the whole sequence. If not, then edit the view until you are happy with the camera setup.

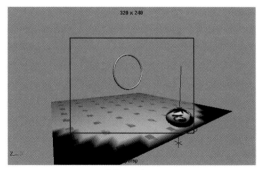

New view

4 Test render the scene

- Select **Display** → **UI Elements** → **Time Slider**.

- Go to frame 30.

- In the Render View panel, click with the right mouse button and choose **Render** → **Render** → **persp**.

Close-up of rendering

- In the Render View panel, click with your right mouse button and choose **View** → **Real Size**.

Rendered scene

5 Zoom into the rendering

You can view the rendering using the **Alt** key and the zoom and track hotkeys.

- Use the **Alt** key and the left and middle mouse buttons to zoom in to the view.

  Now you can evaluate in more detail how your rendering looks at the pixel level.

Rendering animations

Once you are happy with your test rendering, it is time to render an animation. This will be accomplished using Maya's *batch renderer*. In preparation, you will add motion blur to your scene to simulate the blur generated in live action film and video work.

1 Set the Image output

To render an animation, you must set up the scene's file extensions to indicate a rendered sequence. You must also set up the Start and End Frames.

- From the Hotbox, select **Window** → **Rendering Editors** → **Render Globals...**

- Select the **Common** tab.

- From the **Image File Output** section, set the following:

  File Name Prefix to **bounce**;

  This sets the name of the animated sequence.

Frame/Animation Ext to:

name.#.ext (for Windows, Mac)

name.ext.# (for IRIX);

This sets Maya up to render a numbered sequence of images.

Start Frame to **1**;

End Frame to **60**;

By Frame to **1**.

This tells Maya to render every frame from 1 to 60.

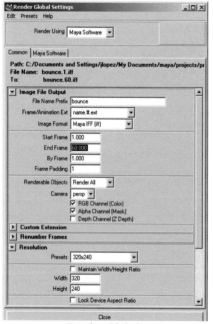

Render Globals

2 Turn on motion blur

- Select the **Maya Software** tab.
- Under the **Motion Blur** section, click on the **Motion Blur** button to turn it on.
- Set the Motion Blur Type to be 2D.

This type of motion blur renders the fastest.

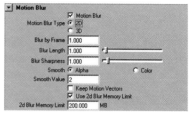

Motion blur check box

3 Save your work

- From the **File** menu, select **Save Scene As...**
- Enter the name *bounce_03* next to the file's path.
- Press the **Save** button or press the **Enter** key.

4 Batch render the scene

- Press **F5** to change to the **Render** menu set.
- Use the hotbox to select **Render → Batch Render**.

5 Watch the render progress

The sequence will be rendered as a series of frames.

- Use the hotbox to select **Window → General Editors → Script Editor.**

In this window, you can watch a series of status entries for your animation.

6 View the resulting animation

After the rendering is complete, you can preview the results using the *fcheck* utility.

On Windows, Mac

- Open the fcheck utility by clicking on its icon.

- Select **File** → **Open Animation**.
- Navigate to the `projectOne\images` folder.
- Select the file *bounce.1.iff* then click **Open**.

  This is the first frame of your rendered animation.

On IRIX

- In a shell window, set your current directory to the `maya/projects/learningMaya/projectOne/images` directory.
- Type the following:

  ```
  fcheck bounce.iff.
  ```

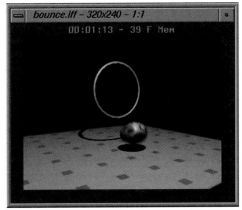

Animation previewed with fcheck utility

In both cases, the animation will load one frame at a time then playback more quickly once in memory.

Tip: To learn more about the capabilities of fcheck for previewing your animations, enter `fcheck -h` in a shell window.

Conclusion

You have now touched some of the basic concepts in texturing and rendering a scene. Maya's shading groups offer a lot of depth for creating the look of your scenes. In later lessons, you will learn how to make use of some of this power.

The resulting animation shows a ball with a texture map of a face. In the next lesson, you will use particles to create a ring of fire that helps explain the concerned look on the ball's face.

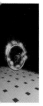

4 Particles

Particles are small object types that can be animated using dynamic forces in place of traditional keyframes. These effects are in essence *simulations* of physical effects such as water, smoke and fire.

To add particle effects to the scene, you are going to add flames to the ring. These flames will be created using Maya's default particle fire effect. You will then create sparks that will be animated to appear when the ball touches the fire.

The ring of fire

In this lesson you will learn the following:

- How to add a fire effect to a NURBS torus
- How to collide the ball and the flames
- How to set up a particle event
- How to define a particle attribute using a ramp
- How to define a particle attribute using an expression
- How to software render a particle animation
- How to hardware render a particle animation

Project set-up

If you are continuing from the last lesson, then you can begin working right away. If not, then open the Maya file you saved in that lesson. You will continue to use the menu-less user interface to explore the use of hotkeys and the hotbox.

1 Set up your Perspective panel

To simplify the workspace, you will focus on a single Perspective view. You will also turn off the resolution gate to let you focus on the particles.

- Use the spacebar to make the Perspective view panel full screen.

- Select **View** → **Camera Settings** → **No Gate** to turn off the resolution gate.

2 Change menu sets

- Press **h** and click with the left mouse button. Choose **Dynamics** from the marking menu.

Note: You could have also used the **F4** hotkey to change menu sets.

Ring of Fire

Using one of Maya's preset particle effects, you will add fire to the ring. This preset creates everything needed to make the particles act and look like fire.

1 Adding the Fire Effect

- Select the *ring* torus.

- Select **Effects** → **Create Fire**.

2 Playback the simulation

- Select **Display** → **UI Elements** → **Range Slider**.

- Click the **Animation Preferences** button found at the right side of the Range slider.

- In the **Playback** section, set the following:

  Playback Speed to **Play Every Frame.**

  When working with particles it is *very important* that the playback speed is set to play every frame. Otherwise your simulations may act unpredictably.

- Click the **Save** button.

- Go back to frame 1 and playback the simulation.

  The particles are generated from the ring. The simulation plays back at the same time the ball is animating. In Maya, you can combine animated objects with your particle simulations.

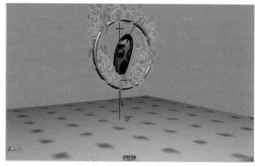

Default fire particles

The fire effect is the result of a particle object that is controlled by several dynamic fields such as

gravity and turbulence. The fire
preset added these elements to your
scene and lets you easily control
them.

Note: Particle simulations should always start
at frame 1 for you to see accurate
results.

3 Editing the fire attributes

To control the various parts of the fire
effect, you can simply edit attributes that
are designed specifically for the fire effect.

- Playback the simulation to a point
  where particles are visible then
  stop.
- Select the fire particles.
- In the Attribute editor, make sure
  that the *particleShape* tab is pressed.
- Rename the particles *flame*.
- Scroll down to the bottom and open
  the **Extra Attributes** section.
- Set the following attributes:

    Fire Density to **15**;

    Fire Lifespan to **1.5**.

- Go back to frame 1 and playback
  the simulation.

    Now there are more fire particles
    and they last longer.

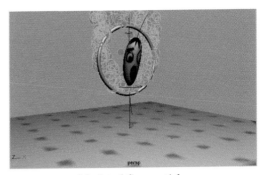

Updated fire particles

4 Setting the Initial state

One problem you may notice with the
simulation is that there are no particles
when the animation starts. Since the ring of
fire needs to be lit at all times, you must set
the particle's initial state.

- Playback the scene until around
  frame 30 then stop playback.
- Select the particles.
- From the **Solvers** menu, select **Initial
  State → Set for Selected**.
- Go back to frame 1 and playback
  the simulation.

    By setting the initial state for the
    particles, you can see that at frame
    1, the particles are already created.

5 Test render the particles

- Playback the scene until around
  frame 35 then stop playback.
- Press **F5** to go to the **Rendering**
  menu set.
- From the **Render** menu, select
  Render current frame...

The scene is now rendered with the fire particles included. Some particles can be rendered using the software renderer which allows them to be automatically integrated into the scene.

Software rendering

Note: The flame's shadows don't look very convincing because the depth map shadows don't work well with the fire's volumetric shader. Also, there is a strange halo around the fire that is caused by the 2D motion blur. You will fix these problems later in the lesson.

Sparks

As an added effect, you will set up more particles that will represent emitted sparks when the ball touches the flames. You will set up this effect to occur at exactly the point where the ball touches the flames.

1 Set up particle collisions

To make the ball and the particles collide, you must define them as colliding objects.

- **Select** the *flame* particles.

- Press the **Shift** key then **select** the ball.

Note: It is very important that the ball is selected last.

- Press **F4** to go back to the **Dynamics** menu set then from the **Particles** menu, select **Make Collide**.

2 Preview the results

- Select **Panels** → **Orthographic** → **front**.

- Playback the simulation.

  When the ball collides with the flames they are pushed a little forward.

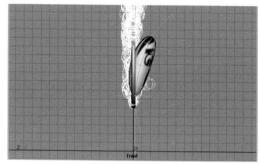

Minimal collisions

Note: If you are not getting a strong collision, you may want to adjust the ball's Y translate animation curve in the graph editor so that it jumps just over the bottom of the ring or you can raise the Y translate of the ring.

3 Adding friction

- **Select** the fire particles on their own.

- In the Attribute editor, click on the *geoConnector* tab.

- Set the following attributes:

  Resilience to **0.3**;

  Friction to **0.9**.

- Playback the simulation.

  Now the flames react a little more when they collide with the ball. The lower resilience allows them to react more and the friction is allowing the ball to drag the flames forward.

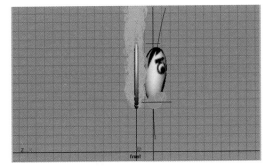

Stronger collisions

4 Create a Particle Event

To generate the sparks, you will use the collision between the ball and the flames to emit a new particle object.

- **Select** the fire particles.

- From the **Particles** menu, select **Particle Collision Events...**

- In the Particle Collision Events window, go to the Event Type section and set the following.

  Type to **Emit**;

  Random # Particles to **On**;

  Num particles to **6**;

  Spread to **0.2**;

  Inherit Velocity to **0.8**.

- Click **Create Event** and close the Particle Collision Events window.

- Playback the simulation.

  Several small particles are emitted after the ball touches the flames. These particles float forward based on the momentum they received from the collision. Now you will adjust how they react and how they look.

- Stop at a frame where the new particles are visible.

Particle collision event

5 Add Gravity to the particles

- Select the new particles.

- From the **Fields** menu, select **Gravity**.

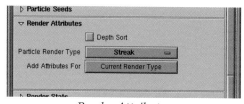

- In the Attribute editor, set the **Magnitude** to **25**.

  This will make them drop more quickly.

- Playback the simulation.

  Now the particles drop to the ground after the collision. The gravity field is pulling them down.

Designing the look of the sparks

To create particles that look like sparks, you need to adjust various particle attributes. In this case, you will create particles that will be streaks that die fairly quickly after being emitted. Their color will start out white, and then turn to a yellow-orange.

1 Change Render Type to streak

Particles can have their render type set from a list of possible looks. You can switch between the different types until you get one that suits your needs.

- Select the new particles.
- Rename them *sparks*.
- In the Attribute Editor, go to the **Render Attributes** section and set **Render Type** to **Streak**.

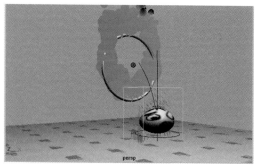

Render Attributes

This render type is designed to work with hardware rendering. This means that later, you will have to composite the final hardware rendered particles with software rendered scenes.

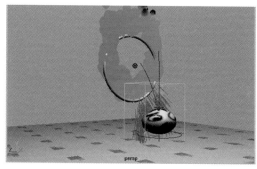

Streak particles

2 Add and edit render attributes

- Click on the **Current Render Type** button.
- Set the **Render Attributes** as follows:

    Line Width to **1**;

    Tail Fade to **0.67**;

    Tail Size to **3.0**.

  This gives the sparks a much stronger presence. The higher tail fade value means that it doesn't taper off too strongly and the tail size value lengthens the sparks.

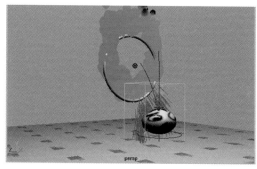

Streak particles

3 Add color per particle

The particle node has the ability to have new attributes added to it as they are needed. This lets you add complexity to a particle node when you need to.

You can use this technique to add color to the particles that will affect the particles individually instead of as a group.

- In the **Add Dynamic Attributes** section, click on the **Color** button.

- From the Particle color window, select **Add Per Particle Attribute** then click the **Add Attribute** button.

  This adds a *rgbPP* line to the **Per Particle Attributes** section.

- Click on the *rgbPP* field with your right mouse button and select **Create Ramp**.

- Click again on the *rgbPP* field with your right mouse button and select **<-arrayMapper.outColorPP → Edit Ramp**.

  In the Ramp window, you will find three markers each with a square and a circular icon.

- Click on the circle icon at the bottom of the ramp then click on the color swatch next to **Selected Color**.

- Change the color to white.

- Complete the same steps to change the middle marker to a yellow and the top marker to a yellow-orange.

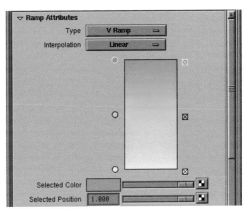

Particle color ramp

- Playback the simulation.

  Now the particles start out white then become yellow and orange over time.

4 Particle Lifespan and Randomness

The Lifespan attribute lets you determine how long the particle will remain in the scene before it disappears or dies. You will then add a slight randomness to the lifespan of the particles.

- With *sparks* selected, go to the **Lifespan Attributes** section in the Attribute editor.

- Change **Lifespan Mode** to **Random range**.

- Change the **Lifespan** to **0.4**.

- Change the **Lifespan Random** to **0.25**

  The lifespan is uniformly distributed with lifespan as the mean and lifespan Random as the width of the distribution.

Therefore the particles in this case have a lifespan between .15 and .65. This gives the sparks a more random look.

5 Save your work

- From the **File** menu, select **Save Scene As...**

- Enter the name *bounce_04* next to the file's path.

- Press the **Save** button or press the **Enter** key.

Rendering Particles

It was discussed earlier that the sparks used a particle type that could only be rendered using hardware rendering while the fire used software rendering. The question, therefore, is how do you bring hardware rendered particles together with software rendered scene?

The answer is to render them separately, and then bring them together using a compositing package.

To composite the particles with the ball, you will need to render the top layer – in this case the sparks – with a matte, or *mask*.

The mask is a grayscale channel that defines what areas are to be masked out when layered on top of the background. In this scene, the background is the bouncing ball, the ring of fire, and the floor.

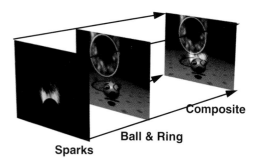

Diagram of compositing layers

Software rendering

The flames created using the fire effect can be rendered using software rendering. This means creating another batch rendering of your scene. This will represent the first render pass that can then be later composited together with the sparks.

1 Change your motion blur type

Since the 2D motion blur used in the last lesson doesn't render well with the flame particles, you will switch to the 3D motion blur type.

- Select **Window → Rendering Editors → Render Globals**.

- Open the **Motion Blur** section and change the **Motion Blur Type** to **3D**.

  This type of motion blur renders more slowly but is more accurate and works better with software rendered particles.

2 Fix the flame shadows

Earlier it was noted that the shadows generated from the flames didn't look correct. The depth map shadows can not recognize the subtleties of the volumetric shader used for the flames and raytrace shadows are needed.

- **Select** the spotlight that is illuminating the scene.

- In the Attribute editor, open the **Shadows** section, scroll down to **Raytrace Shadow Attributes** and set **Use Ray Trace Shadows** to **On**.

- Set the **Ray Depth Limit** to **2**.

  This sets up the light, but to use raytraced shadows, you will need to turn on raytracing itself.

- Open the Render Globals.

- Open the **Raytracing Quality** section and turn **Raytracing** to **On**.

Note: Maya uses a selective raytracer and only objects that require reflections, refractions or Raytrace shadows will use this technique.

---

3 Limiting the Reflections

When Raytracing is turned on, any shader that has a reflectivity value will render with reflections. It is therefore a good idea to set Reflectivity to 0 for some objects so that the rendering be as fast as possible.

- Open up a Hypershade panel.

- **Select** the ball, the floor and the ring in the perspective view.

- In the Hypershade, use the hotbox to select **Graph → Graph Materials on Selected Objects**.

- Select the *ballM* material node in the work area.

- In the Attribute editor, go to the Specular shading section and set **Reflectivity** to **0**.

  Now the ball won't reflect anything.

- Set **Reflectivity** to **0** for the *ring*.

- Set **Reflectivity** to **0.33** for the *floor* so that you do see some reflectivity in the scene.

4 Re-size of the floor surface

To make the floor larger so that it extends beyond the spotlight's influence, you will scale it out then update its texture placement to match the new size.

- Select the *floor* surface.

- In the Attribute editor, set the following:

  Scale X to **4**;

  Scale Y to **4**;

  Scale Z to **4**.

Note: The three columns in the Attribute Editor represent X, Y, Z.

- In the Hypershade, select the *floorM* shader.

- Click on the **Input connections** button.

- Click on the *place2Dtexture* node.

- In the Attribute editor, set the following:

  Repeat U to **32**;

  Repeat V to **32**.

5 Batch render the scene

- Select **File → Save Scene as...**

- Enter then file name *fire_bounce* then click **Save**.

- Press **F5** to change to the **Render** menu set.

- Use the hotbox to select **Render** → **Batch Render.**

  This will create a render pass that includes the geometry and the fire. You will now render the sparks using hardware rendering.

Hardware rendering

You have been using hardware rendering in the Perspective view panel to help preview the scene. You can also use hardware rendering to render the spark particles so that they match the rendered scene.

1 Set the opacity of the fire

Since you only want the sparks to appear in the hardware rendering, you will need to hide the flames by setting an opacity value to 0.

- Select the *flame* particles.

- In the Attribute editor, scroll down to the **Add Dynamic Attributes** section and click on **Opacity**.

- Choose **Add Per Object Attribute** then click on the **Add Attribute** button.

- This adds an opacity attribute to the **Render Attributes** section.

- Set **Opacity** to **0**.

  Now the particles will not be visible in the hardware rendering. You can set opacity to 0 when you want to

hardware render the scene and to 1 when you want to software render the scene.

2 Set the hardware render attributes

- Select **Window** → **Rendering Editors** → **Hardware Render Buffer**...

- In the Hardware Render Buffer window, select **Render** → **Attributes**...

- In the Attribute editor, set the following attributes:

  Filename to *sparks*;

  Extension to **name.1.ext** (Windows, Mac)

  or to **name.ext.1** (IRIX)

This should match the extension setting you chose for your software rendering.

  Start Frame to **1**;

  End Frame to **60**;

  Resolution to **320x240**;

This sets the length and size of the animation.

  Alpha Source to **Luminance**;

  Geometry Mask to **On**.

This will use the ring, floor and the ball as mask objects and the particle luminance to define the alpha. An alpha channel, otherwise known as a matte channel, is important for layering images in a compositing package later.

■ Open the **Multi-Pass Render Options** section and turn

> **Multi-Pass Rendering** to **On**;
>
> **Anti-Alias Polygons** to **On**.
>
> This will soften the look of the rendering.

Note: In some ways, these attributes are similar to the Render Globals, except that these settings only affect hardware rendering.

---

3 Test a frame

■ Playback the simulation until you hit a frame where some of the sparks appear.

■ Click on the **Test** button in the middle of the Render Buffer's time controls.

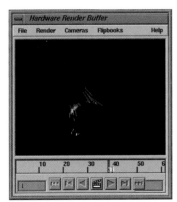

Hardware render buffer

Tip: The resolution gate must be off when performing a hardware render if it is to be composited with the batch render.

---

4 Render a sequence

You can now render a whole animation using this window. Compared to software rendering, this window lets you use the speed of hardware rendering to generate animations quickly.

■ Select **Render → Render Sequence**.

5 Preview the resulting flipbook

Once the sequence is complete, you can preview the results.

■ Select **Flipbooks → sparks.1-60**

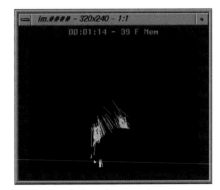

Animation preview

6 Composite rendered animations

You now have an animation of a bouncing ball and a sequence of particles embedded with an alpha channel. You can now use your compositing software to layer all the elements together.

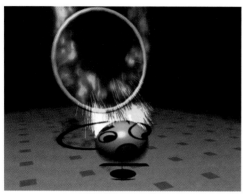

Final composite

The next chapter is a more in-depth look into some of the user interface elements that you have been using in these lessons. Once you have read this chapter, you will be able to make your own decisions on how you want to configure the UI for your needs.

In the projects that follow, the instructions will not specify whether or not you should use the hotbox or menus to complete an action. The choice will be left up to you.

There are several advantages to compositing your layers instead of rendering them all into one scene:

- by separating background and foreground elements and rendering them individually, rendering times can be greatly reduced;

- by rendering different elements on different layers, it is easier to later make revisions to one layer without having to re-render the whole scene;

- when working with particles, interesting effects can also be achieved by compositing hardware and software rendered particles; and

- by using different layers, you can use your compositing software to adjust the color for a particular layer without affecting other layers.

Conclusion

Congratulations, you now have a complete scene that includes objects, shaders and visual effects. You have also begun to develop skills that you will use throughout your use of Maya.

5 Working with Maya

If you have just completed the first four tutorials, then you have worked with Maya from modeling and animating to rendering and particles. Now is a good time to review some of the user interface concepts that you have worked with to give you a more complete overview of how Maya works.

It is recommended that you work through this chapter before proceeding with Learning Maya. This chapter explores the basic user interface actions that you will use in your day-to-day work.

The Workspace

You have learned how to build and animate scenes using different view panels and user interface tools. The panels offer different points of view for evaluating your work – such as perspective views, orthographic views, graphs and Outliners – while the tools offer you different methods for interacting with the objects in your scene. Shown below is the workspace and its key elements:

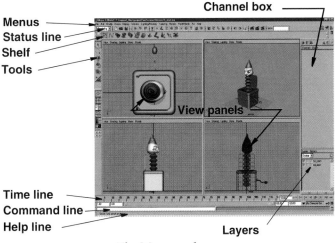

The Maya workspace

Layouts

When Maya is first launched, you are presented with a single Perspective view panel. As you work, you may want to change to other view layouts.

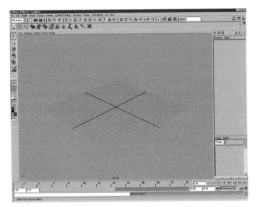

The default layout

To change your view layouts:

- Go to the view panel's **Panels** menu and select a new layout option from the **Layouts** pop-up.

The Layouts pop-up menu

You can set up various types of layouts ranging from two to four panels.

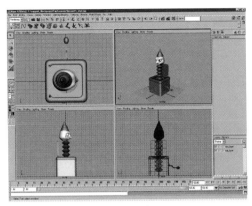

A four view layout

Tip: If you are looking at several view panels at the same time and you want to focus on one of them, tap the space bar and the view will become full screen. Tap the spacebar again and the panels will return to the previous layout.

View panels

As you begin to build and animate objects, you will want to view the results from various points of view. In Maya, you can place either perspective or orthographic views in each panel.

To change the content of a view panel:

- Go to the view panel's **Panels** menu and select a view type from either the **Perspective** or **Orthographic** pop-ups.

View tools

When you are working with perspective and orthographic views, you can change your view point by using hotkey view tools.

To tumble in a Perspective view:

- Press the **Alt** key and click-drag with the left mouse button.

Tip:	The ability to tumble an orthographic view is locked by default. To unlock this feature, you need to select the desired orthographic view and open the Attribute Editor.

To track in any view panel:

- Press the **Alt** key and click-drag with the middle mouse button.

To dolly in any view panel:

- Press the **Alt** key and click-drag with both the left and middle mouse buttons.

These view tools allow you to quickly work in 3D space using a simple hotkey.

Tip:	You can also track and dolly in other view panels such as the Hypergraph, the Graph Editor, Visor, Hypershade, and even the Render View window. The same view tools work for most panel types.

Other panel types

You can also change the content of the view panel to display other types of information such as the Hypershade or the Graph Editor.

To change the content of a view panel:

- Go to the view panel's **Panels** menu and select a panel type from the **Panel** pop-up.

The Panel pop-up menu

In the workspace below, you can see a Hypershade panel for helping you organize your shading groups and a Graph Editor for working with animation curves.

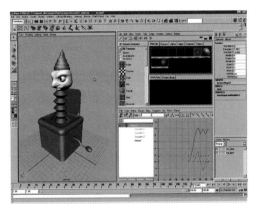

The workspace with various panel types

Saved layouts

As you become more familiar with Maya, you may want to set up an arrangement of panels to suit a particular workflow. For example, you may want a Dope sheet, a Perspective view, a Top view and a Hypergraph view all set up in a particular manner.

To add a new layout of your own:

- Go to the view panel's **Panels** menu and select **Saved Layouts** → **Edit Layouts...**

  In the Edit window, you can add a new saved layout and edit the various aspects of the layout.

To add a new layout to the list:

- Click on **New Layout**.

- Select and edit the layouts name.

- Press the **Enter** key.

To edit the configuration of a saved layout:

- Press the **Edit Layouts** tab.

- Choose a configuration, then click-drag on the center bars to edit the layout.

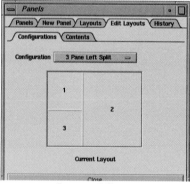

Layout Editor

- Press the **Contents** tab.

- Choose a panel type for each of the panels set up in the configuration section.

Display options

Using the Shading menu on each view panel, you can choose which kind of display you want for your geometry.

To change your panel display:

- Go to the panel's **Shading** menu and select one of the options.

Or

- Make the panel you wish to change the active panel.

- Use one of the following hotkeys to switch display types:

  4 for wireframe;

  5 for smooth shaded.

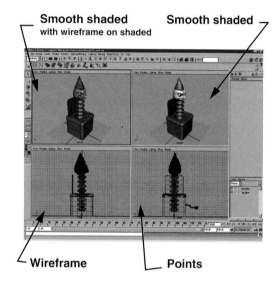

Various display styles

Texturing and lighting

Another important option found on this menu is hardware texturing. This option allows you to visualize textures interactively in the view panels.

To use hardware texturing:

- Build a shader that uses textures.

- Go to the panel's **Shading** menu and select **Hardware Texturing**.

Or

- Press the following hotkey:

    6 for hardware texturing.

To display different textures:

It is possible to display different texture maps on your surface during hardware texturing. For instance, you could display the color map or the bump map.

- Select the material that is assigned to your objects.

- In the Attribute editor, open the **Hardware Texturing** section and set the **Textured channel** to the desired channel.

- You can also set the **Texture quality** for each material node.

To add hardware lighting to your scene:

- Add a light into your scene.

- Go to the panel's **Lighting** menu and select one of the options.

Or

- Press the following hotkey:

    7 for realistic lighting.

| Texturing | Lighting |

Hardware lighting and texturing

Display smoothness

By default, NURBS surfaces are displayed using a rough smoothness setting in order to enhance playback and interactivity of scenes.

To increase objects smoothness:

- Go to the **Display** menu and under **NURBS Smoothness** choose one of the options.

Or

- Use one of the following hotkeys to switch display types:

    1 for rough;

    2 for medium;

    3 for fine.

Or

- Hold the **d** key, **LMB** click and choose an option from the marking menu.

Fine

Medium

Rough

Surface smoothness

Tip: If you want to set a particular smoothness when you first place a piece of geometry into the scene, go to the **Window** → **Settings/Preferences** → **Preferences**. In the **Display** section, you have various options for setting defaults.

Show menu

The Show menu is an important tool found on each view panel's menu. This menu lets you restrict what each panel can show on a panel-by-panel basis.

Restricting what each panel shows, lets you display curves in one window and surfaces in another to help edit construction history. Or you can hide curves when playing back a motion path animation while editing the same curve in another panel.

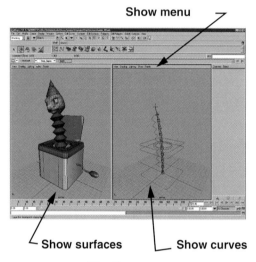

The Show menu

UI preferences

The Maya workspace is made up of various user interface elements which assist you in your day-to-day work. By default, this interface puts all of these on the screen for easy access.

To reduce the user interface to only view panels and menus:

- Go to the **Display** menu and select **UI Elements → Hide UI Elements.**

With less user interface clutter, you can rely more on hotkeys and other user interface methods for accessing tools while conserving screen real-estate.

To go back to a full user interface:

- Go to the **Display** menu and select **UI Elements → Restore UI Elements.**

Menus

Most of the tools and actions you will use in Maya are found in the main menus. The first six menus are always visible, while the next few menus change depending on which UI mode you are in.

Menus and menu pop-ups that display a dotted line at the top can be 'torn off' for easier access.

To tear off a menu:

- Pull down on the menu then release as your mouse hits the top of the menu.

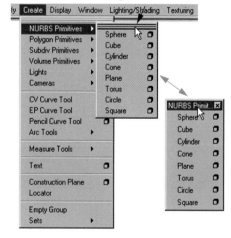

A tear-off menu

Later in this chapter, you will look at the difference between the two main types of menu items – *tools* and *actions*.

Menu sets

There are four menu sets in Maya: *Animation, Modeling, Dynamics* and *Rendering*. These allow you to focus on tools appropriate to a particular workflow.

To choose a menu set:

- Select the menu set from the pop-up menu found at the left of the Status Line bar.

To choose a menu set using hotkeys:

- Press the **h** key and choose the desired UI mode from the radial marking menu.

To choose a menu set using function keys:

- Press **F2** for Animation;
- Press **F3** for Modeling;
- Press **F4** for Dynamics;
- Press **F5** for Rendering.

The shelf

Another way of accessing tools and actions is using the shelf. You can move items from the menu to the shelf to begin combining tools into groups based on your personal workflow needs.

To add a menu item to a shelf:

- Press **Ctrl+Alt+Shift** then select the menu item. It will appear on the active shelf.

To edit the shelf contents and tabs:

- Go to the **Windows** menu and select **Settings/Preferences → Shelves...**

Status Line

The Status Line provides feedback on settings that affect the way the tools behave. The display information consists of:

- the current menu set
- icons that allow you to create a new, open a saved, or save the current
- the selection mode and selectable items
- the snap mode, the history of the selected lead object (visible by pressing the input and output buttons)
- the construction history flag
- Render into new window and IPR button
- quick selection field

To collapse part of shelf buttons:

- Press the small handle bar next to a the button set.

Selection mode

Collapsing handle

The Select modes before collapsing

Select modes button collapsed

Hotbox

As you have learned, pressing the spacebar quickly pops a pane between full screen and its regular size. If you press a little longer, you gain access to the hotbox.

The hotbox is a user interface tool that gives you access to as much or as little of the Maya UI as you want. It appears where your cursor is located and offers the fastest access to tools and actions.

To access the hotbox:

- Press and hold the spacebar.

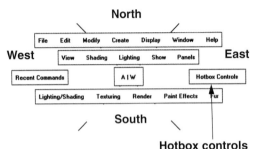

The hotbox with four quadrants marked

The hotbox offers a fully customizable interface element that provides you with access to all of the main menus as well as your own set of marking menus.

You can use the **Hotbox Controls** to display or show as many or as few menus as you need, and you can configure up to 15 different marking menus for fast interaction.

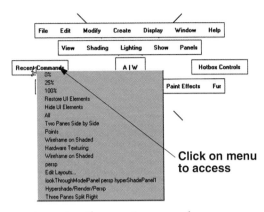

Accessing the recent commands menu

Hotbox marking menus

You can access marking menus in five areas of the hotbox. Since each of these areas can have a marking menu for each mouse button, it is possible to have 15 menus in total. You can edit the content of the marking menus by going to the **Window** menu and selecting **Settings/Preferences** → **Marking menus...**

To access the center marking menu:

- Press the spacebar.

- Click and drag in the center area to access the desired menu.

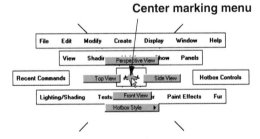

The center marking menu

To access the edge marking menus:

- Press the spacebar.

- Click and drag in the top quadrant to access the desired menu.

North marking menu

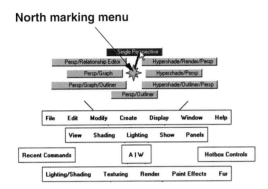

A quadrant-based marking menu

Customizing the hotbox

You can customize the hotbox to make it as simple or as complex as you need. You can choose which menus are available and which are not.

If you want, you can reduce the hotbox to its essentials and focus on its marking menu capabilities.

A reduced hotbox layout

Alternatively, you could hide the other UI elements, such as panel menus, and use the hotbox for access to everything. You get to choose which method works best for you.

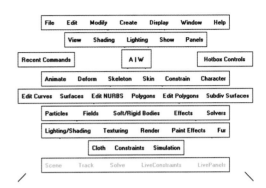

A complete hotbox layout

To customize the hotbox:

- Use the Hotbox controls.

Or

- Use the center marking menu.
- Choose an option from the Hotbox Styles menu.

Tool manipulators

To the left of the workspace you have access to important tools. These include the **Select**, **Move**, **Rotate**, **Scale** and **Show manipulator** tools. Each of these is laid out to correspond to a related hotkey that can be easily remembered using the QWERTY keys on your keyboard.

PROJECT ONE

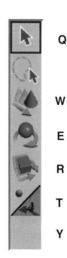

Q

W

E

R

T

Y

The QWERTY tool layout

These tools will be used for your most common tool-based actions—like selecting and transforming.

Note: The Y key drives the last spot on the QWERTY palette which is for the last tool used. The advantages of this will be discussed later in the *Tools and Actions* chapter of this document.

Transform manipulators

One of the most basic node types in Maya is the *transform node*. This node contains attributes focused on the position, orientation and scale of an object. To help you interactively manipulate these nodes, there are three transform manipulators which make it easy to constrain along the main axes.

Each of the manipulators uses a color to indicate their axes. RGB is used to correspond to XYZ. Therefore, red is for X, green for Y

and blue for Z. Selected handles are displayed in yellow.

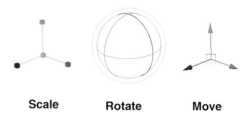

Scale   **Rotate**   **Move**

Transform manipulators

To explore some of the options available with manipulators, you will use the transform manipulator.

To use a transform manipulator in view plane:

- Click-drag on the center of the manipulator.

To constrain a manipulator along one axis:

- Click-drag on one of the manipulator handles.

Drag on handles to constrain

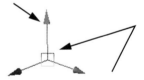

**Drag in center for all axes
(based on view plane)**

The move manipulator

To constrain a manipulator along two axes:

- Press the **Ctrl** key and click-drag on the axis normal to the desired plane of motion.

  This now fixes the center on the desired plane, thereby letting you click-drag on the center so that you can move along the two axes. The icon at the center of the manipulator changes to reflect the new state.

To go back to a view plane focus for center:

- Press the **Ctrl** key and click on the center of the transform manipulator.

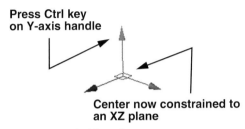

Press Ctrl key on Y-axis handle

Center now constrained to an XZ plane

Working along two axes

Note: The ability to constrain in two axes at a time is available to only the move manipulator.

Using the mouse buttons

When working with manipulators, you can use the left mouse button to select objects and interact directly with manipulators. The middle mouse button is for the active manipulator and lets you click-drag without direct manipulation.

To select objects:

- Set up selection masks.
- Click with the left mouse button.

To select multiple objects:

- Use the left mouse button and click-drag a bounding box around objects.

Or

- Press **Shift,** and with the left mouse button click on multiple objects.

To manipulate objects directly:

- Click-drag on a manipulator handle.

To manipulate objects indirectly:

- Activate a manipulator handle.
- Click-drag with the middle mouse button.

Shift gesture

The manipulators allow you to work effectively in a Perspective view panel when transforming objects.

If you want to work more quickly when changing axes for your manipulators, there are several solutions available.

To change axis focus using hotkeys:

- Press-hold on the transform keys:

    w for move;

    e for rotate;

    r for scale.

- Choose an axis handle for constraining from the marking menu.

To change axis focus using shift key:

- Press the **Shift** key.
- Click-drag with the middle mouse button in the direction of the desired axis.

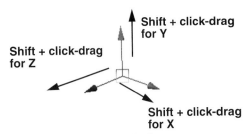

Shift + click-drag for Y

Shift + click-drag for Z

Shift + click-drag for X

Transform manipulators

Set pivot

The ability to change the pivot location on a transform node is very important for certain types of animation.

To change your pivot point:

- Select one of the manipulator tools.

- Press the **Insert / Home** key.

- Click-drag on a manip to move pivot.

- Press **Insert / Home** to return to the manipulator tool.

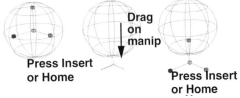

Drag on manip

Press Insert or Home

Press Insert or Home

Setting pivot using Insert / Home key

Numeric Input

To add values to your transformations using accurate values, you can use the numeric input box. This allows you to apply exact values to the attributes associated with the current manipulator. You can use the Command Feedback line to check out current values and to confirm your results.

To access the Help Line:

- From the **Display** menu, select **UI Elements** → **Help Line.**

To change focus to the coordinate box:

- Click on the box.

Or

- Press the **Alt** - ~ keys

To change all values at once:

- Enter three values in a row, with spaces in between.

abs▾ 8 1 6

Numeric input field

Note: Beside the coordinate box is a button to toggle between absolute and relative values. The default is absolute.

To enter a value for the active manipulator.

- Click on the desired handle. (e.g. - Z-translate)

- Enter a single value.

abs▾ 8

Inputting active manipulator value

Note: If no manipulator handle is active, then the single value will be applied to X.

To enter a value while preserving others:

- Type in periods (.) for channels that you want to stay the same. remember to add spaces in between.

- Enter a numeric value for the channels that will change.

  The example below would keep the X and Y values constant and change only the Z information.

Entering periods to keep values constant

Channel box

Another way of entering accurate values is the Channel box. This powerful panel gives you access to an object's transform node and any associated input nodes.

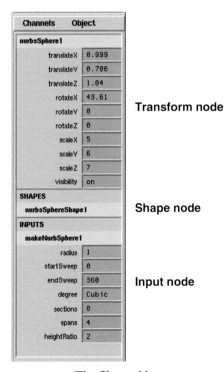

Transform node

Shape node

Input node

The Channel box

If you have multiple objects selected, then your changes to a channel will affect all the nodes which share that attribute.

To put one of the selected objects at the top of the Channel box so that it is visible, choose the desired node from the channel box's **Object** menu.

If you want to work with a particular channel, you can use the **Channels** menu to set keys, add expressions and complete other useful tasks. You can also change the display of the Channel box names to short MEL-based names.

Channels menu

Note: To control what channels are shown in the Channel box, you must go to the **Window** menu, and choose **General Editors → Channel Control**.

Channel box and manipulators

One of the features of the Channel box is the way in which you can use it to access manipulators at the transform level.

By default, the Channel box is set to show manipulators each time you tab into a new Channel box field. You will notice that as you select the channel names such as *Translate Z* or *Rotate X*, the manipulator switches from translate to rotate.

One fast way of working is to select the name of the desired channel in the Channel box, then use the middle mouse button to edit the value by click-dragging in a view panel.

There are three options for the Channel box manipulator setting:

Default manipulator setting

This setting lets you activate the appropriate field in the Channel box, and then modify the values with either the left or the middle mouse buttons.

To use the default method, complete the following steps:

- Click on the desired channel name or within the channel's input field.

- Click-drag directly on the active manipulator with the left mouse button.

Or

- Click-drag in open space with the middle mouse button.

  This may be the easier method since you can click remotely.

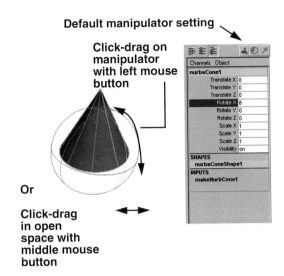

Channel box default manipulator setting

No-manipulator setting

You can click on the manipulator icon over the Channel box to turn manipulation off which leaves the Channel box focused on coordinate input. With this setting, you cannot use the middle or left mouse buttons for manipulation. To manipulate objects in this mode, you must do one of the following:

- Click in the channel's entry field and type the exact value.

Or

- Use one of the normal transform tools such as move, rotate and scale.

No-manipulator setting

No-visual manip setting

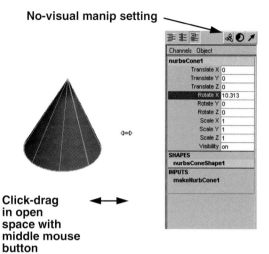

No interactive
manipulation
possible unless you
use a transform tool

Channel box no-manipulator setting

Click-drag
in open
space with
middle mouse
button

Channel box no-visual manipulator setting

No-visual manipulator setting

A third option found on this manip button
returns manipulator capability to the Channel
box – but now you won't see the manipulator
on the screen, as shown in the icon at the
bottom of the Channel box.

- Click on the desired channel name
  or within the channel's input field.

- Click-drag in open space with the
  middle mouse button.

  You can now use the two new
  buttons that let you edit the speed
  and dropoff of the manipulations.

The first button that becomes available with
the No-visual setting is the speed button
which lets you click-drag with your middle
mouse button either slow, medium or fast.

Channel speed controls

The second button is the drop-off button
which lets you choose between a linear
motion, as you click-drag with the middle
mouse button, or a click-drag that is slow at
first then faster as you drag further.

Channel drop-off options

Attribute Editor

If the Channel box lets you focus on attributes
that are keyable using **Set Key**, then the
Attribute Editor gives you access to all the
rest of the attributes/channels.

The Attribute Editor is used for all nodes in Maya. This means that shaders, textures, surfaces, lattices, render globals, etc. can all be displayed in this one type of window.

To open the Attribute Editor window:

- Select a node.
- Go to the **Window** menu and select **Attribute Editor**.

To open the Attribute Editor panel:

- Select a node.
- Go to the **Display** menu select **UI Elements → Attribute Editor**. The Channel box is now replaced by an Attribute editor panel.

When you open up the Attribute Editor, you get not only the active node, but also related nodes based on dependency relationships. In the example below, a sphere's transform, shape and *makeNurbSphere* nodes are all present. These are the same input and shape nodes shown in the Channel box.

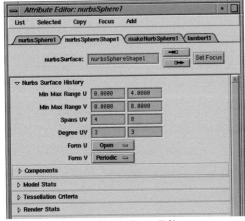

A typical Attribute Editor

SELECTING IN MAYA

One of the most important tasks when working in Maya is your ability to select different types of nodes and their key components.

For instance, you need to be able to select a sphere and move it, or you need to select the sphere's control vertices and move them. You also need to distinguish between different types of objects so that you can select only surfaces or only deformers.

Selection masks

To make selecting work in Maya, you have a series of selection masks available to you. This allows you to have one Select tool that is then *masked* so that it can only select certain kinds of objects and components.

The *selection mask* concept is very powerful because it allows you to create whatever combination of selecting types that you desire. Sometimes, you only want to select joints and selection handles, or maybe you want to select anything but joints. With selection masks, you get to set up and choose the select options.

The selection user interface

The user interface for selecting offers several types of access to the selection masks. You can learn all of them now and then choose which best suits your way of working down the line.

Grouping and parenting

When working with transform nodes, you can build more complex structures by building hierarchies of these node types.

To build these structures, you can choose to *group* the nodes under a new transform node or you can *parent* one of the nodes under the other so that the lower node inherits the motion of the top node.

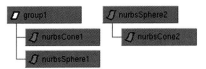

Grouped and parented nodes

Selection modes

At the top of the workspace, you have several selection mask tools available. These are all organized under three main types of select modes. Each of these gives you access to either the hierarchy, object type or components.

The select modes

Scene hierarchy mode

Hierarchy mode gives you access to different parts of the scene hierarchy structure. In the example shown below, the leaf node and the root node are highlighted. This mode lets you access each of these parts of the hierarchy. You can select root nodes, leaf nodes and template nodes using the selection masks.

Root nodes

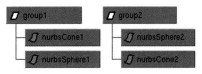

Leaf nodes

Hierarchy types

Object mode

Object mode lets you perform selections based on the object type. Selection masks are available as icons which encompass related types of objects.

With your right mouse button, you can access more detailed options that are listed under each mask group. If you create a partial list, the mask icon is highlighted in orange.

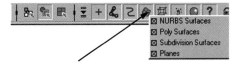

Click with RMB on icon for list

Object mode with selection masks

Tip:	Once you choose selection masks, Maya gives priority to different object types. For instance, joints are selected before surfaces. You will need to use the **Shift** key to select these two object types together. To reset the priorities, select **Window → Settings/ Preferences → Preferences** and click on the **Selection** section to modify the **Priority.**

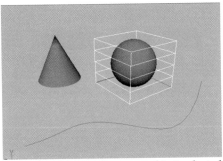

A lattice object and a curve object selected

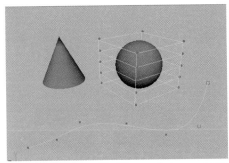

CV components and lattice point components

Component mode

The shape nodes of an object contain various components such as control vertices or isoparms. To access these, you need to be in component mode.

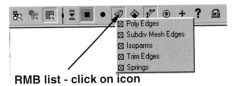

RMB list - click on icon

Component selection masks

When you select an object in this mode, it first highlights the object and shows you the chosen component type; you can then select the actual component.

Once you go back to object mode, the object is selected and you can work with it. Toggling between object and component mode allows you to reshape and position objects quickly and easily.

Tip: To toggle between object and component modes, press the **F8** key.

RMB select

Another way of accessing the components of an object is to select an object, then press the right mouse button. This brings up a marking menu that lets you choose from the various components available for that object.

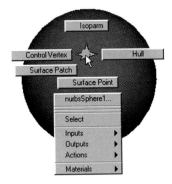

The right mouse button select menu

If you then select another object, you return to your previous select mask selection. This is a very fast way of selecting components when in hierarchy mode, or for components that are not in the current selection mask.

Combined select modes

Just in front of the selection mask mode icons is a pop-up menu that gives you different preset mask options. These presets let you combine different object and component level select options.

An example would be the NURBS option. This allows you to select various NURBS-based mask types such as surfaces, curves, CVs, curve control points and isoparms.

Note:	In this mode, if you want to select CVs which are not by default visible, then you must make them visible by going to the **Display** menu and selecting **NURBS Components → CVs**.

When using a combined select mode, objects and components are selected differently. Objects are selected by click-dragging a select box around a part of the object while components can be selected with direct clicking.

Note:	If you have CVs shown on an object and the select box touches any of them, then you will select these components instead of the object. To select the object, you must drag the select box over part of the surface where CVs are not.

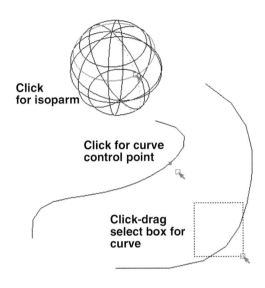

Click for isoparm

Click for curve control point

Click-drag select box for curve

NURBS select options

TOOLS AND ACTIONS

In Maya, there are a large number of menu items that let you act on your scenes in a number of ways. These menu items can be broken down into two types of commands: *tools* and *actions*, each working in their own particular way. Almost every function in Maya can be set to be a Tool or an Action.

Tip:	If a menu item says "Curve tool" then it uses tool interaction. If the word "tool" is not mentioned then the menu item is set as an action.

Tools

Tools are designed to remain active until you have finished using them. You select a tool, use it to complete a series of steps then press the **Select Tool**, or another tool. In most cases,

PROJECT ONE

the Help line at the bottom of the workspace can be used to prompt your actions when using the tool.

Earlier you were introduced to the **y** key on the QWERTY palette. By default, this button is blank because it has been left over to show the last tool used. When you pick a tool from the menus, it's icon inserts itself into the QWERTY menu.

To use as a tool:

- Pick a menu item and go to the options.

- Under the **Edit** menu, select **As Tool**.

  By default you will remain in this tool until you pick the Select tool, or another tool. There is also a setting that will remove you from the tool after the first completion.

To return to the last tool used:

- Press the **y** key.

Actions

Actions follow a selection-action paradigm. This means that you have to first pick something and then act on it. In Maya, this allows you to choose an action, return to editing your work, and lets you refine the results immediately.

Actions require that you have something selected before acting on it. This means that you must first find out what is required to complete the action.

To find out selection requirements of an action:

- Move your cursor over the menu item.

- Look at the Help line at the bottom left of your workspace.

The selection requirements are displayed. For instance, a **Loft** requires *curves, isoparms* or *curves on surfaces* while **Insert Isoparm** requires that isoparms be picked.

To complete the action:

- If the tool is not already set as an action, select **Edit → As Action** from the menu items' options.

- Use either pick modes or the right mouse button pick menu to make the required selections.

- Choose the action using either the hotbox, shelf or menus.

  The action is complete and your focus returns to your last transform tool.

A typical action: 2D fillet

A good example of a typical action is a 2D fillet. As with all actions, you must start with an understanding of what the tool needs before beginning to execute the action.

1 Draw two curves

- Select **Create → CV Curve Tool**.

- Place several points for one curve.

- Press **Enter** to complete.

- Press the **y** key to refocus on curve tool.

- Draw the second curve so that it crosses the first.

- Press the **Enter** key to complete

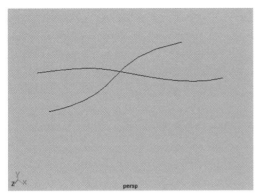

Two curves for filleting

2 Find out 2D fillet requirements

- In the Modeling menu set, move your cursor over the **Edit Curves** → **Curve Fillet** menu item.

- Look in the Help line to find out what kind of pick is required.

  The Help line is asking for *curve parameter points*.

3 Pick the first curve point

- Click on the first curve with the right mouse button.

- Pick **Curve Point** from the selection marking menu.

- Click on the curve to place the point on the side you want to keep.

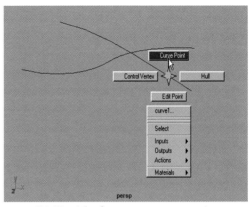

RMB pick of curve parameter point

4 Pick the second curve point

- Click on the second curve with the right mouse button.

- Pick **Curve Point** from the selection marking menu.

- Press the **Shift** key and click on the curve to place the point on the side of the curve you want to keep.

  The **Shift** key lets you add a second point to the selection list without losing the first curve point.

Note: You must first use the marking menu then use the **Shift** key to add a second point to the selection list, otherwise the selection menu will not appear.

Two curve points in place

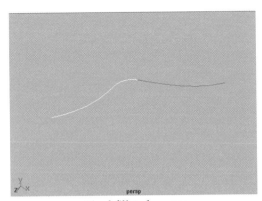

Final filleted curves

5 Fillet the curves

- Select **Modeling** → **Edit Curves** → **Curve Fillet** - ❏ to open the tool options.
- Turn the trim option on.
- Click on the **Fillet** button.

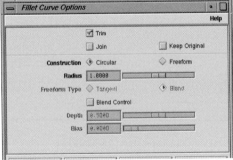

Fillet tool options window

A typical Tool: 2D fillet

With this example you will use the menu item as a Tool rather than an Action.

1 Draw two curves

- In a new scene, draw two curves as in the last example.

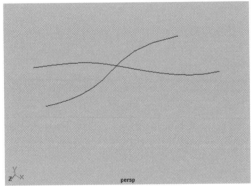

Two curves for filleting

2 Change Curve Fillet to Tool

- Select **Edit Curves** → **Curve Fillet** - ❏.
- Select **Edit** → **As Tool** from the options window.
- Set **Trim** to **On**.

- Press the **Fillet Tool** button.

3 Pick the first curve

- Click with the left mouse button on the first curve.

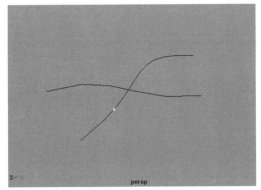

First curve selected

4 Pick the second curve

- Click with the left mouse button on the second curve.

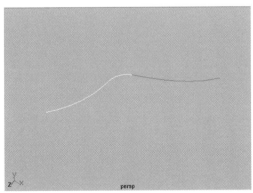

Final filleted curves

Conclusion

You now know how to navigate the Maya user interface and how the tools and actions work. The skills you have learned here will be applied throughout the rest of this book. It is now up to you to choose how you want to use the interface. Try out the different techniques taught here as you work through the Learning Maya projects.

In the next chapter, you will explore Maya's Dependency graph. You will learn about the different Maya nodes and how to build them into hierarchies and procedural animations.

PROJECT ONE

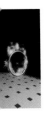

6 The Dependency Graph

In the first four lessons of this book, you were able to interactively animate a ball bouncing. Along the way, you encountered many nodes which helped you build up and animate the scene. You came across input nodes, hierarchy nodes, shading group nodes and texture nodes, as well as emitter and particle nodes. These nodes represent key elements within Maya – each node containing important attributes which help you define and animate your scenes.

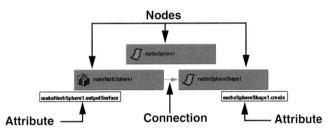

Nodes, attributes and connections

Maya's architecture is defined by this node-based system that is known as the *Dependency graph*. Each of your nodes contains attributes which can be connected to other nodes. If you wanted to reduce Maya to its bare essentials, you could basically describe it as *nodes with attributes that are connected*. This node-based approach gives Maya its open and flexible procedural characteristics.

In this chapter, you are going to explore nodes, attributes and connections by animated objects at various levels. You will explore how attributes are connected by Maya and how you can connect them yourself. You will also learn how to distinguish scene hierarchies from object dependencies.

This chapter will at first seem a bit abstract, but in the end you will be able to see how the various nodes contribute to an animated scene which will help you in later lessons.

Hierarchies and dependencies

If you understand the idea of *nodes with attributes that are connected,* then you will understand the Dependency graph. By building a simple primitive sphere, you can see what this means in Maya.

1 Set up your view panels

To view nodes and connections in a diagrammatic format, the Hypergraph panel is required along with a Perspective view.

- Select **Panels → Layouts → 2 Panes Side by Side**.

- Set up a Perspective view in the first panel and a Hypergraph view in the second panel.

- Dolly into the Perspective view to get closer to the grid.

2 Create a primitive sphere

- Select **Create → NURBS Primitives → Sphere**.

- Press **5** to turn on smooth shading and **3** to increase the surface smoothness of the sphere.

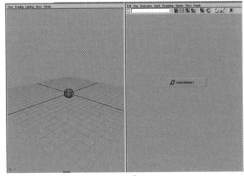

New sphere

3 View the shape node

In the Hypergraph panel, you are currently looking at the scene view. The scene view is focused on *transform nodes*. This type of node lets you set the position and orientation of your objects.

Right now, only a lone *nurbsSphere* node is visible. In actual fact, there are two nodes in this hierarchy but the second is hidden by default. At the bottom of most hierarchies, you will find a *shape node* which contains the information about the object itself.

- In the Hypergraph, select **Options → Display → Shape nodes**.

  You can now see the *transform node* which is in effect the positioning node, and the *shape node* which contains information about the actual surface of the sphere. The transform node defines the position of the shape below.

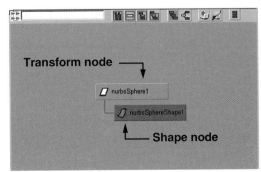

Transform and shape nodes

- In the Hypergraph panel, select **Options → Display → Shape nodes** to turn these off.

  Notice that when these nodes are expanded, the shape node and the transform node have different icons.

When collapsed, the transform node takes on the shape node's icon to help you understand what is going on underneath.

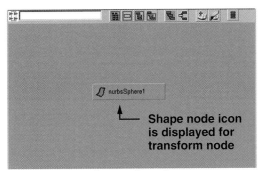

Transform node on its own

4 View the dependencies

To view the dependencies that exist with a primitive sphere, you need to take a look at the up and downstream connections.

- In the Hypergraph panel, click on the **Input and Output Connections** button.

  The original transform node is now separated from the shape node. While the transform node has a hierarchical relationship to the shape node, their attributes are not dependent on each other.

  The *input node* called *makeNurbSphere* is a result of the original creation of the sphere. The options set in the sphere tool's option window, have been placed into a node that feeds into the shape node. The shape node is dependent on the input node. If you change values in the input node, then the shape of the sphere changes.

You will also see the initial Shading group connected to the sphere. This is the default grey lambert that is applied to all new objects.

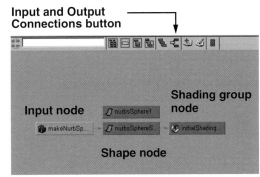

Sphere dependencies

5 Edit attributes in the Channel box

In the Channel box, you can edit attributes belonging to the various nodes. All of the node types can be found in the Channel box. This lets you affect both hierarchical relationships and dependencies.

If you edit an attribute belonging to the *makeNurbSphere* node, then the shape of the sphere will be affected. If you change an attribute belonging to the *nurbSphere* transform node, then the positioning will be changed. Use the Channel box to help you work with the nodes.

- For the transform node, change the **Rotate Y** value to **45**.

- For the *makeNurbSphere* input node, change the **Radius** to **3**.

  You can set attribute values to affect either the scene hierarchy or the Dependency graph.

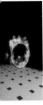

Shading group nodes

In earlier lessons, the word *node* was used a great deal when working with shading groups. In fact, shading group nodes create dependency networks which work the same way as shape nodes.

1 Create a shading group

When you create a shading group you are creating two main nodes that are connected – the shading group node and the material node.

- Select **Window** → **Rendering Editors** → **Hypershade**.

- In the Hypershade window, select **Create** → **Materials** → **Phong**. Assign this material to the sphere.

- Select the sphere in the perspective panel then click on the **Input and Output Connections** button.

   In the Hypergraph view, you will notice how the input node is connected to the shape node which relates to the phong shading group.

   A line is now drawn between the sphere's shape node and shading group node. This is because the shading group is dependent on the surface in order to render.

   Every time you assign a shading group to an object you make a dependency graph connection.

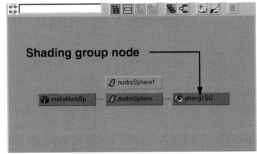

Shading group dependencies

- Select the *nurbSphere* node and the *phongSG* node in the Hypergraph.

- Again, click on the **Input and Output Connections** button.

   You can now see how the *phong* material node and the sphere's shape node both feed the shading group. You can move your cursor over any of the connecting lines to see the attributes that are being connected.

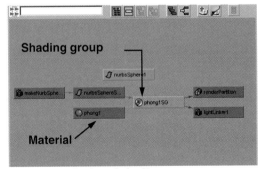

Assigned shading group

2 Open the Attribute Editor

You have seen how the nodes in the Hypergraph and the Channel box have been used to view and edit attributes on connected nodes. Now you will see how the Attribute Editor displays nodes, attributes and connections.

- Click on the **Scene Hierarchy** button in the Hypergraph Panel to go back to a scene view.

- Select the sphere's transform node.

- Press **Ctrl-a** to open the Attribute Editor.

  In this important window, you will see several tabs each containing groups of attributes. Each tab represents a different node. All the tabs displayed represent parts of the selected node's Dependency graph that are related to the chosen node. By bringing up several connected nodes, you have easier access to particular parts of the graph.

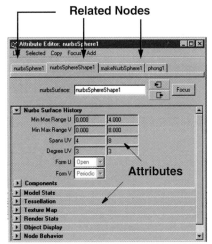

Nodes and attributes in Attribute Editor

- Close this window.

Note: In Maya, the Dependency graph lets you focus on one part of the graph at a time.

Making your own connections

To help you understand exactly what a Dependency graph connection is, you are going to make your own connection and see how it affects the graph.

1 Open the Connection Editor

- Select **Window** → **General Editors** → **Connection Editor...**

- Click on the **Reload Left** button.

  The selected transform node is loaded into the left column. All of the attributes belonging to this node are listed.

Note: There are more nodes here than you saw earlier in the Channel box. The Channel box only shows attributes that have been set as keyable. Other nodes can be found in the Attribute Editor.

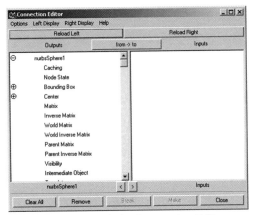

Transform node in Connection Editor

2 Add phong as the output node

- In the Hypergraph, select **Rendering → Show Materials**.

- Select the *phong1* material node.

- In the Connection Editor, click on the **Reload Right** button.

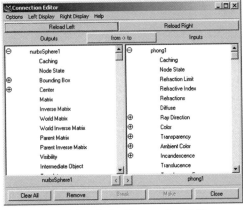

Material node in Connection Editor

3 Make connections

You will now connect some attributes in from the transform node to the material node.

- In the left hand column, scroll down until you find the *Translate* attributes.

- Click on the plus sign to open this attribute type and see the *Translate X, Y* and *Z* attributes. Be sure not to click on the name.

- In the right hand column, scroll down until you find the *Color* attribute.

- Click on the plus sign to open this attribute type and see the *Color R, G* and *B* attributes.

- Click on the **Translate X** attribute in the left hand column.

- Click on the **Color R** in the right hand column.

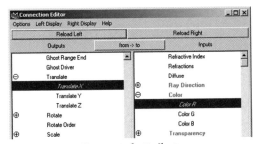

Connected attributes

- Use the same method to connect:

  Translate Y to **Color G**;

  Translate Z to **Color B**.

4 View the connections

- In the Hypergraph panel, select the *phong* node then click on the **Input and Output Connections** button.

- Move your cursor over one of the arrow connections between the transform node and the material node.

The arrow is highlighted and the connected attributes are displayed. You now see the diagrammatic results of your action. Now you should see the effect in the Perspective view.

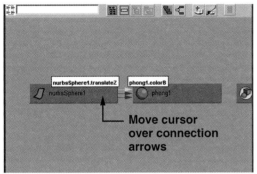

Viewing attribute connections

5 Move the sphere

- In the Perspective view, **select** the sphere.
- **Move** the sphere along the X-axis.

  The color of the sphere changes to red. By increasing the value of the translation along X, you add red to the color.

- Try moving the sphere along each of the three main axes to see the colors change.

Adding a texture node

While it is a fun and educational exercise to see the material node's color dependent on the position of the ball, it may not be very realistic. You will now break the existing connections and map a texture node in their place.

1 Delete connections

You can delete the connections in the Hypergraph view.

- In the Hypergraph view panel, select one of the three connection arrows between the transform node and the material node.
- Press the **Backspace** key to delete the connection.
- Repeat for the other two connections between these nodes.

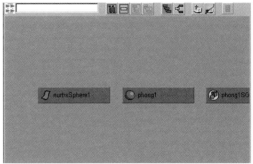

Broken connections

2 Add a checker texture map

You will now use the Attribute Editor to help you add a texture to the existing shading group.

- Click on the *phong1* material node.
- Press **Ctrl a** to open the Attribute Editor.
- Click on the **Map** button next to Color.
- Choose a *Checker* texture from the Create Render node window.
- Move your cursor over the Perspective view panel and press **6**.

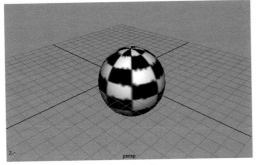

Textured sphere

In the Hypergraph, you can see the dependencies building up for the shading group. The texture is built using two nodes. The checker node which contains the procedural texture attributes, and the placement node which contains attributes that define the placement of the texture on the assigned surfaces.

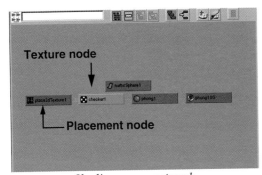

Texture node

Placement node

Shading group network

Animating the sphere

When you animate in Maya, you are changing the value of an attribute over time. Using keys, you set these values at important points in time, then use tangent properties to determine how the attribute value changes in between the keys.

The key and tangent information is placed in a separate animation curve node that is then connected to the animated attribute.

1 Select the sphere

- In the Hypergraph panel, click on the **Scene Hierarchy** button.

- **Select** the *nurbsSphere* transform node.

2 Return the sphere to the origin

Since you earlier moved the sphere along the three axes, it's a good time to set it back to the origin.

- In the Channel box, set the **Translate X, Y** and **Z** to **0, 0, 0**.

- In the Channel box, change the **Rotate Y** attribute to **0**.

3 Animate the sphere's rotation

- In the Time slider, set the playback range to **120** frames.

- In the Time slider, go to frame **1**.

- Click on the **Rotate Y** channel name in the Channel box.

- Click with your right mouse button and select **Key Selected** from the pop-up menu.

   This sets a key at the chosen time.

- In the Time slider, go to frame **120**.

- In the Channel box, change the **Rotate Y** attribute to **720**.

- Click with your right mouse button and select **Key selected** from the pop-up menu.

- Playback the results.

   The sphere is now spinning.

4 View the dependencies

- In the Hypergraph panel, click on the **Input and Output Connections** button.

    You see that an animation curve node has been created and then connected to the transform node. The transform node is now shown as a trapezoid to indicate that it is now connected to the animation curve node. If you click on the connection arrow, you will see that the connection is to *Rotate Y*.

    If you select the animation curve node and open the Attribute Editor, you will see that each key has been recorded along with value, time and tangent information. You can actually edit this information here, or use the Graph Editor where you get more visual feedback.

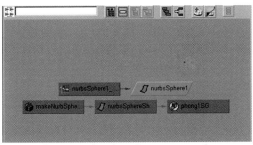

Connected animation curve node

Building scene hierarchies

So far, you have worked a lot with the dependency connections but not with the scene hierarchy. In a hierarchy, you always work with transform nodes. You can make one transform node the *parent* of another node, thereby creating a child which must follow the parent.

You will build a hierarchy of spheres that are rotating like planets around the sun. This example is a helpful way to understand how scene hierarchies work.

1 Create a new sphere

- Go to frame **1**.

- In the Hypergraph panel, click on the **Scene Hierarchy** button.

- Select **Create → NURBS Primitives → Sphere**.

- **Move** the sphere along the Z axis until it sits in front of the first sphere.

- Press **3** to increase the display smoothness of the sphere.

- Go to the **Rendering** menu set.

- Select **Lighting/Shading → Assign Existing Material → phong1**.

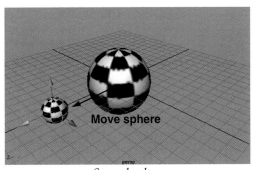

Second sphere

2 Parent the sphere

- Press the **Shift** key and select the first sphere.

- Press the **p** key to parent the new sphere to the first.

    The **p** key does the same thing as selecting **Edit → Parent**.

- Play back the scene.

  The second sphere rotates along with the first sphere. It has inherited the motion of the original sphere.

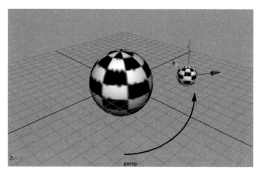

Rotating hierarchy

3   Animate the new sphere's rotation

While child nodes in a hierarchy inherit the motion of the parent, they can also contain their own animation.

- Go to frame **1**.

- With the new sphere selected, go to the Channel box and select **Key Selected** for the **Rotate Y** channel.

- Go to frame **120**.

- In the Channel box, change the **Rotate Y** attribute to **-1440**.

- **Key Selected** for the **Rotate Y** channel.

- Playback the scene.

  The second sphere rotates in the opposite direction as it revolves around the first sphere.

Note: One way of thinking of the hierarchy is to think of a person walking on our own planet. As the planet revolves around its axis, the person revolves too. The person can also walk, jump or spin.

4   Create another sphere

To make this point more clear, you will add a third sphere to the hierarchy to see what happens.

- Go to frame **1**.

- Select **Create** → **NURBS Primitives** → **Sphere**.

- **Move** the sphere along the Z-axis until it sits in front of the second sphere.

- **Scale** the sphere in all three axes to about one third its size.

- Press **3** to increase the display smoothness of the sphere.

- Go to the **Rendering** menu set.

- Select **Lighting/Shading** → **Assign Existing Material** → **phong1**.

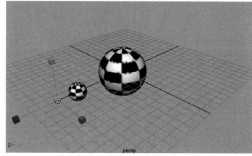

Third sphere scaled down

5 Parent the sphere

- In the Hypergraph panel, click on the **scene hierarchy** button.

- Now use the middle mouse button to click-drag the new transform node onto the second sphere's transform node. This is another method for parenting nodes.

- Play back the scene.

   The third sphere revolves with the rotation of the second sphere. This hierarchy is then revolved around the first sphere.

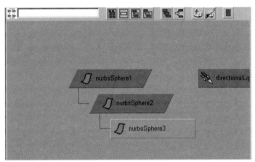

Scene hierarchy view

6 Move and rotate the hierarchy

- In the Perspective view panel, **select** the first sphere.

- Select **Edit → Group** to add another node to the hierarchy.

   This node is now the root of the hierarchy. You can use this to position the nodes below.

- **Move** the hierarchy up along the Y-axis about 5 units.

- **Rotate** the hierarchy around the X-axis about 15 degrees.

- Play back the results.

The hierarchy is now rotating at an angle. You have changed the axis of the whole system.

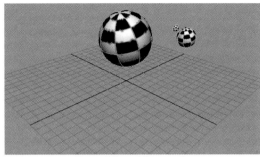

Repositioned hierarchy

Understanding how hierarchies work will be an important part of working with Maya. In upcoming lessons, keep an eye on how hierarchies are built, especially when you begin building characters.

Hiding objects

Before moving onto a more complex animation, you will hide the existing hierarchy. This will let you focus on the second part of this lesson.

1 Hide the grouped hierarchy

- With the new group selected, select **Display → Hide → Hide Selection**.

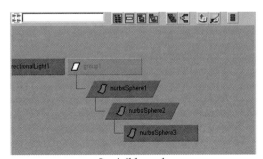

Invisible node

Procedural animation

If Maya's procedural nature is defined as *nodes with attributes that are connected*, then a procedural animation would be set up by animating attributes at various levels of a Dependency graph network.

You will now build a series of animated events that build on each other to create the final result.

1 Create an edit point curve

- Select **Create → EP Curve Tool**.
- Press the **x** key to turn on grid snap.
- Draw a curve as shown below.
- When you are finished, press **Enter** then select **Modify → Center Pivot**.

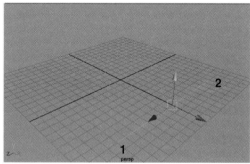

New curve

2 Duplicate the curve

- Select **Edit → Duplicate**.
- **Move** the new curve to the opposite end of the grid.

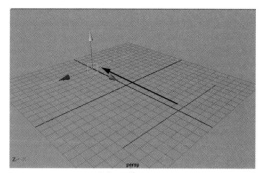

Moved curve

3 Create a lofted surface

A lofted surface can be created using two or more profile curves.

- Click-drag a selection box around both of the curves.
- Select **Surfaces → Loft**.
- Press **3** to increase the surface display smoothness.

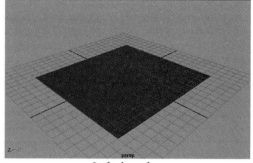

Lofted surface

4 Change your panel display

- In the Hypergraph panel, select **Panels → Perspective → persp**.
- In the Perspective panel, select **Show → None** then **Show → NURBS Curves**.

Now you have two Perspective views. One shows the surface in shaded mode and the second shows only the curves. This makes it easier to pick and edit the curves in isolation from the surface itself.

5 Edit CVs on the original curves

- **Select** the first curve.

- Click with your right mouse button to bring up the selection marking menu and select **Control Vertex**.

- Click-drag a pick box over one of the CVs and **Move** it down.

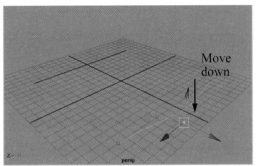

Edited profile curve

In the original Perspective view, you can see the effect on the lofted surface. Since the surface was dependent on the shape of the curve, you again took advantage of the Dependency graph.

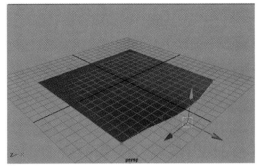

Resulting surface update

Note:	The dependencies associated with models are sometimes referred to as construction history. By updating the input shape, you have in effect updated the history of the lofted surface.

Creating a curve on surface

You will now build a curve directly onto the surface. This curve will become dependent on the shape of the surface for its own shape.

The surface was built as a grid of surface lines called *isoparms*. These lines help define a separate coordinate system specific to each surface. Whereas world space coordinates are defined by X, Y and Z, surface coordinates are defined by U and V.

1 Make the surface live

So far, you have drawn curves into the world space coordinate system. You can also make any surface in Maya into a *live* surface and draw into the UV space of the surface.

- **Select** the lofted surface.

  The CVs on the curve disappear and you are able to focus on the surface.

- Select **Modify** → **Make Live**.
- Select **Display** → **Grid** to turn off the ground grid.

2 Draw a curve on the surface

- Select **Create** → **EP Curve Tool**.
- Draw a curve on the live surface.

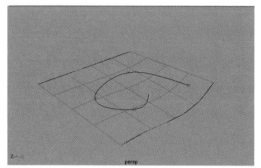

New curve on surface

3 Move the curve on surface

- Press the **Enter** key to complete the curve.
- Select the **Move** tool.

The move manipulator looks a little different this time. Rather than three manipulator handles, there are only two. One is for the U direction of the surface and the other is for the V direction.

- Click-drag on the manipulator handles to move the curve around the surface space.

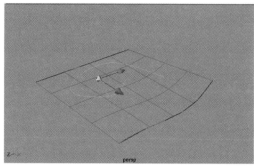

Moving the curve on surface

Tip: This UV space is the same used by texture maps when using 2D placement nodes.

---

4 Make the ground grid live

- Click in empty space to deselect the curve on surface.
- Select **Modify** → **Make Not Live**.

With nothing selected, the ground grid becomes the active or live grid.

Create group hierarchy

You are now going to build another hierarchy. This time you will group two primitives, then animate the group along the curve on surface using path animation.

1 Create a primitive cone

- Select **Create** → **NURBS Primitives** → **Cone**.
- Press the **3** key to increase its display smoothness.

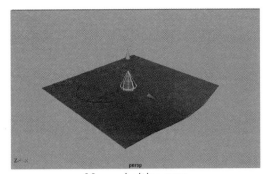

New primitive cone

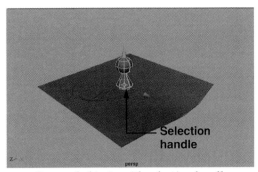

Selection handle

Grouped objects with selection handle

2 Create a primitive sphere

- Select **Create → NURBS Primitives → Sphere**.

- Press the **3** key to increase its display smoothness.

- **Move** the sphere above the cone.

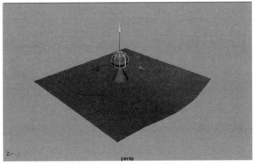

Second primitive object

3 Group the two objects

- **Select** the cone and the sphere.

- Select **Edit → Group**.

- Select **Display → Component Display → Selection Handles**.

    The selection handle is a special marker that will make it easier to pick the group in object selection mode.

Create a path animation

To animate the new group, you will attach it to the curve on surface. You can use the curve on surface to define the group's position over time.

1 Attach to the curve on surface

- With the group still selected, press the **Shift** key and select the curve on surface.

- Go to the **Animation** menu set.

- Select **Animate → Motion Paths → Attach to Motion Path - ❑**. In the option window, make sure that the **Follow** option is turned **Off**.

- Click **Attach**.

- Play back the results.

As the group moves along the path curve, you will notice that it is always standing straight up.

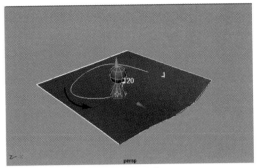

Path animation

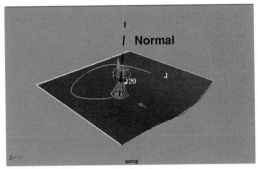

Constrained orientation

2 Constrain to the surface normal

You will now constrain the orientation of the group to the normal direction of the lofted surface. The normal is like the third dimension of the surface's UV space.

- Click in open space to deselect the active objects.

- **Select** the loft surface.

- Press the **Shift** key and select the grouped primitives using the selection handle.

- Select **Constrain** → **Normal** - ❑. In the option window, set the following:

    Aim Vector to **0, 1, 0**;

    Up Vector to **1, 0, 0**.

- Click **Add/Remove** then **Close**.

- Play back the results.

Now the group is orienting itself based on the normal direction of the surface. The group is now dependent on the surface in two ways. Firstly, its position is dependent on the path curve, which is dependent on the surface for its shape. Secondly, its orientation is directly dependent on the surface's shape.

Layer the animation

In Maya, the various parts of the Dependency graph can all be animated to create exciting results. To see the Dependency graph in motion, you will animate different nodes within the network to see how the dependencies react.

1 Edit the loft curve shape

Since the shape of the surface is dependent on the original loft curves, you will start by animating the shape of the second curve.

- **Select** the second loft curve. You may want to use the second Perspective panel which is only displaying curves.

- Click with your right mouse button to bring up the selection marking menu and select **Control Vertex**.

    Control vertices help define the shape of the curve. By editing these, you are editing the curve's shape node.

- Click-drag a pick box over one of the CVs and **Move** it up to a new position.

As you move the CV, the surface updates its shape, which in turn redefines the curve on surface and the orientation of the group. All the dependencies are being updated.

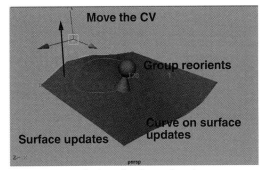

Updating the dependencies

2 Set keys on the CV position

- Go to frame **1** in the Time slider.
- Press **s** to set key.
- Go to frame **120** in the Time slider.
- Press **s** to set key.
- Go to frame **60** in the Time slider.
- **Move** the CV down to a new position.
- Press **s** to set key.
- Play back the results.

  You can see how the dependency updates are maintained as the CV is animated. You are animating the construction history of the lofted surface and the connected path animation.

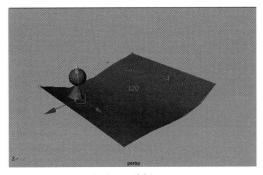

Animated history

3 Animate the curve on surface

To add another layer of animation, you will key the position of the curve on surface.

- **Select** the curve on surface.
- Go to frame **1** in the Time slider.
- Press **s** to set key.
- Go to frame **120** in the Time slider.
- **Move** the curve on surface to another position on the lofted surface.

  Press **s** to set key.

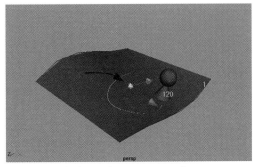

Animated curve on surface

4 Assign the phong shading group

To make it easier to see the animating objects, apply the checker shading group to the primitive group. You will also make visible the animated hierarchy to see all the pieces together.

- **Select** the primitive group using its selection handle.
- Go to the **Rendering** menu set.
- Select **Lighting/Shading → Assign Existing Material → phong1**.
- Select **Display → Show → Show Last Hidden**.
- Play back the scene.

5 Connect two of the spheres

To add your own connection into the equation, you will now connect the rotation of the large sphere from the original hierarchy with the sphere that sits on the cone.

- Select **Window → General Editors → Connection Editor**.
- **Select** the large sphere from the original hierarchy.
- In the Connection Editor, click on the **Reload Left** button.
- Select the sphere that is sitting on top of the cone *without* using the selection handle.
- In the Connection Editor, click on the **Reload Right** button.
- In the left hand column, scroll down to the **Rotate** section.
- Click on the plus sign next to **Rotate** to open this section then click on **Rotate Y**.

- Repeat these steps for the right hand column. When you click on the **Rotate Y** attribute for the second sphere, the two are connected.

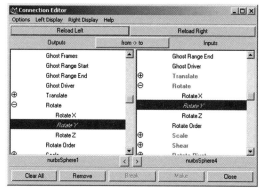

Connected attributes

- Play back the scene.

Now the sphere on top of the cone animates in relation to the larger sphere.

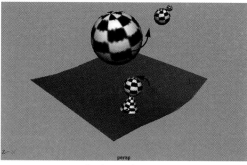

Animated scene

6 View the dependencies

Of course, you can view the dependency network that results from all these connections in the Hypergraph view, which will probably be a bit more complex than anything you have seen so far.

- **Select** the primitive group that is attached to the motion path.

- Open the Hypergraph panel and click on the **Input and Output Connections** button.

The resulting network contains the various dependencies that you built during this example.

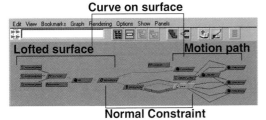

Curve on surface

Lofted surface

Motion path

Normal Constraint

The dependency network

Conclusion

Maya's procedural qualities are tied to how the Dependency graph uses nodes, attributes and connections. You can see how deep these connections can go and how they are maintained throughout the animation process. Similar techniques can be used on other node types throughout Maya.

Obviously, you don't have to use the Hypergraph and the Connection Editor to build, animate and texture map your objects. But in most cases, you will be thinking more about the motion of your character's walk or the color of their cheeks. In this way, it is a good idea to know that the Dependency graph underlies everything that you do and can always be used to your advantage.

PROJECT TWO

PROJECT TWO

In this project, you will animate a Jack-in-the-box. You will begin by modeling the box. You will then use CV pulling and Maya Artisan tools to create Jack's face and head.

To animate the whole scene, you will set keyframes on the rotation of the box's lid and crank then you will use inverse kinematics to animate Jack emerging from the box. Deformations will then be added for some squash and stretch.

1. A Jack-in-the-box sits quietly in the corner of the little boy's room.

2. The crank starts to rotate and the box begins to bulge in anticipation of something big.

3. Suddenly the box burst open and Jack emerges, bouncing up and down.

4. Jack settles down to sit quietly in the corner as if nothing had ever happened.

STORYBOARD

Curves and Surfaces

This lesson will introduce you to modeling with NURBS (Non-uniform rational B-spline) surfaces. This geometry type lets you create curves and surfaces to build up your models. In this lesson, you will build the jack-in-the-box using tools such as revolve, loft and extrude. You will also begin learning about how to use existing geometry to help you build new geometry.

The Jack in the box

In this lesson you will learn the following:

- How to build a box from filleted curves

- How to work with layers

- How to duplicate curves from an existing surface

- How to draw curves

- How to use tools such as loft, revolve and extrude

- How to group your objects to prepare for animation

BUILDING THE BOX

Set up your project

Since this is a new project, you must set a new directory as your project directory. This will let you separate the files you generate in this lesson from other lessons.

1 Set the courseware project

To manage your files, you can set a project directory that contains sub-directories for different types of files that relate to your project.

- Go to the **File** menu and select **Project → Set...**

  A window opens that points you to the Maya projects directory.

- Open on the folder named *learningMaya*.

- Click on the folder named *projectTwo* to select it.

- Click on the **OK** button.

  This sets the learningMaya directory as your current project.

2 Make a new scene

- Select **File → New Scene.**

  This makes sure that your current scene is part of the new project.

3 Restore all UI settings

Before beginning this lesson you will restore all the UI settings.

- Select **Display → UI Elements → Restore UI Elements**.

Building the base

You will build the base by creating a square with rounded corners which will then be duplicated to create a lofted surface.

1 Create a square

- Select **Create → NURBS Primitives → Square**.

  The primitives square is made of four curves.

- In the Channel Box, set the **Scale XYZ** to **10**.

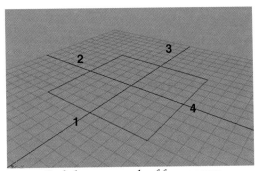

Scaled square made of four curves

2 Round the corners with Fillet Curve

- Select the first two curves.

- In the Modeling menu set, select **Edit Curves → Curve Fillet - ▢**.

- From the **Edit** menu, select **Reset Setting** and **As Action**.

- Check the **Trim** option to **On**.

- Press **Fillet**.

  These curves will now be filleted.

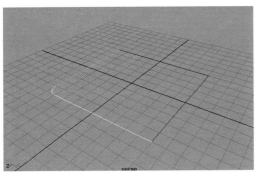

Filleted curves

- With only the second and third curve selected, press **g**.

  The **g** key will invoke the last tool used.

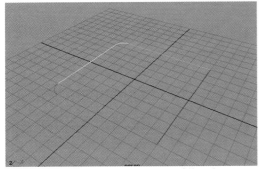

Second and Third curves filleted

- Select only the third and fourth curve.
- Press **g**.

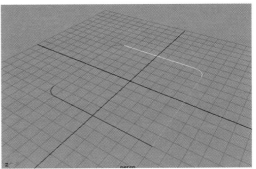

Third and fourth curve filleted

- Select only the fourth and first curve.
- Press **g**.

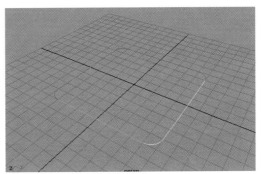

The fourth and first curve filleted

3 Attach the curves

All of the curves and fillets are separate pieces and need to be attached.

- Select the first curve and fillet.

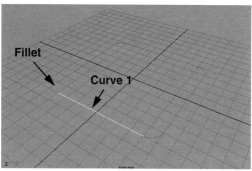

Selected curve and fillet

- Select **Edit Curves** → **Attach Curves** - ❐.
- Change **Attach Method** to **Connect**.
- Turn **Keep Originals** to **Off**.
- Press **Attach**.
- **Shift-select** the next curve.
- Press **g**.

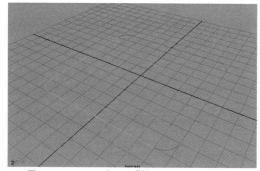

Two curves and one fillet curve attached

- Continue attaching the other curves and fillets until they become one curve.

Note: If the last segment joins or attaches to itself, select the curve and select **Edit Curves** → **Reverse Curve Direction**

- With the curve selected, select **Edit** → **Delete by type** → **History**.

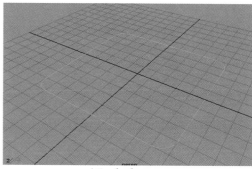

Attached curves

4 Duplicate the curve

- Select the newly attached curve.
- Select **Edit** → **Duplicate**, or **Ctrl-d**.

5 Move the duplicated curve up

You will move the curve in the Y direction using the Numeric Input.

- Select the **Move** tool.
- With the duplicated curve selected, set the Field entry mode to **Numeric Input: Absolute**.

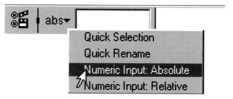

Changing Numeric Input to Absolute

- Enter **0 8 0** in the field. Press the **Enter** key.

The curve has moved in the Y direction by eight units.

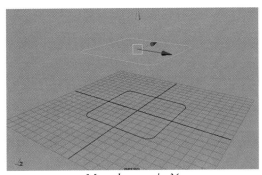

Moved curve in Y

6 Loft the curves

- Select both curves.
- Select **Surfaces** → **Loft**.
- Rename this surface *base*.

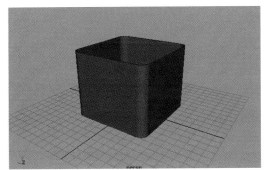

Lofted surface

Note: Throughout this lesson, you will want to press 3 to increase the smoothness of any new object. All of the images in this book will reflect this setting.

---

7 Delete History

- Select the new surface.
- Select **Edit** → **Delete by Type** → **History**.

This gets rid of any extra nodes so that the model is as light as possible for animation down the line.

8 Save your work

- Select **File** → **Save Scene As** and name the new file *jack_01*.

Creating the top surface

To build the top surface, you will use the top curve as one of the generation curves for the top surface.

1 Create a new layer

- Click on the Create a new layer icon.
- Double-click on the layer then enter the name *box_layer* in the option window. Press **Save**.

Create new layer icon ───

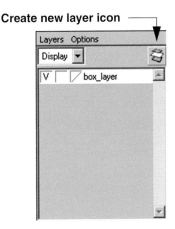

New layer

2 Assign surface to the box layer

- **Select** the *base* surface.
- Right-click over the *box_layer* and select **Add Selected Objects** from the pop-up.

- Press **1** to change to a lower smoothness.
- Click on the empty box beside the V in the *box_layer*. This will put a T in the box and **Template** the *base*.

  Now you can focus on the top of the box while keeping the base around as a visual reference.

3 Offset the curve

- Select the top curve.
- Select **Edit Curves → Offset → Offset Curve**.

  This creates a second curve that is offset from the original. The default offset seems a little big.

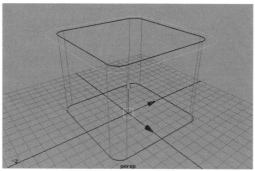

Offset curve to large

- Click on the *offsetCurve* input node in the Channel box.
- Set the **Distance** to **0.2**.

Note: Depending on the direction your original curves were created, the offset may need to be **-.02**.

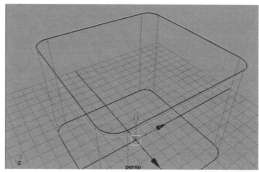

Modified offset curve

4 Duplicate the curve

- Select **Edit → Duplicate**.
- **Move** the new curve up along the Y axis about **1.5** units to create the depth of the box's top surface.

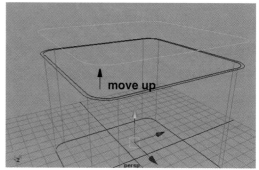

Duplicated curve moved up

5 Create another duplicate curve

- Select **Edit → Duplicate**

  You can see that the pivot of the curve lies at the origin. It would be more useful if the pivot was at the center of the curve.

- With the curve selected, select **Modify → Center Pivot**.

- **Scale** the new curve with the center manipulator in a little to create a border.

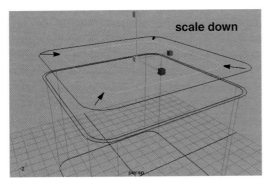

Scaled curve

6 Create another duplicate curve

- Again, select **Edit** → **Duplicate**
- **Move** the new curve slightly down.

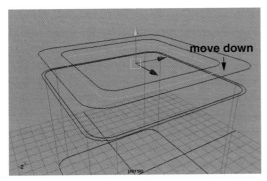

Duplicated curve

7 Delete History

- Select all the curves.
- Select **Edit** → **Delete by Type** → **History**.

8 Save your work

Creating the top edge surface

You will now build the top of the box using these curves to create several lofted surfaces that will then be attached with blending. In the end you will have two surfaces that will make up the top of the box.

1 Set up your view panels

- Select **Panels** → **Layouts** → **Two Panes Side by Side**.
- Set up both panels as perspective views.
- For the first panel, select **Show** → **None** then **Show** → **NURBS Curves**.
- For the second panel, select **Show** → **None** then **Show** → **NURBS Surfaces**.
- Select **Show** → **Grid** to turn off the grid for both the view panels.

  You will use one of the panels for selecting curves and the other to preview the resulting surfaces. This is a useful technique for easily picking different object types.

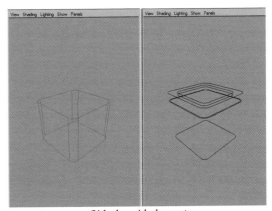

Side-by-side layout

PROJECT TWO

2 Delete the bottom curve

- Select the bottom curve and press **Delete**.

  This curve was only needed to create the base.

3 Create a lofted surface

- In the perspective panel that only shows curves, **select** the first and second curves that you created.

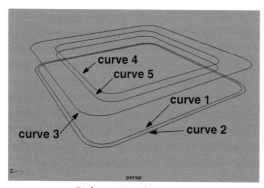

Referencing the curves

- Select **Surfaces** → **Loft**.

  A surface is generated that uses the curves as edge isoparms.

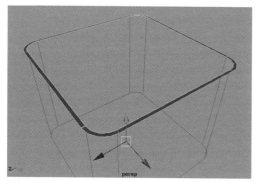

Lofted surface

4 Create a second lofted surface

- **Select** the second and third curves.
- Press **g**.

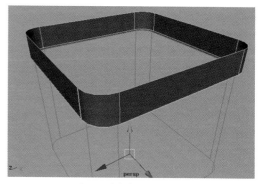

Second lofted surface

5 Create a third lofted surface

- **Select** the third and fourth curves.
- Press **g**.

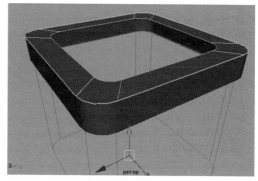

Third lofted surface

6 Create a fourth lofted surface

- **Select** the fourth and fifth curves.
- Press **g**.

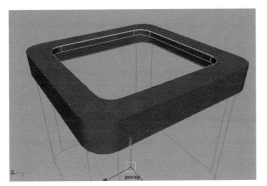

Fourth lofted surface

7 Attach the surfaces using blend

- **Select** the first two surfaces in the perspective panel that only shows surfaces.

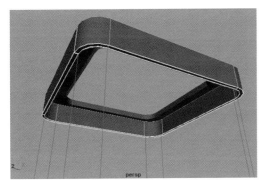

First two surfaces selected

- Select **Edit NURBS → Attach Surfaces - ◻**.
- In the option window, set the following:

     Attach Method to **Blend;**

     Keep Originals to **Off.**

- Click **Attach.**

   Now the two surfaces are blended together smoothly.

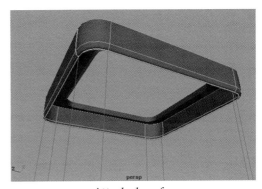

Attached surface

8 Attach the third surface

- With the new attached surfaces selected, shift-select the top surface.
- Press **g**.

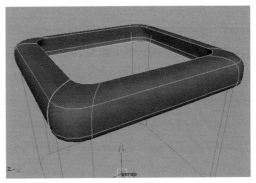

Attached surface

9 Complete the shape

- With the new attached surfaces selected, Shift-select the inner surface.
- Press **g**.

   You will notice that the surfaces have attached at the wrong end. By using Maya's history node you can change this setting.

PROJECT TWO

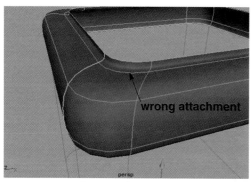

Wrong ends attached

- In the Channel Box Inputs, click on the *attachSurface3* node.
- Set both **Reverse1** and **Reverse2** to **Off**.

Note:	You could also have selected the edge isoparms using the right mouse button to make sure that you attach the surfaces properly.

Final shape

10 Delete History
- **Select** the surface.
- Select **Edit → Delete by Type → History**.

Again, you don't want the history to interfere with your animation later.

11 Save your work

Creating middle section

To create the middle section of the top, you will loft the last of the existing curves with a primitive circle. The circle will act as the hole from which Jack will emerge.

1 Create and place a circle primitive
- Select **Create → NURBS Primitives → Circle**.
- In a top view, **Scale** the circle to fit in the middle of the top surface.

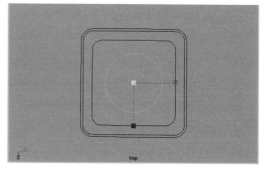

Circle

2 Snap-Constrain the circle
- Select the **Move** tool.
- In a side view, click on the Y-axis handle to activate it.
- Place your cursor over the curve that you want to match the circle to.
- Press the **c** key then *with your middle mouse button* click-drag on the curve.

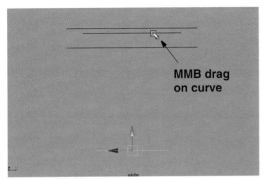

MMB click-drag on curve

By using the **c** key, this constrains the circle so that it only moves along the Y axis while it snaps to the curve.

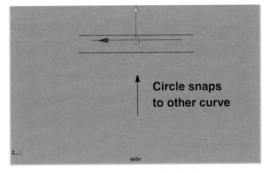

Curve snapping the circle

3 Loft between the curves

- Return to your two perspective layout.
- **Select** curve 5 and the circle.
- Select **Surfaces** → **Loft**.

  The resulting surface is twisted. The circle is not oriented correctly.

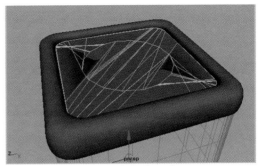

Strange lofted surface

4 Update the surface using history

You can update the surface by editing the profile curves. If you rotate the circle then you can remove the twisting.

- **Select** the circle.
- In the Channel box, highlight **Rotate Y**.
- In the left panel, **click-drag** in the viewport left and right with *middle mouse button* until the surface looks correct.

Tip: It helps to view the surfaces as wireframe when fixing the loft.

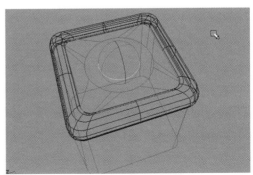

Corrected loft

5 Duplicate and position the circle

- **Select** the circle.
- **Duplicate** the circle.
- **Move** the circle down just below the first.
- Select the two circles.
- Select **Surfaces → Loft**.

  You will keep these surfaces as two separate surfaces instead of attaching them together.

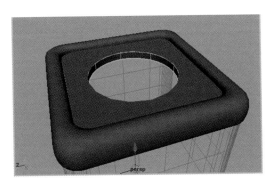

Inner ring

6 Delete History

- **Select** the two new surfaces.
- Select **Edit → Delete by Type → History**.

7 Add the surfaces to the box layer

- **Select** the three top surfaces.
- From the *box_layer's* pop-up menu, select **Add Selected Objects**.

  They will be templated to match the chosen layer state.

8 Save your work

Creating the lid

The box's lid will be constructed using one of the existing curves that will be turned into a planar surface.

This surface will then be duplicated and the two surfaces will be joined using another lofted surface.

1 Set up the starting curve

- **Select** all the curves except curve five.

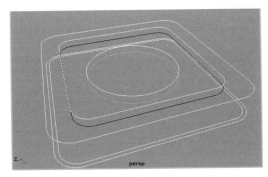

Selected curves

- Press the **Backspace** key to delete them.
- In the panel that only displays curves, select **Show → NURBS Surfaces**.
- Select the remaining curve.
- **Scale** it a little bit smaller and **Move** it up slightly above its original position.

  This will be the base for the bottom of the lid.

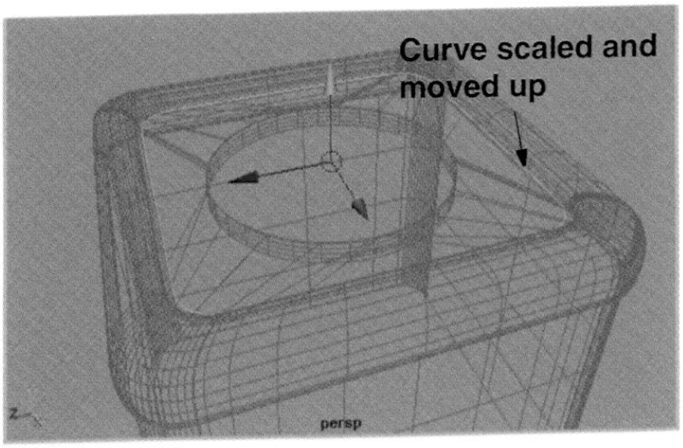
Curve scaled and moved up
persp

Base curve for lid

2 Create a set planar surface

- With the curve selected, select **Surfaces → Planar**.

  This creates a trimmed surface. This means that the surface actually extends outside of the boundary curve then the curve is used to trim the surface.

- **Delete History** on the surface

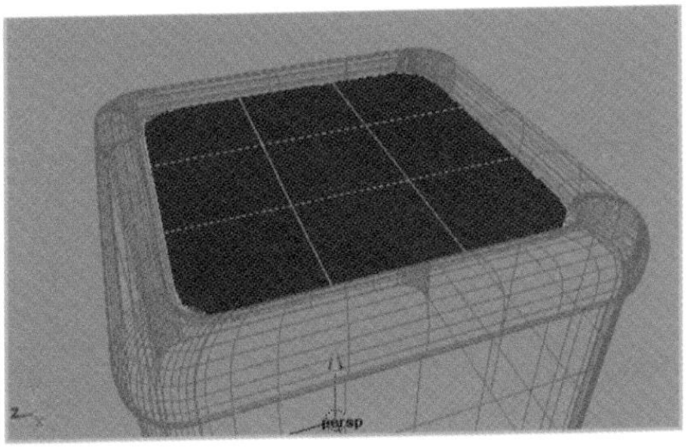

Planar surface

3 Duplicate the surface

- Select the planar surface.
- Press **Ctrl-d** to create a second surface.
- **Move** the surface above the first surface.

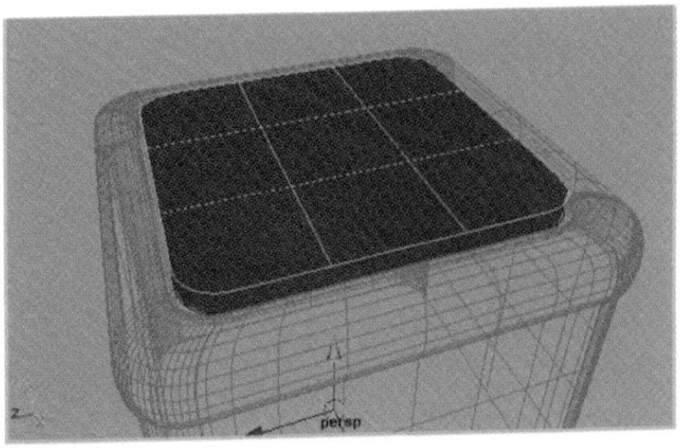

Two surfaces

4 Select the trim edges

- Click with your right mouse button on the first planar surface and select **Trim edge** from the marking menu.
- Click on the edge of the surface to select the trim edge.

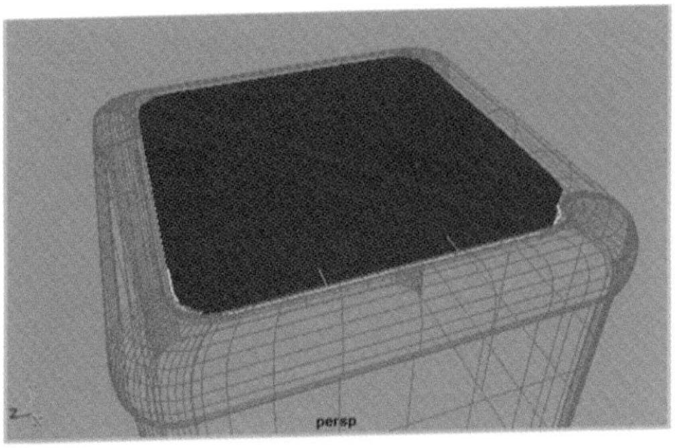
persp

Trim edge

- Click with your right mouse button on the second planar surface and select **Trim edge** from the marking menu.
- Press the **Shift** key and click on the edge of the surface to select the trim edge.

PROJECT TWO

- Select **Surfaces → Loft**.

Very Important! Do not delete history for this surface. The history will play a role later if you decide to deform the planar surfaces.

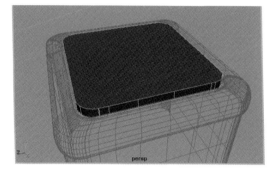

Lofted surface

The Hinge

To act as the hinge for the box's lid, you will create and position a cylinder. This surface will also act as the parent for the other surfaces to help define the rotation of the lid.

1 Create and place a cylinder

- Select **Create → NURBS Primitives → Cylinder - ❑**.

- From the option window select **Edit → Reset Settings** then set the following:

    Axis to **Z**;

    Radius to **0.25**;

    Height to **6**;

    Caps to **Both**.

- Click **Create**.

- **Move** the cylinder back in **X** to about **-4** and up in **Y** to about **9.3**.

- Rename the cylinder to *hinge*.

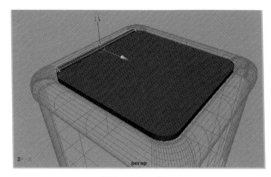

Hinge in place

2 Freeze the hinge's transforms

- Select the *hinge*.

- Select **Modify → Freeze Transformations**.

    This sets the transform values to 0, 0, 0 for translation and rotation, and 1, 1, 1 for scaling while leaving the object in its current location. This gives a good starting point for the animation of the hinge.

3 Parent the lid surfaces

- **Select** only the top and bottom planar surfaces, then press the **Shift** key and click on the *hinge*.

- Press the **p** key to parent them.

Note: Do not parent the lofted surface to the hinge. It does not need to since it is relying on the history from the two planar surfaces. Not including it will also give more predictable results when deforming.

---

4 Test the rotation of the hinge

- **Select** the *hinge*.

- Select the **Rotate** tool.
- Click drag on the axis manipulator to rotate the lid.

Note: Notice that while the lofted surface between the two planar surfaces is not selected, it will rotate along with the hinge. This is because it is parented to the hinge and will inherit any transformations on the parent node.

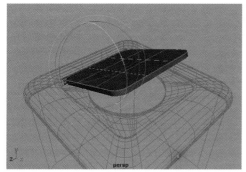

Rotated hinge

5 Add the new group to box layer

- Select the *hinge* and the lofted surface.
- **Assign** the new surfaces to the *box_layer*. They will be templated.

The Handle

To create a handle for the jack-in-the-box, you will extrude a circle along a path.

1 Create and place a primitive circle

- Select **Create** → **NURBS Primitives** → **Circle - ▢**.

- Select **Edit** → **Reset Settings** then set the following:

    Normal Axis to **Z**;

    Radius to **0.20**;

    Degree to **Linear**.

    Number of Sections to **6**;

    This Linear setting creates a curve that has flat spans. This will give the look of a faceted metal.

- Click **Create**.

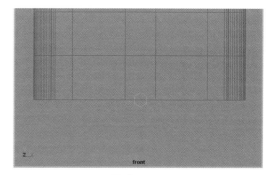

Path curve

2 Draw a path curve

- In a side view, zoom in to the origin.
- Select **Create** → **CV Curve Tool**.

    Press the **x** key to use grid snapping and draw the following curve placing the 6 points as shown:

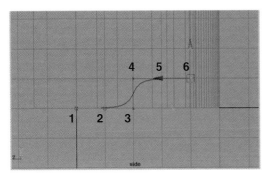

Path curve

- Press the **Enter** key to complete the curve.

3 Extrude the circle

- **Select** the circle and the path curve. Make sure that you select the path curve last.

- Select **Surfaces → Extrude**.

  The resulting surface is a result of the circle being passed along the path curve. The resulting surface is faceted (Linear) in one direction and smooth (Cubic) along the other.

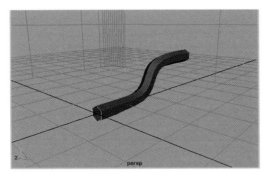

Extruded surface

- **Delete History** from the surface.

- **Delete** the circle and the path curve.

- Rename the surface to *crank*.

4 Add a sphere to the end

- Create a primitive sphere.

- **Scale** it into an egg-like shape.

- **Move** it to the end of the *crank* handle.

- Press the **Shift** key and add the *crank* to the selection.

- Press the **p** key to parent the *sphere* to the *crank*.

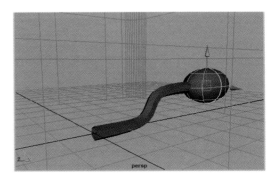

Crank handle

5 Position the crank

- **Move** the crank to the side of the box near the middle. You may need to look at both a top and a side view at the same time to position the crank successfully.

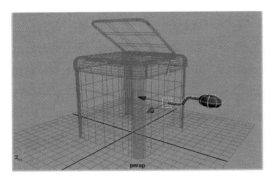

Completed crank

6 Add the crank to box layer

- Select the *crank*.

- **Add** the new surfaces to the *box_layer*. They will be templated.

Jack's body

You are going to create an accordion-like surface for Jack's body. This will include a Linear (degree 1) profile curve that is revolved into shape.

1 Create a Linear NURBS curve

Like the profile of the crank, you will create the body surface using a faceted (Linear) curve in one direction and a smooth (Cubic) curve along the other

- Select **Create → CV Curve Tool - □**.

- In the Option window, set **Curve Degree** to **1 Linear.**

  By using a *linear* setting, a curve will be created with straight lines drawn between CVs.

- In the side view panel, use grid snapping to help you draw a zig-zag curve to act as the profile for the body surface.

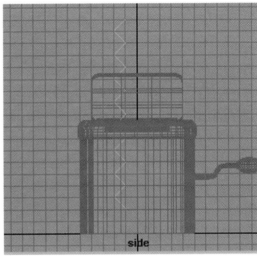

Profile curve

2 Revolve the curve into a surface

- Select **Surfaces → Revolve**.

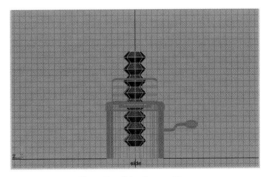

Revolved body surface

3 Delete history

- **Select** and **Delete** the profile curve.

  By removing the profile curve, you have deleted the surface's history.

Jack's head

Using a Cubic (degree 3) curve, you are going to create another revolved surface. This surface will start out very simple then it will be used in the next lesson to sculpt facial features for Jack.

1   Create a degree 3 curve

- Select **Create → CV Curve Tool - ❏.**

- In the Option window, set **Curve Degree** to **3 Cubic.**

  The *cubic* setting will create a smooth curve that is interpolated from the CVs.

- In the side view, draw a curve from the end of the body surface up to the Y axis line.

  Use grid snap to make sure that your last two CVs are lined up perpendicular to the Y axis line. This will prevent Jack's head from being pointy when it is revolved.

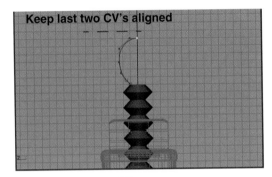

CV curve

2   Revolve the curve into a surface

- Select **Surfaces → Revolve.**

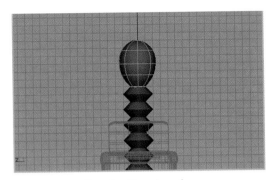

Revolved head surface

3   Delete history

- **Select** and **Delete** the profile curve.

Adding some color

In another lesson, you will set up the rendering for the Jack-in-the-box. For now, you will create a few shaders and assign them to the parts of the model to give your model some basic color.

1   Reveal the box layers

- In the *box_layer,* click on the **T** twice to untemplate the geometry assigned to it.

  Now the objects are visible.

2   Create and assign color shaders

- Use the methods you learned in Project one to create five Blinn materials for the scene.

- Edit the color of the shaders as shown below:

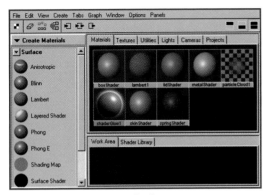

New shaders

- Name the shaders as shown below and assign them to the following surfaces:

    boxShader to base surface;

    lidShader to lid, box top and the crank handle;

    springShader to Jack's body;

    skinShader to Jack's head;

    metalShader to the hinge and the crank stem.

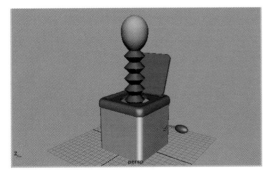

Box with shaders

Conclusion

You now have some experience working with curves and surfaces. You have seen how

profile curves can be used to generate surfaces with the help of tools such as revolve, loft and extrude.

In the next lesson, you will sculpt Jack's face by manipulating the surface at a component level. You will also learn about Maya's Artisan functionality that lets you mold the surface using a brush-like interface.

Organic Modeling

In this lesson, you will sculpt facial features onto Jack by manipulating the surface's control vertices (CVs). At first you will use the transform manipulators to edit the CVs, then you will put Maya's Artisan tools to work using a brush paradigm as you push, pull, and smooth the surface.

Jack's sculpted face

Maya's Artisan tools offer a different approach to how you work in Maya. Rather than typing in values, Artisan lets you use a paint-like interface to edit shapes in Maya. In later lessons, you will also learn how to use Artisan for other important functions.

In this lesson you will learn the following:

- How to rebuild a surface
- How to pull CVs using the Move tool's Normal setting
- How to sculpt surfaces by painting with Artisan
- How to use different brush operations
- How to use the Texture Paint Tool

Getting started

For this lesson, you will continue to work with the model you produced in the last lesson. You are going to work on the face area to define Jack's character.

Editing Control Vertices

Control Vertices represent points on a surface or a curve that help define its shape. By repositioning these important points, you can sculpt the surface.

1 Rotate the surface

Since the curve you used to revolve the head surface was created on the side, this means that the surface's seam is at that point. You want the seam at the back of the head.

- Select the *head* surface.
- In the Channel box, set **Rotate Y** to -90.

  In the shaded view, this didn't seem to change anything. But by moving the seam to the back of the head, you can take advantage of some of Artisan's symmetry tools used later in the lesson.

2 Change to component mode

CVs are part of the surface's shape node and can only be selected by going to component selection mode.

- Make sure that **Show** → **NURBS CVs** is **On** for the perspective panel.
- On the status line, click on the **Select by Component Type** button.
- Turn the **Points** button to **on** and the **Lines** button to **off**.

Now the CVs are shown on the head's surface.

- **Select** the *base* surface of the box.

  Now this surface is displaying its CVs. As you select surfaces, you can focus on editing their CVs.

- Again **Select** the *head* surface.

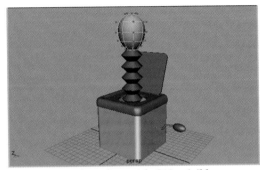

Head surface with CVs visible

3 Select CVs

- From the side view, **select** the row of CVs that lie just under the center of the shape.

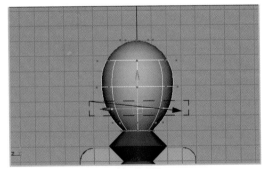

Edited CVs

4 Move and Scale some CVs

- **Move** the CVs down a little.
- **Scale** the CVs out to tighten the shape.

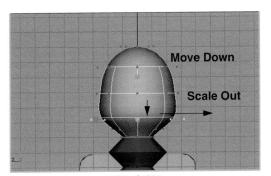

Edited CVs

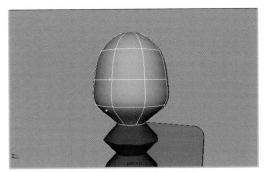

Focusing on the two CVs

5 Focus on a few CVs

- In the perspective view, **select** the two CVs that lie on and just below the middle of the head on its centerline.

- Be careful that you don't select CVs at the back of the character's head.

6 Move using world space

- **Select** the bottom CV.
- Select the **Move** tool.
- **Move** the CV into the head.

  You are moving the CV in world space using the XYZ coordinates to guide you.

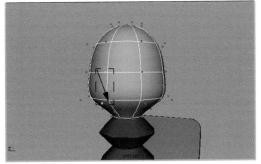

Selected CVs

- Select **Display** → **Hide Unselected CVs**.

  Now you can only see the selected CVs which will make it easier to work with them.

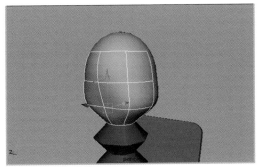

Moving the bottom CV

7 Move CV normal

Sometimes moving a CV in world space can be difficult to control. You will now use the **Move** tool's **Normal** setting to work more closely with the surface.

- **Select** the upper CV.
- Double-click on the **Move** tool to open the Tool options.

PROJECT TWO

- Set your **Move Options** to **Normal**.

  The manipulator now displays new axes that are labelled U, V and N. The U and V labels represent the two dimensions of the surface as represented by the isoparm lines. The N represents the normal direction off of the surface.

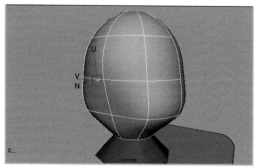

Move CV normal manipulator

- Drag on the **N** axis of the manipulator to **Move** the CV out of the head.

  You are moving the CV in world space using the XYZ coordinates.

- Drag down on the **U** axis of the manipulator to **Move** the CV down along the surface of the head.

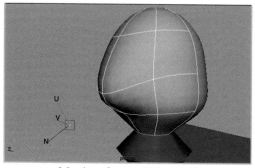

Moving the top CV normal

Now the CV is moving along the shape of the surface.

8 Return to object mode

- Press **F8** to go back to object mode.

  Oops, there is a warning in the feedback line. It is telling you that the **Move → Normal** option does not work in Object mode.

- Double-click on the **Move** tool to open the Tool options.

- Click the **Reset Tool** button to go back to the default settings.

9 Save your work

- Select **File → Save Scene As...**

- Enter the name *jack_02* and **Save**.

USING MAYA ARTISAN®

You could now continue pulling CVs until you have sculpted a head out of this surface. Instead you will use Maya's Artisan tools. These will let you push and pull on the surface as if it were a piece of clay.

Setting up the surface

To work effectively with Artisan tools it is important that the surface has a large number of CVs. You must therefore rebuild the surface so that it has more available CVs for Artisan to work with. You will also change the material qualities on the head to show stronger highlights. This will help you work in hardware shading when using Artisan.

1 Rebuild the surface

- Select the *head* surface.

- Select **Edit NURBS → Rebuild Surfaces -** ❐.

- In the option window, select **Edit** → **Reset Settings** button then set the following:

  Number of Spans U to **30**;

  Number of Spans V to **30**.

- Click **Rebuild**.

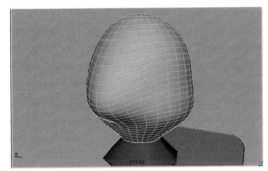

New surface topology

2 Edit the surface's material

- Open up a **Hypershade** panel.

- With the *head* selected, select **Graph** → **Graph Materials on Selected Objects**.

- Double click on the *skinShader* icon to open the Attribute editor.

- Set the following material attributes:

  Eccentricity to **0**;

Updated material node

This puts a strong highlight on the surface that will help evaluate the Artisan sculpting.

Start sculpting the surface

You will now sculpt the surface of the mask by painting on it using the Artisan Sculpt Surfaces tool. At first, you will just test the tools to get a feel for them. Later, you will erase these brush strokes so that you can paint real facial features.

1 Open the Tool Settings window

- **Select** the *head* surface.

- Select **Edit NURBS** → **Sculpt Surfaces Tool** - ◻.

  This opens the Tool Settings window which includes all of the Artisan's sculpting options.

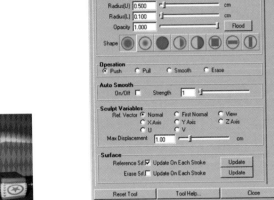

Tool Settings window

- Click on the **Reset Tool** button to make sure that you are starting with Artisan's default settings.

- Set the following attributes:

Under **Stamp Profile**:

Radius (U) to **0.3**;

Under **Sculpt Variables**:

Max Displacement to **0.8**.

- Place the new window to the right of the mask model.

You will work with this window open, until you are familiar with how to use hotkeys.

2 Paint on the surface

- Move your cursor over the *head* surface. The cursor icon changes to show an arrow surrounded by a red circular outline. The arrow indicates how much the surface will be

pushed or pulled while the outline indicates the brush radius.

Artisan's brush icon is context sensitive. It changes as you choose different tool settings.

- Click-drag on the surface. You are now *painting* on the surface to sculpt it.

You can either click-drag using a mouse, or preferably, draw directly with a stylus.

Tip: Artisan works more intuitively with a tablet and stylus, since the input device mimics the use of an actual paintbrush.

This brush stroke pushes in the surface. The brush stroke is sculpting the surface.

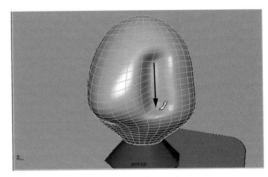

First brush stroke

3 Change the Artisan display

- Click the **Display** tab in the Tool Settings window.

- Click on **Show Wireframe** to turn this option **Off**.

Now you can focus on the surface without displaying isoparm lines.

4 Paint another stroke

- Paint a second stroke across the mask surface.

  Now it is easier to see the results of your sculpting.

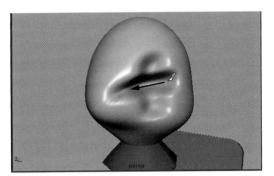

Second brush stroke

The sculpting tools

You will now explore some of the Artisan sculpting operations to see how they work. So far, you have been pushing on the surface. Now you will learn how to pull, smooth and erase.

1 Pull on the surface

- In the Tool Settings window, click on the **Sculpt** tab.

- Under **Operation**, click on **Pull**.

- Tumble around to the other side of the model.

- Paint on the surface to create a few strokes that pull out.

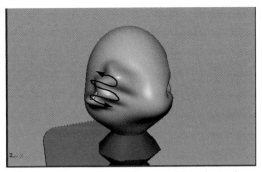

Pulling the surface with several brush strokes

2 Smooth out the results

- Under **Operation**, click on **Smooth**.

- Under **Stamp Profile**, change the **Radius (U)** to **0.6**.

  This increases the size of your brush. You can see that the red outline has increased in size. This is the brush feedback icon.

- Paint all of the strokes to smooth the details. If you stroke over an area more than once, the smoothing becomes more evident.

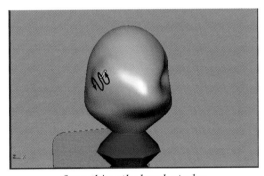

Smoothing the brush strokes

3 Erase some of the brush strokes

- Under **Operation**, click on the **Erase** option.

- Paint along the surface to begin erasing the existing sculpt edits. Don't erase all the edits.

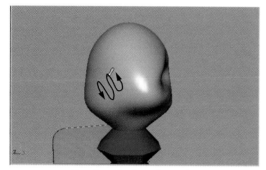

Erasing the brush strokes

4 Flood erase the surface

- In the **Stamp Profile** section, click on the **Flood** button next to **Opacity**.

   This uses the current operation and applies it to the whole surface using the current opacity setting.

Fully erased surface

Updating the reference surface

When you paint in Artisan, you paint in relation to a *reference surface*. By default, the reference surface updates after every stroke so that you can build your strokes on top of each other. You can also keep the reference

surface untouched until you decide to update it manually.

1 Change the brush attributes

- Under **Operation**, click on **Pull**.

- Set the following attributes:

   Under **Stamp Profile**:

   Radius (U) to **0.5**;

   Under **Sculpt Variables:**

   Max Displacement to **0.4**.

2 Pull the surface with two strokes

- Paint on the surface to create two crossing strokes that pull out.

   The second stroke built on top of the first stroke. Therefore, where the two strokes intersect, the height of the pull is higher.

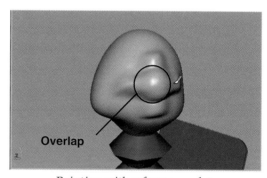

Overlap

Painting with reference update

3 Change the reference update

- In the Tool Settings window, scroll down to the **Surface** section, and click on the **Reference Srf: Update On Each Stroke** to turn this option **Off**.

4 Paint more overlapping strokes

- Paint on the surface to create a few strokes that pull out. This time, the strokes do not overlap. The reference surface does not update, therefore the strokes can only displace to the **Maximum Displacement** value. You cannot displace beyond that value until you update the reference surface.

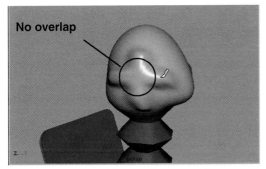

Painting with no reference update

5 Update the reference layer

- In the **Surface** section, click on the **Update** button next to **Reference Srf**.

6 Paint on the surface

- Paint another stroke over the last set of strokes.

  The overlapping strokes are again building on top of each other.

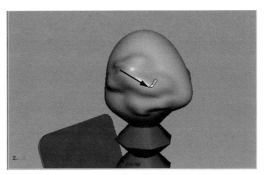

Painting on updated reference layer

7 Flood erase the surface

- Under **Operation**, click on the **Erase** option.

- Click on the **Flood** button.

Sculpting the eye sockets

Now that your surface is clean again, you can sculpt two eye sockets. Ideally, you want the strokes you apply to the left eye to be mirrored on the right eye. Artisan makes painting symmetrical strokes very simple.

1 Turn reference updating back on

- In the **Surface** section, click on the **Reference Srf: Update On Each Stroke** to turn this option to **On**.

  This will let you build up the facial details as the reference surface updates.

2 Change your stylus pressure setting

If you are working with a tablet and a stylus, you can set up your stylus to create more subtle results.

- Click on the **Stroke** tab.

- Under **Stylus Pressure**, click on **Radius**.

PROJECT TWO

This means that the harder you press, the larger the radius of the brush stroke. You can now set the upper radius (**Radius (U)**) and lower radius (**Radius (L)**) sizes that will be used by the stylus.

As you work through this lesson, explore the various stylus settings to see how they can help you paint.

3 Change your Stamp Profile settings

- Click on the **Sculpt** tab.
- Change the **Radius(U)** to **0.7**.
- Change the **Radius(L)** to **0.3**.

This means that the lowest your stroke will go is 0.3 and the largest will be 0.7.

- Change the **Opacity** to **0.2**.

This means that each stroke will only have 0.2 of the effect. This lets you use softer strokes to build up a shape.

- Change your stamp setting to the second icon, which has more feathering at the brush's edge.

New brush shape

4 Turn Reflection on

- Click on the **Stroke** tab.
- Under **Reflect Paint**, set **Reflection** to **On**.

By default, it is set to reflect around the U-axis.

- Move your cursor over the surface. You can see that the reflection is going the wrong way.

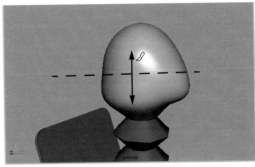

Reflecting in U

- Click on **V Dir** for reflecting. Now the two stroke icons are visible on the two sides of the face.

5 Push the eye sockets in

- In the **Operation** section, select **Push**.
- Paint one of the eye socket areas to push it in. The other socket is pushed by the reflection.

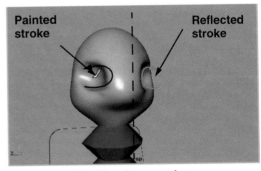

Pushing in eye sockets

6 Pull the eyebrows out

- In the **Sculpt Variables** section, change the **Ref. Vector** to **Normal**.

- In the **Operation** section, select **Pull**.
- Paint the eyebrow areas to pull them out.

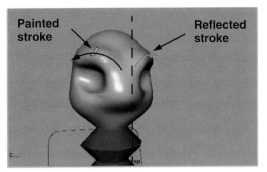

Pulling out eyebrows

7 Flood smooth the surface

- In the **Operation** section, select **Smooth**.
- Click on the **Flood** button two times.

8 Save your work

- Select **File → Save**

Sculpting the Nose

You will now sculpt the nose. You will work with the Artisan hotkeys to change brush attributes.

1 Change the brush radius

- Press the **b** key and click-drag to make the upper radius smaller. This hotkey gives you quick access to the brush radius.

Note:	Artisan has a couple of hotkeys that makes it easier to edit key brush attributes. These include: **b** - **Radius (U)** **m** - **Maximum Displacement**

2 Paint the length of the nose

- In the **Operation** section, select **Pull**.
- Paint from the top of the nose to the tip. Use several strokes to build up the bridge of the nose and the nostril areas. You may need to tumble your view to complete these strokes.

  If you don't like any of your strokes, you can undo the action using the **z** key, or you can **Erase** back to the original surface. Artisan gives you this flexibility in order to let you explore design alternatives.

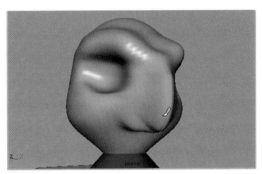

Sculpting the nose

3 Flood smooth the shape

Since these strokes appear somewhat bumpy, you can smooth all the strokes using the Flood button.

- In the **Operation** section, select **Smooth**.

- In the Tool Settings window, click on **Flood** twice.

This smooths out some of the bumps. Because the opacity setting is set to 0.2, the smoothing is more subtle. It is a good idea to smooth your shape regularly to clean up your strokes.

Sculpting the mouth

You will now sculpt the mouth by pulling out the lips.

1 Pull out two lips

- Select **Pull** from the Tool settings window.
- **Paint** the lip area to pull two lips out.

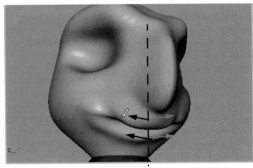

Pulling out two lips

2 Add the upper lip detail

- Set your **Radius (U)** and **Radius (L)** to **0.1**.
- Select **Push** from the Tool settings window.
- Paint the area above the upper lip to push it in.

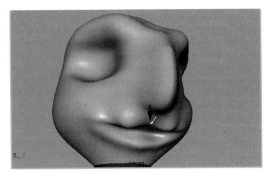

Pushing in the upper lip

3 Continue sculpting

- Keep working with the Artisan tools until you get the face that you want.

Remember to adjust the upper and lower radius of your brush as well as your maximum displacement.

Complete the hat and eyes

To complete the head, you will add a hat and two eyes. These extra surfaces can be parented to the head.

1 Add a hat

- Now add a primitive **Cone** for a hat and **Move** it to the top of Jack's head.
- **Assign** the *lidShader* to the *hat*.
- Use Artisan's tools to add some detail to the *hat*.
- **Select** the *hat* then select the *head* surface.
- Press **p** to parent the hat to the head.

2 Create eyes for Jack

- Add two primitive **Spheres** for eyes and **Move** them into the eye sockets.
- Make sure that the *eye* spheres have a **Rotate z** of **-90** so that their polar axis is pointing out from the head.
- **Select** the *eyes* then select the *head* surface.
- Press **p** to parent the eyes to the head.

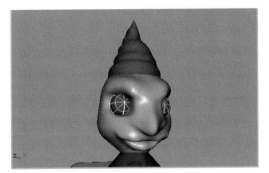

Head with eyes and hat

3 Add a phong material to the eyes

- Open the Hypershade.
- Create and apply a *phong* material to the eyes.
- Press **6** to see Hardware texturing.
- Double click on the new material node.

4 Add a Ramp texture to the eye's color

- Click on the **Map** (checker) button next to **Color**.
- Select **Ramp** from the Create Render Node window.

5 Edit the Ramp indicators

- Click on the square icon next to the middle color indicator. This deletes the marker.
- Click on the round icon next to the top color indicator.
- Click on the color swatch next to **Selected color** then change the color to black.
- Use the same technique to change the lower color indicator to white.
- Click drag on the white round icon to move it near the top of the ramp.
- Move the black round icon closer to the white one.
- Change the **Type** to **U Ramp**.

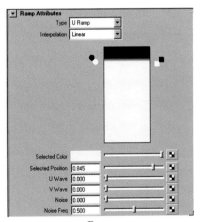

Ramp

If this doesn't look accurate on your model then the black bar may need to be at the bottom of the ramp.

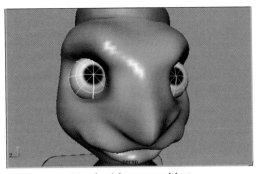

Head with eyes and hat

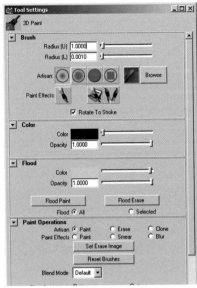

Paint Textures window

Painting Textures

To add a color texture to the face, you will use Maya's 3D Paint tool. This will allow you to create and assign a texture to the face then use a brush to add color.

1 Get the Texture paint tool

- **Select** the *head*.

- Using the **Rendering** menu set, select **Texturing → 3D Paint Tool - ❐**.

  This opens the 3D Paint tool window. You are now able to set the brush's color and assign textures to your surfaces.

2 Assign a color texture to the face

- Press the **Assign/Edit Textures** button.

  This will open an options window for the texture.

- Keep the default settings and press **Assign/Edit Textures**.

Assigning the texture

3 Start painting the cheeks

- In the tool settings window set the **Flood Color** to a skin color.

- Select **Flood All** and press the **Flood Paint** button to fill the surface with this color.

- Under the **Display** section, turn **Show Wireframe** to **Off**.
- Under the **Color** section change the **Color** to pink.
- Paint the cheeks with the brush.

Painting the cheeks

4 Save Textures

- As you are working you will need to press the **Save Textures** button.

  This will save your file to disk.

5 Paint eyebrows on the face

- Change the **Color** to black.
- Paint some eyebrows on the head.

Painting the eyebrows

When you are finished, you can continue to add whatever color you want to enhance the look of the face.

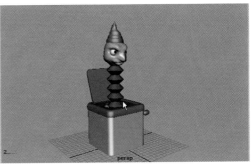

Head with eyes and hat

6 Save your work

Conclusion

You have now edited a surface using its control vertices. You have also used Maya's Artisan tools to help give the face a more organic quality. Generally, you will use CV pulling to get the basic shape of a surface then use Artisan to give it a more natural look. You have also used the 3D Paint Tool to add further paint to the face. In the next lesson, you will begin to animate Jack and his box.

PROJECT TWO

Animation

In the last two lessons, you modeled various pieces of the Jack-in-the-box. You can now set keyframes on the various parts to bring Jack to life. To start, you will build some skeleton joints that will help you control Jack. You will then add inverse kinematics to animate Jack's release.

In this lesson, you will also use Maya's character definition tools that will help you create a pose-based animation that lets you quickly block out the motion.

The Jack in the box

In this lesson you will learn the following:

- How to set up skeleton joints
- How to bind geometry onto joints
- How to set up a Spline IK solution
- How to create a new attribute
- How to constrain an object to a joint
- How to set up a character
- How to set keys on characters

Adding skeleton joints

Skeleton joints offer a great tool for controlling how a character moves. By moving the skeleton, you will move the surface.

1 Prepare your scene

- **Open** the scene file that you saved in the last lesson.

- Place the head and the body surfaces on a new layer. Call the new layer *Jack_layer*.

- **Template** the *box_layer*.

  Now you are focused on the Jack character.

2 Draw two skeleton joints

- Select **Display** → **Joint Size** → **50%**.

- Go to the **Animation** menu set.

- Select **Skeleton** → **Joint Tool**.

- In a side view, press the **x** key to use grid snapping then click near the ground to place the first joint.

- Click two grid units above the first joint to place the second joint.

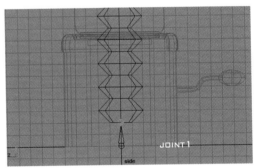

First Joint

3 Draw 8 more joints

- Use grid snap to place several more joints at two grid intervals until you reach the head.

- Press the **Enter** key to complete the skeleton.

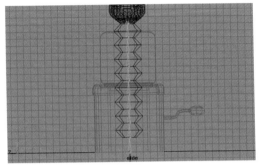

Second Joint

IK Spline Handle

Later you will want to control Jack's head so that it sways back and forth after emerging from the box. You will use an Inverse Kinematics solution called IK Spline.

An IK Spline handle uses a curve to control the shape of the skeleton. As you move the curve, the Inverse Kinematics solver rotates the joints to match.

1 Create IK spline for the joints

- Select **Skeleton** → **IK Spline Handle Tool**.

- Click on the base of the skeleton when prompted for the *start joint for handle*.

- Click on the end of the skeleton when prompted for the *end joint or end effector*.

This adds an IK handle to the skeleton and a curve for controlling the joints.

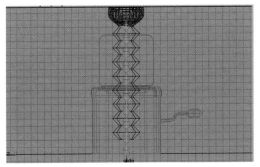

Spline IK handle

2 Add a Point on Curve Deformer

You now have a single span curve that can be used to control the joints. You could edit the CVs on the curve, but instead you will add a Point on Curve Deformer for higher level control.

- From the side view panel, select **Show → None, Show → Grid** then **Show → NURBS Curves**.

- Click on the curve with your right mouse button.

- Select **Curve Point** from the pop-up marking menu.

  Click and hold on the curve then drag up to the top. This is your selected curve point.

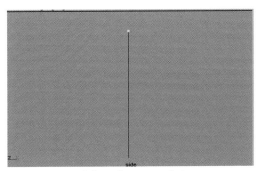

Selected curve point

- Select **Deform → Point on Curve**.

- Select **Show → Locators** and **Show → Joints.** Now you can see a locator at the top of the IK spline that will be used to control the curve.

- Select **Modify → Center Pivot**.

- **Move** the *Locator* to control the Spline.

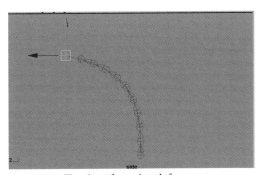

Testing the point deformer

3 Skinning the neck surface

- Press **z** to undo the move.

- Select **Show → All**.

- With the Locator still selected, select **Display → Component Display → Selection Handles**.

PROJECT TWO

This will make it easier to select the locator later, since these handles have a higher selection priority than other objects.

Skinning

To make the body surface move with the skeleton joints, it needs to be bound to the joints using Maya's skinning tools.

1 Skin the body surface

- **Select** the root joint of the skeleton.
- Press the **Shift** key and select the body surface.
- Select **Skin** → **Bind Skin** → **Smooth Bind**.

2 Testing the results

- In the Handles Pick mask, right-click and turn **IK Handles** off.

Turning IK Handles off

- Click-drag over the area where the locator is to select it.

  Since you added the selection handle, the *Locator* is selected over all the other objects when you click-drag to select.

- **Move** the *Locator* to test the bind.

  The smooth bind is very effective at giving good results very quickly. This bind is exactly what is needed.

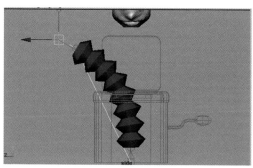

Testing the bind

Set up the joint scaling

In order for Jack to pop out of the box, you need to set up the body so that it can extend out of the box or pull back into it.

1 Add an attribute to the locator

To control the extending of the body, you will add an attribute to the locator. This will give you a single attribute that will be linked to the joints using Set Driven key.

- With the *Locator* selected, select **Modify** → **Add Attribute...**
- In the Add Attribute window, set the following:

  Attribute Name to *extend*;

  Data Type to **Float**;

  Minimum to **0**;

  Maximum to **10**;

  Default to **10**.

- Click **OK**.

  In the Channel box, you will see that a new attribute named *Extend* has been added to the list. You will use this to control Jack moving in and out of the box.

2 Load the Set driven key window

Since the extending of the skeleton joints requires the scaling of several nodes, you will use Set Driven key so that editing the *Locator's* **extend** attribute does all the work.

- Select **Animate** → **Set Driven Key** → **Set - ☐**.

- In this window, click on the **Load Driver** button.

- Click on **Locator** in the left hand column.

- Click on **extend** in the right hand column.

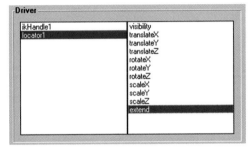

Loading the driver attribute

3 Load all the joints as the driven

- Select **Window** → **Outliner**.

- Press the **Shift** key and click on the square box next to *joint1*. This will expand the hierarchy so that you can see all the joints.

- Press the **Shift** key and select all the joints in the skeleton.

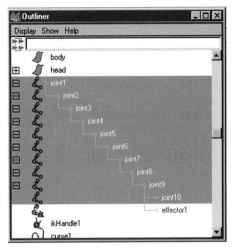

Outliner

- Click **Load Driven** in the Set Driven Key window.

- In the left hand column, select all of the **joints**.

- In the right hand column select **scaleX**.

By default, the joints' X-axes are pointing along the joints. For this reason this is the axis that needs to be modified.

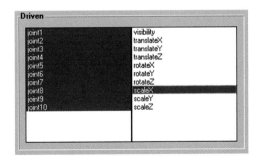

Loading the driven attributes

4 Key the start position

- Click on the **Key** button so that when the **extend** attribute is set to 10, the joints will be scaled to 1 in X.

5 Key the end position

- **Select** the *Locator*.

- Set the **extend** attribute to **0**.

- Re-select all the joints in the Outliner.

- In the Channel box, set **ScaleX** to around **0.15**. This squashes the body into the box.

- Click on the **Key** button.

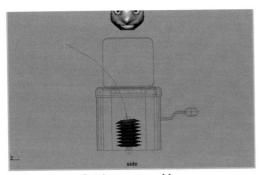

Setting a second key

6 Test the results

- Select the *Locator*.

- Click on the **Extend** attribute in the Channel box.

- With your middle mouse button, click-drag left to right to adjust the body surface.

- **Move** the Locator to see how the extending action works with the spline curve.

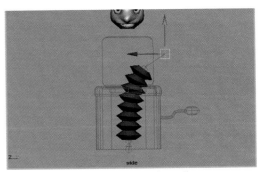

Testing the Expand attribute

Constraining the head

You now want the head to move with the skeleton, but you don't want it to squash with the body. Therefore instead of binding the head into the skeleton, you will constrain the head's position and orientation to match the skeleton's top joint.

1 Edit the head's pivot location

- **Select** the *head* surface.

  This will also select the eyes and hat which are children of the head.

- Select **Modify → Center pivot**.

- Select the **Move** tool.

Note:	If you are using a Mac, use the **Home** key instead of the **Insert** key to edit the pivot location.

- Press the **Insert / Home** key to go into edit mode.

- **Move** the head's pivot to the base of head.

- Press the **Insert / Home** key to go back to object mode.

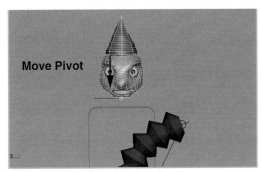

Setting the pivot location

2 Point constrain the head

- **Select** last *joint*. You may want to use the Outliner to help you.

- Press the **Shift** key and select the *head* surface.

- Select **Constrain** → **Point**.

  Now the head sits in the same position as the top joint. Right now it isn't oriented properly.

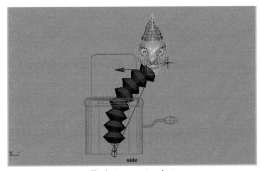

Point constraint

3 Orient constrain the head

- With the joint and the head still selected, select **Constrain** → **Orient**.

  Now the head is oriented to match the joint. One problem is that it has been rotated sideways. This is

because the head's local axis and the joint's local axis work slightly differently.

Every node has a local axis that determines its orientation in space. You can view and edit the axis to correct the rotation of the head.

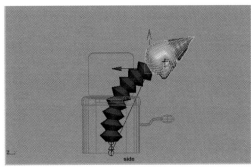

Orient constrain

4 Rotate the local rotation axis

- **Select** the head surface.

- Press **F8** to go into component mode.

- Click on the **Points** selection mask button to turn it off then click on the **Miscellaneous** button to turn it on.

  This selection mask option displays the local rotation axes for all the parts of the head.

- Select the axis near Jack's neck and open the Attribute Editor.

- Select the *head* tab.

- Under **Transform Attributes**, change the value of **Rotate Y** to **-90**.

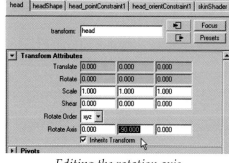

Editing the rotation axis

- Click on the **Miscellaneous** selection mask button to turn it off then click on the **Points** button to turn it on.

- Press **F8** to go back to object mode.

Set up a character

Before animating the whole scene, you are going to create several Maya character definitions. A Character definition is a collection of attributes that you need to animate for your chosen character.

1 Create the main character

This Character node will be the main one which will contain two sub-characters.

- Make sure nothing is selected.

- Select **Character** → **Create Character Set** – ❑.

- Change the name to *jack_in_box*.

- Press **Create Character Set**.

2 Create a sub-character

The locator is going to be a sub-character of *Jack_in_box*. In order to create a sub-character, the main character node needs to be set. This can be verified by viewing what character is active in the field in the bottom right hand corner.

Active character

- Select the *Locator*.

- Highlight all the **Translate** and **Extend** attributes in the Channel Box.

Selected attributes

- Select **Character** → **Create Subcharacter Set** – ❑.

- Change the name to *Jack*, and set **SubCharacter Set Attributes** to **From Channel Box**.

- Press **Create Subcharacter Set**.

Only the selected attributes from the locator are now part of the *Jack* Character and *Jack* is a sub-character of *Jack_in_box*.

3 Create a second sub-character

To animate the parts of the box, you will create another character that uses other attributes that you would associate with the box.

- In the Outliner select *hinge*.

- Highlight the **Rotate Z** attribute in the Channel Box.

- Select **Character** → **Create Subcharacter Set** – ❐.

- Change the name to *Box*, and set **Subcharacter Set Attributes** to **From Channel Box**.

- Press **Create SubCharacter Set**.

   Only the selected attributes from the hinge are now part of the *Box* Character and *Box* is a sub-character of *Jack_in_box*.

4 Add another attribute to the Box character

You will now add the *crank* rotateZ attribute to the *Box* sub-character.

- Select **Character** → **Set Current Character Set** → **jack_in_box** → **Box**.

- In the Outliner select *crank*.

- In the Channel Box highlight the **RotateZ** attribute.

- Select **Character** → **Add to Character Set**.

5 View in the Relationship Editor

The procedure of adding attributes through the Channel box could have also been completed using the Relationship Editor. Take a look at how the characters are set up in this editor.

- Select **Character** → **Set Current Character Set** → **Character Sets...**

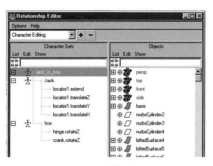

Expanded character

Tip:	This method can also be used to create definitions for a character's body parts such as arms and legs.

Setting up for animating

You are almost ready for animating the scene. Before you start, you need to get Jack and the box into their starting positions.

1 Position the Locator

To set up Jack, you need to set the locator's extend attribute so that Jack is hiding in the box.

- **Move** the *Locator* so that it is sitting directly above the box.

- Set the *Locator's* **extend** attribute to **0**.

- You may notice that Jack's hat is sticking up past the top of the box. You will need to scale the head down when it is in the box.

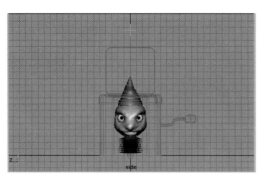

Locator positioning

2 Untemplate the box layer

- Untemplate the *box_layer*.

  Now you can see all of the parts of the model.

Open position

3 Set head to scale with the hinge

To set up the scaling of Jack's head, you will use Set Driven key. This will allow you to control the scaling of the head by the rotation of the hinge.

- Select **Animate** → **Set Driven Key** → **Set** - ❑.

- Select the *hinge* then click on the **Load Driver** button.

- Click on *rotate* Z in the right hand column.

- **Select** the *hat* surface then press the **up arrow** to navigate the hierarchy to the *head*.

  You can use the up and down arrows to navigate between children and parent nodes in a hierarchy.

- Click **Load Driven**.

- Click on *scale* Y in the right hand column.

- **Rotate** the hinge to about **90** degrees around the Z axis.

- Click on the **Key** button so that when the lid is all the way open the head will be scaled to 1 in Y.

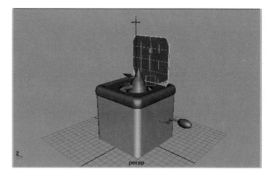

Open position

4 Key the end position

- **Select** the *hinge* and set **Rotate Z** to **0**.

- Select the *head* and set its **Scale Y** so that the hat is sitting inside the box.

- Click on the **Key** button.

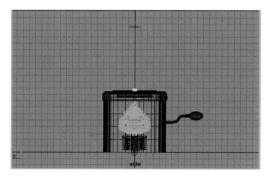

Closed position

5 Set up the box

- Set the **Rotate Z** of both the *hinge* and the *crank* to **0**.

  You are now ready to animate the Jack-in-the-box.

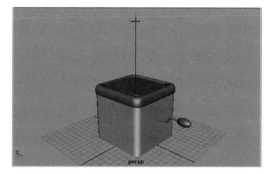

Starting position for box

Animate the Jack in the box

Because you set up the Jack-in-the-box as a character, you can quickly flesh out your animation using a pose-based technique. This means that you set up a series of poses for the character then set keys for all the attributes.

1 Set up for the animation

- In the time range, set the **Start time** and **Playback start time** to 1 and the **End time** and **Playback end time** to 120.

- In the Character menu, select **jack_in_box**. This does not highlight the character in the modeling view. It only indicates it as the active character.

Character menu

Now when you set keys using the **s** key, all the character's attributes will be keyed. When working with a character, it is important to remember that you can set keys on the active character even if the related nodes are not selected in the modeling views.

2 Set your tangent defaults

You will edit your tangent defaults so that all keys are created with **Flat** tangents. This tangent option gives a good starting point for the pose-based animation being used here.

- Select **Window → Settings/ Preferences → Preferences**.

- In the Settings section click on **Keys**.

PROJECT TWO

- Set the following:

    Default In Tangent to **Flat**;

    Default Out Tangent to **Flat**.

3 Set an initial key

- Move the Time slider to frame 1.

- Press the **s** key to set keys.

4 Create a pose at frame 60

- Move the Time Slider to frame 60.

- Select the *crank*.

- Set its **Rotate Z** to **900**.

- With your middle mouse button, click in a modeling view then press the **s** key to set keys.

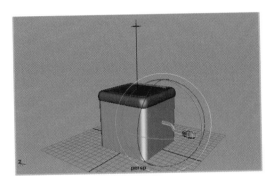

Rotated crank

Note: Even though the crank is selected in the modeling view, the keys are being set for all the attributes in the *jack_in_box* character.

---

5 Create a pose at frame 70

- Move the Time Slider to frame 70.

- Select the *hinge*.

- Set **Rotate Z** to around **100**.

- With your middle mouse button, click in a modeling view then press the **s** key to set keys.

Now the lid is open and the head has scaled back to its normal size.

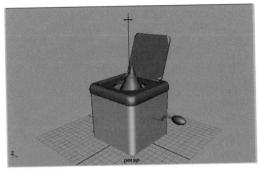

New Pose at frame 70

6 Create a pose at frame 80

- Move the Time Slider to frame 80.

- Select the *Locator* and set **Extend** to **10**.

- **Move** the *Locator* to the left.

- Set another key.

New Pose at frame 80

7 Create a pose at frame 85

- Move the Time Slider to frame 85.

- Select the *Locator* and set **Extend** to **7**.
- **Move** the *Locator* to the middle.
- Set another key.

- Select the *Locator* and set **Extend** to **6**.
- Set another key.

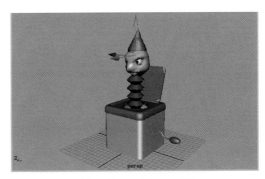

New Pose at frame 95

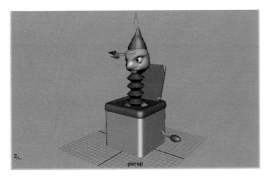

New Pose at frame 85

8 Create a pose at frame 90

- Move the Time Slider to frame 90.
- Select the *Locator* and set **Extend** to **10**.
- **Move** the *Locator* to the right.
- Set another key.

10 Create a pose at frame 100

- Move the Time Slider to frame 100.
- Select the *Locator* and set **Extend** to **10**.
- **Move** the *Locator* to the left.
- Set another key.

New Pose at frame 100

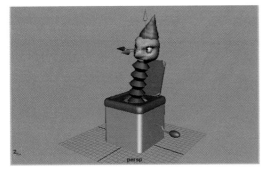

New Pose at frame 90

9 Create a pose at frame 95

- Move the Time Slider to frame 95.

11 Preview the results

- Make sure that your perspective panel is active.
- Select **Window → Playblast...**

This creates a quick preview animation that is good for reviewing the look of an animation.

Playblast window

For the Jack-in-the-box, you will see that the motion is a little mechanical. While the pose-based animation has not given you a finished product, it did offer a quick way of blocking out the action. In the next lesson, you will fix the look of the animation using several secondary motion techniques.

12 Save your work

Conclusion

By creating a character definition for the Jack-in-the-box, you were able to quickly set up poses to get a quick look at the motion. The character definition lets you bring different attributes from a number of different nodes and put them in one easy to organize place.

In the next lesson, the character will be used to help you edit the animation curves. You will then add some deformers to your surfaces to create some anticipation and follow-through for the action.

Secondary Animation

This lesson is about adding some life to the mechanical motions generated by the pose-based animation of the last lesson. You are going to use traditional animation techniques such as anticipation, overlapping action and squash and stretch to enhance the quality of the motion.

In Maya, you have a lot of flexibility when it comes to refining your animations. You can edit the curves in the graph editor or you can add deformers to give life to a scene. By combining several of these techniques you will create a more effective animation.

The Jack in the box

In this lesson you will learn the following:

- How to create overlapping actions in the graph editor
- How to use breakdown keys
- How to insert in-between keys
- How to use a lattice deformer
- How to lock an object to a deforming surface

OVERLAPPING ACTIONS

When you look at the animation of the Jack-in-the-box, each action follows directly after the last. The crank rotates. As it stops the lid opens. After the lid opens, Jack emerges. This breaks down the flow of the animation by giving distinct start and stop points.

You are now going to adjust the animation curves belonging to these actions so that each one flows into the other. You will continue working with the file you completed in the last lesson.

Extending the crank rotation

The first place where you can overlap the action is the crank rotation. Currently it stops just as the lid is being opened. You will extend the crank rotation to overlap the lid.

1 Open a graph editor panel

- Set up a panel layout where you have a perspective view, a Graph editor and any other panel type that you want.

2 View box curves in the graph editor

- From the character menu below the playback controls, select the *jack_in_box* character.

  The character now appears in the Graph editor. This is another advantage of using the character definitions. You can have the character loaded in the Graph editor even if no objects are selected in the modeling views.

- Click on the square plus sign next to *jack_in_box* to expand the character.

You now see the two sub-characters and all of their attributes.

- Press the **Ctrl / Command** key and click on the *Jack* and the *box* characters.

- From the Graph editor, select **View → Frame All** or press **A**.

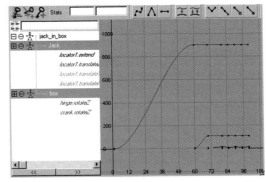

Graph editor

3 Delete extra keys on crank curve

- Click on the *crank.rotateZ* channel in the Graph editor. Now it is the only visible channel.

- **Select** the keys at the end of the curve. Leave only the first two unselected.

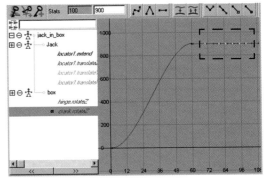

Selected keys

- Press the **Backspace** key to remove these keys.

4 Move the last key

- Select the last key on the curve.
- In the **Stats** section of the Graph editor, change the **Selected Key's Time** to **95**.

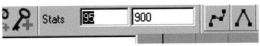

Graph editor stats

- Press the **Shift** key and click on the *hinge.rotateZ* channel in the Graph editor.

  You can see that the rotation of the crank is now overlapping the opening of the lid in time.

- Playback the results in the perspective panel to see the overlap.

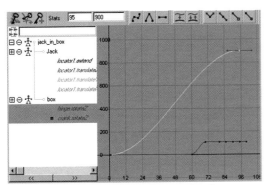

Viewing overlap in the Graph editor

Editing Tangent Weights

Since the *crank.rotateZ* channel is only described by two keys, the quality of its motion will be defined by what is happening between the keys. The Flat tangents set in the last lesson ensure that the crank accelerates

into motion at the beginning and decelerates to a stationary position at the end.

To control these two actions, you need to edit the weighting of the existing tangents so that you can either lengthen or shorten the action at the end points.

1 Convert the keys to weighted keys

- Click on the *crank.rotateZ* channel in the Graph editor so that it is again the only visible channel.
- Select both keys in the Graph editor.
- From the Graph editor, select **Curves → Weighted Tangents**.
- Next, click on the **Free tangent weight** button. This lets you edit the tangent weight on one side of a key without editing the tangent weight on the other.

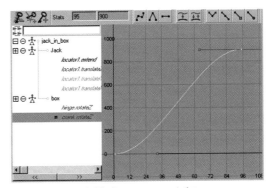

Added tangent weight

2 Adjust the tangent weight

- **Select** the first key on its own.
- **Select** the Tangent weight handle to the right of the key.
- Select the **Move** tool.

- Press the **Shift** key and click-drag with the MMB to the right.

This increases the weighting.

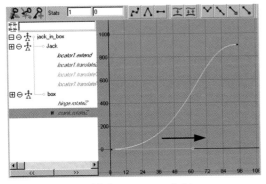

Added tangent weight

3 Adjust the end key tangents

- **Select** the second key on its own.
- **Select** the Tangent weight handle to the left of the key.
- Press the **Shift** key and click-drag with the MMB to the right.

This decreases the weighting.

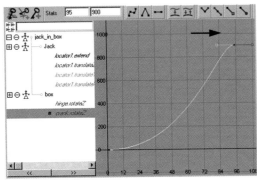

Added tangent weight

- Playback the results.

Now the handle takes longer to start up but stops more abruptly.

Overlapping Jack's extending

Another place where you could use some overlap is where Jack begins to extend up from the box. Right now, Jack doesn't emerge from the box until after the lid is actually opened. This is a result of the pose-based animation that was used. By deleting just one key, you can get some overlap here.

1 Select the extend channel

- In the Graph Editor, click on the channel labelled *locator.extend*.
- Select **View** → **Frame All**.

2 Select the extra key

- **Select** the key at frame 70.

This is the key that matches the point where the lid is fully opened.

- Press the **Backspace** key to delete the key.
- Playback the results.

Now Jack begins to emerge as the lid is opening.

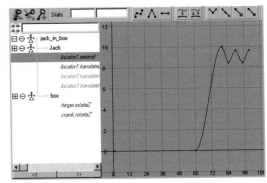

Extend animation curve

Add follow-through to the lid

When the hinge rotates, it goes from a closed position to an open position directly. To help emphasize the force of the lid's opening, you will now create some follow-through when the lid is fully opened. Rather than stopping it will sort of bounce back and forth to suggest a reverberation from the opening.

1 Move the extra keys

- **Select** the *hinge.rotateZ* attribute in the Graph Editor.

- From the Graph editor, select **View → Frame All**.

  This curve has a number of extra keys after the point where the lid opens. Rather than deleting these, you will modify them to create the back and forth motion.

- **Select** the last six keys on the curve.

- From the Graph editor, select **View → Frame Selection**.

- **Select** and **Move** the frames as shown below. Notice how the key at frame 70 has had its value increased to about 140 degrees. The goal is to have the lid open extra wide at frame 70 then oscillate back and forth for the next few frames:

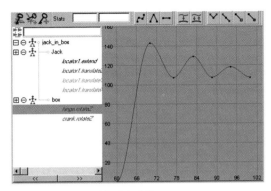

Updated frames

- Playback the results.

2 Convert keys to breakdown keys

Now that the final 6 keys are working correctly, you want to work with them as a grouped action. By converting the middle keys to Breakdown keys, you can control them all using the last key.

- **Select** the four keys that sit between the key at frame 70 and the end key.

- From the Graph editor, select **Keys → Convert to Breakdown**.

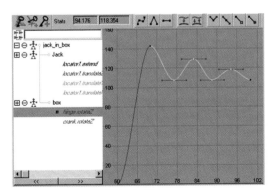

Selected keys

PROJECT TWO

3 Test the breakdown keys

A breakdown key is a special key in Maya that maintains a relationship to the keys around it. If they move, then the breakdown key is adjusted to suit.

- **Select** the end key.

- Press the **Shift** key and with your middle mouse button, **Move** the key left and right to move it in time.

- You can see that now the breakdown keys maintain an appropriate relationship to the keys around it.

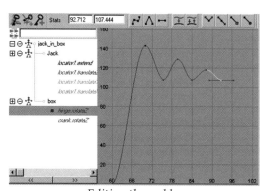

Editing the end key

- Playback the scene. If you are happy with the look of the lid then move on. If not, then continue to edit the keys until you are happy.

ANTICIPATION

Another important animation concept is anticipation. If you playback the Jack-in-the-box scene, you will notice that your audience is given no clue that Jack is going to emerge. One way to offer some anticipation would be to add a cartoon-like squashing of the box. As the crank begins to wind, the box begins to bulge until at the last minute it bursts with Jack emerging.

Add lattice to box

To create the bulging of the box, you will use a lattice deformer. This deformer type allows you to reshape one or more surfaces using a special frame. By working with the Lattice points, you can deform the look of the surface.

1 Select the surfaces

- Go to frame 68 or the frame where the lid is in an upright position.

- Select **Window** → **Outliner**.

- **Select** the base surface and the three lofted surfaces and the hinge.

Essentially, you should have all the surface for the box selected except for Jacks head and body.

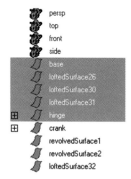

Selected surfaces

2 Make sure side loft is not selected

Since this loft is using the history from the trim edges, you will not be including it in the lattice. This will minimize problems if the lid ever swings outside the lattice area.

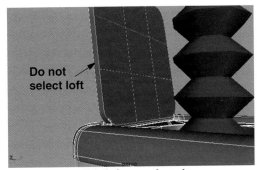

Side loft not selected

3 Add the Lattice

- Select **Deform** → **Create Lattice**.

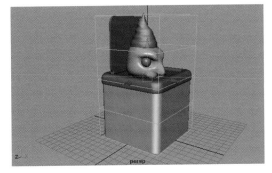

Box Lattice

Animate the box deformations

To animate the bulging of the box, you need to animate the lattice points themselves.

1 Set keys for frame 1

- Go to frame 1.
- From the **Character** menu, select **Set Current Character Set** → **none**.

  Setting this to none is *very important* to make sure that any keys you set do not get set on other character nodes.

- Press **F8** to go into component mode.
- **Select** all the Lattice points.
- Press **s** to set keys for the points.

2 Set keys for frame 50

- Go to frame 50.
- Edit the Lattice points to get the following shape. You will need to pick Lattice points either one at a time or as a group then either **Move** or **Scale** them. The goal is for the box to appear squashed with its front end tilted slightly lower than the back end:

Note: You do not need to adjust the top two rows of CV on the lattice at this point.

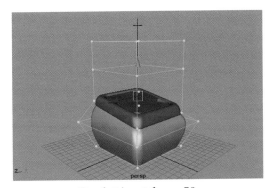

Box lattice at frame 50

- **Select** all the Lattice points.
- Press **s** to set keys for the points.

3 Set keys for frame 72

- Go to frame 72.
- Edit the Lattice points to get the following shape:

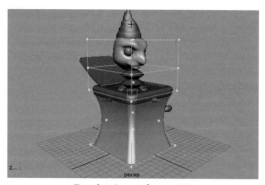

Box lattice at frame 72

- **Select** all the Lattice points.
- Press **s** to set keys for the points.

4 Set keys for frame 82

- Go to frame 82.
- Edit the Lattice points to get the following shape:

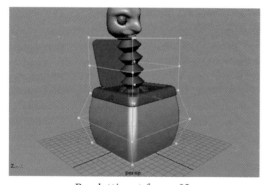

Box lattice at frame 82

- **Select** all the Lattice points.
- Press **s** to set keys for the points.

5 Set keys for frame 95

- Go to frame 95.
- Edit the Lattice points to get the following shape:

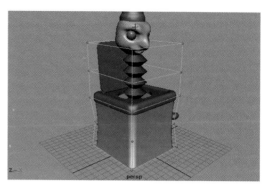

Box lattice at frame 95

- **Select** all the Lattice points.
- Press **s** to set keys for the points.

6 Set keys for frame 100

- Go to frame 1.
- With your middle mouse button, drag the current time indicator in the time slider to frame 100.

  By using the middle mouse button, the time was updated but the objects stay in their frame 1 positions.

- **Select** all the Lattice points.
- Press **s** to set keys for the points.

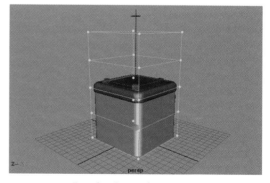

Box lattice at frame 100

Constrain crank to box surface

As you playback the scene, you will notice that the base of the box bulges but the crank remains stationary. You can use a single frame motion path to add the crank to the bulging action.

1 Draw a curve on surface

- Press **F8** to go back into object selection mode.
- Select the *base* surface of the box.
- Select **Modify → Make Live**.
- Hide the grid for the perspective view panel.

 Now the base surface is the working surface. Its isoparm lines will be the grid on which you will draw.

- Select **Create → EP Curve Tool**.
- Press the **x** key and click on the isoparm crossing at the center of the side face.
- Click a second point somewhere else on the surface.
- Press the **Enter** key to complete the curve.

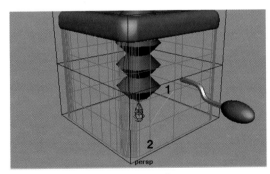

Curve on surface

- Click in an empty area to select nothing.
- Select **Modify → Make Not Live**.

2 Attach Crank to path

- **Select** the *crank*, then select **Edit → Group**.
- Select the **Move** tool, press the **Insert / Home** key and move the pivot point to the end of the crank. Press the **Insert / Home** key to exit pivot point mode.

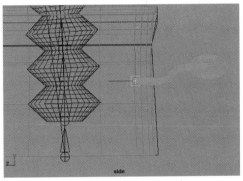

Pivot point repositioned

- With the group node selected press the **Shift** key and select the curve on surface.
- Select **Animate → Motion Paths → Attach to Motion Path - □**.
- In the option window, set the following:

 Time Range to **Start**.

- Click **Attach**.
- Playback the results.

 Now the crank is locked to the curve on surface and follows the surface during its deformations.

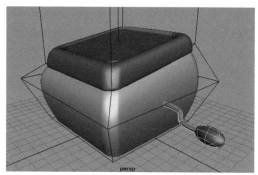

Crank attached to surface

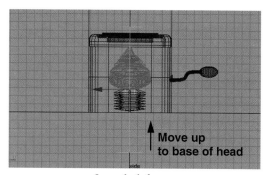

Move up
to base of head

Squash deformer

SQUASH AND STRETCH

In the bouncing ball example, you learned about squash and stretch. This principle will also be useful when Jack's head reaches the peak of his extension. Right now you notice that the head reaches the peak with no visible reaction. By adding a squash deformer to the head, you will be able to stretch the head at these points to give the feeling that the head is following through with the action.

Add squash deformer to head

To make the deformer work with the head, you will have to add it to the appropriate shapes then parent it into the hierarchy.

1 Add the deformer

- Go to frame 1.
- Select the *head* surface. This also selects the eyes and the hat.
- Select **Deform** → **Create Nonlinear** → **Squash**.
- Move the center *squashHandle* up to the base of the head.

2 Parent the deform handle

- In the Outliner window, click with your middle mouse button on the *squashHandle* and drag it to the *head* node. This action parents these together.

Animate stretching of head

You can now set keys on the squash attribute to complete the animation.

1 Set a key for frame 50

Since the box is itself a little squashed at frame 50, you will start here so that you can squash the head enough to make sure that the hat is not poking through the lid.

- Go to frame 50.
- With the *squashHandle* selected, click on the squash input node in the Channel box.
- Select the **Show Manipulator** tool.
- Click-drag on the squash manipulator to squash the head down.
- In the Channel box, click on the squash input node's **Factor** attribute's name to highlight it.

- From the Channel box menus, select **Channels → Key Selected**.

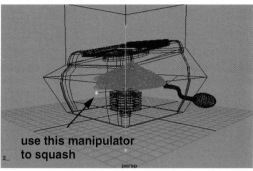

use this manipulator to squash

Squash setting

2 Set a key at frame 80

To set the remaining keys, you will use Auto keying.

- Turn on **Auto Keyframe toggle**.
- Go to frame 80.
- Use the *squashHandle* manipulators to stretch out Jack's head.

  A key is automatically set.

Squash at frame 80

3 Set more keys

- Now follow the animation and wherever Jack's head hits a peak in

its bouncing, add some stretch, and wherever his head hits a low point, add some squash.

- Your final animation curve for the Factor attribute might look something like this.

- When you are finished turn **Auto Key** to off.

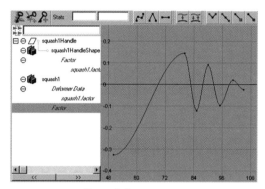

Squash factor curve

4 Save your work

Finishing touches

If you playback the animation at this point, you may be happy with some parts of the motion and unhappy with others. It is now up to you to complete the animation by tweaking the various keys to create the perfect animation.

Here are some examples of what you might want to do:

1 Make the head bounce for longer

Right now the head only bounces up and down for a short time. Extend these keys beyond the point where the box stops deforming. You may even want to add a few more bounces.

Remember that if you edit the timing of the Locator's **extend** attribute you must do the same for the squash's **factor** attribute since these work together.

2 Make the head flop around more

You may want to be more dramatic with where the Locator is positioned during the final bounces of the head. You could make these edits in the Graph editor or by setting new keys on top of old ones.

Conclusion

This lesson shows how time taken to add secondary animation to your work is very important to its success. Maya has many tools for adding these kinds of tweaks and adjustments and you should learn to use them effectively. Becoming an expert with the Graph editor is an important step to becoming a master animator.

Rendering

In this lesson, you will set up materials, textures and lighting for Jack. You will explore the make-up of a typical shading group including its material node and any texture maps.

This lesson will make extensive use of Maya's Interactive Photorealistic renderer (IPR). This tool allows you to create one rendering of the scene that can then be used to interactively update changes to the lighting and texturing of your scene. You will see how fast and intuitive it is to texture in Maya's IPR world.

The Jack in the box

In this lesson you will learn the following:

- How to set up and tweak multiple lights in a scene
- How to set up an Interactive Photorealistic Rendering
- How to add bump and specular maps
- How to make connections in the Hypershade panel
- How to texture map a deforming object
- How to create a texture reference object
- How to set up camera attributes

CREATE A SIMPLE SET

To create a backdrop for Jack, you will build a simple set with some props. These will all be built with primitives and will get their look from texture maps.

Create a three sided backdrop

You will create a cube then remove some of the faces to create a backdrop. Two walls and one floor surface is all you need to create a simple set for your action.

1 Create and position a primitive cube

- Select **Create → NURBS Primitives → Cube**.

- Set the *cube's* **Y translate** to **0.5**.

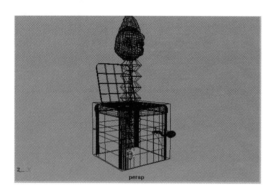

New cube

2 Set the cube's pivot

- Select the **Move** tool.

- Press the **Insert / Home** key so that you can edit the cube's pivot point.

- Use grid snapping to move the cube's pivot point back to the origin.

    Now you will be able to scale the cube from its base.

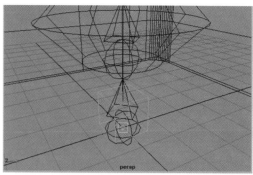

Pivot location

3 Scale the cube to desired size

- Press the **Insert / Home** key again.

- **Scale** the cube until it is big enough to cover a fairly large area round Jack.

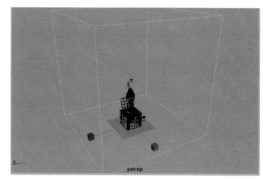

Scaled cube

4 Remove the three unwanted faces

- Press **5** to turn on hardware shading.

- Select the top face and the two front faces and press the **Backspace** key.

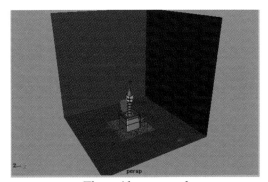

Three sides removed

Add some props

To add some extra detail to the scene, you will add some primitive shapes to act as props.

1 Create a ball

- Select **Create → NURBS Primitives → Sphere**.

- **Move** and **Scale** the sphere and place it to the left and behind the jack-in-the-box.

- **Rotate** it off its axis so that it looks more interesting when you texture it later.

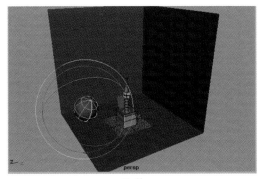

Ball

2 Create some blocks

- Create another primitive cube.

- Position it to the right of the jack-in-the-box.

- **Duplicate** the box three times and create a stack of blocks.

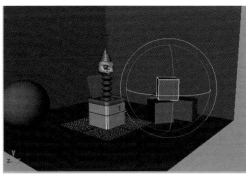

Blocks

A Directional Light

Before you can start rendering your scene, you will need some light. The easiest light to set up is a directional light which works with parallel rays of light much like the sun.

1 Create a directional light

- Select **Create → Lights → Directional Light**.

- Click in your perspective panel with your middle mouse button then press the **7** key to turn on hardware lighting.

  At first, only the sides of your objects are illuminated because of the light's default direction.

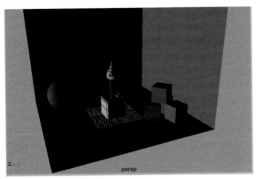

Directional light

2 Position and Orient the light

- Select the **Show Manipulator** tool.

- Click drag on the light manipulator handle to move the light up and to the left.

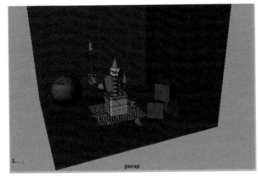

Repositioned light

Camera setup

To see how your rendering will look when rendered, you can set up some display tools that will help guide your action.

1 Set up resolution gate

- From the perspective panel menus, select **View** → **Camera Settings** → **Resolution Gate**.

This sets up a bounding box to show you what will get rendered.

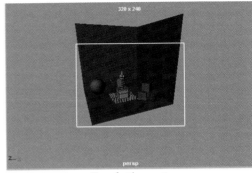

Resolution gate

2 Adjust the camera's overscan

- From the perspective panel menus, select **View** → **Camera Attribute Editor**.

- In the Film Back section of the perspShape node, set the following:

    Film Fit to **Vertical**;

    Overscan to **1.2**.

    Now you can see more of the scene.

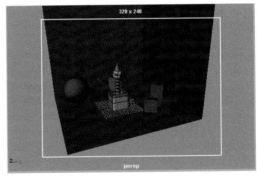

Resolution gate

Note: If your panel was more vertical then your Film Fit would have to be set to Horizontal.

3 Set up display guides

- From the perspective panel menus, select **View** → **Camera Settings** → **Safe Action**.

  This shows a second bounding box that defines the area that would be visible if you rendered to video.

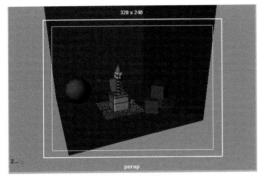

Safe Action box

4 Set up a view for rendering

- From the perspective panel menus, select **View** → **Camera Attribute Editor**.

- In the **Camera attributes** section, set the following:

  Focal Length to **28**;

  This adjusts the Angle of view and lets you see a more wide angle view of the scene.

- Tumble, Track and Dolly into the view to get a nice view of the Jack-in-the-box extended. Scroll in the

time slider to check your view at different times.

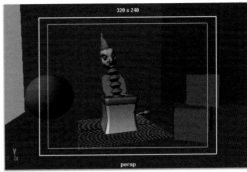

New view

IPR

You are now ready to render your scene. To give you access to interactive updating capabilities, you will set up an IPR (Interactive Photorealistic Rendering) rendering.

An IPR rendering creates a special image file that stores not only the pixel information about an image but also information about the surface normals, materials and objects associated with each of these pixels. This information is then updated as you make changes to your scene's shading.

1 Panel setup

- Set up a four panes view panel layout and set up the panels to include a Hypershade, Perspective view, Render View and a Top view.

2 IPR setup

- From your Render view panel, open the Render Globals.

- Click on the **Maya Software** tab.

- From the **Anti-aliasing quality** section, set **Quality** to **Production quality**.

  For IPR, you can use the best settings if desired. Your initial IPR rendering will be slower but the interactive updates will still be fast.

- Close the Render globals.

3 Create an IPR rendering

- From your Render view panel, select **IPR** → **IPR Render** → **persp**.

  Now what seems to be a regular rendering of the scene appears. You will learn how to work with this rendering interactively.

- Click drag to select an area of the IPR rendering that includes both walls and the floor. This is the area that will be updated as you make changes.

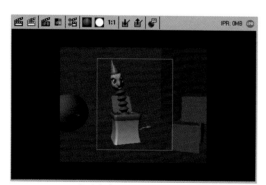

Initial IPR rendering

4 Create two new materials

- In your Hypershade panel, create a new **Lambert** material.

- Name it *wall* and change its color.

- Create a new **Phong** material.

- Name it *floor* and change its color.

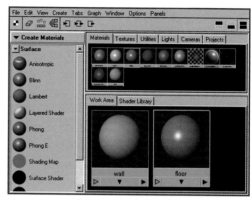

New material nodes

5 Assign the materials

- With your middle mouse button, click-drag the floor material onto the floor surface in the Render View panel within the selected area.

  In the Render View, the new color is updated quickly.

- Repeat for the *wall* material. Be sure to assign it to both wall surfaces.

Drag material into bounded area

IPR update

6 Edit the Floor material's color

- Open the Attribute editor. Click on the floor in the IPR window. This loads the floor's material into the Attribute editor.

- Click on the Color swatch and in the Color wheel, start trying out different colors.

  As you click-drag around the color wheel, the IPR window will update automatically.

Click to load shader in Attribute editor

Updated color

7 Refresh the IPR image

- Click on the **Refresh the IPR image** button.

  Now the color and material changes are visible on the whole scene.

Refresh IPR image

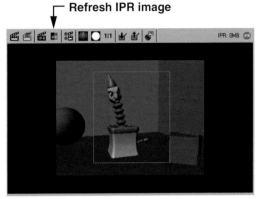

IPR update

Lighting

You can also use the IPR window to explore different lighting possibilities. You will now set up three light sources with shadows to make the scene more interesting.

1 Change the existing light type

- In the Hypershade, click on the Lights tab and double-click on the Directional light icon.

- In the Attribute editor, change the **Type** to **Spot light**.

  In the IPR update area, you will see that the light is now restricted to a cone angle. This is one of the key properties of a spotlight.

PROJECT TWO

Spotlight in IPR window

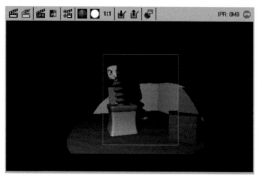

Updated IPR window

2 Edit the light properties

- In the Attribute editor, change the **Cone Angle** of the light to **60**.

- Open the Shadows section and turn **Use Depth Map Shadows** to **On**.

  You will notice that the cone angle adjustment did update in the IPR window but the shadows did not. Some attribute changes may require that you redo the rendering. This takes longer than a refresh.

- Select **IPR → Redo Previous IPR Render**.

  Now the shadows are visible.

- Re-select an update area for your IPR view.

3 Edit the Shadow position

- Zoom out in the perspective view panel.

  You will notice that this does not update in the IPR update area. View changes are not reflected until the rendering is redone. This can be a good thing since you can change views temporarily to edit lights without losing your rendering.

- **Select** the spotlight then select the **Show Manipulator** tool.

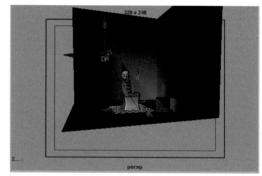

Perspective view

- Move the light around until you get a lighting view that you like in the IPR window. You may need to click on the **Refresh** button from time to time to get an overall view of the changes.

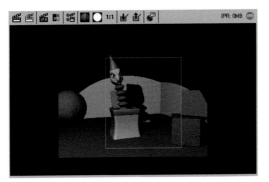

Perspective IPR view

- When you are finished, be sure to click in the perspective panel with your middle mouse button then press the [key to undo your view changes to get back to your chosen render view.

4 Edit the Shadow properties

- View the spotlight in the Attribute editor and set the following values:

In the Spot Light Attributes section:

Penumbra Angle to **5**.

In the Depth Map Shadow Attributes section:

Dmap Filter Size to **3**.

These settings soften the edge of the spotlight and the shadow.

Note: Be careful of setting the Dmap Filter Size too high. It slows down rendering time significantly.

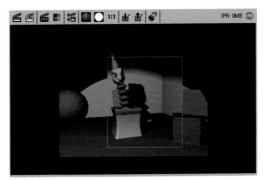

Updated IPR window

5 Add a second spot light

- Select **Create** → **Lights** → **Spot light**.
- With the **Show Manipulator**, set up the light to look up at Jack from the ground.

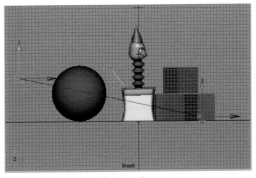

Front view

6 Edit the light

The shadows from this low light will look dramatic on the back wall.

- Turn on **Depth Map shadows** for this light.
- Redo your IPR rendering.
- Set the light's **Intensity** to about **0.75** then play with its light attributes to get the look that you want for the

PROJECT TWO

light. Use the IPR update area to
assist you.

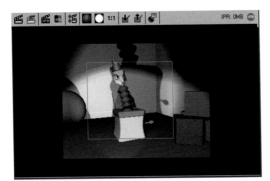

Two lights

TEXTURE MAPS

You are now going to add texture maps to
some of your materials. Starting with the
walls and the floor, you will see how to create
color maps that add detail to your rendering.

Texturing the wall

You are going to add a simple checker pattern
to the wall using one of Maya's procedural
textures. A procedural texture gives you a
node that has attributes for you to adjust. You
can also edit the positioning of the texture to
get a more interesting pattern.

1 Add a texture to the wall

- In the Hypershade, click in the
  Work Area panel to make it active.
  Select **Graph → Clear Graph** to
  remove everything from the view.

- Click on the Materials tab. With
  your middle mouse button drag the
  wall shader to the work area.

- Click on the **Create Materials** menu
  of the Hypershade and select **Create
  Textures** from the pop up menu.

- Use your middle mouse button to
  drag a checker texture onto the *wall*
  material.

- When you release the mouse, select
  color from the pop-up menu.

  The texture is now added to the
  material node in the Hypershade
  panel and you can see it in the
  update area of the IPR view.

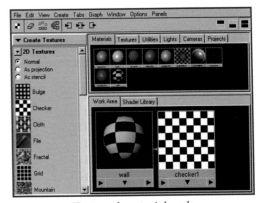

Textured material node

2 Update the textures attributes

The checker texture is a procedural texture
that has editable attributes. You can
change the color of the opposing parts of
the checker.

- In the Attribute Editor, click on the
  Color1 swatch and change the color
  as you see fit.

- Repeat for **Color2**.

Updated colors

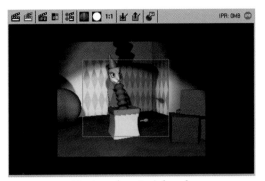

Textured material node

3 Reposition the texture

▪ In the Hypershade panel, click on the *checker* node to select it then click on the **Input Connections** button. This displays the texture's placement icon.

Show Input Connections

Show Input Connections Icon

▪ Double click on the *place2Dtexture* icon in the Hypershade to open the Attribute Editor.

▪ Set the following:

> **Repeat U V** to **4** and **12**;
>
> **Rotate UV** to **45**.

In the IPR update area, you will see the effect that these changes have to the pattern.

Texturing the floor

To texture map the floor you will use a file texture of a wood pattern. While procedural textures give you a lot of flexibility, a painted or scanned texture can add significant realism to a scene.

1 Create a file texture

▪ Open the Attribute editor for the *floor* material.

▪ Click on the **map** button next to **Color**.

▪ Select **File** from the 2D Texture section of the **Create Render Node** window.

▪ In the Attribute editor, click on the folder icon next to **Image Name** and choose the *teak.iff* file from the *sourceimages* directory.

Now you have this texture mapped to the floor.

PROJECT TWO

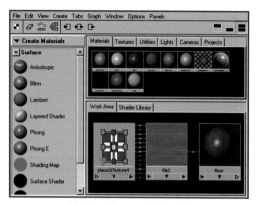

Textured material node

2 Position the texture

- In the Hypershade panel, click on the *teak* node to select it then click on the **Input Connections** button. This displays the texture's placement icon.

- Click on the *place2Dtexture* icon and in the Attribute editor, set the following:

   Repeat U to **2**;

   Repeat V to **2**;

   Rotate UV to **45**.

Incorrectly positioned texture

3 Texture the props

- Now use the technique you have just learned to add texture maps to the ball and the blocks. Try out different texture types.

   Remember to move the IPR update area to preview the texture changes.

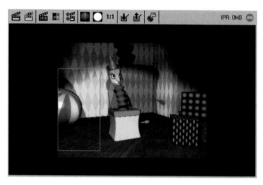

Correctly positioned texture

TEXTURING THE BASE

You are now going to texture map the base of the jack-in-the-box. You will accomplish this with a projected texture map. Projection maps are positioned using a 3D placement icon instead of sitting directly on the surface. You will set up this map type then explore the implication for the base surface which is a deforming surface.

Projection mapping

To set up a projection map, you must first set up the material then place the texture in relation to the surface.

1 Set up IPR window

- Go to frame 1.

- Select **IPR** → **Redo Previous IPR Render**. Select an update area.

2 Texture map the base's color attribute

- Drag *boxShader* to the Work Area.
- In the Attribue Editor, click on Map button next to color.
- Set **2D Textures** to **As projection**.
- Click on **File**.
- In the Attribute editor, click on the folder icon next to **Image Name** and choose the *base.iff* file from the *sourceimages* directory.

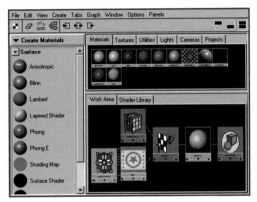

Texture icons

3 Position the texture

- In the Attribute editor, make sure that you are looking at the *projection* node and set the following:

    Set **Projection Type** to **TriPlanar**.

  This map type will project your texture along all three axes.

- Click on the **Interactive placement** button then click on the **Fit to BBox** button.

Now the texture is surrounding the base of the box.

Positioning icons

In the IPR window, you will see that the texture is now mapped to the sides of the box.

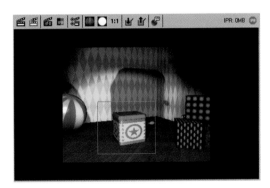

Rendered texture

Texture Reference Objects

While the projected texture works for frame 1, it will not necessarily work later when the box begins to squash and stretch. You therefore need to set up a non-deforming object as a reference for the texture.

1 Test the texture at frame 55

- Go to frame 55.

- Redo the IPR rendering.

  You can see that the texture is not following the surface. The stars are not bulging and the top bar of the texture has disappeared. This is because it is using the texture placement node to determine the projection.

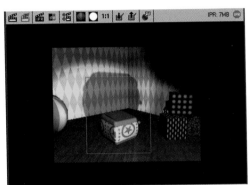

Incorrectly Positioned texture

2 Create a texture reference object

- Go to frame 1.

- Select the *base* surface.

- Select **Texturing** → **Create Texture Reference Object**.

  You will notice that there is a now a templated version of the box.

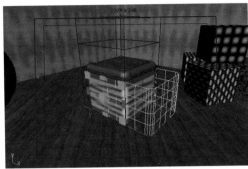

New reference object

3 Test render the texture reference object

- Go to frame 55.

- Redo the IPR render.

  Now the texture is working with the surface. When you deform a surface, there is a templated un-deformed surface that is being referred to during deformations. Your projection is now being applied to that template object instead of the deforming one.

  You are now ready for the final rendering.

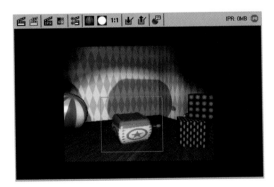

Positioned texture

4 Save your work

- From the **File** menu, select **Save Scene As...**

- Enter the name *jack_final* next to the file's path.

- Press the **Save** button or press the **Enter** key.

Rendering the animation

Once you are happy with your test rendering, it is time to render an animation. This will be accomplished using Maya's *batch renderer*. In preparation, you will add motion blur to your scene to simulate the blur generated in live action film and video work.

1 Set the Image output

To render an animation, you must set up the scene's file extensions to indicate a rendered sequence. You must also set up the Start and End Frames.

- Select **Window → Rendering Editors → Render Globals...**

- Click on the **Common** tab.

- From the **Image File Output** section, set the following:

     File Name Prefix to **jack**;

This sets the name of the animated sequence.

  Frame/Animation Ext to:

    name.#.ext (for Windows, Mac)

    name.ext.# (for IRIX);

This sets Maya up to render a numbered sequence of images.

  Start Frame to **1**;

  End Frame to **120**;

  By Frame to **1**.

This tells Maya to render every frame from 1 to 120.

2 Turn on motion blur

- In Render Globals, click on the **Maya Software** tab.

- In the **Motion Blur** section, click on the **Motion Blur** button to turn it on.

- Set the **Motion Blur Type** to be **2D**.

3 Batch render the scene

- Press **F5** to change to the **Rendering** menu set.

- Use the hotbox to select **Render → Batch Render...**

   Maya is now rendering out each frame of your animation. You can view the progress in the Command Feedback line or by opening the Script editor.

4 View the resulting animation

After the rendering is complete, you can preview the results using the *fcheck* utility.

On Win, Mac

- Open the fcheck utility by clicking on its icon.

- Select **File → Open Animation**.

- Navigate to the `projectTwo\images` folder.

- Select one of the frames of your animation then click **Open**.

On IRIX

- In a shell window, set your current directory to the `maya/projects/learningMaya/projectTwo/images` directory.

- Type the following:

```
fcheck jack.iff.
```

Conclusion

You are now finished the Jack-in-the-box lesson. Maya's IPR has helped speed up the creative process and allowed you to explore a number of lighting and texturing very quickly.

You are now finished with this project. Next you will build two spaceships and send them into battle.

PROJECT THREE

Project Three

In this project, you will explore how to model with both NURBS and polygonal geometry. This will give you a chance to explore some of the possibilities inherent in the two types of geometry. You will then animate the ships along two path curves so that you can easily build and edit a space animation.

You will then create a rendered image of a space scene to use as an animated backdrop. You will then add OptiF/X thrusters and explosions. Particles will also be used for some effects.

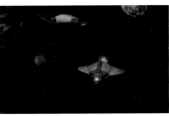

1. A spaceship tries desperately to escape the pursuit of an approaching fighter ship.

2. The fighter shoots one photon torpedo at the fleeing ship.

3. A quick, last second dodge barely clears the resulting explosion.

4. The spaceship breaks away with a trail of smoke emitting from her wing.

12 **Polygonal Spaceship**

In this lesson, you will build and texture map a polygonal spaceship. Starting with a polygonal cube, you will extrude Poly Faces until you have a completed ship. You will then be able to edit the construction history of the modeling actions to update the model and edit the results.

You will then apply texture projections in order to create UV coordinates on the polymesh. These will let you texture map the ship using a series of texture maps imported as file textures.

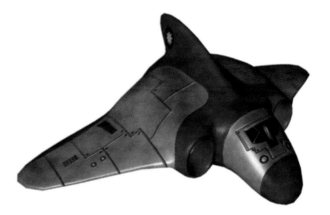

Polygon spaceship

In this lesson you will learn the following:

- How to model using polygons
- How to smooth a polygonal mesh
- How to work with procedural modeling attributes
- How to model using lattices
- How to work with procedural modeling attributes
- How to set up files for referencing

Initial set-up

You will use an existing project directory which contains all of the required texture files for the next few lessons.

1 Set the current project

- Select **File → Project → Set...**

- Locate and select the *projectThree* directory in the *learningMaya* directory.

- Click **OK**.

2 Set up the modeling panels

- Start a **New Scene**.

- In the view panel menu bar, select **Panels → Saved Layouts → Edit Layouts...**

- In the **Panels** window, open the **Edit Layouts** tab.

- Set the **Configuration** to **4 Panes Split Left**.

- Set the large panel to the Perspective view with the Top, Front and Side view panels along the side.

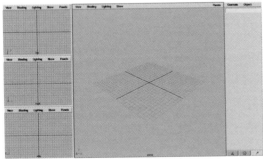

Recommended layout for this tutorial section

Starting the ship

This spaceship will be built starting with a simple polygonal cube. The Poly Faces will then be extruded to create a more complex shape.

1 Place and position a primitive cube

- Select **Create → Polygon Primitives → Cube**.

- Set each view to **Smooth Shade All**.

- Select the **Scale** tool.

- Click-drag on the **Scale** handles to create the following shape:

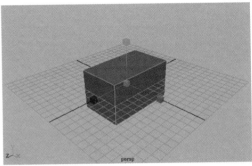

Scaled primitive polygon cube

2 Turn on backface culling

During the process of modeling the polygonal spaceship, it is important that you do not accidentally select and modify Poly Faces that are on the opposite side of the object. To prevent this, *backface culling* can be turned on so that the Poly Faces that are facing away from the view are not displayed and cannot be selected.

- Select **Display → Custom Polygon Display - □**.

- In the option window, set **Backface Culling** to **On**. Click **Apply and Close**.

3 Select the two side faces of cube

- Press **F8** to go into **Select by Component** mode.
- Turn off the **Points** selection mask.
- Turn on the **Faces** selection mask.
- **Select** the facet handle on the right side of the cube.

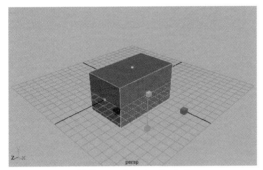

Polygon facet selected

- **Tumble** the view to the other side of the cube.
- Press the **Shift** key and **Select** the opposite facet handle.

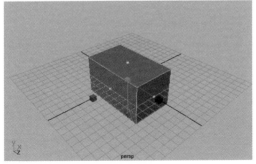

Opposite polygon facet selected

4 Extrude and scale Poly Faces

- Select **Edit Polygons** → **Extrude Face**.

A manipulator appears which gives you access to translation, rotation and scaling all at the same time.

- Tumble the view to get a better view of the manipulator.
- Click-drag on the blue **Move** handle to extrude a new facet.

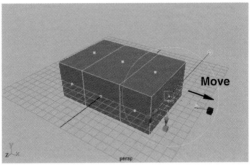

Opposite Poly Faces extruded

- Click-drag on green **Scale** handle to taper the edges.

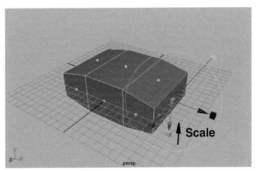

Extruded Poly Faces scaled in one direction

Note: When you manipulate the handle associated with one facet, the other facet reacts equally. Both extrusions are working based on the normals of the original Poly Faces.

PROJECT THREE

5 Add wing base

- Press the **g** key to reactivate the **Extrude** tool and start a new extrusion.

- **Click-drag** on the green **Scale** handle to create a long, thin polygon centered about the edge facet.

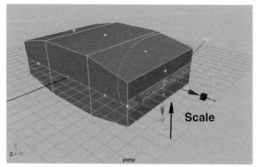

Thin facet extruded as the base of the wing

6 Extrude and shape wing

- Press the **g** key.

- Click-drag on the blue **Move** handle.

- Click-drag on red **Scale** handle.

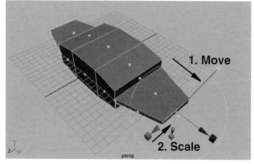

Wing tip extruded and scaled

- Click-drag on red **Move** handle.

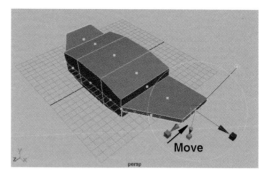

Wing tip scaled and moved into position

7 Add a top wing

- **Select** the facet handle belonging to the top surface of the shape.

- Press the **g** key.

- Click-drag on red **Scale** handle to create a long thin polygon centered in the top facet.

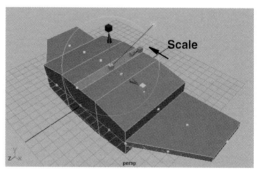

Thin facet extruded as the base of the fin

- Press the **g** key.

- Click-drag on the blue **Move** handle.

- Click-drag on green **Scale** handle.

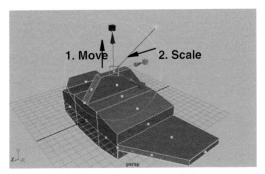

Fin extruded and scaled

- Click-drag on green **Move** handle.

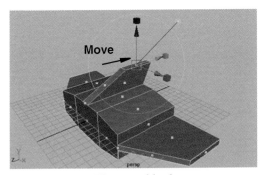

Fin moved back

Air intake ports

In addition to extruding out, you can use the extrusion tool to push a polygonal facet into a surface to create an opening. For the ship's air intake ports, this technique will be used.

1 Create the front of the ports

- **Select** the facet handle belonging to the side thruster port.
- Press the **Shift** key and **Select** the opposite facet.

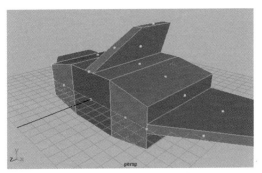

Two Poly Faces selected to create thruster ports

- Press the **g** key to re-evoke the **Extrude** tool and start a new extrusion.
- Click-drag on the green **Scale** handle to create a little lip at the edge of the top and bottom of the thruster ports.
- Click-drag on red **Scale** handle to create a similar lip at the side edges of the thruster ports.

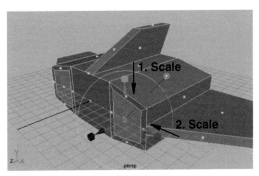

Front edge of the thruster ports

2 Add a lip to the ports

To give the thruster a little bit of an edge, you will next create a little lip using the extrude tool.

- Press the **g** key.

PROJECT THREE

- Click-drag on green **Scale** handle to create a little lip at the top and bottom edges of the thruster ports.

- Click-drag on red **Scale** handle to create a similar lip at the side edges of the thruster ports.

- Click-drag on blue **Move** handle to push this extruded facet back a little.

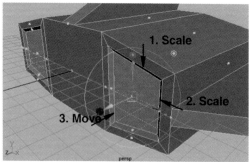

Lip added to the thruster ports

3 Extrude the hole

- Press the **g** key.

- Click-drag on blue **Move** handle to push this facet back deep into the spaceship.

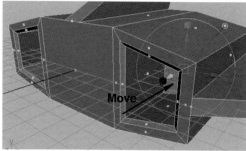

Hole extruded for thruster port

4 Add the rear thruster

- **Tumble** the view around to see the back of the ship.

- **Select** the facet handle belonging to back facet of the ship.

- Press the **g** key.

- Click on one of the **Scale** handles.

The center of manipulator changes to a **Scale** manipulator.

- Click-drag on the center **Scale** handle to create the edge to the exhaust port.

All four sides scale to the same value and proportion.

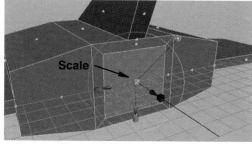

Front edge of exhaust port

- Repeat the steps used to create the front thruster ports to finish the back exhaust hole.

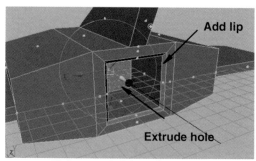

Hole extruded for exhaust port

The front cockpit

You can now continue to use the extrude tool to pull out a cockpit area for the spaceship.

1 Pick the front facet

- **Tumble** around to see the front of the ship.
- **Select** the facet handle belonging to front facet of the ship.

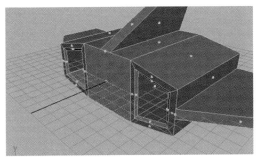

Front facet to be extruded for the cockpit

2 Extrude the front facet twice

- Press the **g** key.
- Click-drag on blue **Move** handle to pull this facet out.
- Press the **g** key.
- Use blue **Move** handle to pull a second facet out.

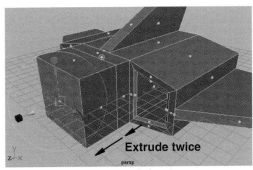

Facet extruded twice

3 Scale and move the facet

- Use the green **Scale** handle to scale the front facet down.
- Use the red **Scale** handle to scale this facet in.
- Use the green **Move** handle to move this piece down.

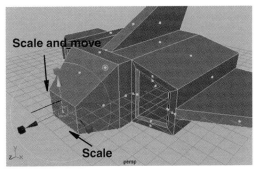

Front facet scaled and moved down

Creating a more organic look

At this point, you might be thinking that this will be a very simplistic looking spaceship. You will now apply a smooth node on the polygons to create a more organic look and improve the look of the ship. You will then apply a lattice and deform the lattice points to achieve a more streamlined look.

1 Turn off Backface Culling

To make it easier to select all the Poly Faces in one selection it will be necessary to turn off Backface Culling.

- Select the *polyShip*.
- Select **Display** → **Custom Polygon Display** - □.
- Set **Backface Culling** to **Off**.
- Click **Apply and Close**.

2 Smooth the Ship

The whole polyset can be smoothed into a more organic shape.

- While in **Component Mode**, **Select** all facets on the ship.
- Select **Polygons** → **Smooth**.

The planar polymesh that was created out of the series of extrusions is now smoothed and rounded

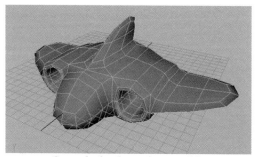

Smoothed polymesh spaceship

3 Edit the extrude history

The smooth has been applied as an input node to the polymesh. All of the original extrusions have been recorded in a series of *polyExtrudeFace* nodes that you can find in the Channel box.

By selecting one of these input nodes and invoking the show manipulator tool, you can edit the history of the extrusion.

- In the Channel box, **Select** the *polyExtrudeFace1* node.
- Select the **Show Manipulator Tool**.

  The manipulator for the first extrusion is displayed.

- Use the blue **Move** handle to move the extrude in towards the center.

Both the extrude history and smooth action update, as the exhaust ports become more narrow.

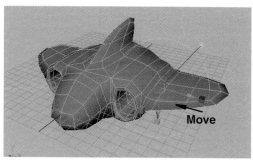

Width of thrusters updated through history

Note:	Any of the other extrusions can be adjusted by selecting the relevant input node and using show manipulator, or by editing the values in the Channel box. This is a good example of Maya's procedural modeling capabilities.

4 Edit the smooth history

Since the smooth action is also saved as an input node, you can edit a parameter on this node to increase the smoothness of the ship's surface.

- **Select** the *polySmoothFace1* input node in the Channel box.
- Set **Divisions** to **2**.

  The detail and smoothness of the spaceship increases.

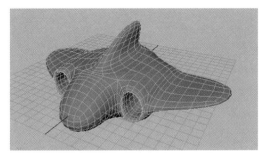

Level of smoothness increased

5 Add a lattice

- Change to the **Animation** menu set.
- Go to object mode.
- Select **Deform** → **Create Lattice**.
- In the Channel box, set the following under the *ffd1LatticeShape* node:

    S Divisions to **4**;

    T Divisions to **2**;

    U Divisions to **6**.

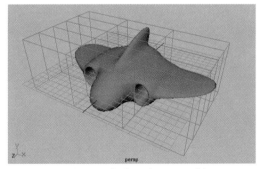

Lattice applied to the spaceship

6 Edit the lattice points

To reshape the spaceship, you will use the lattice by editing the lattice points. By editing the simple lattice frame, you can easily make edits to the polymesh surface.

- Press **F8** to go into **Select by Component Type** mode.
- Turn on the **Points** selection mask.

    The **Poly Faces** selection mask should be turned off.

- In the Top view, use the **Shift** key and click-drag to **Select** the twelve control points near the tips of the wings as shown.

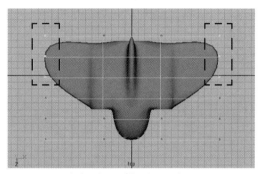

Selection of lattice points

- Select the **Scale** tool.
- Click-drag on the red **Scale** handle to scale the points out.

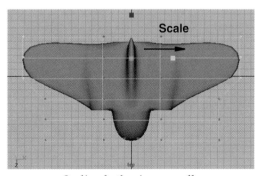

Scaling both wings equally

7 Move the tail

- In the Perspective view, **Select** the six control points closest to the tail.

Make sure that you do not select
any of the control points at the
bottom of the lattice.

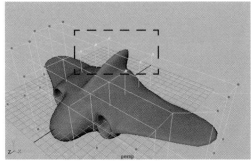

Control points selected

- Select the **Move** tool.
- Use the green and blue handles to
  Move the control points up and
  towards the back.

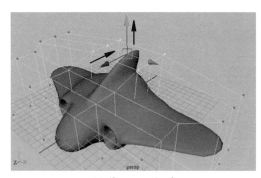

Tail area raised

8 Move the lower back edge down
  - In the Side view, **Select** the four
    control points at the back lower
    edge.
  - **Move** these points down.

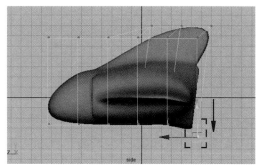

Back area lowered

9 Move the wings tips down
  - In the Front view, **Select** all the
    control points on the right and left
    sides of the lattice.
  - **Move** these points down.

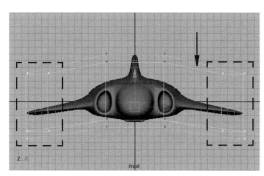

Wing tips moved down

10 Curve the nose forward and down
  - In the Side view, **Select** the front
    two rows of control points.
  - **Move** these points forward and
    down.

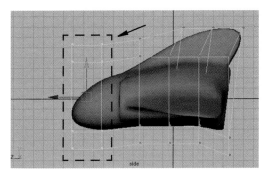

Cockpit area moved forward and down

- **Select** the front row of the control points.
- **Move** these points forward and down.

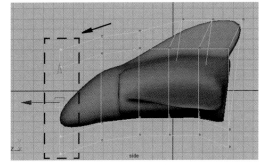

Nose moved forward and down

Finishing the model

Now that you are happy with the shape of the ship, you can delete history. This will remove the input nodes. You could keep them around, but they can add extra complexity to the model which is not required.

1 Delete history

- Press **F8** to go back to **Select by Object Type** mode.
- **Select** the spaceship.

- Select **Edit → Delete by Type → History**.

  The lattice and the input nodes are deleted and the history of the polymesh spaceship can no longer be adjusted.

2 Rename the polymesh

- Rename the polymesh *polyShip*.

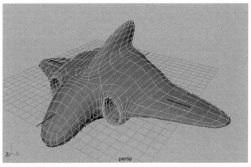

History deleted on spaceship

3 Save the file

- Select **File → Save Scene As...**
- Save the file as *polyShip*.

TEXTURING THE SHIP

You now have a polygonal mesh that requires texturing. Although, polygons have a default setting for UV parameters, onto which textures can be applied, you will need to adjust these settings for each specific application. You can use special polygon tools to assign/modify these kinds of values to the ship.

Creating the polyShip shading

The polyShip will be textured using a single shading group that contains several texture maps. The method of positioning the texture on the surface will be accomplished using the polygon texturing tools.

1 Set up view panels

- Select **Panels** → **Saved Layouts** → **Four View** or select the four view layout in the Tool Box.

- Select **Display** → **Grid** to hide the grid in the view panels.

  This will help you see the texture projection planes.

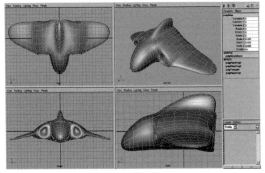

Recommended layout for this tutorial section

2 Create and assign a new shading group

- Open the Hypershade window.

- Create a Blinn Material node.

- **Assign** the Blinn Material to the polymesh object.

- Rename the material node *polyShipBlinn*.

3 Turn on hardware texturing

- Turn on hardware texturing in each view panel.

  The display of the model does not change because there are no textures assigned.

4 Map an image file to the color

- Open the attributes for the *polyShipBlinn* node.

- **Map** the **Color** attribute with a 2D **File** texture node. Make sure that the **Normal** option is selected.

- Rename the *file1* node *polyColor*.

- Click on the **Folder Icon** button next to **Image Name**.

- In the sourceimages directory of the *projectThree* project, locate the *polyColor.iff* image file in the *sourceimages* directory.

  The image file is a bitmap image that was created in a paint package.

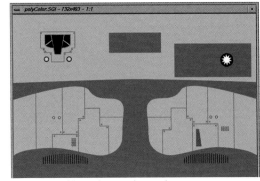

Bitmap file to be used as color texture map

- Click **Open**.

  The texture has been placed on the polymesh surface using the default UV mapping inherited from the original poly cube.

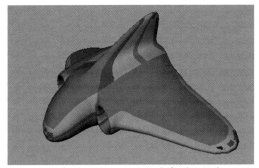

Applied texture using default UV's

Projecting the texture

The texture you are mapping onto the spaceship has been created as a sort of *decal* sheet. You will be using the polygon projection methods to map the parts of the decal sheet to different parts of the ship. Shown below are the main parts of the ship labeled. Later, you will see how the decal sheet will work.

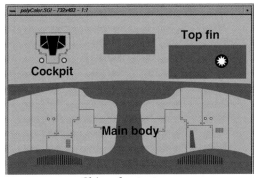

Ship color texture

1 Select all the Poly Faces

The Poly Faces of the polymesh surface must be mapped with a projection to create UV coordinates on the polymesh.

- Select the *polyShip*.

- Click on the ship with the **RMB**, and select **Face** from the pop-up marking menu.

- Click-drag a selection box around the entire object to **Select** all of the poly faces.

  It is important that you do not miss any Poly Faces. The color of the Poly Faces turn slightly yellow when selected.

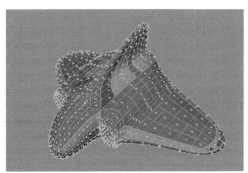

Selection of all the Poly Faces of the polymesh

2 Create planar mapping

- From the main menu bar, make sure that **Edit Polygons → Texture → Assign Shader to Each Projection** is turned off. There should be no check mark beside the menu item.

- Select **Edit Polygons → Texture → Planar Mapping**.

  A large projection plane icon appears in the in front of the object which projects the texture map from the front of the object. The texture is mapped onto the surface which can be seen with hardware texturing.

PROJECT THREE

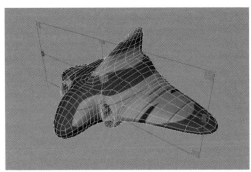

Projection plane manipulator and texture

3 Rotate the direction of planar projection

- Dolly the Top view out.

  The entire texture projection plane should be within view.

- In the Channel box, set **Rotate X** to **-90** and the **Rotation Angle** to **180**.

  The texture is now projected onto the surface from above.

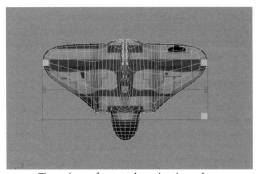

Top view of rotated projection plane

4 Position the planar projection

- Click-drag on the thin green line of the manipulator to move the projection plane along the Z-axis.

The center of the projection plane should be positioned over the approximate center of the polyShip.

- Click-drag on the red and green **Scale** handles to scale the projection plane to slightly larger than the polyShip.

  With hardware texturing, the color texture moves across the surface with the projection plane.

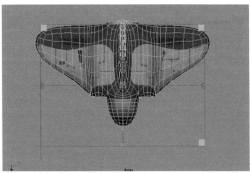

Projection plane moved and scaled

Note: If the projection manipulator disappears, reselect the polyShip, click on the *polyPlanProj1* input node in the Channel box and select the show manipulator tool.

---

5 Open Texture View

- Select **Window → UV Texture Editor...**

  The window opens with the mapped Poly Faces of the polyShip visible, shown from the view of the texture projection.

- From the Texture View menus, select **View → Grid** to hide the grid in the window.

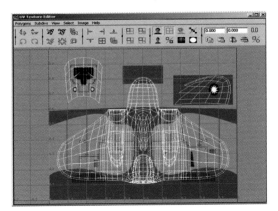

Texture View window

Note: The view of the mapped Poly Faces and the loaded texture are both initially displayed in the Texture View window with a square proportion – regardless of the proportion of the planar projection positioned in the 3D space of the model and the proportion of the texture image file.

6 Position texture icon

You can now move the texture icon to position it properly in relation to the surface. You have the option of using the manipulator in the workspace or the Texture View window.

- Dolly in the Texture View until you see the full extent of the positioning manipulator.

- Use the green box handle to scale the proportion of the polyShip profile.

- Use the green arrow to move the profile into position.

The polyShip outline should be centered on the texture, with the red box covering the tip of the nose, the wings stretching between the horizontal red bands, and the vertical black lines should overlap the back edge of the wings.

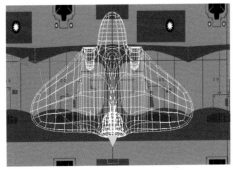

Outline positioned correctly over the texture

7 Examine the texture positioning

- Press the **F8** key to change selection mode.

- Click in one of the view panels to deselect the polyShip.

  You can now see the texture more clearly.

- Tumble in the Perspective view to see the position of the texture on the polyShip surface.

PROJECT THREE

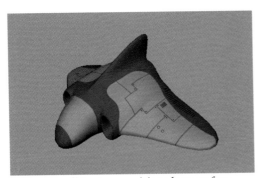

Overall texture positioned on surface

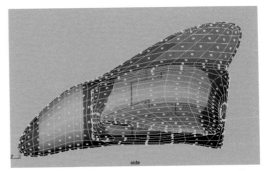

Fin Poly Faces selected for secondary mapping

Note: To make any refinements to the texture positioning, select the *polyPlanProject1* input node and select show manipulators.

Mapping the fin

The projection of the map down onto the ship does not let you map the fin from the side. You can create a separate projection to these Poly Faces to map the fin with the ship's logo.

1 Select the fin Poly Faces

- Press the **F8** key to return to component selection mode.

- Click on the polyShip to display the Poly Faces.

- In the Side view, click-drag to **Select** the Poly Faces that form the main area of the tail.

  By click-dragging, you select the Poly Faces on both sides of the fin.

2 Map the fins with a planar projection

- Select **Edit Polygons** → **Texture** → **Planar Mapping**.

A small projection plane manipulator is positioned in front of the selected Poly Faces, which are outlined with a heavy line. The texture is projected from the front of the polyShip.

Projection plane positioned in front of the Poly Faces

3 Position mapping manipulator

- In the Channel box, set **Rotate Y** to **90**.

The texture is now projected from the side, and the texture pattern repeats several times across the Poly Faces.

- Click-drag on one of the red horizontal lines of the manipulator to move the projection plane.

It should be at the approximate center of the outlined Poly Faces.

Projection plane rotated and centered

- **Scale** the projection plane.

It should cover the outlined Poly Faces.

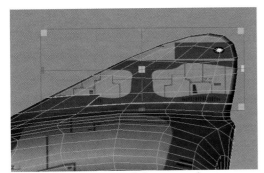

Projection plane scaled to cover facet area

4 Position Texture View

- Dolly the Texture View out so that the entire placement icon is visible.

- Use the blue **Scale** handle to scale the placement icon down.

- Use the **Move** handles to position the icon over the red area in the top right corner of the texture.

- Refine the scale and position of the placement icon.

The Poly Faces should be completely within the red area of the texture and the black and white logo should be centered on the tail profile.

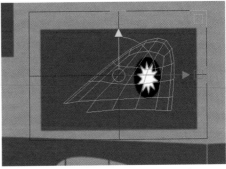

Refined position of fin projection on the texture

5 Evaluate the second projection

- Deselect the polyShip.

- Tumble the Perspective view to see the effect of the second projection.

PROJECT THREE

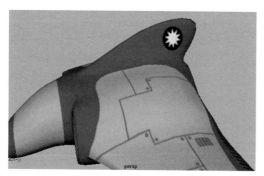

Second projection on fin

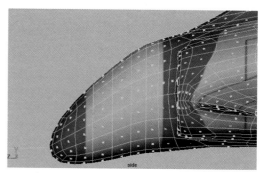

Side view of Poly Faces selected for cockpit

Mapping the cockpit

You may be wondering why the cockpit portion of the texture was not part of the original projection. Since the projection goes right through the ship, you didn't want the cockpit appearing on the top and bottom. You will now remap the cockpit onto the top of the ship only.

1 Select nose Poly Faces for cockpit

- Select the polyship.

- Click with **RMB** over the polyship and select **Face**.

- In the Side view, click-drag to **Select** the Poly Faces on the top part of the nose.

  Use the **Shift** key to make multiple selections.

  Make sure that you do not select Poly Faces that are mapped with red areas of the texture.

Note: If you do not have hardware texturing, you can see the selected Poly Faces displayed with a yellow hatching in the Texture View window. Make sure that the selected Poly Faces do not overlap with the red bands of the texture.

2 Create planar mapping

- Select **Edit Polygons** → **Texture** → **Planar Mapping**.

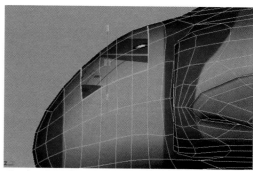

Projection plane positioned in front Poly Faces

3 Position the projection plane

- Click on the red line handle at the bottom corner of the manipulator.

The manipulator changes to move, scale and rotate handles.

- Click-drag on the circular blue rotate handle to rotate the projection plane.

The plane should be roughly parallel to the top face of the cockpit area.

- Use the green **Move** handle to move the projection plane up along the nose.

It should be positioned so that the projection covers the outlined Poly Faces of the cockpit.

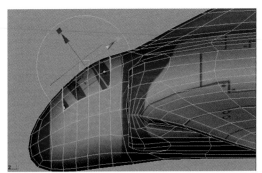

Side view of projection plane in position

4 Position texture view

- In the Texture View window, **Scale** and **Move** the positioning icon, so that it is centered over the cockpit area at the top left corner of the texture.

- Refine the position and scale.

The outline of the Poly Faces encompasses all the cockpit details of the texture.

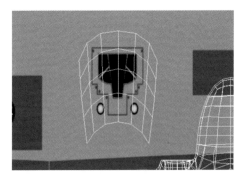

Texture View of cockpit Poly Faces position

5 Examine the three texture projections

You have now used three different planar projections to map one file texture on the Poly Faces of the polymesh of the spaceship. This mapping can be seen in the Texture View window and with hardware texturing, you can examine the results in the Perspective window.

- Press the **F8** key.

- Dolly out of the Texture View window to see the mapping of the three projections on the texture.

- If the projections are not visible, **Select** the polyShip object.

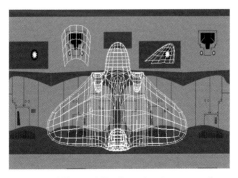

Texture View of final projection mapping

- Deselect the polyShip.

- Tumble the Perspective view to examine the areas where one projection meets another.

  The texture colors should be consistent around the fin and cockpit projection areas.

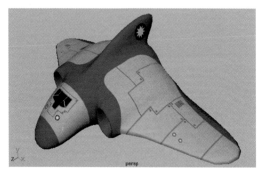

Perspective view of combined projection mapping

Note: To modify any texture mapping, select the appropriate *polyPlanProj* input node in the Channel box and select the show manipulator tool.

Rendering the ship

To confirm that the texturing is working correctly, you can now render the scene. To render you will create and place some lights in your scene.

1 Add directional lighting

- Change to the **Rendering** menu set.
- Select **Create → Lights → Directional Light**.
- **Move** and **Rotate** the light so that it is pointing towards the front of the polyShip from above.

- In the Attribute editor, set the **Color** to a light yellow.
- Open the **Shadows,** and then the **Depth Map Shadow Attributes** sections.
- Turn on **Use Depth Map Shadows**.

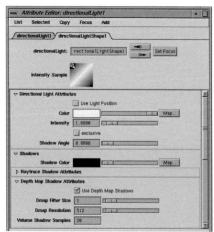

Depth Map Shadows set for directional light

- From the Perspective panel menus, select **Lighting → Use All Lights**.

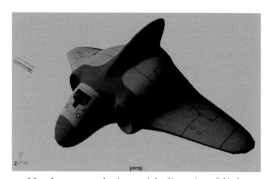

Hardware rendering with directional light

2 Add ambient lighting

- Create an **Ambient Light**.

- In the Attribute Editor:

  Change the **Color** to blue;

  Reduce the **Intensity** to **0.3**;

  Set **Ambient Shade** to **0.2**.

By reducing the ambient shade, the light will slightly illuminate surfaces that are facing away from the source.

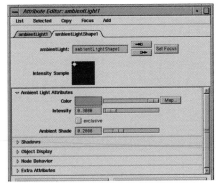

Ambient light attributes

3 Set Render Globals

- Open the **Render Globals** window.
- Select the **Maya Software** tab.
- Open the **Anti-aliasing Quality** section.
- Set the **Presets** to **Intermediate Quality**.

4 Render the scene

- Set up the Perspective view.
- Open the Render View window.
- **Render** the Perspective view.
- **Keep** the image.

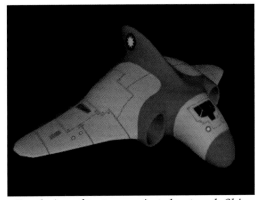

Rendering of texture projected onto polyShip

Adding different texture maps

You can now begin refining the shading group to include other types of texture maps. A reflection map for the cockpit, a bump map for the grooved joints, and a specularity map for the different material effects.

1 Map the bump attribute with a file

The next texture map you are going to use is a bump map that raises and lowers parts of the model.

- Open the Attribute Editor for the *polyShipBlinn* material node.
- **Map** the **Bump Mapping** attribute with a **File** 2D texture node.
- Click the *file1* tab.
- Rename the node *polyBump*.
- Click the **Folder Icon** button.
- In the *sourceimages* directory, open the *polyBump* file.

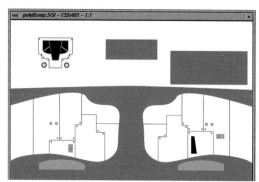

Bitmap file for material bump map texture

Note: Because the color texture map used the default texture placement node settings, you will not need to adjust the values of the placement nodes for the other file textures.

2 Refine the bump map

To create a high quality bump, you should set the depth to define how deep the bump is going to be, and set the filter to define the sharpness or softness of the bump map.

- Open the *bump2d* tab.
- In the **2d Bump Attributes** section:

   Set the **Bump Depth** to **0.25**.

- In the **Effects** section:

   Set **Bump Filter** to **0.2**.

   This setting makes sure that the map is sharp instead of blurred.

3 Map specularity

The next map is going to be used to map the specularity on the surface. Darker areas will produce less specularity while lighter areas produce more.

- From the Attribute editor menus, select **Focus** → **polyShipBlinn**.

   This returns the window to the material node attributes.

- In the **Specular Shading** section set:

   Eccentricity to **0.2**;

   Specular Roll Off to **0.9**.

- **Map** the **Specular Color** attribute with a **File** texture node.

- Rename the *file* node *polySpec*.

- Connect the *polySpec* node to the *polySpec* image file.

- In Render View **Render** → **Redo Previous Render**.

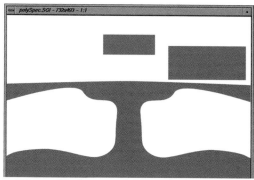

Bitmap file for material specularity texture

4 Map reflectivity

The reflectivity map is quite simple. Where the map is black, you will not get reflections – but where the map is white, you do. This map will not show you any results until you either raytrace the scene or add a reflection map.

- Return to the attributes for the *polyShipBlinn* node.

- Hold down the right mouse button on the **Reflectivity** attribute.

- Select **Create New Texture...** from the pop-up menu.
- Create a **File** texture node.
- Rename the *file* node *polyReflect*.
- Connect the *polyReflect* node to the *polyReflect* image file.
- In Render View select **Render** → **Redo Previous Render**.

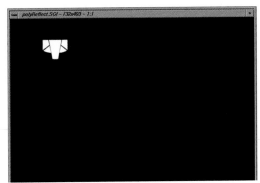

Bitmap file for material reflectivity texture

5 Add dirt to the spaceship color

The spaceship textures render to show a clean surface as if the spaceship just left the factory floor. You will now map a 3D fractal map to the color map's Color Gain attribute to roughen up the look of the ship.

- Navigate to the attributes for the *polyColor* file texture node.
- Open the **Color Balance** section.
- **Map** the **Color Gain** attribute with a **Solid Fractal** 3D texture.
- In the **Solid Fractal Attributes** section, set:

    Threshold to **0.2**;

    Amplitude to **0.75**.

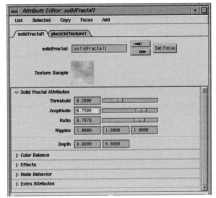

Solid fractal set to add dirt to the color map

6 Scale the 3D texture placement

You need to scale the icon to scale up the effect of the fractal on the surface.

- Click on the *place3dTexture1* tab.
- At the bottom of the Attribute Editor, click on **Select**.

    This selects the 3D placement node in the modeling views.

- In the Perspective view, **Scale** the placement icon to half the size of the polyShip.

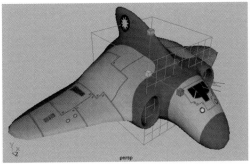

Solid fractal 3D texture placement icon scaled

PROJECT THREE

7 Parent the texture placement node

Right now, if you were to animate the spaceship, the dirt would stay behind. You need to parent the node to the ship so that if the ship moves then the texture moves too.

- Press the **Shift** key and **Select** the polyShip.

  It is important that the icon was selected first, ahead of the ship. This means that the icon will be parented to the ship.

- Select **Edit** → **Parent**.

  This parents the placement node into the hierarchy of the polyShip. When the polyShip is animated in a later lesson, the placement node will also be animated. This is necessary so that the fractal dirt does not move on the surface.

8 Render the scene

- In Render View select **Render** → **Redo Previous Render**.

  Notice the effect of the bump map, and the difference in the specular qualities between the main color areas of the surface. The layer of grime that is produced by the solid fractal texture is also clearly visible.

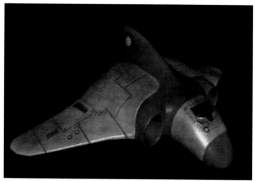

Rendering of polyShip with textures and dirt

Note: The effect of the reflectivity texture will not be seen until later in the project, when an environment map of a starfield will be used as the reflected color instead of using raytraced rendered reflections.

9 Save your work

You should save this file as *polyShip*. You will reference this file into another file in a future lesson.

Conclusion

In this lesson, you have learned how to model a complete spaceship out of a primitive cube. In the process, you used polygon modeling tools to create the form. Each tool created an input node that you were able to edit later to change the construction history of the ship.

In the next lesson, you will model another spaceship using NURBS geometry. This will let you compare the two modeling techniques. Later, you will animate the two ships in a space battle.

13 NURBS Spaceship

In this lesson, you will build a second spaceship using NURBS surfaces. You will start by drawing spline curves that will be used to construct the surfaces. Your model will be built out of several pieces that will then be combined to make the final ship.

In the end, you will apply shading groups. For some parts of the spaceship, you will use projection map textures to achieve the desired look.

NURBS spaceship

In this lesson you will learn the following:

- How to draw a spline curve
- How to build a revolved surface
- How to build a birail surface
- How to build a lofted surface
- How to attach surfaces
- How to rebuild a surface
- How to use projection maps

Initial set-up

To create this spaceship, start a new file where you can focus on the new model.

1 Create a new file

- Make sure that your *polyShip* is saved then select **File** → **New**.

2 Set the display options

- Select **Windows** → **Settings/Preferences** → **Preferences...**

- Click on **Display**.

- In the **Nurbs** section, set the **Shaded Divisions** to **4**.

- Click **Save**.

  Now your surfaces will have a higher surface smoothness and you don't have to press the **3** key every time you create a surface.

Main thruster

The first part of this spaceship is the main thruster. This will be built by revolving a curve around the Z-axis.

1 Draw the revolve profile

- Select the **Modeling** menu set.

- Select **Create** → **CV Curve Tool**.

- In the Side view, track the view to the left.

- Press and hold the **x** key to use grid snapping and click on the Z-axis line to start drawing a curve.

- Release the **x** key to stop using grid snapping and draw the next six CVs as shown in the following:

The curve is shown with a box icon representing the first CV and a U icon representing the direction of the curve. Just like X, Y and Z are used to represent spatial dimensions, U is used to represent measurements along a curve.

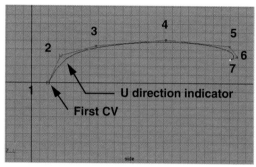

CV curve points

- Press **Enter** to complete the curve.

2 Revolve the curve

- Select **Surfaces** → **Revolve** - ❑. In the option window, set the following:

  Axis Preset to **Z**.

- Click **Revolve**.

  The curve has now been used to generate a revolved surface.

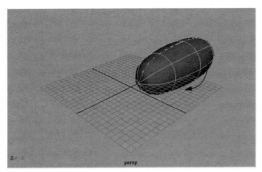

Revolved shape

Construction history

The shape of the surface is dependent on the shape of the curve. You can therefore edit the shape of the surface by editing the curve.

The end of the thruster comes to a point. You will now fix the tangency at the end of the curve to smooth out the revolved shape's end point.

1 Change your Side view display

- In the Side view panel, select **Show → None** then **Show → NURBS Curves.**

  Now you can focus on the curve and then preview the shaded surface as it updates in the Perspective view.

2 Get the Curve Editing Tool

- Select **Edit Curves→ Curve Editing Tool.**

- Click on the curve in the Side view.

  A manipulator appears with several handles used to edit your curves. These include the following:

the **parameter handle** which lets you move the editor to a particular point on the U direction of the curve;

the **position handle** that lets you move the chosen point of the curve and the CVs will update to suit;

the **tangent** and **tangent scale handles** let you scale and position the curve's tangent; and

the **axes lines** can be used to snap the tangent handle to either the X, Y or Z axes.

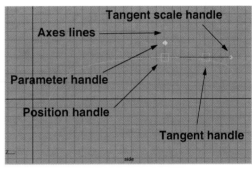

Curve editing tool

- Click-drag on the yellow parameter handle to move the manipulator to the left end of the curve.

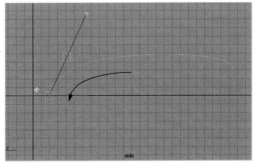

Edited parameter handle

3 Align the end of the curve

- Click on the dotted axis line as shown in the following diagram.

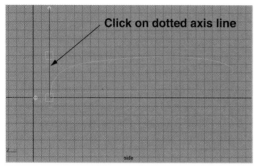

Tangent aligned to axis

The handle's tangent line snaps to align with the axis. In the shaded view, you can see that the end of the shape is more rounded.

4 Scale the length of the tangent handle

- In the Perspective view, click on the tangent scale handle to make it active.

  Click-drag with your middle mouse button to edit the length of the tangent.

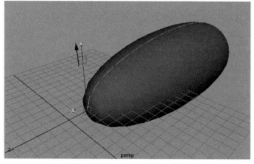

Scaled tangent handle

- Press **Enter** to accept the edits.

5 Delete the construction curve

- Select the curve in the Side view.

- Press the **Backspace** key to delete it.

6 Create a new layer and template the main thruster

- Create a new layer called *mainBody*.

- Select the revolved surface.

- Rename it *mainThruster*.

- Add *mainThruster* to the new layer.

- Template the *mainBody* layer.

7 Save your work

- Select **File → Save Scene As...** and name the file *nurbShip*.

THE HULL

The hull of the spaceship will be created by using the birail tool. This tool creates a surface by tracking one or more profile curves along two rail curves.

Drawing character curves

To build the shape of the spaceship's hull, you will start with *character* curves. These curves will define the shape of the surfaces. When working with NURBS models, the quality of your surface is dependent on the character curves.

One approach for creating efficient curves is to start with simple single span curves. When working with NURBS curves, the fewer CVs you have the easier it is to control the curve. You can then insert more spans if you need more complexity.

For now, you will only be building half of the spaceship. Once completed, you will mirror the other half and join together the surfaces.

1 Draw main character curve

- In the Side view panel, select **Show** → **All**.
- In the Side view, dolly out to see about **25** units on each side of the main Y-axis line.
- Select **Create** → **EP Curve Tool**.
- Click and hold in the Side view. Now as you drag, you can use the feedback line to help you place the following points using approximately the values shown below:

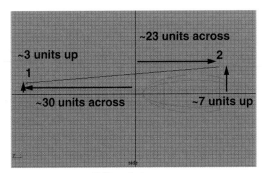

Edit point curve

2 Edit the shape of the curve

- Press **Enter** to complete the curve.
- Press **F8** to go into component selection mode.
- **Select** the middle two CVs.
- **Move** them up and to the left.
- Press **F8** to go back to object selection mode.

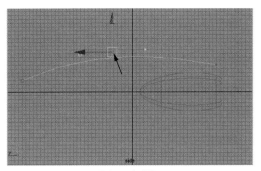

Moved CVs

3 Create the lower rail curve

- Use the method outlined in the last two sections to create the following rail curve:

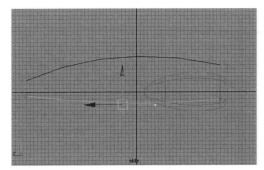

Second rail curve

4 Duplicate and move the curves

- **Select** the two curves.
- Select **Edit** → **Duplicate**.
- **Move** the curves about 11 units along the X-axis.

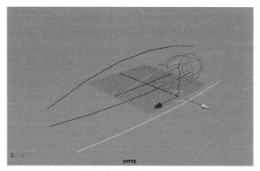

Duplicated curves

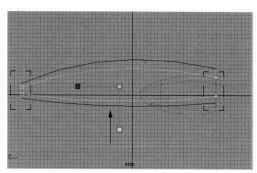

Scaled end CVs

5 Scale the new curve CVs

- Press **F8** to go into component selection mode.

- **Select** all of the CVs on the two curves.

- **Scale** them along the Y-axis to scale them down a little.

6 Reshape the new curve

- **Select** the first two CVs on the new curves.

- In the Top view, **Move** the CVs about 4 units toward the main axis line.

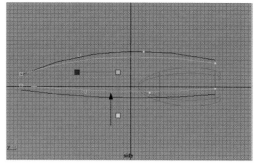

Scaled CVs

- **Select** the end CVs on the two curves.

- **Scale** them along the Y-axis to scale them down a little.

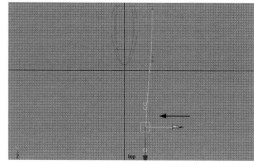

Moved CVs

- **Select** the first CV on the new curves.

- In the Top view, **Move** the CVs about 2 units toward the main axis line.

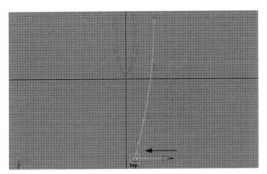

Moved end CV

- Press **F8** to go back to Object selection mode.

Profile curves

You now have four rail curves defining half the spaceship body. The next step is to connect the *rails* with *profile* curves. You will be creating three surfaces: a top surface, side surface, and bottom surface.

1 Add the top profile curve

- Select **Create → EP Curve Tool.**

- In the Perspective view, press and hold the **c** key to temporarily use curve snapping.

- Click and drag onto the back of the center rail curve.

- Drag until this point stops at the end of the curve then release the mouse button.

- Repeat to place a second edit point at the end of the second rail curve.

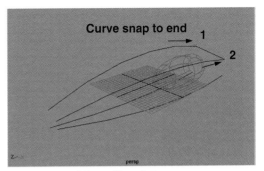

New edit point curve

- Press **Enter** to complete the curve.

Tip: By using curve snapping, you are sure that the new curve is touching the two rail curves. This is important to successfully use the birail tool later.

2 Edit curve tangency

To ensure surface tangency at the centre, of the spaceship, you will use the curve editor.

- Select **Edit Curves → Curve Editing Tool.**

- Click-drag on the top handle and drag towards the center axis until it stops at the end of the profile curve.

- Click on the X-axis crosshair (red line) to modify projection.

PROJECT THREE

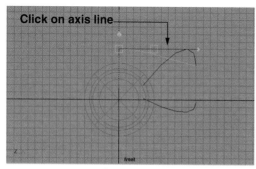

Aligned curve

- Select the **Move** tool.
- Press **F8** to go into component selection mode.
- **Move** the third CV on the curve to reshape the curve.

  Don't touch the second CV.

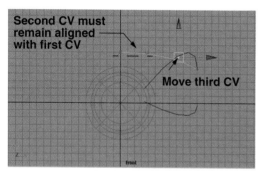

Edited CV position

3 Add the front profile curve

- Use the steps outlined above to add a second profile curve to the front of the rail curves.
- Adjust the curve tangency as outlined above as well.

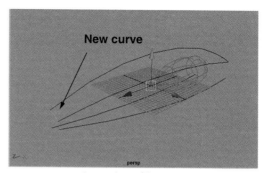

Second profile curve

Birail surface

A birail surface is created using the two profile curves and the two rail curves. The rails define the sides of the surface while the cross sections are derived from the two profile curves. A birail surface can only be built if all the curves are connected.

1 Create top birail surface

The top surface is now defined by two rail curves and two profile curves. You can now use these to build a birail surface.

- Select **Surfaces** → **Birail** → **Birail 2 Tool.**
- Click on the four defining character curves in the following order:

  back profile curve;

  front profile curve;

  center rail curve;

  side rail curve.

- A surface is created along the top of the spaceship.

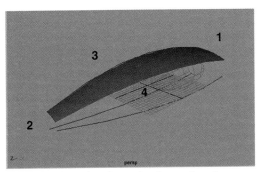

Birail surface showing selection order of curves

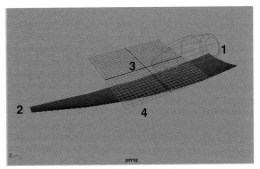

Second birail surface

- Select **Display → Show → Show Last Hidden**.

The side surface

The side of the ship will again be built using a birail surface. This time, you will use three profiles in order to control what the surface looks like at the beginning, middle and end.

Note: If no surface is produced, the profile curves may not be touching the rail curves. Should this be the case, undo your surface creation then go back and rebuild the rails. Also note that you must have **Show → Surfaces** on for your view panels to see them correctly.

- **Select** the first surface and the four creation curves.

- Select **Display → Hide → Hide Selection**.

2 Create bottom birail surface

- Create two profile curves for the bottom of the spaceship using the techniques taught for the first two rail curves.

- Create a birail surface using these curves.

1 Create a side profile curve

- In the Perspective view, dolly into the end of the spaceship.

- Select **Create → EP Curve Tool**

- In the Perspective view, press and hold the **c** key to temporarily use curve snapping.

- Click-drag onto the back of the top rail curve.

- Repeat to place a second edit point at the end of the second rail curve.

PROJECT THREE

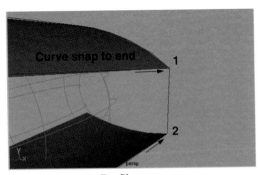

Profile curve

2 Project tangent for profile curve

Before creating the side birail surface, you will create a tangency from the top and bottom surface to the side profile curve.

- **Select** the top surface and the side profile curve.
- Select **Edit Curves → Project Tangent.**
- Repeat these steps using the bottom surface and the profile curve.
- You will notice that the profile curve is now projecting with a tangency from the top and bottom surface.

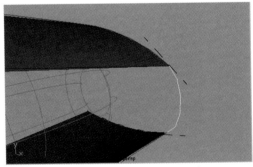

Curve projected on both ends

3 Edit tangency scale

Since the projected tangency curve has history, you can edit the project tangent attributes using the input node and the show manipulator tool.

- **Select** the profile curve on its own.
- In the Channel box, click on *projectTangent1*.
- Select the **Show Manipulator Tool.**
- Click-drag on the **Scale** handle until the **Tangent Scale** is set to about **2.0**.

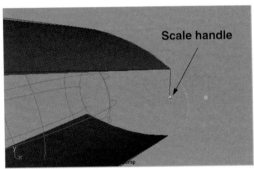

Scaled tangent handle

As you modify this manipulator handle, you can see the value change in either the Channel box or the Coordinate Feedback line.

- Use the same workflow to edit the **Tangent Scale** for *projectTangent2* to about **2.0**.

4 Insert CVs to the back side profile curve

You will add two more isoparm spans to this profile curve. This will let you create a more complex profile.

- Press **F8** to go into component selection mode.

- Click with **RMB** over the profile curve and select **Curve Point** from the pop-up menu.

- Click on the profile curve about one third of the curve down to place a curve point.

- Press the **Shift** key and click on the curve to place a second curve point.

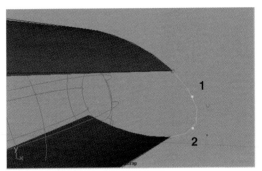

Curve points

5 Insert knots

- Select **Edit Curves → Insert knot**.

6 Move the middle curve points

- **Select** the middle two CVs.

- **Move** the CVs in towards the center axis of the ship.

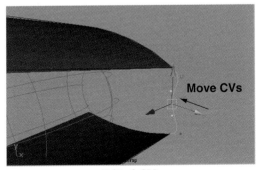

Edited CVs

- Press **F8** to go back into object selection mode.

7 Create the front profile curve

- Draw a single span edit point curve at the front of the ship using curve snapping.

- Use **Project Tangent** to make the curve tangent to the existing surfaces.

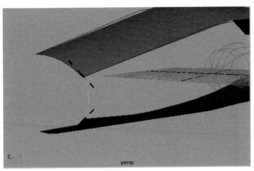

Projected edit point curve

8 Create a middle profile curve

- Draw a single span edit point curve in the middle of the ship using curve snapping.

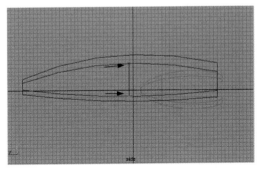

Curve snap new curve

- Use **Project Tangent** to make the curve tangent to the existing surfaces.

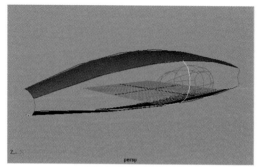

Projected curve

9 Create the side birail surface

- Select **Surfaces** → **Birail** → **Birail 3+ Tool**.
- Click on the three profile curves to select them.
- Press **Enter** to accept these curves.
- Select the outer edges of the existing surfaces as the rail curves.

  The birail surface is created.

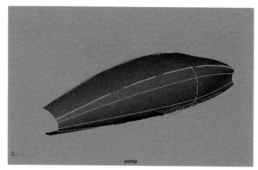

Birail surface

Aligning surfaces

When you projected the profile curves off the top and bottom surfaces, you started to build a tangential relationship for the middle surface. Between the profile curves, this relationship is broken. To fix this, you will align and attach the surfaces to make them more continuous.

1 Align and attach surfaces

- **Select** the top surface first, and with the **Shift** key select the side surface second.
- Select **Edit NURBS**→ **Align Surfaces -** ❑ and make sure that the following options are set:

  Attach to **On**;

  Modify Position to **Second**;

  Modify Tangent to **Second**.

- Press **Align.**

  The top and side surfaces are one surface now.

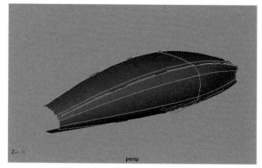

Aligned and attached surfaces

- **Select** the bottom surface first, and the middle surface second.
- Select **Edit NURBS** → **Align Surfaces**

All three surfaces are now one complete surface.

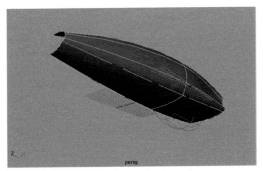

Aligned and attached surfaces

2   Duplicate and mirror the surface

- **Select** the new surface.
- Press **Ctrl-d** to **Duplicate** it.
- Enter **-1** in the **Scale X** field in the Channel Box.

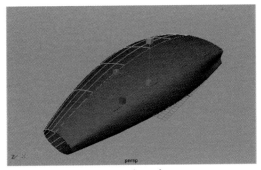

Mirrored surface

3   Align and attach the two halves

- **Save** your work before this next step.
- **Select** the two surfaces.
- Select **Edit NURBS → Align Surfaces.**

You may have noticed that the seam of the two surfaces is on top of the ship. You can control this by selecting the edges that you want to align and attach.

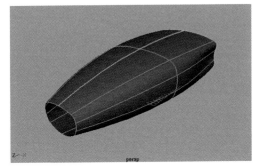

Aligned surfaces with seam on top

4   Undo the last align

- Undo your last step or close file and reopen, without saving new changes.

5   Select the edge isoparms

- **Select** the new surface.
- Click on the new surface with your right mouse button and select **Isoparm** from the pop-up menu.
- Click-drag on one of the longitudinal isoparms and drag to the edge of the surface.
- When you release your mouse button, a yellow line will indicate your selection.

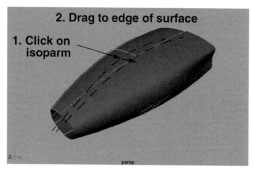

Selected isoparm

- Click on the other surface with your right mouse button and select **Isoparm** from the pop-up menu.

- Press the **Shift** key and click-drag on one of the longitudinal isoparms and drag to the edge of the surface.

- When you release your mouse button, a yellow line is placed at the newly selected edge.

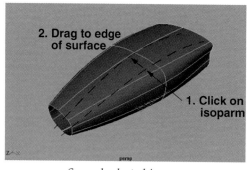

Second selected isoparm

6 Align and attach the two halves

Now that you have chosen which edges are to be aligned, you will get the proper results.

- Select **Edit NURBS → Align Surfaces - ❑** and make sure that the following options are set:

    Attach to **On**;

    Modify Position to **Both**;

- Press **Align**.

    The seam will now appear at the bottom of the ship.

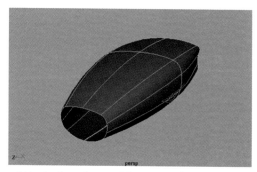

Attached surfaces with seam at bottom of ship

7 Close the surface

You will now close the surface so that the edges are connected properly.

- Select the nurbs ship.

- Select **Edit NURBS → Open/Close Surfaces**.

8 Delete history

- With the surface selected, select **Edit → Delete by Type → History**.

- In the Side view, select **Show → None** then **Show → NURBS Curves**.

- In this view, **Select** the various profile curves.

- Press the **Backspace** key to delete the curves.

TRIM SURFACES

The surfaces you have built so far have all been created so that you can add them together. If you want to cut a section out of your surface, then you will need to trim it.

Trimming requires that you define a trim region on the surface using curves on surface. In an earlier lesson, you made the surface live and then drew the curve on surface directly. In this lesson, you will create curves on surface by intersecting existing surfaces.

The back surface

Slightly recessed from the back of the ship's hull, you will next need to place a surface. This surface will intersect the hull and the thruster. You will create curves on surface and then trim.

1 Untemplate and move the thruster

- Untemplate the *mainBody* layer.

- Move the thruster until it intersects the top of the ship's hull.

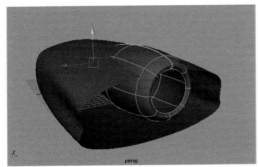

Untemplated thruster

2 Create and place a primitive plane

- Select **Create** → **NURBS Primitives** → **Plane**.

- **Move** the plane along the Z-axis to the back of the ship.

- **Scale** the plane along the X and Z axes to make it about the same size as the ship.

- **Rotate** the plane 90 degrees around the X-axis.

- **Move** it until it is intersecting the end of the hull.

- Select **Edit** → **Delete by Type** → **History**.

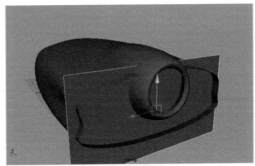

New plane intersecting main body

3 Intersect the plane and the body

- Press the **Shift** key and select the ship's hull.

- Select **Edit NURBS** → **Intersect Surfaces** - ❏ and set the following options:

    Create Curves for to **First Surface**;

    Curve Type to **Curve on Surface**.

- Click **Intersect**.

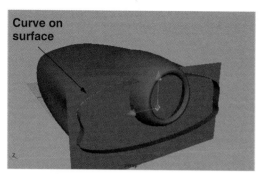

Intersecting curve on surface

4 Intersect the plane and the thruster

- **Select** the plane then press the **Shift** key and **Select** the thruster surface.

- Select **Edit NURBS → Intersect Surfaces**.

Second curve on surface

5 Trim the plane surface

- **Select** the plane.

- Select **Edit NURBS → Trim Tool.**

  The surface is displayed with its trim regions identified. This lets you choose which areas to keep or discard.

- Click in the middle area to place the trim indicator. This means that this area will be kept.

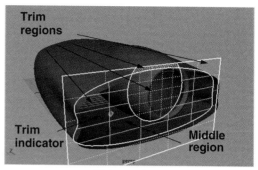

Trim regions

- Press **Enter**.

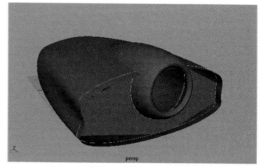

Trimmed surface

6 Increase the surface smoothness

You will now increase the smoothness so that the surface will look better in the interactive view panels.

- Select **Display → NURBS Smoothness → Custom - ❑** and in the **Shaded** section, set the following:

  Surface Div per Span to **8**.

- Click **Apply and Close**.

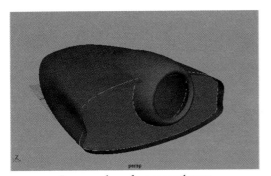

Increased surface smoothness

7 Increase the surface tessellation

While the smoothness will look good interactively it may not render properly. You must set the surfaces tessellation to ensure that the trimmed surface will render nicely.

- Press **Ctrl-a** to open the Attribute Editor.

- Click on the *nurbsPlane1trimmedSurfaceShape1* tab in the Editor.

- Open the **Tessellation** section, and set the following:

   Display Render Tessellation to **On**

- Open the **Options** section and set the following:

   Smooth Edge to **On**

   You can now see the effect that the smooth edge has on the surface. You do not need to have the **Display Render Tessellation** set on to have it render with the settings. This is only a visual feedback

- Set **Display Render Tessellation** to **Off.**

8 Intersect the body and the thruster

- **Select** the hull and then the thruster surface.

- Select **Edit NURBS → Intersect Surfaces**.

   This creates a curve on surface. Right now you won't trim the hull surface back. You will wait until later when you have other curves on the surface; and therefore more trim regions to choose from.

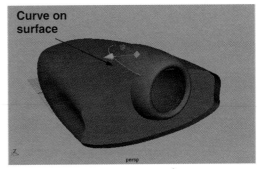

New curve on surface

A circular fillet

You will now create a circular fillet to define a softer look for the front of the ship. The fillet will be created between a primitive plane and the hull surface.

1 Create and place a primitive plane

- In the Perspective view, tumble until you see the front of the ship.

- Select **Create → NURBS Primitives → Plane**.

- **Rotate** the plane in **X** to **70** degrees.

- **Move**, and **Scale** the plane until it is intersecting the end of the ship body at a slight angle.

- Select **Edit** → **Delete by Type** → **History**.

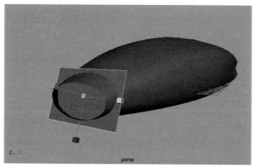
New plane

2 Fillet the two surfaces

- Press the **Shift** key and add the main ship body to the selection.

- Select **Edit NURBS** → **Surface Fillet** → **Circular Fillet** - ❑ and set the following options:

  Create Curve On Surface is **On**;

  Radius to **0.5**.

- Click **Apply** but do not close the option window.

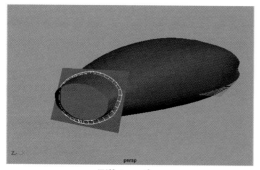
Fillet surface

- Press the **z** key to undo the fillet.

- In the Circular Fillet options window, set the following:

  Reverse Secondary Surface Normal to **On**.

  And if the fillet is in front of the plane, then also set:

  Reverse Primary Surface Normal to **On**;

- Click **Fillet** then **Close**.

- Press the **4** key to go into wireframe mode where you can see the new filleted surface.

Note:	The new surface may be created in pieces and may extend pass the hull. If this is the case, leave it and it will be fixed later.

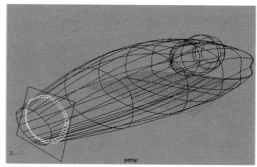
Corrected fillet

3 Trim the center piece

- **Select** the plane.

- Select **Edit NURBS** → **Trim Tool**.

- Click in the middle area to place the trim indicator.

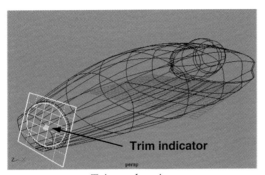

Trimmed region

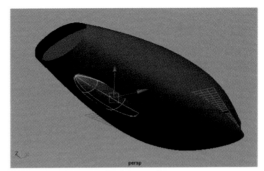

Primitive sphere

- Press **Enter**.

- Select **Display** → **NURBS Smoothness** → **Custom**.

- Use the method taught earlier to edit the **Tessellation Criteria** in the Attribute Editor.

  Again, you will wait to trim the surface of the ship until all curves on surface have been placed.

The photon recess

To create an area for the ship to shoot photon blasts, you will create a recess at the bottom of the hull using a primitive sphere. You will intersect this shape and then trim both the surfaces.

1 Create and place a primitive sphere

- In the Perspective view, **Tumble** until the bottom of the ship is in view.

- Select **Create** → **NURBS Primitives** → **Sphere**.

- **Rotate** the sphere **90** degrees around the X-axis.

- **Move** and **Scale** the sphere to place it as shown below:

- Select **Edit** → **Delete by Type** → **History**.

2 Intersect the two shapes

- Press the **Shift** key and add the ship's body to the selection.

- Select **Edit NURBS** → **Intersect Surfaces** - ❑ and set the following options:

  Create Curves for to **Both Surfaces;**

  Curve Type to **Curve on Surface.**

- Click **Intersect**.

3 Trim the sphere

- **Select** the sphere surface.

- Select **Edit NURBS** → **Trim Tool**.

- Click on the area at the top of the sphere to place the trim indicator.

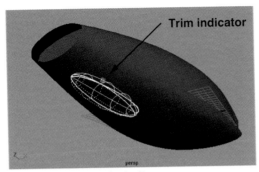

Trim indicator

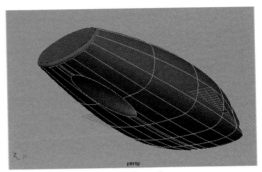

Trimmed surfaces

- Press **Enter**.

4 Trim the ship's body

- **Select** the ship's body surface.
- Press the **y** key to get the last tool.
- Click on the area in the middle of the surface to place the trim indicator.

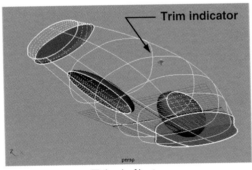

Trim indicator

- Press **Enter**.
- Select **Edit** → **Delete by Type** → **History**.

5 Template the surfaces

- Select all of the surfaces.
- Assign the surfaces to the *mainBody* Layer.
- Template the *mainBody* layer.

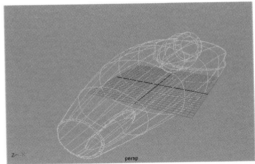

Templated surfaces

6 Save your work

Building the wing

Like the main body, character curves will be created. This time the curves will act like the ribs of the surface which will then be connected using the loft tool. Construction history will then be used to tweak the surface by editing the curves.

1 Draw a primitive circle

You will start with a primitive circle which is simply a premade curve.

- In the Side view, select **Show → All**.
- Select **Create → NURBS Primitives → Circle**.
- In the Channel box, set the following:

  Rotate Z to **90**;

  Scale Z to **12**;

  Scale X to **0.85**.

- **Move** the circle to back of the ship as shown below:

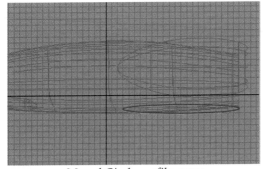

Moved Circle profile curve

2 Reshape the circle

- Press **F8** to go into component selection mode.
- **Select** the middle 6 CVs.
- **Scale** the CVs out to push them closer to the edge of the profile to create a rounded square shape.

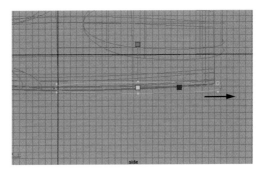

Scaled CVs

3 Move the profile's pivot location

- Press **F8** to go back to object selection mode.
- Press the **Insert / Home** key to go into edit mode.
- **Move** the pivot along the Z-axis to the end of the profile.
- Press the **Insert / Home** key to exit edit pivot mode.

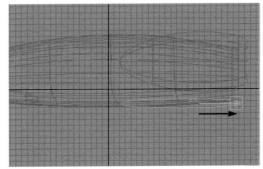

Relocated pivot

4 Duplicate and move the new profile curve

- Select **Edit → Duplicate**
- **Move** the new profile along the X-axis to about 2 times the width of the ship.

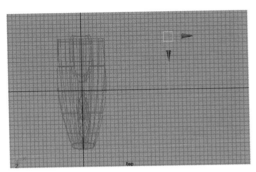

Repositioned profile curve

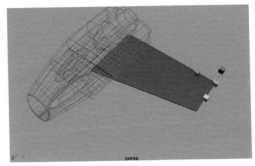

Modified surface

5 Loft the two profile curves

- Select both curves.
- Select **Surfaces** → **Loft**.
- Name the new surface *wing*.

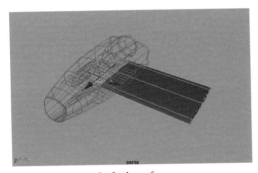

Lofted surface

6 Use construction history to modify surface

- Select the outside profile curve at end of the wing.
- **Scale** the curve in Z to **7.5.**

  With construction history, the surface will update as you are modifying the curve.

7 Rebuild the surface

You will be modifying the end of the wings even further. For more control, this will require more density of isoparms. You can achieve this by rebuilding the surface with more isoparms while retaining the shape.

- Select the *wing* surface.
- Select **Edit NURBS** → **Rebuild Surfaces - ❑**, and set the following:

  Number of Spans U to **8;**

  Number of Spans V to **10**

- Press **Rebuild.**
- Delete the two profile curves.

8 Bend the end of the wings

You will be modifying CVs by rotating them to curl the end of the wing upward.

- Select the *wing* surface.
- Press **F8** to go into component mode.
- Select the end three rows of CVs.
- Select the **Rotate** Tool.
- Press the **Insert / Home** key to enter edit pivot point mode.

- In the front window, **Move** the pivot point in X until it is in line with the third row of CVs.

- **Move** the pivot point in Y until it is just above the top row of CVs.

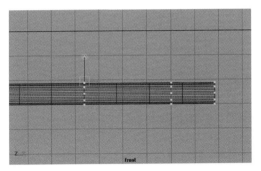

Repositioned pivot point

9 Rotate the selected CVs

- Press **Insert / Home** to exit edit mode.

- Rotate the CVs around Z until the end of the wing is pointing 45 degrees.

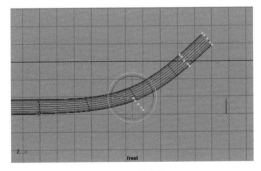

Rotated CVs

10 Deleting history

- Press **F8** to go back to object mode.

- Select the wing surface and choose **Edit → Delete by type → History**.

11 Duplicate and mirror the wing

- Select the wing surface.

- Select **Edit → Duplicate**.

- **Scale X** to **-1** to mirror.

Details

To finish off the spaceship, you will add several details that will add to the look of the spaceship. To give you a chance to work on your own, you will build these elements yourself.

1 Create the wing thrusters

- Untemplate the *mainBody* layer

- Create two wing thrusters just above the wing. You can build these by either duplicating the existing thruster and scaling it down or by revolving new shapes from scratch.

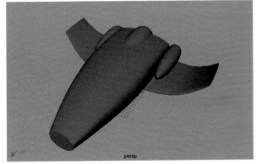

New thrusters

2 Add two wing torpedoes

- Create two wing torpedoes using either elongated spheres or revolved surfaces.

PROJECT THREE

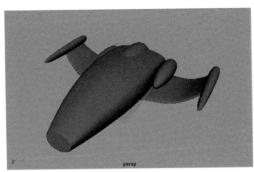

Wing torpedoes

3 Create a cockpit

- Create a cockpit surface in the center of the hull. You can use a half sphere and edit the CVs or you can revolve a profile.

  This surface does not have to be trimmed because it will properly intersect with the hull surface when rendered. Only use trimming when it is required visually.

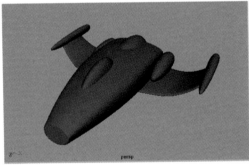

Cockpit surface

Deleting history

To animate this spaceship, you will not be needing any of the construction history. While it is possible to maintain and even animate history, it is not required for this

sequence. History can slow things down somewhat, and therefore should be deleted.

1 Delete history on the surfaces

Even though you have removed history from some of the surfaces, you can make sure by deleting history from all of the surfaces at the same time.

- Select all of the ship surfaces.
- Select **Edit** → **Delete by Type** → **History**.

Grouping the shapes

You will now organize the ship surfaces into a hierarchy. While only the root node will be used during the animation, it is a good idea to organize your work so that others can understand your models later on.

1 Group the thruster pieces

- **Select** all three of the thruster surfaces.
- Select **Edit** → **Group**.
- Rename the new group *thrusters* in the Channel box.

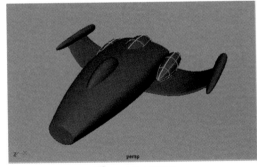

Thruster group

2 Group the hull pieces

- **Select** the parts of the hull and cockpit excluding the thrusters.
- Select **Edit → Group**.
- Rename the new group *hull* in the Channel box.

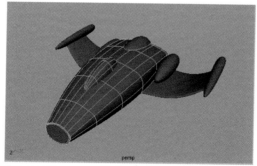

Hull group

3 Group the wing pieces

- **Select** the two wing surfaces and the two torpedoes.
- Select **Edit → Group**.
- Rename the new group *wing* in the Channel box.

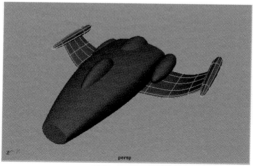

Wing group

4 Group the various groups

- Click on the **Select by hierarchy** button, then click on the **Select by hierarchy: Root** button.

  This will make sure that you are picking the top node of each group.

- Click-drag a selection box around the parts of the ship.
- Select **Edit → Group**.
- Rename the new group *nurbShip* in the Channel box.
- Open the Hypergraph to see the results. You can double-click on the group nodes to collapse them and make the graph easier to read.

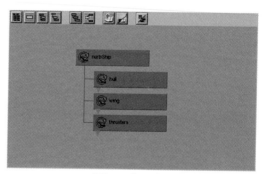

Hierarchy view

5 Add a selection handle

- Make sure that the *nurbShip* node is selected.
- Select **Display → Component Display → Selection Handles**.

  This handle will make it easier to select the whole hierarchy later.

PROJECT THREE

TEXTURING SURFACES

You are now going to texture the NURBS surfaces using projection maps. Projection maps use an external texture placement node to place the texture in relation to the surfaces. Your map will then be projected onto the surface based on your chosen projection technique.

Texturing the thrusters

You will start by texturing the thrusters with a basic colored shading group.

1 Create a blinn shading group

- Open the Hypershade.

- Create a **Blinn** material node.

- Rename the Blinn node to *thrustersBlinn*.

- Change the **Color** to red.

2 Assign it to the thruster surfaces

- Press **F8** to go back into object selection mode.

- **Select** the three thruster surfaces and the two torpedo surfaces.

- Select **Lighting/Shading → Assign Existing Material → thrustersBlinn**.

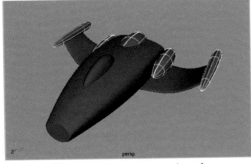

First shading group assigned

Texturing the cockpit

The cockpit will be textured using another simple color material.

1 Create a blinn material

- Create a **Blinn** material node, and rename it *cockpitBlinn*.

- Change the **Color** to black.

2 Assign it to the cockpit surfaces

- **Select** the cockpit surface.

- Select **Lighting/Shading → Assign Existing Material → cockpitBlinn**.

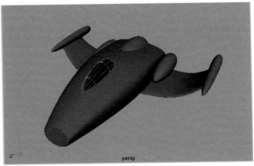

Cockpit blinn assigned

Cylindrical projection map

To texture map the hull of the ship, you will use a cylindrical projection map. Because you want the texture to cover the main hull, the circular fillet and the front face a projection map is required.

A cylindrical projection is similar to wrapping a label around a tin can. The texture will be aligned with the length of the ship.

1 Create a blinn material

- Create a **Blinn** material node and name it *hullBlinn*.

2 Apply a projected color map

- Open the Attribute Editor for *hullBlinn*.

- Click on the **Map** button next to **Color**.

- In the 2D Textures section, click on the **As projection** option and click on the **File** button.

- Set **Proj Type** to **Cylindrical**.

- Click on the *file1* tab.

- Click on the folder icon button next to **Image name**.

- Click on the file named *hull*, then click on the **Open** button.

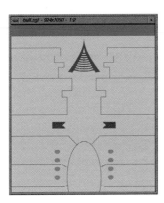

Texture map

3 Assign the shading group

- **Select** the main hull surface, the circular fillet surface and the front face of the ship.

- Select **Lighting/Shading** → **Assign Existing Material** → **hullBlinn**.

- If you have hardware texturing, press the **6** key to preview the

results. Press the **3** key to increase the surface display.

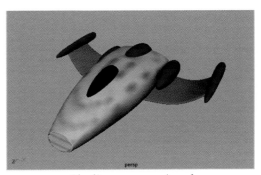

Shading group assigned

4 Position the projection icon

- Select **Lighting/Shading** → **Assign Existing Material**→ **hullBlinn -** ❐.

  This opens the material node in the Attribute Editor.

- Click on the Map button next to **Color**.

- Click on the *place3DTexture1* tab.

- Under **Transform Attributes**, set the following:

  Translate to **0, 0, 3**;

  Rotate to **-90, 0, 0**;

  Scale to **28, 28, 14**.

  This places the projection icon so that it surrounds the spaceship surface. If it is not quite right for your model, tweak the values interactivley or enter different numbers.

PROJECT THREE

Texture placement icon

Note: You will notice that the placement icon has manipulator handles. For this lesson, the coordinate entry was used because the handles were too small.

5 Add a directional light

- Select **Create → Lights → Directional Light**.
- **Rotate** the light until the light is looking down at the ship from the front.
- Press the **7** key.

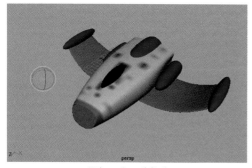
Directional light

6 Test render the surface

Now that you have a light, you can render the scene using software rendering.

- Open a Render View panel.
- In the Render View panel, select **Render → Render → persp**.

Rendered surface

7 Parent the 3D placement node

You will now parent the *place3dtexture* node to the hull surface so that it moves with the ship when it is animated later.

- In the Hypershade, Hypergraph, or Outliner, select the *place3dtexture* projection placement node.
- **Select** the main hull surface.
- Select **Edit → Parent**.

Now the icon will move with the ship when it is transformed.

Planar projection map

Another projection technique is planar mapping where the placement of the texture is a plane that is then projected down onto the surface.

1 Create a Blinn material

- Create a **Blinn** material node and name it *wingBlinn*.

2 Apply a projected color map

- Open the Attribute Editor for *wingBlinn*.

- Click on the **Map** button next to **Color**.

- In the **2D Textures** section, click on the **As projection** option then click on the **File** button.

- Click on the *projection2* tab in the Attribute Editor.

- Set **Proj Type** to **Planar**.

- Click on the *file2* tab.

- Click on the **Folder** icon button next to **Image name**.

- Click on file named *wing.iff* then click **Open**.

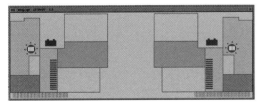

Wing texture map

3 Assign the shading group

- In the perspective window, press **6** for shaded view.

- **Click-drag** with **MMB** the *wingBlinn* material node from the Hypershade to over the left wing in the perspective window and release the button.

- Repeat for the right wing.

4 Position the planar projection

- Open the Attribute Editor for *wingBlinn*.

- Click on the arrow icon button next to **Color**.

- Click on the *place3DTexture2* tab.

- Under **Transform Attributes**, set the following:

  Rotate to **90, 0, 0**.

- Click on the **Fit to group bbox** button in the **3D Texture Placement attributes** section.

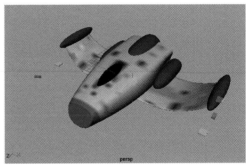

Projection icon

5 Test render the surface

- Open a **Render View** panel.

- Select **Render → Render →persp**.

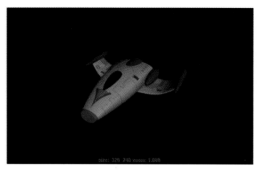

Rendered wings

In the next lesson, you will animate the two ships along motion paths.

6 Parent the place3DTexture node

You will now parent the placement node to the wing surface so that it moves with the ship when it is animated later.

- **Select** the *place3DTexture* node for *wingBlinn*.

- **Select** the wing surface.

- Select **Edit** → **Parent**.

  Now the icon will move with the ship when it is transformed.

7 Reuse textures as bump maps

- Use techniques taught in earlier lessons to reuse the *projection* node textures as bump maps. You can use either the Hypershade or the Hypergraph to help you.

8 Save your work

Conclusion

You now know how to begin working with NURBS modeling tools. You can lay down character curves and then use these to generate surfaces. You have also learned how to use construction history to edit your shapes after creation.

14 Animating the Ships

In this lesson, you will animate two spaceships using *path animation*. You will also add an image plane to the scene to help create a setting for the battle. The planets will be created using simple primitives which will be rendered out. Using paint effects, you will add some galaxy and space nebula to your rendered image. These ships will then be exported out so that they can be detailed in later lessons.

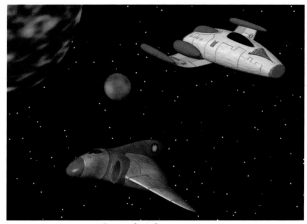

Space battle sequence

In this lesson you will learn the following:

- How to render a space scene with planets
- How to use paint effects to paint on a 2D image
- How to use the rendered space scene as an image plane
- How to create a reference to the ship files
- How to use path animation
- How to update the path markers
- How to shape the path to edit the animation

STARS AND PLANETS

To create a context for your spaceships, you will render a scene that contains a starfield and some planets. This simple space scene will then be rendered and used as an image plane backdrop for your duelling spaceships.

Initial set-up

You are going to create a new file in which you will create the starfield image plane.

1 Start a new scene

- Make sure that your NURBS spaceship has been saved.

- Select **File** → **New Scene**

- Set up four panels containing the Perspective view, two orthographic views and the Hypergraph.

  In this lesson, the Hypergraph will be used to select various nodes of the shading groups that are to be created. This method of working with shading groups will be shown as an alternative to the Hypershade.

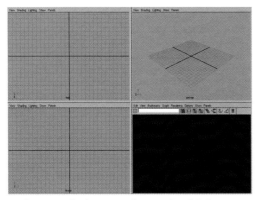

Suggested view pane layout for this lesson

Creating the planets

To populate the space scene, you will need some planets which will act as the backdrop for the final scene.

1 Create the planets

- Create 2 **Primitive NURBS Spheres**.

- Rename the spheres as follows:

  planet1

  planet2

- Turn on the resolution gate by selecting **View** → **Camera Settings** → **Resolution Gate** from the perspective window pane.

- **Scale** and **Move** the spheres as shown below.

  The relative size and position of the spheres in the 3D space of the scene is not important because they will be rendered into a 2D image plane later. Set them up so that their perceived relationships create the desired look in the Perspective view.

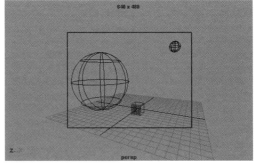

Spheres scaled and positioned as planets

Creating the planet texture

You will now texture the planet. You will use various procedural textures to refine a particular look, and then connect these to a shading group. In some cases, you will use a special window called the Connection Editor to make a direct connection between two attributes.

In previous lessons, you used the Hypershade to visualize how a shading group works. This time you will use the Hypergraph to work with these nodes.

1 Create and assign the first planet shading group

You will now create and assign a shading group using the Hypershade.

- Select **Window** → **Rendering Editors** → **Hypershade...**
- Create a **Lambert** material.
- Rename the material node *planetLambert*
- **Click-drag** with **MMB** *planetLambert* onto *planet1.*

2 Display and rename the nodes

You can use the Hypergraph to see the shading group and material nodes.

- In the Hypergraph, select **Rendering** → **Show ShadingGroups**.
- Select the *lambert2SG* node.
- Click on the **Graph** → **Input and Output Connections** button.

  You can see the material node and the sphere surface connected to the shading group

- Rename the shading group node *planetSG1.*

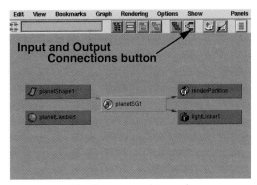

Shading group hierarchy

3 Map the material's color

To create the surface of the planet, you will use a solid fractal texture.

- **Select** the *planetLambert* node.
- Open the Attribute Editor.
- In the Attribute Editor, click on the **Map** button next to the **Color** attribute.
- In the **3D Texture** section, select a **Solid Fractal** node.
- Rename the texture node *color1.*

  The Solid Fractal Attributes can remain set to the defaults.

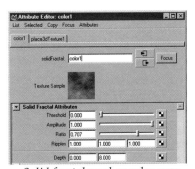

Solid fractal used as color map

4 Remap the color of the fractal

Currently, the fractal is only a grayscale image. You will use the Color Remap option to add color to the fractal.

- Open the **Effects** attributes section.

- Click on the **Insert** button next to **Color Remap**.

  A *RemapRamp* node is connected between the texture and the material nodes. The different positions on the ramp represent the grayscale values of the original texture. By changing the color on the ramp at the different values, you are setting a color on the original texture.

- In the **Ramp Attributes** section, set the ramp **Selected Colors** and **Selected Positions** as shown.

  Click on the top round icon and set the following:

  Selected Position to **0.84**;

  RGB to **0.62, 0.54, 0.41**.

  Click on the middle round icon and set the following:

  Selected Position to **0.57**;

  RGB to **0.87, 0.74, 0.63**.

  Click on the bottom round icon and set the following:

  Selected Position to **0.43**;

  RGB to **1.0, 0.87, 0.66**.

Note: To change RGB values, open the color chooser. Under the HSVA values is a drop down menu where you can set the color values to be either in HSVA or RGB mode.

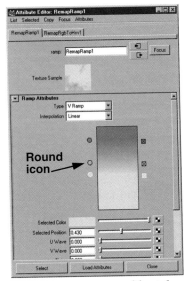

Round icon

Remap ramp of fractal

5 Map the material's bump

You now want to create a bump map node. This node will be used later to reconnect the color remap node as a bump.

- Open the *planetLambert* material node in the Attribute Editor.

- Click on the **Map** button next to **Bump Mapping**.

- In the Create Render Node window, open to the **Utilities** tab.

- Under **General Utilities**, select a **Bump 3d** node.

- In the **3d Bump Attributes** section:

  Set **Bump Depth** to **-1.0**

- In the **Effects** section:

  Set the **Bump Filter** to **0.5**.

6 Connect the remap node to the bump

To connect the remap node to the bump, you need to drag the texture onto the bump node.

- In the Hypergraph, drag with **MMB** the *RemapRamp1* node over the *bump3d1* node. If a menu pops up, select **default**.

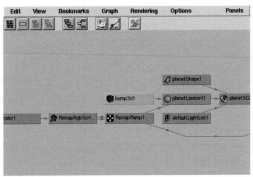

Connecting remap ramp node to 3D bump node

Note: The nodes are now connected in the Hypergraph. You can move your cursor over the arrow lying between the nodes, and the connected attributes will be highlighted.

---

7 Map a glow to the material

You can achieve a nice lighting effect by using a utility called the Sampler Info node mapped into the glow attribute. In this case the Sampler Info node will create a slight glow on the surface of the planet

where the light is most intense and then dissipate to darkness as the planet falls into shadow.

In the Hypershade, create a Sampler Info node by selecting **Create** → **General Utilities** → **Sampler Info.**

- Create a Ramp in the Hypershade window. Make sure that the **As Projection** option is set back to **Normal**.

- In the Hypershade, drag with **MMB** the *SamplerInfo1* over the *ramp*.

  A pop-up window will open, Select **Other**. . . The Connection Editor opens. You can use this window to connect various attributes.

- In the **Outputs** column, highlight **Facing Ratio.**

- In the **Inputs** column, click the plus sign beside *UvCoord* and select **V Coord.**

- With the Connection Editor still open, Click the **Clear All** button. Drag with **MMB** *ramp* into the Outputs window. Drag the *planetLambert* into the Inputs window.

- **Connect** *Out Alpha* in the Outputs window and *Glow Intensity* in the Inputs window.

  Close the Connection Editor.

- Open the Attribute Editor for *ramp1*. Press the square icon beside the middle color icon to delete it.

- Set the ramp **Selected Colors** and **Selected Positions** as shown:

Click on the top round icon and set
the following:

  Selected Position to **0.90**;

  RGB to **0.50, 0.50, 0.50**.

Click on the bottom round icon and
set the following:

  Selected Position to **0.00**;

  RGB to **0.00, 0.00, 0.00**.

Tip: You can make fine adjustments to the
final look of this material by adding a
light and creating an IPR render and
adjusting various attributes on the ramp
node.

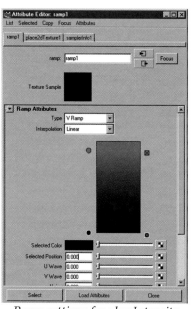

Ramp settings for glowIntensity

Create the planet2 material

To texture map planet2, you will duplicate
the first shading group, then edit the various
texture nodes to produce different effects.

1 Duplicate the planet's shading group

  ▪ In the Hypergraph, **Select** the
  planetSG1 node.

  ▪ From the main menu, select **Edit** →
  Duplicate - ❑, and in the Duplicate
  Option window:

    Turn on **Duplicate Input Graph**;

    Click on **Duplicate**.

  A duplicate copy of the network of
  nodes that make up the shading
  group is made.

Tip: This is the same as selecting **Duplicate**
→ **Shading Network** from the
Hypershade's **Edit** menu.

---

2 Assign the new Shading Group

  ▪ **Click-drag** with **MMB** *planetSG2* from
  the Hypergraph onto *planet2* in the
  view panel.

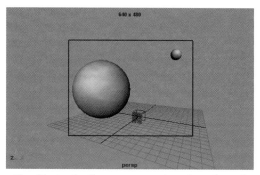

Duplicate shading group assigned to planet2

3 Change the color of planet2

Modifying the fractal, as seen in the
Texture Sample, will create different planet
images.

- In the Hypergraph, select **Rendering → Show Textures**.

  All of the texture nodes in the scene are displayed. Notice that all of the texture nodes for the planet shading group have been duplicated.

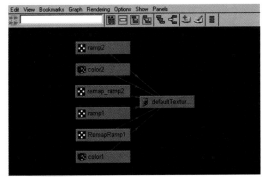

Hypergraph view of the texture nodes in the scene

- **Select** the *color2* node.
- In the Attribute Editor, change the values for **Threshold**, **Amplitude** and **Ratio** to whatever you like.
- **Select** the *RemapRamp2* node.
- Change the **Colors** and **Positions** to produce a new map.

  Remember that the value of the remap colors will also be used by the bump map.

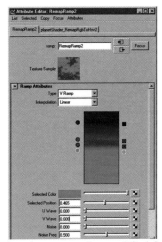

Fractal and remap nodes modified for planet2.

Tip: The material for planet2 should have more detail to account for the smaller size. This could be done by adjusting the scale of the 3D texture placement icon.

Render the scene

You will now render the space scene to create a bitmap image. This is the image that you will use to add some 2D Paint Effects and eventually use as an image plane in the final battle scene.

1 Place lights in the scene

- Create a **Directional Light**.
- **Rotate** the light so that the direction is coming from the right of the view and from above.
- In the Attribute Editor, set the **Color** to a pale yellow.

PROJECT THREE

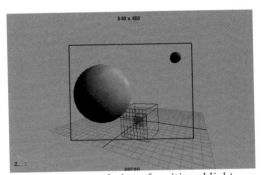
Hardware rendering of positioned light

Note: When adding lights, plan ahead to determine how the lights will be positioned in the final scene. Keep in mind that they should be consistent with the lighting of the background image.

---

2 Fine tune the look of the planet

- Create an **IPR** render of the scene. Click-drag a region around *planet1*.

  You may notice that the light on the planet is shining a little too bright. Using IPR you can adjust this to get the look you want.

- Open the Attribute Editor for the Directional Light. Lower the **Intensity**.

3 Increase sphere tessellation

- **Select** the sphere for the largest planet.

- Open the **Tessellation** section of the Attribute Editor.

- Set the **Display Render Tessellation** button to **On**.

- Set the following:

  Set **Curvature Tolerance** to **Highest Quality**

  Set **U Divisions Factor** to **2**;

  Set **V Divisions Factor** to **2**;

- Set the **Display Render Tessellation** button to **Off**.

  Depending on their size in relation to the overall view, you may want to increase the tessellation of the other sphere.

4 Render the background image

- In the Render View window, select **Options → Render Globals**.

- Click the **Maya Software** tab.

- In the Resolution section set the **Render Resolution** to **640x480**

- In the Anti-Aliasing Quality section, set the **Presets** to **Production Quality**.

- In the Render View window, select **Render → Render → Persp**.

Rendered background image

5 Save the rendering

- From the Render View window, select **File** → **Save Image...**

- Name the image *background* and save it into the *sourceimages* directory.

6 Save your Maya file

- **Save** the file as *planets* in the *scenes* directory.

ADD SPACE AND NEBULA

You are now ready to import your rendered planet image into Paint Effects and use some preset brushes to paint starfields and nebulas.

1 Create a new file

- Make sure that your planets file has been saved then select **File** → **New Scene**.

2 Paint in the Maya Paint Effects® window

- Press **8** to go to the Maya Paint Effects preview window.

- Select **Paint** → **Paint Canvas**.

  This will change the canvas into 2D paint mode.

- In the Paint Effects window, Select **Brush** → **Get Brush**.

- Open a brush section, select a brush and paint on the canvas.

  You can now experiment with different brushes and sizes.

- Select **Canvas** → **Clear**.

3 Import your render into Paint Effects

- Select **Canvas** → **Open Image**. From the *sourceimages* directory, select *background*.

Imported Image

4 Paint your image

- In the Visor window, open the *galactic* folder.

- Select the *space* brush and paint some space onto your image.

- Continue painting space elements to your image using the different preset brushes.

- If you make a mistake you can Undo the last brush stroke by selecting **Canvas** → **Canvas Undo**.

Final background image

Tip: You can change the size of your brushes by using the hotkey **n**.

5 Save the image

- When you are done with your image, in the Paint Effects window select **Canvas** → **Save As -** ❑.

- In the Option window, make sure that **Save Alpha** is turned **Off**.

- Click on **Save Image** and highlight the *background.iff* in the *sourceimages* directory.

THE SPACESHIP SCENE

You will now start to create and animate the duelling spaceship scene. You will start with the polygonal spaceship from the last lesson. Then you will animate a proxy object for the NURBS spaceship. Lastly, you will import and animate the background image as an image plane.

Creating a reference

You are now going to start a new file, then create a reference to the first spaceship. By referencing the file, you begin to create a situation where files can be shared by multiple users.

1 Create a new file

- Make sure that your painted image file has been saved then select **File** → **New Scene**.

2 Create a reference to the polyShip

- Select **File** → **Create Reference...**

- Select the *polyShip* file from the file window then click **Reference**.

- Select **File** → **Reference Editor...**

- Click on the arrow to see that the new file is a reference in the new

scene. Highlight the path for more info.

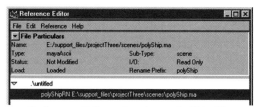

Reference Editor showing polyShip file

- Close this window.

3 Hide the referenced lights

When the reference was created, all the lights from the scene were also referenced. Since this scene will have its own lights, you will hide the reference lights.

- Select the lights.

- Select **Ctrl -h** to hide selection.

Path animation

Path animations are created by assigning an object or series of objects to a path. This creates a special *motionPath* node that allows you to key its motion along the path.

1 Scale the spaceship

- **Select** the polyShip surface.

  In the Channel box, you will see that the name of the ship is *polyShip_polyShip*. This is because the file's name has been used as a prefix for all referenced nodes. This helps recognize referenced nodes and prevents name conflicts.

- Select **Edit** → **Group**.

- In the Channel box, rename the group as *polyShipAnim*.

- Select **Display** → **Component Display** → **Selection Handles**.
- **Scale** the selected node to **0.3** in all directions.

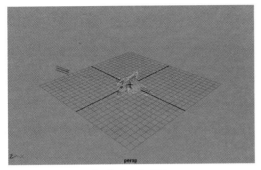

Scaled polyShip

2 Draw a path animation curve

- Select **Create** → **EP Curve Tool**.
- Click three times to draw a curve diagonally across the ground grid then press the **Enter** key.

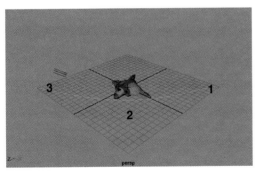

Path curve

3 Attach the ship to the path

- Change the **Time slider** range to **120** frames.

- **Select** the *polyShipAnim* node using its selection handle and then press the **Shift** key and select the path.

Note: In order to create a path animation, the path must be picked last. The last object picked is indicated in green.

- Go to the **Animation** menu set.
- Select **Animate** → **Motion Paths** → **Attach to Motion Path - ❏**
- Set **Time Range** to **Time Slider**.
- **Attach** and playback the results.

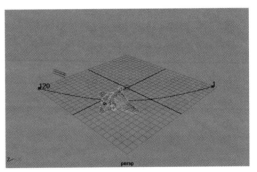

Ship attached to path

Note: If you want to preview the correct playback timing, remember to set your playback speed to normal in the General Preferences window.

4 Edit the motion path input node

The ship is moving down the path but it is not aimed in the correct direction. You can change this using the *motionPath* input node.

- With the *polyShipAnim* node selected, open the Attribute Editor.

- Click the tab for *motionPath1* and set the following:

   Follow to **On**;

   Front Axis to **Z**;

   Up Axis to **Y**.

- Play back the results.

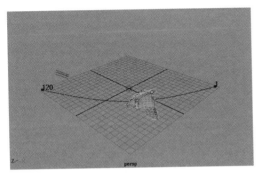

Spaceship with follow

5 Edit the path's shape

You can edit the shape of the path using the curve's control vertices and the object will follow the path.

- **Select** the path curve.
- Press the **F8** key to go into component select mode.
- **Select** the middle CV.
- **Move** it down along the Y-axis.

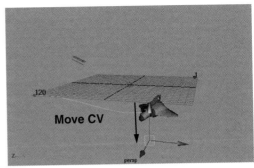

Move CV

Edited path curve

- Press the **F8** key to go into object select mode.

- Playback the results

Tip: You can press the **Alt** key and tumble in the Perspective window as the animation is playing back. This lets you preview the shape of the path from different angles.

---

6 Key the path's U value

You can set a key on the *motionPath's* U value to add more markers to the path.

- Go to frame **40**.

- **Select** the *polyShipAnim* node using its selection handle.

- In the Channel box, click on the *motionPath* input node.

- In the Channel box, click on the **U Value** channel name to highlight.

- With your right mouse button, select **Key Selected** from the pop-up menu.

   A new marker is placed where the new key is set. You are setting a key on the position of the ship along the

U direction of the curve. The value represents the parameter of the curve.

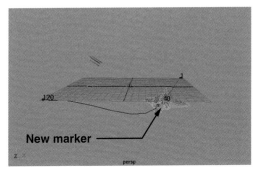

New path markers

7 Key a second value

This time you will key the U value using the show manipulator tool and Auto Key.

- Go to frame **80**.

- Select the **Show Manipulator** tool.

  A manipulator appears with handles for positioning the object along the path and twisting. You will use the middle handle to move the ship along the path.

- Click on the **Auto Key** button at the right end of the Time slider to turn it **On**.

- Click-drag on the yellow manipulator handle to drag the ship back. Be sure not to click-drag on the arrow.

- Another path marker is placed on the curve.

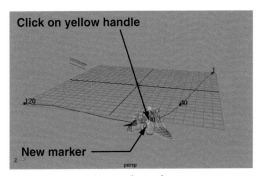

New path marker

Tip: It is always good to remember that input nodes may have manipulators which you can access using the show manipulator tool.

8 Edit the path marker's position

The position of the markers can be moved to edit the animation of the ship.

- Click on the **Auto Key** button to turn it **Off**.

- **Select** the path marker that is labeled as **40**. Click on the number without touching the curve to select the marker on its own. It will be colored yellow when selected.

- Select the **Move** tool.

- **Move** the marker past the marker labeled as **80**.

  The marker is constrained to the curve as you move it.

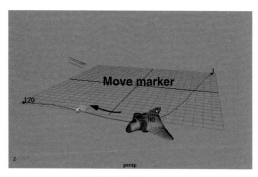

Edited path curve

- Play back the results.

  The ship animates up to the **40** marker, then goes backwards to the **80** marker, and then forward to the end of the curve. The position of the ship at these key frames can be set using the markers.

9 Edit the timing

Since the marker points are simply keys set on the U Value of the *motionPath* node, you can edit the timing of the keys in the Graph Editor.

- **Select** the ship using its selection handle, then click on the *motionPath* input node in the Channel box.

- Open a Graph Editor panel.

- Move your cursor into the Graph Editor window and press **a** to frame all into the panel.

  The position of the attached object in the U direction of the curve is mapped against time. You can see that a key has been set for each of the path markers.

- **Select** the key at frame **80**.

- In the Graph Editor's Stats area change the time from **80** to **100**.

- In the Graph Editor, select **Tangents** → **Flat**.

  You can edit the effect of the in-between frames for path keys using the same techniques as you have used for set keys.

Edit this field

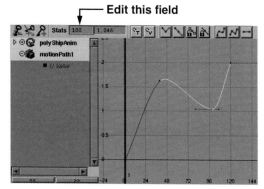

Edited path curve

You can see that the path marker is now labeled as **100** in the view panel.

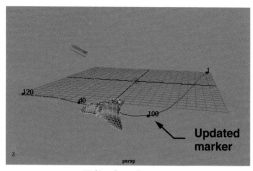

Edited path curve

10 Remove the middle two markers

While the markers have shown you how to make the ship move back and forth, this is not how you want the spaceship to animate. You will remove the middle markers to return to a two marker path.

- **Select** the markers that are labeled as **40** and **100**. Make sure that no other objects are selected.

Tip: You can select the keyframes from the Graph Editor to delete them as well.

- Press the **Backspace** key on your keyboard.

Animate a second ship

You will now animate the NURBS spaceship along a second path.

1 Create a reference to the nurbShip

- Select **File** → **Create Reference**.
- **Select** the *nurbShip* file from the file window.

  Now this file is also referenced into the scene. Just like the polyShip, it is also too big right now.

2 Scale the NURBS ship down

- **Select** the nurbShip using its selection handle.
- **Scale** the ship down by **0.15** in all directions.

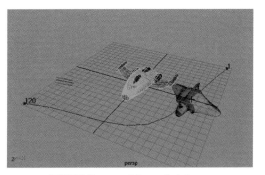

NURBS spaceship scaled down

3 Hide the referenced light

- Hide the light which was referenced with the *nurbShip*.

4 Draw a second path curve

- Select **Create** → **EP Curve Tool**.
- Click five times to draw a curve that snakes diagonally across the ground plane in the opposite direction from the first curve. Press the **Enter** key.

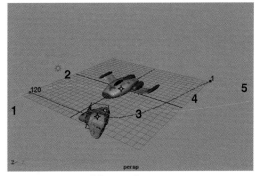

New path curve

- Press **F8** to go into component select mode.
- **Select** the middle CVs and **Move** them up so that this curve passes over the first curve.

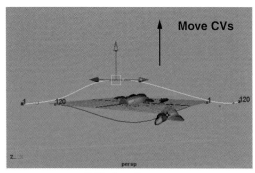

Edited path curve

- Press **F8** to go back to object select mode.

5 Attach the ship to the path

- Go to the **Animation** menu set.
- **Select** the *nurbShip* using its selection handle.
- Press the **Shift** key and **Select** the path curve. Remember that the path must be selected last.
- Select **Animate** → **Motion Paths** → **Attach to Motion Path**.
- Open the Attribute Editor and set the following:

    Follow to **On**;

    Front Axis to **Z**;

    Up Axis to **Y**;

    Bank to **On**.

- Select **Display** → **Grid** to turn off the ground grid.
- From the Perspective view panel, select **Show** → **NURBS Curves** and **Show** → **Textures** to turn these object types off.

    Now you can preview what the ships look like on their own.

- Playback the results.

    With banking turned on, the *nurbShip* tilts to the side as it rounds the corners of the path.

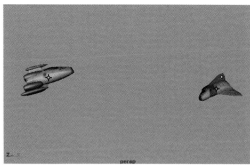

NURBS spaceship with banking

6 Save your work

- From the **File** menu, select **Save Scene As...**
- Enter the name *spaceScene* next to the file's path.
- Press the **Save** button or press the **Enter** key.

Setting up the image plane

You are now going to import the background image plane. This plane will be used behind the spaceships to help compose the final shot. Once it is in place, you will edit the paths to suit the final scene.

1 Create a new camera

You will create a new camera to hold the image plane.

- Select **Create** → **Cameras** → **Camera**.
- This places a camera at the origin.
- Select **Show Manipulator** tool.

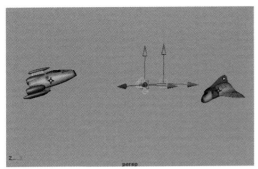

New camera placement

2 Set up your panels

- In one of the orthographic panels, select **Panels** → **Perspective** → **camera1**.

- Press **5** or **6** to shade the *camera1* panel.

- Dolly, tumble and track in the *camera1* panel until you can see both spaceships.

- From the *camera1* view panel, select **View** → **Camera Settings** → **Resolution Gate**.

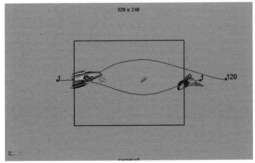

Resolution gate

3 Add the image plane

- From the *camera1* view panel, select **View** → **Image Plane** → **Import Image**.

- Choose the *background* image file from the *sourceimages* directory.

  This is the image file that you rendered earlier in the lesson.

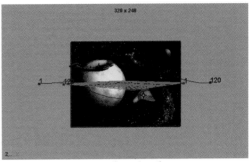

Image plane in place

4 Set up the image plane

- Select *Camera1*.

- In the channel box, click to open the image plane attributes.

- Set the following:

  Size X to **2.83**;

  Size Y to **1.9**;

  Depth to **500**;

  Offset X to **-0.5**;

  Offset Y to **-0.2**.

  The size setting doubles the size of the image in relation to the resolution gate, the depth setting moves it away from the camera and the offset changes the position in relation to the film back.

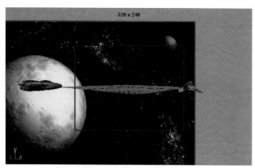

New image plane placement

5 Key the image plane

- In the **Time slider**, go to frame **1**.

- In the Channel box, click on the **Offset X** and **Y** with the right mouse button and select **Key Selected**.

  The two offset fields should become shaded to indicate that they have been keyed.

- In the **Time slider**, go to frame **120**.

- In the Channel Box, set the following:

  Offset X to **0.1**;

  Offset Y to **0.1**.

- Again, click on **Offset X** and **Y** with the right mouse button and select **Key Selected**.

- Playback the results.

  The image plane is now animating from one position to another. This will give the impression that the camera is moving in space.

6 Save your work

Edit the path curves

You are now going to edit the animation of the two ships to create the final sequence.

1 Edit the curve shape for both curves

- Edit the CVs on the two path curves to create an animation where the nurbShip moves up and over the polyShip.

- You can also move the entire curve to set up the timing of animation.

  You can set the shape of the curve to anything you desire. The key is to make sure that at frame 50, the nurbShip is above the polyShip so that it can shoot a photon laser in the next lesson.

Tip: Changing the **display mode** of the Image Plane can make it easier to see the objects in your scene when working.

---

2 Edit the position marker

If required, change the position of the path markers to refine the animation along the paths.

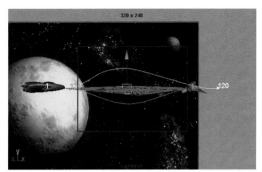

Updated paths

3 Save your work

4 Playblast the final sequence

- In the *camera1* view panel, select **View → Camera Settings → No Gate**.

- Select **Window → Playblast**.

Play back the sequence using the Movie Player controls.

Playblast preview

Conclusion

You now have the two ships animated along two paths. In the next lesson, you will add visual effects to the scene as the nurbShip shoots a photon laser at the polyShip. You will then render the scene with the effects in place.

15 Visual Effects

In this lesson, you will add visual effects to your spaceship scene. The first few effects will use Maya's Digital OptiF/X capabilities. These effects include the photon's explosion and the nurbShip's thruster flame.

Visual effects

In this lesson you will learn the following:

- How to create an OptiF/X fog light thruster
- How to create a photon laser
- How to create an OptiF/X explosion
- How to create a particle-based thruster
- How to add particle smoke to the polyShip wing

Initial set-up

You will continue this lesson using the space scene saved in the last lesson. You will add visual effects to the two animated spaceships. You will set keys on these effects in order to integrate them with the existing sequence.

1 Set up your view panels

- Create four view panels.

- Place the panels as shown below.

- In the Perspective view, select **Show** → **Cameras** to turn off the display of *camera1* and its image plane.

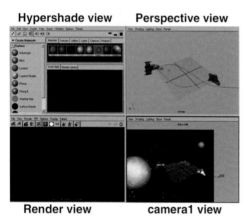

Hypershade view   Perspective view

Render view   camera1 view

View panel layout

In the Hypershade, you will see all the materials belonging to the scene. You may remember that some of these nodes are part of referenced files – in this case, the nurbShip and polyShip files. You can edit attributes for these shaders and assign them to other objects if required. Just remember that the original shader is part of another file.

CREATING OPTI F/X

OptiF/X are visual effects that you can add to your lights. These include, fog, glows and halos. Each of these effects generates nodes with attributes that you can animate.

To start, you will create a thruster for the nurbShip using a fog light. This light will use an animated fractal texture to give it a more interesting look. You then use animated glows to create a photon torpedo and an explosion.

Building a thruster light

The thruster flame is going to be built using a spot light. You want the light to be positioned on the nurbShip so that it is pointing out of the rear thruster.

1 Place spot light in scene

- Select **Create** → **Lights** → **Spot Light**.

  This places a spot light at the origin.

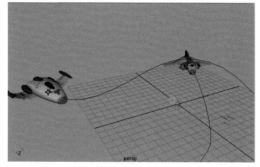

New light at the origin

2 Parent the light into the nurbShip

- Press the **Shift** key and select the nurbShip using its selection handle.

- Select **Edit** → **Parent** - ❏ and set the following;

  > **Preserve Position** to **Off**.

- Click on **Parent**.

- Select the **Move** tool.

Parented light with global move manipulator

The move manipulator is currently oriented to the world space grid. You need it to move in the local space of the light.

- Double-click on the **Move** tool icon or select **Modify** → **Transformation Tools** → **Move** - ❏ and set the following option:

  > **Move** to **Local**.

Now the orientation of the move manipulators are aligned with the ship group.

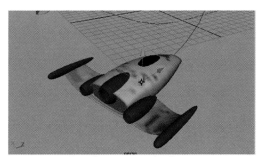

Local move manipulator

3 Position the light

You can now position the light using the local axis to keep yourself aligned with the nurbShip.

- **Move** the light so that it sits in the center of the thruster.

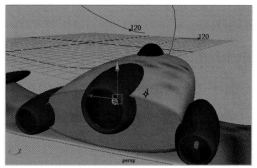

Positioned light

- **Scale** the size of the light.

  The light cone should now protrude outside of the thruster. This will make it easier to select.

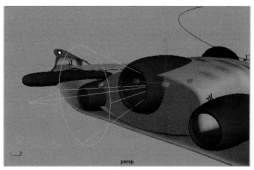

Scaled light icon

4 Add fog to spot light

- Open up the **Light Effects** section in the Attribute Editor and click on the **Map** button next to the **Light Fog**.

PROJECT THREE

5 Test render the effect

You will be using the IPR feature in the Render View window to fine tune the look of the thruster fire.

- Create a directional light and position it to light the side of the ship.

- Select a closeup view of the backside of the ship.

- In the Render View, select **IPR** → **IPR Render** → **Persp.**

    This will generate an IPR file.

- **Click-drag** select a region around the thruster for fine tuning.

    Using IPR, you are able to adjust attributes in the Attribute Editor and see the results instantly in the IPR window

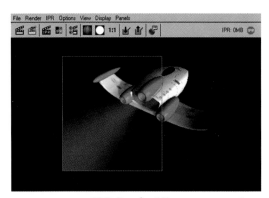

IPR Render View

6 Rescale the light

The fog adds a *coneshape* icon to the spot light to show the extent of the fog. You may want to scale the light back down to shorten the fog's *coneshape* icon.

- **Scale** the *coneshape* icon until the icon is closer to the ship.

- Create another IPR image.

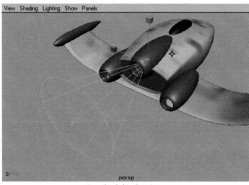

Scaled light icon

Scaled light icon in IPR

7 Adjust the spot light shape node

- In the Attribute Editor, click on the *spotLightShape* tab and in the **Light Effects** section set the following:

    Fog Spread to **0.5**;

    Fog Intensity to **5.0**.

Fog Effects in IPR

8 Change the spot light color

- Set the following in the **Spot Light Attributes**:

  Color of the light to a bright orange using values of **RGB** values of about **1.0**, **0.33**, **0.15**.

  Decay Rate to **Cubic**;

  Penumbra Angle to **2.0**.

- Fine tune the attributes on the thruster fire until you are happy with the results.

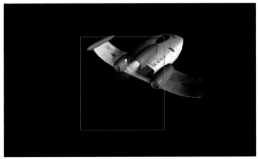

Spotlight Color in IPR

Note: If you change the cone angle, it is recommended that you regenerate the IPR file.

---

9 Save your work

- Select **File → Save Scene As** and enter the name *SpaceScene2*.

Animate the fog effect

To create a thruster flame that has an animated effect, you will apply a 3D fractal texture. You will then animate the position of the fractal to give the fog some motion.

1 Add a fractal map to the fog

- Click on the *lightFog* tab in the Attribute Editor.

- In the **Light Fog Attributes** section of this new node, click on the **Map** button next to **Color**.

- Select a **Solid Fractal** 3D texture.

- **Hide** the 3D texture icon.

  You should notice that the IPR render has updated to reflect the change in fog.

- Fine tune the thruster fire to your liking.

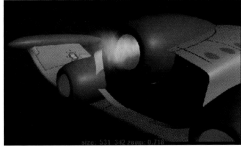

IPR region showing fractal map

2 Animate the fog effect

You do not actually have to do anything to animate the exhaust. Because the fractal map's placement icon is fixed at the origin, the look of the fog will change over time as the ship animates along its path.

In essence, the fog light is passing through the fractal effect as the ship animates. This makes sure that the effect is different for different frames.

Building a photon laser beam

You will now animate a laser beam shooting from the nurbShip to the polyShip. This will be done by using a cylinder and applying a shader with glow to it.

1 Place a cylinder in the scene

- Turn off the IPR updating by pressing the red button in the top right hand corner of the Render View window.

- Select **Create** → **Nurbs Primitives** → **Cylinder**.

2 Parent the cylinder into the nurbShip

- Go to frame **50**.

- Press the **Shift** key and select the *nurbShip* using its selection handle.

- Select **Edit** → **Parent - □**.

- In the option window select **Edit** → **Reset Settings**, then click on **Parent**.

- **Scale** the cylinder very thin in the **Y** direction.

- **Move** the cylinder up into the photon recess of the nurbShip.

  You may need to use different orthographic views to place the cylinder correctly.

- **Rotate** the cylinder so the other end of the laser penetrates the *polyShip*. You may want to move the pivot

point of the cylinder to the end to make rotating it easier.

Tip: You can also move the Motion Path curves to position the ships.

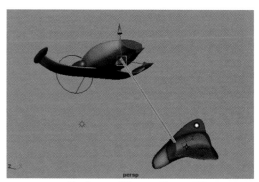

cylinder position at frame 50

3 Animate the cylinder's visibility

You only want to see the cylinder in the frames that the laser beam is shooting at the polyShip. Therefore you will need to key the visibility for the light.

- Go to frame **49**.

- In the Channel box, change the **Visibility** to **Off**.

- Click on the **Visibility** channel with your right mouse button and select **Key Selected** from the menu.

- Go to frame **50**.

- In the Channel box, change the **Visibility** to **On**.

- Click on the **Visibility** channel with your right mouse button and select **Key Selected** from the menu.

- Go to frame **54**.

- In the Channel box, change the **Visibility** to **Off**.

- Click on the **Visibility** channel with your right mouse button and select **Key Selected** from the menu.

- Play back the results in the *camera1* view.

4 Create a laser material

- Go to frame **50**.

- Create an IPR render and select a region around the laser.

- In the Hypershade, create a new *Blinn* material.

- **Assign** the *Blinn* material to the cylinder.

- Open the Attribute Editor and change the **Color** to bright green.

- Open the Special Effects tab and set the **Glow Intensity** to **0.4**.

  You can see the cylinder update in the IPR window.

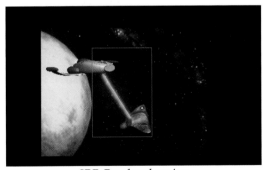

IPR Rendered region

Building an explosion

Using a new point light, you will set keys for a number of light attributes to create the effect of an explosion which will occur as a result of the laser hitting the polyship.

1 Create a new point light

- Select **Create** → **Lights** → **Point Light**.

2 Animate point light coming into scene

- Go to frame **53**.

- **Position** the light at the base of the laser just over the surface of the polyship.

New point light

3 Edit the point light attributes

- In the Attribute Editor, open the **Point Light Attributes** section and set the following;

  Color to bright orange;

  Decay Rate to **Linear**.

  In the **Light Effects** section:

  Fog Type to **Linear**;

  Fog Radius to **2**.

- Click on the **Map** button next to **Light Fog**.

- In the new fog node, click on the **Map** button next to **Color**.

- Select a **Solid Fractal** 3D texture.

4 Scale the fractal map

- In the Perspective view, **select** the green 3D texture icon.
- Press **Shift-r** to set keys for the scale attributes.
- Go to frame **63**.
- **Scale** the icon by **2** units in all three axes.
- Press **Shift-r** to set keys for the scale attributes.

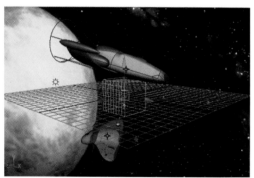

Scaled texture icon

- Go to frame **53**.
- Click-drag with your middle mouse button in the Time slider to go to frame **73**.

  The middle mouse button lets you use the attribute values from frame 53 for your new frame.

- Press **Shift-r** to set keys for the scale attributes.

5 Animating the light Intensity

- Select the explosion point light and in the Attribute Editor, click on the *pointLightShape* tab.

- Go to frame **53**.
- In the **Point Light Attributes** section, set the **Intensity** to **0.0**
- Set a key by using **RMB** over **Intensity** field.
- Go to frame **73**.
- Set another key on the **Intensity** attribute.
- Go to frame **63**.
- Set the **Intensity** to **2** and set a key.

6 Test render the effect

- Go to frame **63**.
- From the Render View panel, select **Render → Snapshot → camera1**.
- Click-drag a selection box around the new point light.

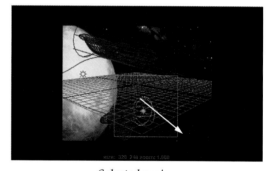

Selected region

- Select **Render → Render Region**.

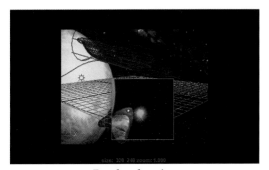

Rendered region

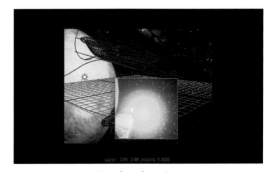

Rendered region

7 Adding and animating halo

- In the Attribute Editor's **Light Effects** section, click on the **Map** button next to **Light Glow**.

- In the new *opticalFX* node, set the following:

     Glow Type to **None**;

     Halo Type to **Linear**.

- Go to frame **53**.

- Open the Halo Attributes and set the **Halo Intensity** to **0**.

- Set a key on this attribute.

- Go to frame **73**.

- Set another key on this attribute.

- Go to frame **63**.

- Open the Halo Attributes and set the **Halo Intensity** to **15**.

- Set a key on this attribute.

8 Test render the effect

- From the Render View panel, select **Render → Render Region**.

  The effect extends beyond the region but the general look can be easily evaluated.

Updating the polyShip animation

At the moment, the polyShip is flying right past the explosion as if nothing is happening. You will now set keys on the path animation's *twist* attribute to animate the ship reacting to the laser blast.

When you set keys on the *motionPath* node's twist attribute, you will create new *orientation markers* that will work similar to the position markers which you learned about in the previous lesson.

1 Select the polyShip's path node

- Select the polyShip using its selection handle.

  This should pick the *polyShipAnim* node.

- In the Channel box, click on the *motionPath* input node.

2 Unlock the front twist node

- In the Channel box, click on the **Front Twist** attribute name with the right mouse button and select **Unlock Selected** from the pop-up menu.

PROJECT THREE

3 Set a key on the twist

- Go to frame **53**.

- In the Channel box, click on the **Front Twist** attribute name with the right mouse button and select **Key Selected** from the pop-up menu.

- Go to frame **73**.

- Set another key.

  These keys place orientation markers onto the path. These markers can be edited using similar methods used on the position markers you learned about in the last lesson.

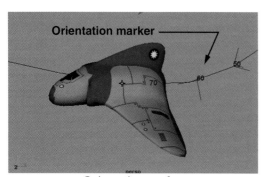

Orientation marker

4 Set a key on the twist at frame 60

- Go to frame **60**.

- Highlight the **Front Twist** attribute in the Channel Box.

- In the *camera1* view, **click-drag** with the **MMB** to twist the polyShip about -30 degrees.

- Set a key on the **Front Twist** attribute.

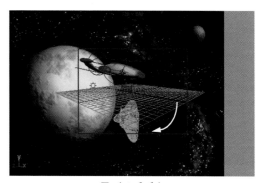

Twisted ship

- Playback the results

PARTICLE EFFECTS

You will now add software particles for the thruster of the polyShip.

Create a particle emitter

You will start with a particle emitter that will be used for the polyShip's thruster. You need to create the emitter and then parent it to the polyShip just as you did with the light and the nurbShip.

1 Set up your Perspective view

- Set up one of your panels in Perspective view.

- Select **Show** → **None** then **Show** → **Polygons, Show** → **Handles, Show** → **Dynamics** and **Show** → **NURBS Curves**.

  Now you can preview only the elements needed for this section of the lesson.

- Move your cursor into the Perspective view panel and press the spacebar to pop it to full screen.

This will make things run a little faster.

2 Create an emitter

- Go to the **Dynamics** menu set.
- Select **Particles → Create Emitter.**
- Play back the animation.

  The particles are emitting, but are not moving with the ship. You need to parent the emitter into the ship.

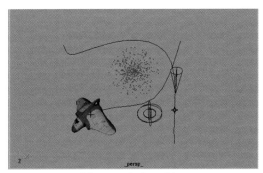

Unparented emitter

3 Parent the emitter to the polyShip

You will now parent the emitter to the ship in order to get them moving together.

- With the emitter selected, press the **Shift** key and select the *polyShipAnim* node using its selection handle.
- Select **Edit → Parent - ❒.**
- In the option window set the **Preserve Position** to **Off.** Click **Parent**.
- Select the **Move** tool. The **Move** option should still be set to **Local**.

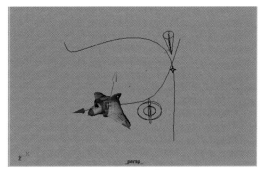

Parented emitter

- **Move** the emitter along the local Z-axis to move it into the polyShip's thruster space.

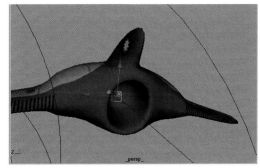

Positioned emitter

- Play back the scene.

  Now the particles are being emitted out of the thruster space.

PROJECT THREE

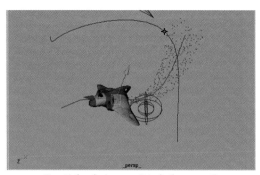

Particles being emitted along path

4 Set the emitter direction
- Go to frame **1**.
- Make sure that the emitter is selected.
- In the Channel box, change the following attributes:

  Direction X to **0**;

  Direction Y to **0**;

  Direction Z to **-1**;

  Spread to **0.4**;

  Speed to **2**;

  Emitter Type to **Directional**;

- Play back the scene.

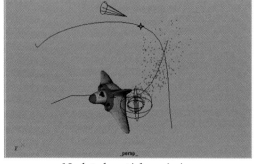

Updated particle emission

Particle attributes

Now that you have particles being emitted in the desired direction, you can start to look at the particle node attributes. These attributes would include *lifespan* and *color*.

1 Set particle attributes
- Select the *particle* node by selecting any of the emitted particles.
- Open the Attribute Editor.
- Click on the *particleShape* tab.

2 Set the lifespan attribute

Right now, the particles are remaining on the screen indefinitely. You can use a lifespan attribute to limit how long the particles live.

- In the Attribute Editor, open the **Lifespan Attributes** section.
- Set **Lifespan Mode** to **Random Range**.
- Set the **Lifespan** to **0.4**.
- Set the **Lifespan Random** to **0.3**.
- Playback the results.

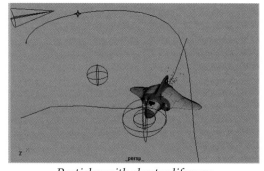

Particles with shorter lifespan

Rendering the particles

You now want to set up the particles for rendering. In Lesson 4, you used hardware rendered particles to add a spark effect to the bouncing ball and software rendered particles for the ring of fire.

For this lesson, you will again use software rendered particles. These will give you particles which will render with your other objects during the batch rendering process.

1 Change the render type

- With the *particleShape* tab active in the Attribute Editor, scroll down to the **Render Attributes** section and set **Particle Render Type** to **Cloud (s/w)**.

  The *(s/w)* label means that this render type will render with software rendering. This offers a different kind of effect than hardware rendered particles.

- Play back the animation to about frame 55 and stop to see the particle display.

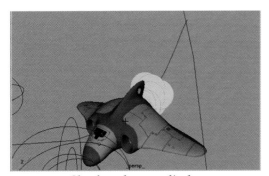

Cloud render type display

2 Add render attributes

Render attributes can be added to the node to help you set up the look of the particles.

- In the **Render Attributes** section, next to **Add Attributes for**, click on the **Current Render Type** button.

This adds new attributes to the node.

- Set the following:

  Radius to **0.6**.

3 Map the particle color

You now want to map the particle with a particle shading group. This will let you define the rendered look of the particles.

- In the Hypershade, select **Create** → **Volumetric Materials** → **Particle Cloud.**

- Rename the Material node *polyThrusterCloud.*

- Open the Attribute Editor for *polyThrusterCloud.*

- Press the **Map** button next to **Life Color.**

  By using the **Life Color** instead of **Color**, it will be connected directly with the lifespan attribute.

- Click on **Ramp.**

- In the Hypershade, highlight the ramp node to see it in the Attribute Editor.

- Delete the color in the middle of the ramp.

- Set the following for the color at the top of the ramp:

  Selected Position to **0.4**;

  Color(HSV) to **240, 0.97, 0.8**.

- Set the following for the color at the bottom of the ramp:

  Selected Position to **0.06**;

  Color(HSV) to **0, 0, 1**.

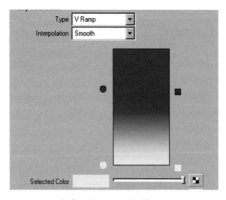

Color Ramp attributes

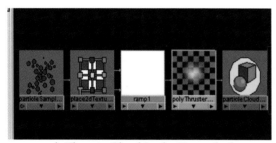

polyThrusterCloud in the Hypershade

4 Make the particles fade out

You will now add transparency to the particles. As they get older, they will become more transparent.

- Open the Attribute Editor for *polyThrusterCloud*.

- Press the **Map** button next to **Life Transparency**.

- Click on **Ramp**.

- In the Hypershade, highlight the new ramp node to see it in the Attribute Editor.

- Delete the color in the middle of the ramp.

- Set the following for the color at the top of the ramp:

  Selected Position to **0.5**;

  Color(HSV) to **0.0, 0.0, 1.0**.

- Set the following for the color at the bottom of the ramp:

  Selected Position to **0.0**;

  Color(HSV) to **0.0, 0.0, 0.0**.

The ramp is now fading from black at the bottom to white at the top.

5 Assign the shading group

- **Select** the particles in the view panels.

- In the Hypershade, click with **RMB** over the *polyThrusterCloud* node, select **Assign Material To Selection**.

The particles turn green to indicate that a shading group has been applied.

6 Test render the particles

- Use **Render** → **Render Region** to test render the particles coming out of the ship.

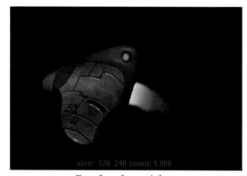

Rendered particles

Particle smoke

The next effect is going to be particle smoke that will be emitted from the polyShip's wing after being grazed by the explosion. This will be created in a similar manner to the last section, except that now you must set the particles to start emitting after frame 63.

1 Create the emitter

- Select **Particles** → **Create Emitter.**

2 Parent the emitter

Again the emitter must be parented to the ship in order to move with it.

- **Parent** the emitter to the polyShip.

- **Move** the emitter in local space to an area where your laser fire hits the ship.

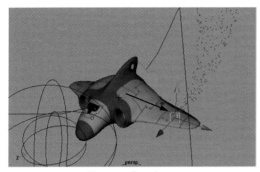

Parented emitter

3 Set keys on the emission

You will now set keys on the rate of emission so that the emitter starts with no particles, then starts up after frame 63.

- Go to frame **63**.

- In the Channel box, set the **Rate** to **0**.

- Use your right mouse button to select **Key Selected** for the **Rate**.

- Go to frame **70**.

- Set the **Rate** to **100**.

- Set another key.

    Now the particles will begin emitting right after the explosion.

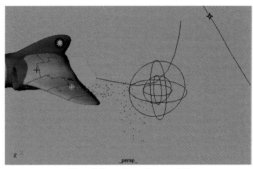

Particles after frame 70

4 Set the particle attributes

You will again use a cloud Render Type. The steps will be almost identical to the thruster particle set-up.

- Select the particles and open the Attribute Editor.

- Set the **Lifespan Mode** to **Constant**.

    This will unlock the Lifespan attribute.

- Set the **Lifespan** to **0.75**.

- Set the **Particle Render Type** to **Cloud(s/w)** then click **Current Render Type** and set the attributes as follows:

    Radius to **0.25**;

    Threshold to **0.75**.

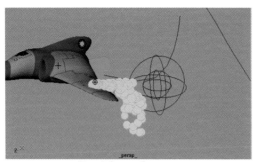

Particle render type

5 Create material for particles

- In the Hypershade, select **Create** → **Volumetric Materials** → **Particle Cloud.**

- Open the Attribute Editor for the Particle Cloud.

- Map a **Ramp** to the **Life Color**.

- Set the ramp colors to be white at the bottom to grey at the top.

- Map a **Solid Fractal** to the **Blob Map**.

- Assign the Material to the smoke particles.

6 Test render the particles

- Use **Render** → **Render Region** to test the particles at around frame 90.

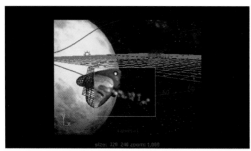

Rendered particles

RENDERING

You are now going to batch render the scene to preview the results. You are going to create a very low quality test of this animation, in order to test all of the cool effects you have integrated into the scene.

It is always a good idea to preview a low resolution/low quality test before committing to a longer rendering. While still image tests may offer you some idea of how the scene may appear, it is always best to see if the sequence animated properly.

Setting the Render Globals

You have already used the Render Globals window to set up some test renderings. This window is where you make your final decisions before sending a rendered animation off to the batch renderer.

1 Open the Render Globals window

- Select **Window** → **Rendering Editors** → **Render Globals...**

2 Set the Image File Outputs

- Set **Frame/Animation Ext** to **name.ext.#**.

- Set the **Start Frame** to **1**, and the **End Frame** to **120**.

- Turn **Alpha Channel (Mask)** to **off**.

- Set **Camera** to **camera1**.

3 Set the Anti-Alias Quality

- Click the **Maya Software** tab.

- Set the **Quality** to **Preview Quality**.

4 Set the size

- Open the **Resolution** Section.

- Set the **Presets** to **320x240**.

5 Set up the Camera

- Change your perspective view to be the *Camera1* view.

- Run through the sequence to check framing and reposition the camera if necessary.

6 Save your work

- Select **File** → **Save Scene As**. Enter the name *spaceSceneComplete* and press **Save**.

7 Batch render the scene

- Select **Render** → **Batch Render**.

  Refer to the Feedback line in the lower right to follow the progress of the rendering.

8 Previewing the animation

Once you have completed the animation, you can view your work as a Playblast animation or by using *fcheck*.

If you are happy with the results, then you can do a final render at a higher quality.

Movie Player preview

The final rendering

While there is no need to create a final high quality rendering of this lesson, it is worthwhile to think about some options:

1 Rendering the whole scene

The first option is to create a finished animation of the whole scene with all of the parts working together. This seems at first to be the easiest solution because it means you would render just once to get the final result.

2 Rendering the scene in layers

The other option is to render each part of the scene separately. These different render *passes* can later be composited. For this lesson, you might render the following layers:

- background space scene
- nurbShip
- polyShip
- photon laser
- explosion OptiF/X
- nurbShip thruster OptiF/X
- smoke particles
- polyShip thruster particles

In the layer's window there is a drop down menu where you have the option to also create *Render Layers*. You can assign objects to render layers in the same fashion as display layers. In the Render Globals window there is a section called Render Layer/Pass Control where you can choose to render each layer separately.

These passes put each key object onto their own layer when you composite. You also avoid rendering the scene with an image plane background which is more easily accomplished in a compositing package.

Now, if changes are to be made to one of the elements – say, a texture map to be modified for one of the ships, or one of the glows to be intensified – then only that layer has to be updated. Also, color corrections can be made to each layer if desired.

To render the OptiF/X and particle layers, you may need to apply a special **Use Background** material so that the mask is more accurate. Refer to the *Using Maya: Rendering* guide to find out more about this shading group type.

Resetting the move tool

Earlier you changed the Move tool options to Local. You should change it back to Global to make sure that upcoming lessons work properly.

1   Change the Move tool options to world

- Double-click on the **Move** tool icon or select **Modify** → **Transformation Tools** → **Move -** ❐ and set the following option:

    Move to **World**.

Conclusion

You have now touched on the visual effects offered by Maya's OptiF/X features, while comparing these to Maya F/X's particle effects.

In the next lesson, you will create a walking biped character called Primitive Man.

PROJECT
FOUR

Project Four

In this project, you are going to model, texture and animate a walking character – Primitive Man. This character will be built using skeleton joints that are controlled using IK solver handles. Expressions and constraints will then be used to create a rolling foot motion.

The surfaces of this character will be built using primitive shapes. These surfaces will then be bound into the skeleton. Character deformers known as *flexors*, and *influence objects* will then be added to control the bending of the knee and elbow, and the bulging of the upper arm.

Finally, Nonlinear Animation techniques using the Trax Editor will provide a way to layer and mix character animation sequences to achieve an animation of Primitive Man walking then climbing a set of stairs.

1. The camera follows as Primitive Man walks in his primitive world.

2. He decides to climb a set of stairs.

3. He briefly looks over his right shoulder on the way up.

4. Satisfied, Primitive Man climbs on with confidence.

In this lesson, you will build a character out of skeleton joints and primitive shapes. The character's motion will be established using IK chains on the arms and legs while Set Driven Key will be used to create a rolling foot hierarchy.

Primitive Man

You will then bind the primitives into the skeleton in order to get skeletal deformations. In cases where the surface is not suited for being bound directly, you will apply a *lattice* and bind the lattice instead. You will then use joint and bone *flexors* and *influence objects* to further refine the surface deformations.

In this lesson you will learn the following:

- How to create skeleton joints with IK handles
- How to create a rolling foot hierarchy
- How to bind surfaces and lattices into skeleton joints
- How to edit the membership of a cluster set
- How to use flexors and influence objects
- How to use influence objects to bulge a surface

Initial set-up

You will now create a new project then create the files from scratch.

1 Create a new project

- Select **File → Project → Set...**
- From the *learningMaya* directory, set the name to *projectFour*.
- Click **OK**.

2 Set up a four view panel layout

- Select **File → New Scene**.
- Set up a four view panel layout that shows the three orthographic views and a Perspective view.

BUILDING A CHARACTER

Building a character usually involves building the character's surfaces, drawing skeleton joints to match the surfaces. The surfaces are then bound to the skeleton and deformations are applied.

For this lesson, you will build the skeleton first, then build surfaces to suit. This will let you explore skeletal issues before worrying about the surfaces.

Drawing a skeleton leg

You will start by creating the joints for the skeleton's legs. Later you will add IK handles and constraints to set up a foot that rotates from heel to toe during walk cycles.

1 Draw the leg joints

- Go to the **Animation** menu set.
- In the Front view, track the view to place the X-axis line at the bottom of the panel.

- Select **Skeleton → Joint Tool - ❐**.
- In the option window, set the following:

    Auto Joint Orient to **None**.

This setting makes sure that the joints constrain properly when you create the foot set-up.

- In the Front view, press the **x** key to use grid snapping, then click three times to place the following leg joints:

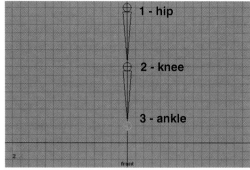

Skeleton leg joints

- Now click two more times using grid snapping to place the following foot joints:

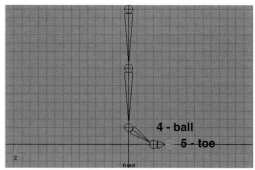

Skeleton foot joints

- Press the **Enter** key to accept the joints.

2 Rename the joints

- Open a Hypergraph view panel.
- Dolly and track to see the new joints.
- Rename the joints as shown below. Use the names as labelled in the last two diagrams:

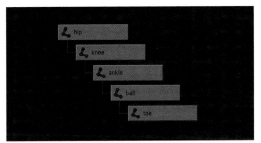

Renamed joints

Note: In this skeleton, the heel joint has been left out. You will add the heel later using a second skeleton hierarchy that will be used to control the foot.

Create a Reverse foot skeleton

When you animate a walking character, you need the character's feet to plant themselves while the other foot is lifted into position. In the time it is planted, the foot needs to roll from the heel to the toe. A Reverse Foot skeleton is the ideal technique for creating these conditions.

1 Draw the reverse foot joints

- Dolly into the area around the foot.
- Select the **Joint Tool** and starting with the heel, draw four joints using

grid snap as shown in the following diagram:

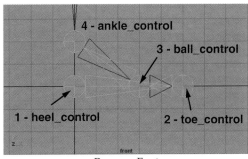

Reverse Foot

- Press the **Enter** key to accept the joints.

2 Rename the joints

- In the Hypergraph, rename the joints as shown below:

Renamed joints

Adding an IK handle to the leg

To control the leg, you will need an IK handle running from the hip to the ankle. This will be used to control the motion of the leg.

1 Prepare the leg for the handle

To correctly apply an IK handle to the joints, you need to slightly rotate the knee then set a preferred angle.

- **Select** the *knee* joint by selecting the bone just below the knee.

- **Rotate** the knee back by about 10 degrees.

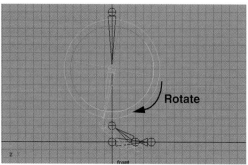

Knee joint rotated

2 Set the joint chain's preferred angle

- **Select** the *hip* joint.

- Select **Skeleton → Set Preferred Angle**.

  This will give the IK handle a starting rotation that will be used as the target rotation by the IK solver.

3 Draw the IK chain

- Select **Skeleton → IK Handle Tool**.

- Click on the *hip* joint.

- Click on the *ankle* joint to create an IK chain.

  This chain uses a *rotate plane* IK solver which offers more control than the single chain solver.

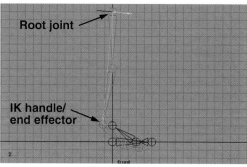

First IK chain

In the Hypergraph, you can see the end effector connected into the hierarchy and the IK handle to the side. The end effector and the IK handle are connected along with the appropriate joints at the dependency node level. When you control the handle, you control the whole IK chain.

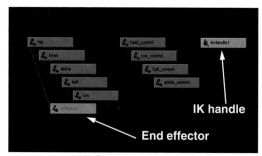

Nodes in Hypergraph

4 Move the IK handles

- **Select** the IK handle.

- **Move** the handle to move the foot.

  You can see that the foot moves while the hip stays in place. You can also see that the foot is rotating a little around the Z axis instead of staying straight.

- Place the IK handle just up and to the right of the reverse foot chain.

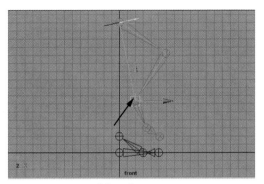
Moved group

Creating a Reverse Foot

To offer better control for the foot and a proper heel to toe rotation, you will now constrain the IK handle, the *ball* and *ankle* joints, to the reverse foot chain. This will allow you to use the reverse foot chain to control the foot and the leg.

1 Point Constrain the IK handle

- **Select** the *ankle_control* joint on the reverse foot chain.
- Press the **Shift** key and **Select** the IK handle.
- Select **Constrain → Point**.

  Now the IK handle is positioned over the reverse foot's *ankle_control* joint.

Tip: You may want to use the Hypergraph panel to help you select the joints.

---

2 Test the reverse foot chain

- **Select** the *heel_control* joint.

- **Move** the joint to test the foot.

  The ankle moves with the reverse foot chain but the joints are not properly aligned.

3 Orient Constrain the ball joint

To align the rest of the foot, you will orient constrain the ball joint to the reverse foot.

- Select the *toe_control* joint on the reverse foot chain.
- Press the **Shift** key and **Select** the *ball* joint from the leg chain.
- Select **Constrain → Orient**.

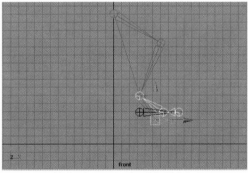
Orient constrained ball joint

4 Orient Constrain the ankle joint

You will now repeat these steps for the ankle joint.

- Select the *ball_control* joint on the reverse foot chain.
- Press the **Shift** key and **Select** the *ankle* joint from the leg chain.
- Select **Constrain → Orient**.

  Now the foot joints and the reverse foot joints are aligned.

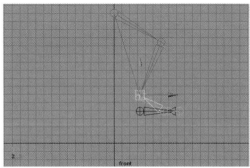

Orient constrained ankle joint

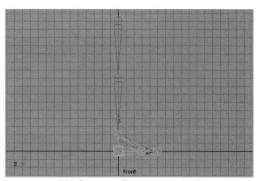

Heel_control joint at origin

5 Test the movement of the reverse foot

- Select the *heel_control* joint.

- **Move** the joint to test the motion.

  If you pull the reverse foot further than the leg chain will allow, the leg will pull away from the reverse foot. This is the desired effect.

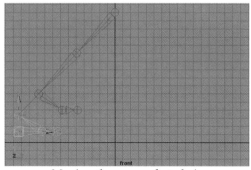

Moving the reverse foot chain

- **Move** the heel_control joint back to the origin.

Creating the Heel to Toe Motion

You could now control the rotation of the foot by rotating the various control joints on the reverse foot. Instead of requiring the rotation of several joints to achieve a heel to toe motion, you will use **Set Driven Key** to control the roll using a single attribute on the *heel_control* joint.

1 Add a Roll attribute

- **Select** the *heel_control* joint.

- Select **Modify** → **Add Attribute**.

- Set the following values in the **Add Attribute** window:

  Attribute Name to **roll**;

  Data Type to **Float**;

  Minimum to **-5**;

  Maximum to **10**;

  Default to **0**.

- Click **OK** to add the attribute.

  You can now see this attribute in the Channel box. The minimum and maximum values give reasonable boundary values for the roll.

- **De-select** the skeleton.

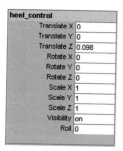

Channel box settings

2 Prepare the Set Driven Key window

- Select **Animate** → **Set Driven Key** → **Set - ❑**.

- **Select** the *heel_control* joint and click **Load Driver** in the **Set Driven Key** window. This loads the heel_control attributes into the upper section of the window.

- **Select** the *heel_control, ball_control and toe_control* joints and click **Load Driven** in the **Set Driven Key** window. This loads these joints into the lower section of the window.

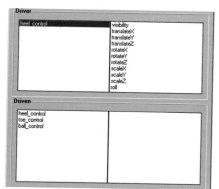

Set Driven Key window

3 Key the Heel rotation

- In the upper section of the **Set Driven Key** window, click on the *roll* attribute to highlight it.

- In the lower section, click on *heel_control* then on *rotateZ*.

- Click on the **Key** button to set the starting rotation.

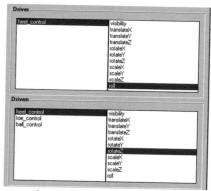

Set Driven Key window

- In the channel box, set the **Roll** value to **-5**.

- Set the **Rotate Z** to **20**.

- Again, click on the **Key** button.

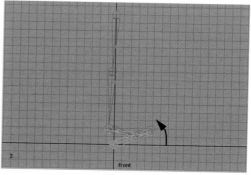

Foot rotated back on heel

- You can now test the roll attribute by clicking on its name in the Channel box then clicking with your middle mouse button in the modeling panels. You can see that the foot rolls from the heel to a flat position.

- When you are finished, set the **roll** attribute to **0**.

4 Key the Ball Rotation

- In the lower section of the **Set Driven Key** window, click on *ball_control* then on *rotateZ*.

- Click on the **Key** button to set the starting rotation.

- Click on *heel_control* and set the **Roll** value to **10**.

- Click on *ball_control* and set the **Rotate Z** to **-30**.

- Again, click on the **Key** button in the Set Driven Key window.

- Click on *heel_control* and set the **Roll** value back to **0**.

Tip: When working with Set Driven key, always set the value of the driver before setting the driven. If you set the driver second, then it will reset your driven value because of earlier keys.

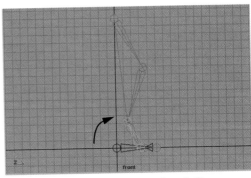

Foot rotated forward on ball

5 Key the Toe rotation

- In the lower section of the **Set Driven Key** window, click on *toe_control* then on *rotateZ*.

- Click on the **Key** button to set the starting rotation.

- Click on *heel_control* and set the **Roll** value to **10**.

- Click on *toe_control* and set the **Rotate Z** to **-30**.

- Again, click on the **Key** button.

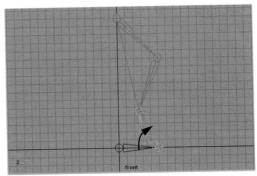

Foot rotated forward on toe

6 Test the foot roll

- Select the *heel_control* joint.

- Click on the roll attribute name in the Channel box then click-drag with your middle mouse button in the front view panel to test the roll.

- When you are finished, set the **Roll** back to **0**.

Creating geometry

The purpose of creating skeleton joints is to drive the movement of geometry that you can either group or bind to the joints. You will now create a half-sphere to use as the foot and a cylinder to use as the leg.

1 Create the foot using a half-sphere

- Go to the **Modeling** menu set.

- Select **Create → NURBS Primitives → Sphere**.

- In the Channel box, name this surface *rightFoot*.

- In the Channel box, set the following attributes for the sphere's transform nodes:

    Rotate Y to **90**;

    Rotate Z to **90**.

- Click on the *makeNurbSphere* input node and set the following:

    End Sweep to **180**;

    Spans to **12**.

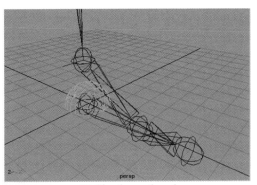

Half-sphere placed

2 Scale the foot

- **Scale** the sphere along the Z axis until it covers the ankle area.

    You will notice that the Z axis is pointing up now that the sphere has been rotated.

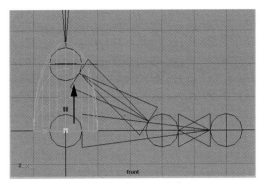

Half-sphere scaled

3 Reshape the CVs

- Press **F8** to go into component select mode.

- In the *Front* view, **select** the CVs on the right half of the sphere.

- Press the **Insert / Home** key to go into edit mode.

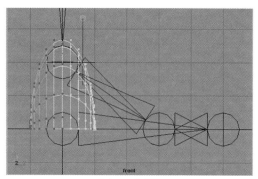

Selected CVs

- Press the **x** key to temporarily turn on grid snap and drag the pivot handle to the origin.

- Press the **Insert / Home** key to go back to the **Scale** tool.

- **Scale** the CVs out to cover the toe and down to form the top of the foot.

- Press **F8** to go back to object mode.

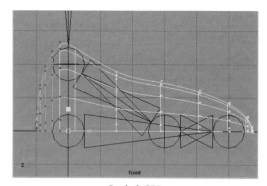

Scaled CVs

4 Create the leg using a cylinder

- Select **Create → NURBS Primitives → Cylinder**.

- In the Channel box, rename this surface to *rightLeg*.

- **Scale** and **Move** the cylinder until it covers the leg joints of the skeleton.

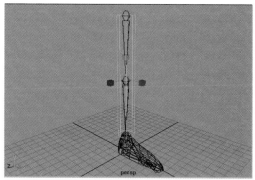

Cylinder covering leg joints

5 Select isoparms on the cylinder

This cylinder is not complex enough to bend properly when you bind it later. You are now going to add sections using the cylinder's input node.

- Click on the cylinder's *makeNurbCylinder* input node in the Channel box.

- Set the number of **Spans** to **7**.

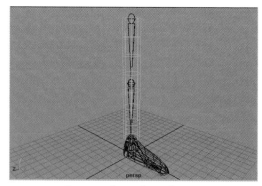

Increased number of spans

6 Delete history

You are now going to delete history on the two primitives. This will remove the input nodes before you bind the surface.

- **Select** the half-sphere and the cylinder.
- Select **Edit** → **Delete by Type** → **History**.

Binding the geometry

To get the surfaces to deform properly, you must bind them to the skeletons. In the case of the sphere, you will apply a lattice and use that object to bind to the joints. You can bind many different object types to skeletons.

1 Add a lattice to the foot

To get nice deformations in the foot, you will use a lattice.

- **Select** the half-sphere surface called *rightFoot*.
- Go to the **Animation** menu set.
- Select **Deform** → **Create Lattice**.
- In the Channel box, set the following shape node attributes:

  S Divisions to **2**;

  T Divisions to **5**;

  U Divisions to **3**.

The lattice is now oriented along the length of the foot. There are now enough lattice points to bind nicely to the skeleton.

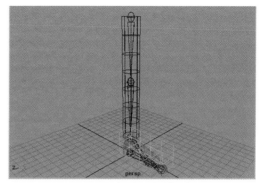

Lattice applied to half-sphere

2 Bind the cylinder and the lattice

- **Select** the lattice and the cylinder.
- Press the **Shift** key and select the leg skeleton's *hip* joint node.
- Select **Skin** → **Bind Skin** → **Rigid Bind** - ❐ and set the following option:

  Color Joint to **On**.

- Click **Bind Skin**.

  The joints and bones are now colored differently. This helps you later when you check the membership of CV and lattice points to the bind sets.

3 Test the results

- **Activate** the Front pane and press **5** to smooth shade that view.
- **Select** the two surfaces and press **3** to increase the surface smoothness.
- **Select** the *heel_control* node.
- **Move** the group to see the effect on the surfaces then adjust the heel_control's roll node to bend the foot.

PROJECT FOUR

The cuff of the leg surface is bending with the ankle and the inside of the knee is pinching. You will need to fix both of these deformation artifacts to create more satisfactory results.

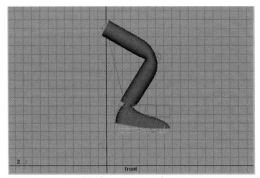

Deforming surfaces

Editing the sets

When you bound the lattice and the cylinder to the joints, sets were created. One set is created for every bound joint. As you move and rotate joints, the sets react accordingly.

In the case of the back of the foot surface, some of the CVs on the leg are associating themselves with the *ankle* joint instead of the *knee* joint. You will now move these CVs to the *knee* joint set to get the expected results.

1 Edit the set membership on the foot

- With the knee in the bent position, **select** the *knee* joint.

- Select **Deform → Edit Membership Tool**. This displays CVs and Lattice points that are associated with the *knee*. Other points on the cylinder and the lattice are displayed with other colors that match the coloring

placed on the skeleton by the bind tool.

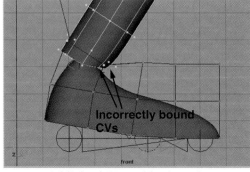

Highlighted CV and lattice points

- Press the **Shift** key and with the left mouse button, **Select** the CVs that make up the leg's cuff.

Once you select the CVs using this method, they become part of the *knee* joint set and are removed from the *ankle* joint set.

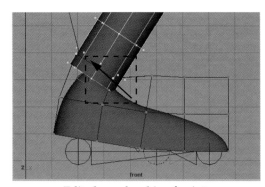

Edited membership of points

2 Test the results

- **Select** the *heel_control* joint.

- **Move** the reverse foot chain to see how the foot reacts now.

- When you are finished, **Move** the chain back to the origin and set the **Roll** attribute back to **0**.

Adding a flexor

The other problem you encountered with the deformations was with the pinching of the knee. You can fix this using a lattice flexor.

A flexor is a deformer that is automatically bound into a joint hierarchy while being applied to the associated surface.

1   Add a flexor to the knee

- **Select** the *knee* joint.
- Select **Skin → Edit Rigid Skin → Create Flexor...**
- In the Create Flexor window, set the following:

    Flexor Type to **lattice**;

    Joints to **At Selected Joints**.

- Click **Create** then **Close**.

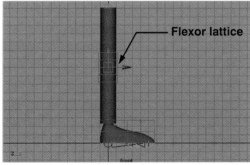

Flexor on knee

2   Test the motion

- **Select** the *heel_control* joint.
- **Move** the group to see how the foot reacts now.

You are getting a more subtle effect on the inner side of the knee while the outer part of the knee becomes more rounded.

- Adjust the **Roll** attribute to see how the foot reacts.

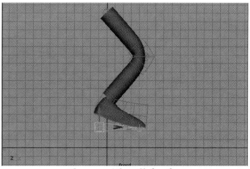

Flexor with roll for foot

- **Move** the reverse foot back to the origin and set the **Roll** attribute to **0**.

Creating the second leg

You will now create a second leg by duplicating all of the existing hierarchies and their connections. This will give you a second deforming leg.

1   Rename the root nodes

Since this leg will be the right leg, you will rename the root nodes of the two joint chains. Since the other joints are below the root joint, they don't have to be renamed.

- **Select** the *hip* joint of the skeleton.
- Rename it *rhip*.
- **Select** the *heel_control* joint of the skeleton.
- Rename it *rfoot* since it will be used to control all the motion of the foot.

PROJECT FOUR

2 Move the first leg

You will move the *rhip* joint and the foot group to one side of the XY plane.

- **Select** the *rhip* joint of the skeleton.
- Press the **Shift** key and **select** the *rfoot* node.
- **Move** these two to the character's right side by 3 units.

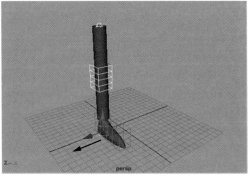

Leg moved to the right side

3 Duplicate the first leg

- In the Hypergraph, **select** all of the pieces built so far.

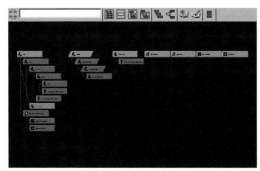

Selected hierarchies

- Select **Edit → Duplicate - ❏** and set **Duplicate Input Graph** to **On**.
- Click **Duplicate**.

- **Move** the new group by selecting the duplicated *rhip1* and *rfoot1* to the character's left side by 3 units.

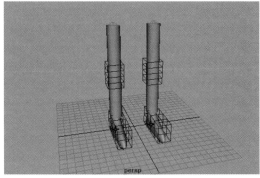

Second leg moved to the left

4 Rename the root nodes

- Rename *rhip1* to *lhip*
- Rename *rfoot1* to *lfoot*.

5 Test the motion on the left leg

- **Select** the *lfoot* joint.
- **Move** the joint chain and edit the **Roll** attribute to test the leg construction.

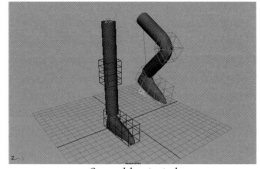

Second leg tested

- **Move** the *lfoot* joint to the starting position and set its **Roll** attribute to **0**.

Create the torso and head

To create the character's head and torso, you will start with a hierarchy of joints that will be used to attach a cube for the body and a sphere for the head. In this case, you will not use any IK chains to control the character. Joint rotations will offer sufficient control for the character's spine.

1 Draw the spine joints

- Select **Skeleton** → **Joint Tool - ❏.**

- In the option window, Click on the **Reset Tool** button then click on **Close.**

- In the Front view, press the **x** key to use grid snapping, then place 5 joints as shown below. Press **Enter.**

- When you finish, rename the joints as labelled:

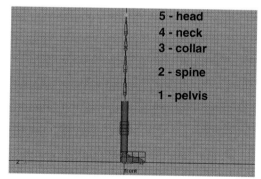

5 - head
4 - neck
3 - collar
2 - spine
1 - pelvis

Spine joints

2 Create a head and a body

- Create a Nurbs primitive sphere for the character's head and a Nurbs primitive **Cube** for the body.

- **Scale** and **Move** these pieces to suit your joints.

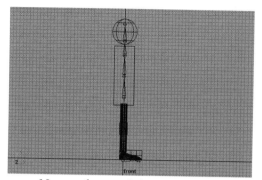

New surfaces scaled and positioned

These surfaces should be positioned as shown below.

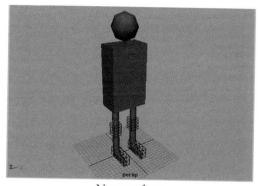

New surfaces

- **Select** the surfaces and press the **3** key to increase their surface smoothness.

- Select **Edit** → **Delete by Type** → **History**.

3 Place a lattice on the cube

- **Select** the cube. In object mode, you will pick one of the cube's faces.

- Press the **up arrow** to go to the root *nurbsCube* node.

- Select **Deform** → **Create Lattice**.

PROJECT FOUR

4 Bind the lattice and the sphere

- With the lattice already selected, press the **Shift** key and **select** the head sphere.

- Press the **Shift** key and select the root node of the spine skeleton.

- Select **Skin** → **Bind Skin** → **Rigid Bind**.

5 Test the binding

- Select one of the middle nodes of the spine skeleton.

- **Rotate** to test the quality of the bound surfaces.

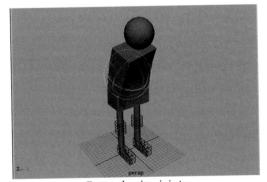

Rotated spine joints

- When you are finished, **Rotate** the joint back to 0 in all three directions.

6 Connecting the legs to the body

- From the *persp* view panel, select **Show** → **NURBS Surfaces**. This turns off the display of NURBS surfaces in this panel.

- Select the *rhip* joint.

- Press the **Shift** key and select the *pelvis* joint of the spine skeleton.

- Select **Skeleton** → **Connect Joint** - ❐ and set **Mode** to **Parent Joint**.

- Click **Connect**.

- Repeat for the *lhip*.

  Now the legs are connected to the spine chain.

- From the *persp* view panel, select **Show** → **NURBS Surfaces** to turn on the display of surfaces in this panel.

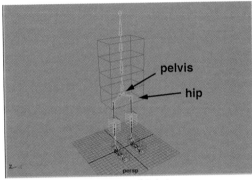

Connected joints

Building arms

You will now build arms for your character. The arms will be built out of cylinders. This time rather than using a Rigid Bind with a flexor, you will set up a Smooth Bind then use an influence object to create the bulging of the arm.

1 Create skeleton joints

- Select **Skeleton** → **Joint Tool** → ❐.

- Make sure **Joint Orient** is set to **None**.

- In the Side view, place 3 joints off to the side as shown below. Press **Enter**. Rename the joints as labelled:

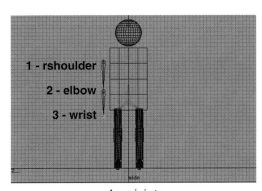

Arm joints

2 Set the preferred angle

- In the Front view, rotate the *elbow* joint forward to put a slight bend in the arm.

- **Select** the *rshoulder* joint.

- Select **Skeleton** → **Set Preferred Angle**.

3 Add an IK chain

- Select **Skeleton** → **IK Handle Tool**.

- Click on the *rshoulder* joint.

- Click on the *wrist* joint to create an IK chain.

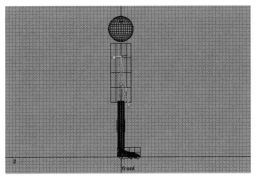

Arm IK chain

4 Move the arm into place

- **Select** the arm's IK handle.

- Rename the IK handle *rArm*.

- **Move** it down to straighten the arm.

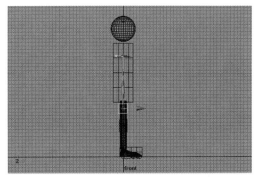

Positioned arm

5 Create a cylindrical surface

- Select **Create** → **NURBS Primitives** → **Cylinder**.

- In the Channel box, rename this surface to *rightArm*.

- **Scale** and **Move** the Cylinder until it covers the arm joints of the skeleton.

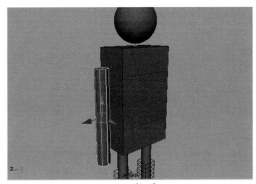

Arm cylinder

6 Add isoparm spans

- Select the *makeNurbCylinder* input node in the Channel box.
- Set the number of **Spans** to **8**.
- Select **Edit** → **Delete by Type** → **History**.

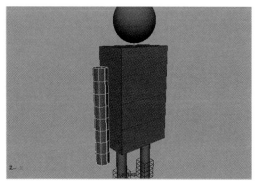

Inserting isoparms

7 Bind the surface

- With the cylinder already selected, press the **Shift** key and **select** the *rshoulder* joint.
- Select **Skin** → **Bind Skin** → **Smooth Bind**.

  This binding method weights the CVs in a way that produces smoother results than a Rigid Bind without requiring flexors.

8 Test the motion

- Select *rArm* IK Handle.
- Select the **Move** tool.
- In the Perspective view, press the **Ctrl** key and click on the Z-axis handle.

Now the middle manipulator is constrained to move only along the X- and Y-axis plane.

- **Click-drag** on the center manipulator to test the arm.

Tip: You may want to select the arm surface and press **3** to increase the display smoothness.

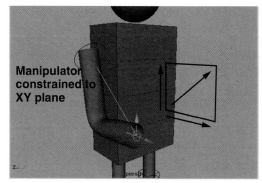

Testing the motion

- When you are finished, return the arm to the character's side.

Building a Bulging Bicep

You will now use a half sphere as an influence object for the arm surface. By connecting the scaling of the sphere to the rotation of the elbow joint, you can create a bulging bicep.

1 Hide the existing surfaces

- Create a new **Layer**.
- Name it *body_layer*.
- Use your pick masks to help you select all of the surfaces and lattices without selecting any joints or handles.

- Right-click on the *body_layer* and select **Add Selected Objects**.
- Click on the V in the *body_layer* to hide the surfaces and lattices.

  This will make it easier to set up the half sphere before assigning it as an influence object.

2 Create and position a half sphere

- Select **Create → NURBS Primitives → Sphere**.
- Rename the sphere to *muscle*.
- **Select** the *makeNurbSphere* node and set the following:

  Start Sweep to **-90**;

  End Sweep to **90**.

- **Move** the *muscle* sphere until it lies in the center of the upper arm.

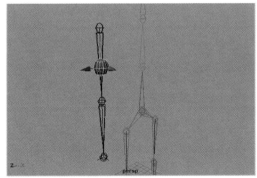

Half Sphere in position

- **Scale** the sphere along the Y axis until it is around the same length as the upper arm.

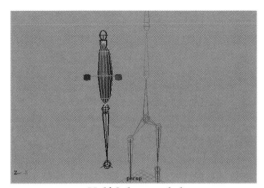

Half Sphere scaled

3 Parent the muscle to the shoulder

- In a Hypergraph panel, click on the *muscle* node with your middle mouse button and drag it onto the *rshoulder* node.

  Now the muscle will move when the shoulder is rotated.

4 Set Driven Key

You will now drive the shape of the *muscle* sphere with the rotation of the *elbow* joint.

- Select **Animate → Set Driven Key → Set - ❑**.
- Click on **Load Driven** to load the sphere.
- Click on the muscle in the left hand column then on **scale X** in the right column.

  This is the attribute that you want to drive.

- **Select** the *elbow* joint.

Note: You may have to adjust your selection masks to allow you to select joints.

- In the Set Driven Key window, click on **Load Driver**.

- Click on **rotate Z** in the right column, and click the **Key** button.

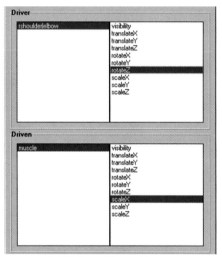

Set Driven Key options

Now the current rotation setting for the *elbow* is linked to the current scaling of the *muscle* object.

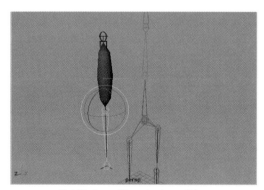

Set Driven Key start position

5 Set a second key

- **Select** the hand's IK handle.

- **Move** the handle to raise the arm until the *elbow* joint is rotated.

- Select the *muscle* node.

- **Scale** it out along the X-axis.

- Click on **Key** button.

  This sets the finish position for the Set Driven Key.

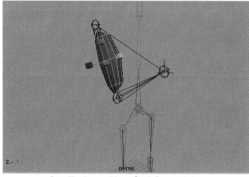

Set Driven Key finish position

- Close the Set Driven Key window.

6 Test the results

- **Select** the hand's IK handle.

- **Move** the handle to watch the muscle bulge.

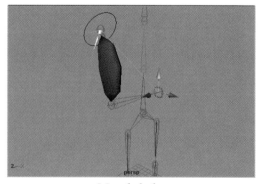

Muscle bulge

7 Add the muscle as an influence object

You now want this surface to deform the arm surface to create the bulge.

- **Select** the *rshoulder* joint.

- Select **Skin → Go to Bind Pose**.

  This rotates your joints back to their position at the point the arm surface was bound to the skeleton.

- Select **Visible** from the *body_layer* to make it visible.

- Select the *rightArm* surface and then the *muscle* surface.

- Select **Skin → Edit Smooth Skin → Add Influence**.

8 Test the Results

- **Select** and **hide** the muscle surface.

- **Select** the hand's IK handle.

- **Move** the handle to raise the arm until the *elbow* joint is rotated.

- You can now see the arm bulging based on the motion of the muscle's influence.

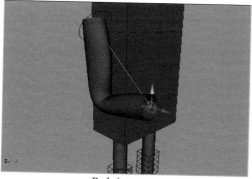

Bulging arm

Duplicate the arm

Now just like the leg, you will need to duplicate the arm, the IK handle, the surface, and any connected nodes.

1 Select the parts

- In the Hypergraph, **Select** the root of the arm skeleton chain, the *rightArm* surface and their associated IK handle.

Selected nodes

2 Duplicate

- Select **Edit → Duplicate - ❑** and make sure that **Duplicate Input Graph** is set to **On**.

- Click **Duplicate**.

- **Move** the new group to the character's left side.

- Rename the *rshoulder1* node to *lshoulder* and *rightArm1* to *leftArm*. and the *rArm1* IK handle to *lArm*.

PROJECT FOUR

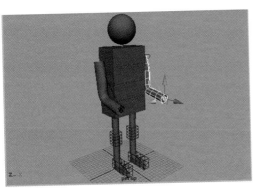

Duplicated arm

3 Connect the joints

- **Select** the *rshoulder* joint.

- Press the **Shift** key and select the
  collar joint of the spine skeleton.

- Select **Skeleton** → **Connect Joint** - ❑
  and set **Mode** to **Parent Joint**.

- Click **Apply.**

- Repeat for the left arm.

  Now the arms are connected to the
  spine chain.

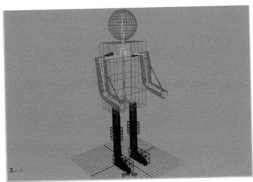

Connected joints

4 Save your work

Conclusion

You now have the basic setup for animating
Primitive Man with a sophisticated foot roll
setup. The next lesson will teach you how to
add further controls using expressions,
selection handles, and Pole Vector constraints.

17 **Character Controls**

In this lesson, you will prepare controls that will make it easier to animate Primitive Man. These controls will allow you to work with a few key character nodes instead of switching back and forth between many joints, IK handles and group nodes. You will also use expressions to allow the feet to drive the general position of the pelvis area.

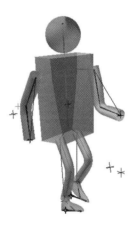

Primitive Man Controls

Eventually, you will build character nodes for Primitive Man that gather important attributes into a single location. The use of character nodes is also a crucial requirement of Maya's non-linear animation system called Trax which you will learn about in the next lesson.

In this lesson you will learn the following:

- How to add selection handles
- How to use expressions to drive the pelvis
- How to work with an IK Rotate Plane controls
- How to set up Pole Vector constraints
- How to create character nodes and sub-character nodes

Selection Handles

Only a few joints and handles will be used to control the skeleton during animation. To make it easier to find and select these nodes, you will add selection handles.

1 Display selection handles

- In Perspective view, select **Show** → **NURBS Surfaces** and **Show** → **Deformers** to turn these off.

- **Select** the *pelvis* joint.

- Select **Display** → **Component Display** → **Selection Handles**.

  It will be colored to match the associated joint and may be hard to find.

- **Select** and **Display** Selection Handles for the following nodes:

  spine joint;

  larm IK handle;

  rarm IK handle;

  lfoot joint

  rfoot joint

2 Edit the handle positions

To make it easier to select the pelvis and spine selection handles, you will move them outside the body.

- Press **F8** to go into component mode.

- **Select** the selection handles pick mask.

- **Move** the pelvis and the spine handles so they are outside and behind the character.

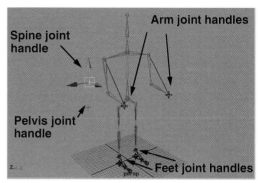

Selection handles labelled

- Press **F8** to go back to object selection mode.

Set up the Pelvis motion

When you begin animating a walk, you will want the pelvis to be positioned about half way between the two feet

1 Lower the pelvis

Select the *pelvis* joint using its selection handle and lower it until Primitive Man's knees are slightly bent.

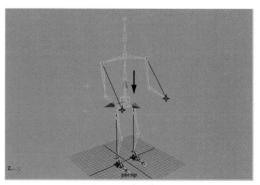

Lowered pelvis

2 Group the pelvis

- Select **Edit** → **Group**.

- Rename the new node to *pelvis_control*.

  This adds a node above the pelvis that has its pivot point at the origin. You can now control this node using expressions while still using the *pelvis* node for secondary motion.

3 Create Expressions

- Click in empty space to deselect everything.

- Select **Window → Animation Editors → Expression Editor**.

- Set the **Expression Name** to *pelvis_expression*.

- In the expression field, enter the following:

```
pelvis_control.tx =
      (rfoot.tx + lfoot.tx)/2;
pelvis_control.ty =
      (rfoot.ty + lfoot.ty)/2;
pelvis_control.tz =
      (rfoot.tz + lfoot.tz)/2;
pelvis_control.ry =
      (rfoot.ry + lfoot.ry)/2;
```

- Click **Create**.

  When writing expressions, you can use an attribute's short name. For instance translateX would be tx. After creating the expression all attributes are recorded using their long name in the editor.

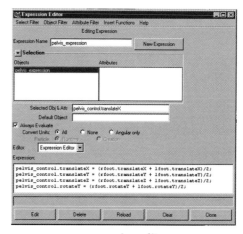

expression editor

4 Move the left foot node

The purpose of the expression was to automate the motion of the pelvis as the feet move.

- **Select** and **Move** the *lfoot* node.

  You can see that the pelvis moves to a point half way between the two feet.

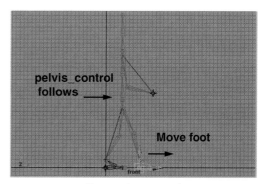

Expression at work

5 Adjust the pelvis node

- **Select** the *pelvis* joint using its selection handle.

- **Move** it down to further bend the knees.

  You can see that the *pelvis* node can be adjusted freely while the *pelvis_control* node works with the expression.

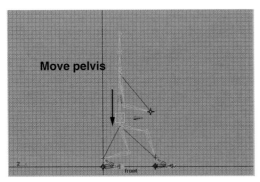

Pelvis node adjustment

6   Rotate the left foot node

- **Move** the *pelvis* node back up.

- **Select** and **Rotate** the *lfoot* node around the Y axis.

  The *pelvis_control* node continues to update as the foot is updated.

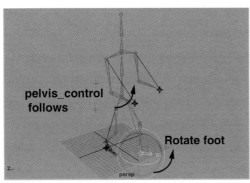

Rotated foot

7   Reset the skeleton

- **Rotate** and **Move** the various nodes back into the starting position.

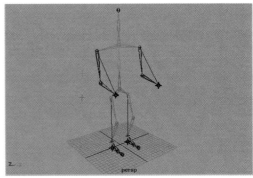

Starting position

The Rotate plane IK solver

When moving the arm IK handles, you will notice that you seem to have limited control over how the elbow moves. Since you created this IK handle using the *rotate plane solver*, you can use manipulator controls to define how the whole arm works.

1   Test the arm motion

- **Select** the *lArm* IK handle.

- **Move** it up along the Y axis, above the shoulder line.

  You will see that the arm flips and you lose control of the elbow.

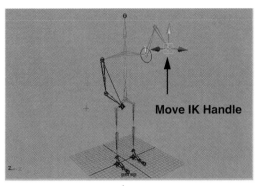

Arm

2 Turn on the Rotate plane manipulators

The rotate plane attributes can be set in the Channel box or you can use the rotate plane manipulators.

- With the *lArm* IK handle selected, select the **Show Manipulator** tool.

- You now get a few manipulator handles to help you control the arm

- Drag the manipulator handle down to adjust the **Pole Vector Axis**.

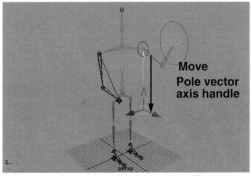

Adjusting Pole Vector Handle

The **Pole Vector Axis** handle lets you manipulate the whole rotate plane. By positioning the handle, you change the orientation of the plane.

When you set up a **Rotate plane IK handle**, the whole length of the chain is controlled by a plane that is defined by the **Pole vector axis handle** which runs between the **Root joint** and the **End effector**, and a secondary vector that is called the **Pole vector**. By default, the IK handle will manipulate the chain so that it works within this plane.

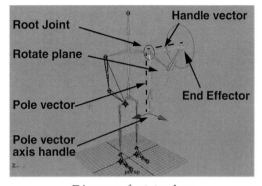

Diagram of rotate plane

3 Adjust the Twist manipulator

- Click-drag on the circular **Twist** manipulator to orient the arm off of the rotate plane.

  The **twist** attribute lets you move the elbows out away from the plane.

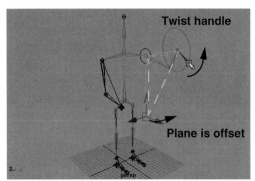

Rotate plane manipulator handles

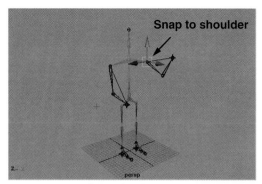

Snapping Locator

- In the channel box, set the *lArm's* **Twist** attribute to **0**. This places the elbow back on the rotate plane.

Pole Vector constraint

You have seen that flipping occurs when the end effector is moved through the rotate plane. To prevent this from happening, you learned how to use the **pole vector axis** handle to move the plane in relation to the End Effector and thereby counter act the flipping.

To avoid having to set keys on the pole vector axis attribute itself, you can create locators that can then act as constraints for the Pole vector. This offers a more visual control for the vector that is easier to control.

1 Create a Locator for the left arm

- Select **Create → Locator**.
- Rename the locator to *lelbow*.
- Press the **v** key to use point snapping and snap **Move** the locator to the left shoulder.

2 Move the locator behind the character

- In the Front view, **Move** the locator behind Primitive man to just under his hip level.

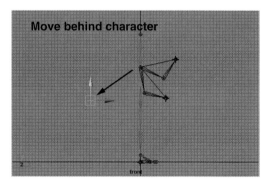

Repositioned Locator

3 Constrain the Pole Vector

- With the *lelbow* locator selected, press the **Shift** key and select the *lArm* IK handle.
- Select **Constrain → Pole Vector**.

  Now the Pole Vector Axis is controlled by the locator.

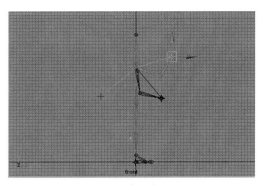

Constrained Pole vector

4 Repeat for the other arm

- Create a **Locator** for the right arm.
- **Move** it into a location that matches the left arm locator
- Constrain the *rArm* handle's pole vector to the new locator.
- When you are finished, rename the second locator to *relbow*.
- Position the two IK handles in front of the body aligned along the Z axis.

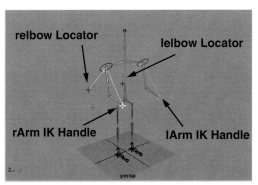

relbow Locator

lelbow Locator

rArm IK Handle

lArm IK Handle

Pole vectors and handles

Parenting to the shoulders

While you want to set keys on the character's feet in world space, arms can be parented into the character to allow for local motion. This means that when the character moves the arms move along with it. Then keys set on the arms would define how the arms move in relation to the body. This technique will work well for a walking character like Primitive man.

1 Parent the right arm

- Make sure the *rArm, lArm, relbow* and *lelbow* nodes are selected.
- Press the **Shift** key and select the *collar* joint.
- Press the **p** key to parent to this joint.

2 Test the Results

- **Select** the *spine* joint using its selection handle.
- **Rotate** the joint to show that the arms and pole vector constraint locators are rotating in the collar's local space.

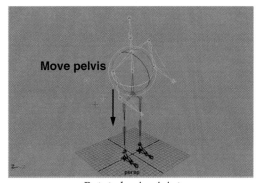

Move pelvis

Rotated spine joint

- **Undo** this rotation or set the **Rotate** values for the *spine* back to 0, 0, 0.

Controlling the Knee

The leg is another area where Pole Vector constraints would be helpful. Right now if you were to rotate the reverse foot controls, the knee would remain pointed forward. Using Locators parented to the reverse foot chains, you can keep the knees pointed in the right direction.

1 Test the knee motion

- **Select** the *pelvis* node.
- **Move** it down to bend the character at the knees.
- **Select** the *lfoot* reverse foot chain.
- **Rotate** it around the Y-axis.

    You can see the problem of the knee still facing forward as you rotate the foot.

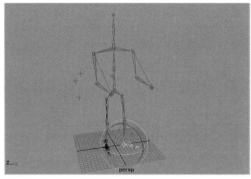

Rotated foot

- **Undo** the rotation until the foot is pointing straight ahead.

2 Add a Locator

- Select **Create → Locator**.
- Rename the locator to *lknee*.

- Press the **v** key to use point snapping and snap **Move** the *lknee* locator to the *knee* joint.
- **Move** the *lknee* locator along the X-axis about **15** units.

    This places the locator in a good position for constraining the **Pole Vector Handle**.

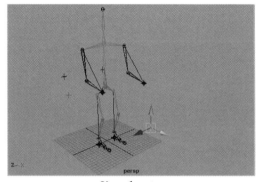

Knee locator

3 Parent the Locator to the foot control

- With the *lknee* locator selected, select **Modify → Freeze Transformations**.
- Press the **Shift** key and **select** the *lfoot* joint.
- Press the **p** key to parent the locator to the foot.

4 Constrain the IK chain's Pole Vector

- With the *lknee* locator selected, press the **Shift** key and **select** the left leg's IK handle.
- Select **Constrain → Pole Vector**.

5 Test the Results

- **Select** the *lfoot* reverse foot chain.

- **Rotate** it around the Y-axis.

You can see that the knee moves with the foot.

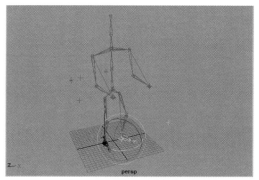

Knee rotating with foot

- **Undo** the rotation until the foot is pointing straight ahead.

Tip: If you want to offset the knee from the foot then you can animate the position of the Locator in relation to the knee.The reason you used Freeze Transformations was to make sure that a value of 0, 0, 0 always places the locator in front of the knee.

---

6 Repeat for the other leg

- Create and position a *rknee* locator.
- Repeat the steps used to set up the *lknee*.

Now you have foot controls that let you drive the motion of the foot, the roll from heel to toe and the rotation of the knee. This will aid in the creation of a walk cycle in the next lesson.

Creating Character nodes

In the next lesson, you will use Non-linear animation techniques to make Primitive Man walk. To make the Trax editor recognize Primitive Man, you must create Character nodes and Sub-character nodes. These nodes let you collect attributes into a single node that can then be keyed and edited as a group.

1 Create a main character node

- Make sure that nothing is selected.
- Select **Character → Create Character Set - ❐**.
- Set the **Name** to *primitiveMan*.
- Click **Create Character Set**.

This character is now active and visible next to the Range slider.

Character menu

2 Select the foot attributes

- Select the *lfoot* and *rfoot* joints nodes.
- In the Channel box, use the **Ctrl / Command** key to highlight the *translate*, *rotate* and *roll* attributes.

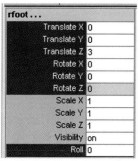

Highlighted channels

3 Create a legs sub character

- Select **Character** → **Create SubCharacter Set** - ❑.

- Set the following:

  Name to *legs*;

  SubCharacter Set Attributes to **From Channel Box**.

- Click **Create SubCharacter Set**.

4 Add attributes to the Legs character

- Select **primitiveMan** → **legs** from the character menu next to the Range slider.

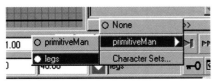

Sub Character

- **Select** the *pelvis* joint node.

- In the Channel box, highlight the *translate* and *rotate* attributes.

- Select **Character** → **Add to Character Set**.

5 Remove attributes from Leg character

- Select **Character** → **Select Character Set Node**→ **legs** to view all the attributes in the Channel box.

  You will notice that *rfoot.rz* and *lfoot.rz* are already connected. This is being driven by the *roll* attribute and therefore they are not needed in the character.

- Use the **Ctrl / Command** key to highlight *rfoot.rz* and *lfoot.rz* in the Channel box.

- Select **Character** → **Remove from Character Set**.

6 Select the arm attributes

- Select **primitiveMan** → **primitiveMan** from the character menu next to the Range slider.

- **Select** the *lArm* and *rArm* IK handles.

- In the Channel box, highlight the *translate* attributes.

7 Create the body sub character

- Select **Character** → **Create Subcharacter Set** - ❑.

- Set the following:

  Name to *body*;

  SubCharacter Set Attributes to **From Channel Box**.

- Click **Create Subcharacter Set**.

8 Add attributes to the Body character

- Select **primitiveMan** → **body** from the character menu next to the Range slider.

- Select the *spine* joint node.

- In the Channel box, highlight the *Rotate* attributes.

- Select **Character** → **Add to Character Set**.

- Select **Character** → **Select Character Set Node**→ **body** to view all the attributes in the Channel box.

Character attributes for legs and body

Conclusion

You now have a biped character all hooked up and ready for a stroll. You can roll the feet and deform the surfaces using the skeleton to control the motion.

While this character's outer shell isn't very sophisticated, the binding and deformation techniques can be translated to other models. Your cylindrical arms could easily be sculpted surfaces while the binding, flexors and influence objects would be similar.

In the next lesson, your Primitive Man will be animated. This will involve setting keys on the character nodes to create animation clips that will be composed using the Trax editor which is based on non-linear animation techniques.

PROJECT FOUR

18 Animating a Walk Cycle

You have now built a character that is ready to be animated. To create a walk cycle, you will build up the motion one part at a time. Starting with the sliding of the feet, you will then lift the feet, use the Roll attribute, and set the twist of the pelvis. When you are finished, Primitive Man will be walking with various levels of motion.

Primitive Man walking

Once you have a cycle ready, you will create a character clip to be used in Maya's Trax editor. This non-linear animation tool will let you build and layer animation clips with a high level of control.

In this lesson you will learn the following:

- How to animate the character's feet
- How to animate the twist of the character's pelvis
- How to animate the roll of the foot
- How to create a character clip
- How to add clips to the Trax editor
- How to cycle and scale the clip in the Trax editor

Initial set-up

For this lesson, you will animate Primitive Man walking. You should start with the file you saved in the last lesson.

1 Set up your view panels

- Set up a Perspective view panel and a Front view panel.

- In the Front view, select **Show** → **None** then **Show** → **Handles** and **Show** → **Joints**.

  This panel will be used to watch the movement of the joints.

- In the Perspective view, select **Show** → **None**, then **Show** → **NURBS Surfaces,** and then **Show** → **Handles**.

  This panel will be used to watch the movement of the surfaces.

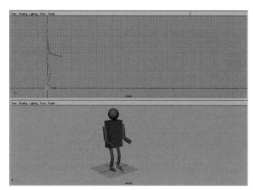

View panel layout

Note: The display of selection handles will make it easier to select the parts of the character that you want to animate – feet, arms, pelvis and spine.

ANIMATING A WALK CYCLE

To create a walk, you will start with a single cycle. To create a cycle you will need the start position and end position to be similar. There are several controls that need to be keyed including the position of the feet, the roll of the feet and the rotation of the pelvis.

Animate the feet sliding

You will now key the horizontal positions of the feet to establish their forward movement. This will result in a sliding motion on the feet.

1 Set your time range

- Set the **Start Time** and **Playback Start Time** to **1**.

- Set the **End Time** and **Playback End Time** to **30**.

  This will give you a smaller time range to work with as you build the cycle.

2 Make the legs character active

- In the Active Character menu, next to the Range Slider, select **primitiveMan** → **legs**.

  Now any keys you set will go to this part of the character.

Active Character menu

3 Position and key the left foot

You will key the starting position of the two feet in the position of a full stride.

- Go to frame **1**.

- In the Perspective window, select the *lfoot*.

- **Move** the handle **8** units forward along the X-axis.

- Press **s** to set a key on all the channels of the *legs* sub-character.

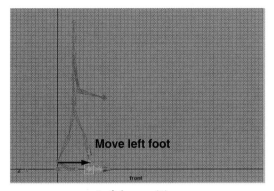

Left leg position

Note: The pelvis_control node moves with the feet. Later you will key the pelvis node to add secondary animation to this area.

---

4 Position and key the right foot

- Go to frame **10**.

- In the Perspective window, select the *rfoot*.

- **Move** the handle forward **16** units along the X-axis.

  This value is exactly double the value of the initial left foot key. This is important to make sure that the two feet cycle together later.

- Press **s** to set a key on all the channels of the *legs* sub-character.

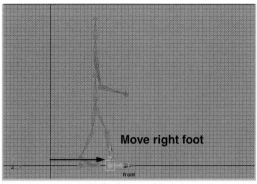

Right leg position

5 Position and key the left foot

You will move the left foot into a position that is similar to the starting position.

- Go to frame **20**.

- In the Perspective window, select the *lfoot*.

- **Move** the handle **16** units forward to a value of **24** along the X-axis.

  Again the value is set using units of 8. This will ensure a connection between cycles later.

- Press **s** to set a key on all the channels of the *legs* sub-character.

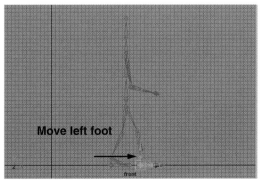

Left leg position

Edit the animation curves

To refine the in-between motion of the feet, you can use the animation curves to view and change the tangent options for the feet.

1 View the curves in the Graph Editor

You will edit the animation curves produced by the keys in the Graph Editor.

- Click in open space to de-select all nodes.

- Open the Graph Editor.

  In the Graph Editor, highlight the legs character.

- Select **View → Frame All**.

  The step pattern of the keys should look as follows. These are all the keys that belong to the *legs* sub character.

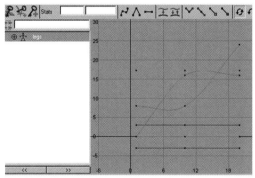

Legs Anim Curves in Graph Editor

- Play back the animation to see the motion.

  By default the curves are drawn using a **Spline** interpolation. This makes the feet slip without planting themselves properly.

Note: The animation channel with keys set in the negative direction is the animation curve connecting the Rotate Z of the foot to the Roll attribute.

2 Change the curve tangents

The tangent curves can be changed to properly plant the feet.

- Click on the plus sign in the circle next to *legs*.

- In the Graph Editor, highlight the two **Translate X** curves for the feet in the outliner portion of this window.

- Select **Tangents → Flat**.

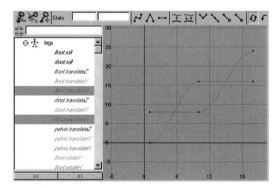

Translate X curves using flat tangent

- Play back the animation to see change in the motion.

  Now the motion of each foot is more deliberate.

Animate the feet up and down

You will now key the vertical raising and lowering of the feet to establish the stepping action.

1 Turn on Auto Key

You will now use Auto Key to help you with the raising of the feet.

- Click on the **Auto Keyframe Toggle** button in the right side of the Time slider to turn it on.

- Open the Animation Preferences window, using the button just to the right of the **Auto Keyframe Toggle** button

- Click on the **Keys** category and set the following:

  Default In Tangent to **Flat**;

  Default Out Tangent to **Flat**.

  This will set all future tangents to match these settings.

2 Raise the right foot at midstep

Key the high point of the raised foot at the appropriate frame.

- Go to frame **5**.

- **Select** the *rfoot*.

- **Move** the foot about 1 unit up along the Y-axis until the left leg is almost straight.

  This sets a new key for the Y-axis channel of the foot using Auto Key.

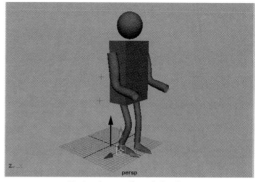

Raised step for right foot

3 Raise the left foot at midstep

- Go to frame **15**.

- **Select** the *lfoot*.

- **Move** the foot about 1 unit up along the Y-axis until the right leg is almost straight.

  Again a key is automatically set.

- Play back the results.

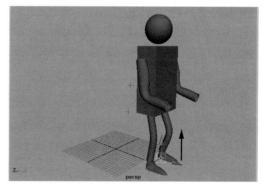

Raised step for left foot

4 View the animation curves

The translate Y channels might need some adjustment in the Graph Editor.

- Click in open space to de-select all nodes.

- Press the **Ctrl / Command** key and click on the **Translate Y** channels for both feet.

  This selects only the Translate Y curves.

- Select **View → Frame All**.

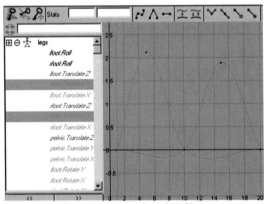

Step curves in Graph Editor

5 Adjust the curves

- With the names of the two translate Y curves highlighted, select **Tangents → Flat**.

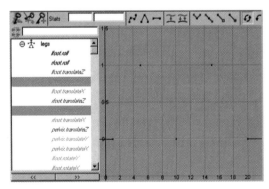

Flattened tangents

6 Save your work

Animate the pelvic rotations

To create a more realistic action, the pelvis' position and rotation will be set to work with each step. These keys will be in addition to the motion of the *pelvis_control* node.

You will again set keys for the translation and rotation of the pelvis using Auto Key.

1 Select the pelvis

You will now animate the pelvis rotation to give the walk a little more motion.

- Go to frame **1**.

- **Select** the *pelvis* node using its selection handle.

2 Set the Y rotation

You will now key the rotation in the Top view using Auto Key, which is still on.

- In the Top view, **Rotate** the pelvis, using the rotation handle, in a clockwise direction.

  This points the left hip towards the left foot and the right hip towards the right foot.

  Another Auto Key is set at this pose.

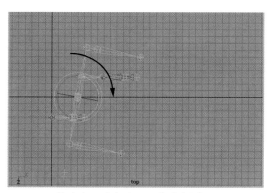

Rotate pelvis toward right foot

3 Rotate in the opposite direction

- Go to Frame **10**.
- **Rotate** the pelvis in the opposite direction.

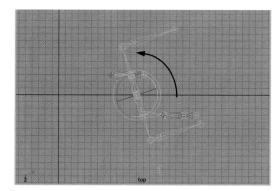

Rotate pelvis toward left foot

4 Set the Y rotation

- Go to Frame **20**.
- In the Top view, **Rotate** the pelvis, in a clockwise direction.

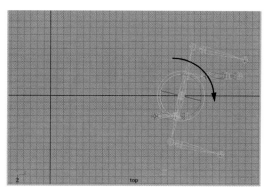

Rotate pelvis toward right foot

5 Auto Key rotation in Side view

- Go to frame **5**.
- In the Side view, **Rotate** the pelvis using the rotation handle to rotate the hips so that the right hip is raising with the right leg.

  Another key is set at this pose.

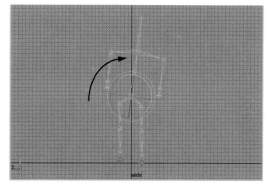

Rotated pelvis with right foot raised

- Go to frame **15**.
- **Rotate** the pelvis in the opposite direction to rotate the hips up as the left foot raises.

PROJECT FOUR

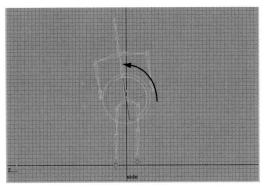

Rotated pelvis with left foot raised

6 Edit the keys

To prepare the file for creating clips later, you will need to make sure that the rotations match at the start and end of the cycle.

- Click in open space to de-select all nodes.

- In the Graph Editor, press the **Ctrl / Command** key and click on the **Rotate X** and **Y** channels for the *pelvis*.

  This selects only these curves.

- Select **View → Frame All**.

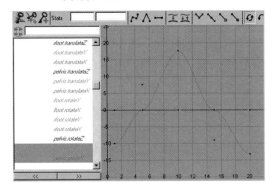

Pelvis curves

7 Edit the rotate X curve

The rotation around X does not match at the beginning and end of the clips. This needs to be edited in the Graph editor.

- Highlight the *pelvis.rotateX* channel.

- Select the first and last keys for this channel.

- Change both their values to match. Use a value around **-12.**

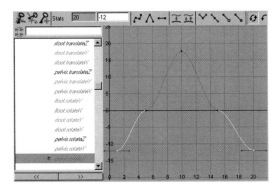

Aligning first and last keys

- Play back the motion to test the results.

8 Save your work

Animate the heel rotation

In the last lesson, you spent a great deal of time preparing the foot for the *heel to toe* motion that a foot goes through when walking. You are now going to use Auto Key to keyframe the foot rotations to take advantage of this work.

1 Set a key on the right foot's roll

- Go to frame **1.**

- **Select** the *rfoot* using its selection handle.

- Set the *rfoot's* **Roll** attribute to **10**.

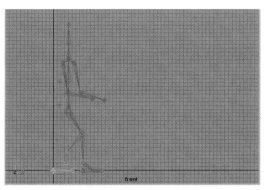

Foot rotated forward

2 Set a second roll key

- Go to frame **10**.
- Set the *rfoot's* **Roll** attribute to **-5**.

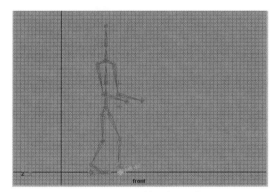

Foot rotated backward

3 Set a third key on the right foot's roll

- Go to frame **20**.
- Set the *rfoot's* **Roll** attribute to **10**.

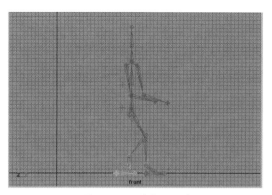

Foot rotated forward

4 Set a key on the left foot's roll

- Use the same technique to set the *lfoot's* **Roll** attribute as follows:

   At frame **1**, set **Roll** to **-5**;

   At frame **10**, set **Roll** to **10**;

   At frame **20**, set **Roll** to **-5**;

5 Save your work

6 Turn Auto Key off

- Turn off the **Auto Keyframe Toggle** button. This will prevent any unwanted keying.

NON-LINEAR ANIMATION

At this point you have one cycle of the walk. You could now repeat this motion by either setting keys directly or by copying and pasting keys. Another tool available to you is the **Trax editor** that uses non-linear animation techniques to compose animation sequences.

The term non-linear refers to the creation of animation clips that are not tied down to the timeline. These clips can be stored in the Visor then applied to the Trax editor.

PROJECT FOUR

Creating your first clip

The walk cycle you now have from frame 1 to frame 20 is perfect for creating your first clip. This clip will be placed in the Visor then used later in the Trax editor to animate Primitive man.

1 Set up your scene

- Go to frame 1.

- Make sure that nothing is selected and that the **Active Character** menu is set to *legs*.

- Set up your views to show a **Perspective** view panel, a **Visor** panel and a **Trax editor** panel as shown below:

Panel setup

2 Create a Walk clip

- Select **Animate** → **Create Clip** - ❑.

- Set the following options:

    Name to *walk*;

    Leave Keys in Timeline to **Off**;

    Clip to **Put Clip in Visor Only**.

- Click **Create Clip**.

3 View the clip in the Visor

- In the Visor, click on the **Character Clips** tab. The *walkSource* is available in this location.

    In the main view you will find that Primitive man no longer has any animation curves assigned. If you playback the scene, you will see that he is no longer animated. The animation curves are now part of the clip.

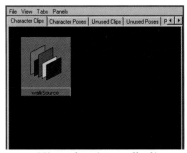

Visor showing walk clip

Cycling the clip

To animate a longer walk cycle, you will bring the *walk* clip into the Trax editor where clips are assigned to their appropriate character or sub-character.

1 Drag the clip to the Trax editor

- With your middle mouse button, click on the *walkSource* clip and drag it onto the *legs* track in the Trax editor.

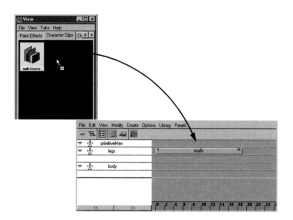

Trax editor with walk clip

2 Move the clip

When the clip is first placed into the editor, it may not be located exactly where you need it.

- Use the **Alt** key to scale and pan until you see about 30 frames in the Trax editor.

- Click-drag on the clip with your left mouse button to move it along the track until the beginning of the clip is at frame 1.

- Playback the animation.

  Primitive man is now moving using the keys set in the original cycle.

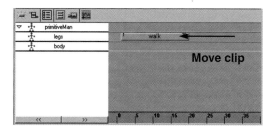

Clip located at frame 1

3 Click drag to cycle the motion

- Use the **Alt + RMB** buttons to scale and pan until you see about 100 frames in the Trax editor.

- Move your cursor to the bottom right of the walk clip in the Trax editor.

- When the cursor changes to a circular arrow and a line, begin dragging to the right until the clip reaches around frame 97.

  The clip is extended with small ticks indicating the timing of each cycle.

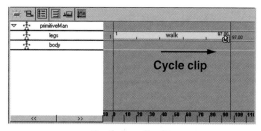

Cycled walk clip

4 Playback the cycled motion

- In the Range slider, set the **End Time** and **Playback End Time** to 100.

- Playback the scene.

  Oops! The clip still goes through its cycle then goes back to the origin. This is not the motion required. You need to create a different cycle offset.

5 Edit the cycle offset

By default the clip is cycled using absolute cycling. This does not allow you to build the values onto each other. You need relative cycling that places each cycle in relation to the last.

PROJECT FOUR

- Double click on the *walk* clip in the Trax editor.

  This selects the clip and makes it available in the Channel box.

- In the Channel box, set the *walk* clip's **Offset** attribute to **relative**.

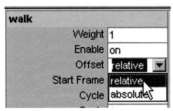

Channel box

6 Playback the scene

- Playback the scene to see Primitive Man moving forward without returning to the origin.

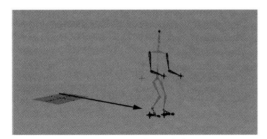

Primitive Man with cycled motion

Scale up the clip

A key feature of the Trax editor clips is the fact that they can be easily scaled to adjust their timing. By scaling the clip, you scale all the animation curves that make up that clip.

1 Speed up the clip

- Move your cursor to the top right of the walk clip in the Trax editor.

- When the cursor changes to a straight arrow and a line, begin dragging to the left until the end of the clip reaches around frame **45**.

- Playback the results.

  The walk is now much faster.

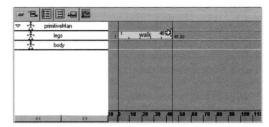

Scaling walk clip

2 Slow down the clip

- Now use the same method to scale the clip out to around frame **260**.

- Playback the results.

  The walk is now much slower.

Scaling walk clip

3 Reset the scaling

- Double click on the walk clip.

- In the Channel box, set the **Scale** attribute back to **1**. This is the value that is affected by the click-drag scaling.

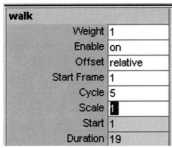
Channel box

Edit the walk source clip

While you can move the clip around, cycle it
and scale it, there might still be a need to
tweak some of the original channels to refine
the motion. This can be accomplished by
editing the curves associated with the *walk*
clip.

1 Open the Graph editor

- Select the *walk* clip in the Trax
  editor.

- In the Trax editor, select **View →
  Graph Anim Curves...**

  This opens the Graph editor.

- In the Graph editor, select **View →
  Frame All**.

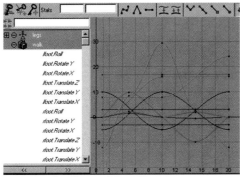
Graph editor with walk anim curves

2 Edit the pelvis height

- Highlight the *pelvis.translateY*
  channel.

- Select the **Insert Keys Tool** found in
  the Graph editor.

- Click on the curve with your left
  mouse button to select the curve
  then with your middle mouse
  button to insert a key.

- Add keys at frames **5** and **15**.

- **Move** them down or enter a value of
  about **14** to add some bounce to the
  walk.

- Playback the results. The edits have
  affected all of the cycles within the
  walk clip.

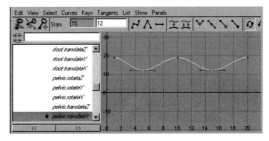
Pelvis Y translate channel

Conclusion

Non-linear animation is one of many
animation tools available in Maya. Beyond
simple walk cycles, you can also add multiple
clips, create poses, add blending between
clips and poses and layer non-destructive
keys to refine the motion.

In the next lesson, you will complete the
Primitive man animation using these
techniques.

19 **Non-Linear Animation**

In the last lesson, you animated Primitive Man walking using a cycled, non-linear animation clip. The power of working with non-linear animation lies in the ability to layer multiple clips freely without worrying about accidentally altering the animation curves. Poses can also be used as single frame clips in the Trax editor.

Primitive Man on the move

In this lesson, you will create a more complex motion by building a second clip of Primitive man climbing a set of stairs that will be set up to follow the walking motion. You will then build clips for the arms.

In this lesson you will learn the following:

- How to work with relative and absolute clips
- How to work with character poses
- How to work with absolute clips
- How to blend between clips
- How to layer non-destructive keys over clips
- How to animate a two-node camera

ANIMATING CYCLES

In the last lesson, you used relative offset to make sure that each cycle of a clip would build on the last. You can also use this technique to put two clips together such as a walk cycle and a stair-climbing cycle.

You will continue working with the file you saved at the end of the last lesson.

Animating a climb cycle

The stair climbing cycle will now be built. This clip will be built independently of the walk clip. Later the two will be composed in the Trax editor.

For this section, you will set keys for all the parts of the climbing motion. This includes the two feet and the pelvis motion. In most cases, exact values are provided to make sure that you create a stepping motion that goes 5 units forward and 2.5 units up with each step. This precision will help ensure proper cycling using relative offsets.

1 Activate the legs character

- In the Active Character menu, next to the Range Slider, make sure that the *legs* sub-character is selected.

2 Go to Frame 1

- Move the Time Slider to Frame 1.

3 Clear the Trax editor

In order to build a new clip, the walking clip is not required. This will be re-applied in the Trax editor later in the lesson.

- Click on the *walk* clip in the Trax editor to highlight it.
- Press the **Delete** key to remove it.

4 Reposition the feet

- **Select** the *lfoot* joint and set the following values:

      Translate X to **0**;

      Roll to **4**.

- **Select** the *rfoot* joint and set the following values:

      Translate X to **5**;

      Translate Y to **2.5**;

      Roll to **4**.

- **Select** the *pelvis* joint and set the following values:

      Translate X to **2**;

      Translate Y to **17**.

      Rotate X to **5**.

These settings set up a starting position for Primitive man to walk up some stairs. The balls of the feet are on the ground and the knees are slightly bent.

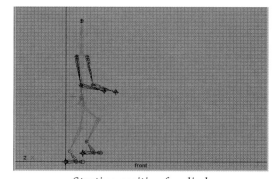

Starting position for climb

5 Set keys for the stepping motion

- Press the **s** key to set a key for the *legs* character at this starting position.

- Go to frame 5.
- **Select** the *lfoot* joint and set the following values:

    Translate X to **10**;

    Translate Y to **5**.

- **Select** the *pelvis* joint and set the following value:

    Rotate X to **-5**.

- Press the **s** key to set a key for the legs character at this new position.

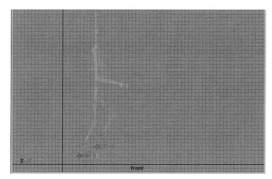

Second position for climb

6 Set keys for the pelvis rotation

- Go to frame 10.
- **Select** the *rfoot* joint and set the following values:

    Translate X to **15**;

    Translate Y to **7.5**.

- **Select** the *pelvis* joint and set the following value:

    Rotate X to **5**.

- Press the **s** key to set a key for the legs character at this new position.

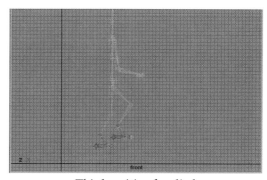

Third position for climb

7 Evaluate the motion

- Set the **Playback End Time** in the Range slider to 10.
- Click-drag in the Timeline to scrub through the ten frames.

    You will see that the feet seem to be sliding to the next step without the being lifted. You will fix this by altering the animation curves.

8 View the left foot's anim curves

- In the Graph Editor, select **View →
Frame All**.

    This puts your focus on the curves belonging to the *legs* sub-character.

- Highlight the *lfoot.translateY* channel.

PROJECT FOUR

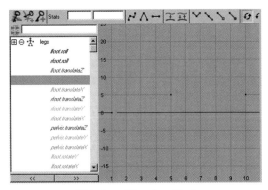

Third position for climb

9 Edit the left foot's anim curves

To make sure that the feet are lifting up and onto the next step, you will

- Select the **Insert Keys Tool** found in the Graph editor.

- Click on the curve with your left mouse button to select the curve then with your middle mouse button to insert a key.

- **Move** the key to around frame **3.5** at a value of about **6**.

Insert Keys tool

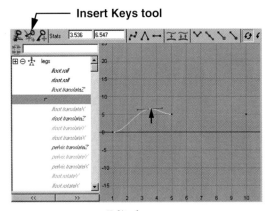

Edited curve

10 Repeat for the right foot's anim curves

- Use the steps shown above to create a similar lifting for the right foot at around frame 8.5.

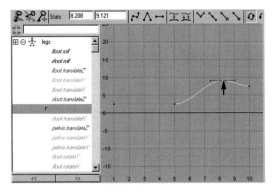

Edited curve

11 Edit the Pelvis's Y translation

- Highlight the *pelvis.translateY* curve.

- **Insert** two keys in-between the existing keys then **Move** them down to around a value of **14**.

This will create a bouncing motion similar to the walk cycle.

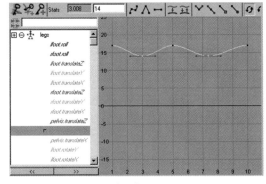

Edited curve

12 Edit the Pelvis's X translation

- Highlight the *pelvis.translateX* curve.

- **Insert** two keys in-between the existing keys then **Move** them up to around a value of around **4**.

  This motion has Primitive man leaning into each step as he climbs.

- Scrub in the Timeline to see the results.

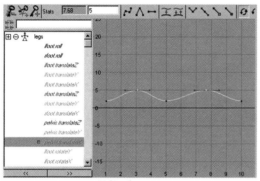

Edited curve

13 Create another clip

Now you want to make a clip that can be cycled to walk up a flight of stairs.

- Select **Animate** → **Create Clip** - ❏.

- Set the following options:

  Name to *climb*;

  Leave Keys in Timeline to **Off**;

  Clip to **Put Clip in Trax Editor and Visor**.

- Click **Create Clip**.

  You will notice that there are now two clips in the visor.

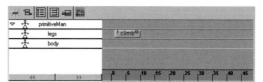

Climb clip in Trax editor

14 Test the clip

- Use the methods taught in the last lesson to cycle the clip **10** times and to set its **Offset** to **Relative**.

- Playback the motion using a frame range of about **100** frames.

  Now Primitive man is walking up an imaginary flight of stairs using the *climb* clip to define the motion of the legs.

Tip: Don't forget that you can also scale the clip to speed up or slow down the motion.

- When you are finished previewing the clip, move the clip out to frame **100** in the Trax editor.

  You will now bring back the *walk* clip and put the two clips next to each other.

Set up the walking clip

You are again going to set up the walk clip with a number of cycles starting at frame 1. You will then put the climb clip next to it.

1 Apply and edit the walk clip

- Increase the Playback Frame Range to **250**.

- Drag with middle mouse button the *walk* clip from the Visor to the *legs* track and position it at frame 1.

- **Cycle** the *walk* clip **5** times and set its **Offset** to **Relative**.

- Move the *climb* clip back to frame 96 so that it touches the *walk* clip.

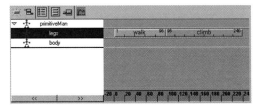

Walk clip in Trax editor

- Scrub in the Trax editor timeline.

As the walk cycle becomes the climb cycle, you see that the feet start to move in an odd way. This is because the climb motion is being added to the last pose of the *walk* clip. Since the last pose of the *walk* is very different from the first pose of the *climb* clip, the relative offset creates a gap between the feet.

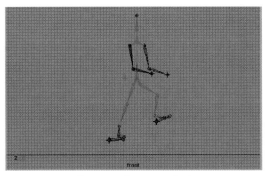

Legs getting stretched

Create a transition clip

You need the pose at the end of the first clip to transition into the start pose of the second clip. Since relative offsets are being used, a non-linear blend will not solve the problem. You need to set up a transition clip that uses the ending of the *walk* and the beginning of the *climb* as its beginning and end. These will be set up as two absolute poses that can be blended and then merged into a new clip.

Poses are single frame clips that can be useful building blocks for more complex clips.

1 Create a climb start pose

- Double click on the *climb* clip and in the Channel box set its **Offset** back to **absolute**.

- Go to frame **96**.

- Select the legs in the Trax editor.

- Select **Animate** → **Create Pose - ❏**.

- In the option window, set the **Name** to *climbStartPose*.

- Click **Create Pose**.

- When you are finished, **Delete** the *climb* clip from the *legs* track.

2 Create a walk end pose

- Stay at frame 96 which is the last frame of the walk clip.

- Select **Animate** → **Create Pose - ❏**.

- In the option window, set the **Name** to *walkEndPose*.

- Click **Create Pose**.

3 View the poses in the Visor

- In the Visor, click on the **Character Poses** tab.

Poses

4 Put the poses into the Trax editor

- Drag the *walkEndPose* from the Visor to the right of the cycled *walk* clip at frame **96** with the **MMB**.

- Drag the *climbStartPose* from the Visor to the right of *walkEndPose* at frame **101** with the **MMB**.

- Scrub in the Trax editor timeline.

  Primitive man starts with the first pose then jumps back to the origin. You need the second pose to follow the first more closely.

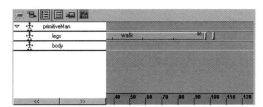

Poses in Trax editor

5 Edit the values of the second pose

To make the two poses work together, you will edit the *climbStartPose* so that the position of the feet immediately follow from the first pose.

- Go to frame 96 and **select** the *lfoot* node. You will notice that its Translate X value is **88**.

- Select *climbStartPose* in the Trax editor.

- Select **View → Graph Anim Curves...**

- In the Graph Editor, select **View → Frame All**.

- Highlight the *lfoot.translateX* channel.

- Select the *lfoot.translateX* key and edit its value to **88**.

- Highlight the *rfoot.translateX* channel.

- Select the *rfoot.translateX* key and edit its value to **93**. Just like the original climb pose, this value is 5 units in front of the left foot.

- Scrub in the Trax editor timeline.

  Now the left foot stays in the same position while the other channels pop into their new position. You now want to create a softer transition between these poses.

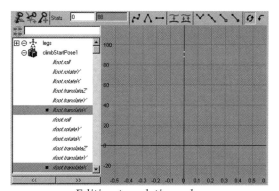

Editing translation value

6 Blend the two poses

- In the Trax editor, select the two poses.

- Select **Create → Blend** from the Trax editor menus.

- Scrub in the Trax editor timeline.

PROJECT FOUR

Now there is a smoother transition from one pose to the other.

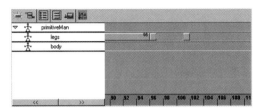

Adding the blend

7 Merge the poses into a clip

To make it easier to work with the transition, you can turn it into a clip.

- In the Trax editor, select the two poses. You don't need to select the Blend

- Select **Edit** → **Merge** from the Trax editor menus.

- Double click on the *mergedClip1* in the Trax editor.

- In the Channel box, rename it *walkToClimb*.

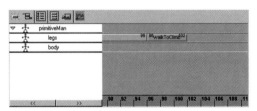

Walk to climb clip in Trax editor

Adjust the transition clip curves

If you view the transition clip from a front view, you will see that the right foot slides up to the first step instead of rising up then dropping down onto the step. You will now adjust the right foot anim curves to correct this motion.

1 Clean up the rfoot Y translation curve

- Select the *walkToClimb* clip.

- In the Trax Editor, select **View** → **Graph Anim Curves...**

- In the Graph Editor, select **View** → **Frame All**.

  You will notice that the curves have keys set for every frame of the blend. This was a result of the merge.

- In the Graph editor, select all the curves then select **Tangents** → **Spline**.

- Highlight *rfoot.translateY*.

- Again select **View** → **Frame All**.

- Select all the keys except the two end keys and the middle key and press the **Delete** key.

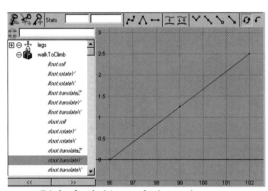

Right foot's Y translation anim curve

2 Edit the middle key

- **Move** the remaining key as shown below.

- Scrub in the Trax editor timeline.

Now there is a smoother transition from one pose to the other as the foot rises up and the down onto the first step.

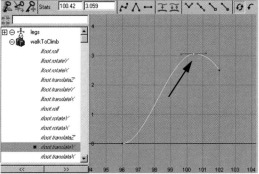

Adjusted anim curve

A problem you may encounter is around frames 98 and 99, you can see that the pelvis is raised too high and the left foot is leaving the ground.

3 Edit the pelvis' Y translation curve

You will need to lower the pelvis in the middle of the transition clip to bring the left foot back to the ground.

- Make sure that the *walkToClimb* curves are in the Graph editor.

- Highlight the *pelvis.translateY* channel.

- In the Graph editor, select **View** → **Frame All**.

- Select all the keys except the two end keys and the middle key and press the **Delete** key.

- Modify the keys until the pelvis looks correct in the middle of the step. You may want to also adjust

the tangent handles to shape the curve.

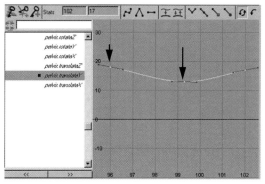

Lowered pelvis key

The pelvis drops down during the transition and the left foot is properly planted on the ground.

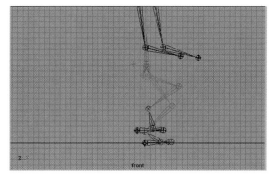

Foot planted on ground

Complete the legs animation

You now have a transition between the walk and the climb. You should first test to see if the transition is the right speed then add the climb clip.

1 Test the animation so far

- Set your Time slider range to cover the animated clips then playback the scene in a perspective view panel.

The transition clip's duration of 6 frames will seem a little quick. It would be more natural if it was a little slower.

2 Adjust the timing of walkToClimb clip

- Click-drag in the upper right corner of the *walkToClimb* clip to scale it out to frame **108**.

- Playback the scene.

  This timing will feel a little more natural. Later you can adjust its scaling if you want a different look.

3 Add and adjust the climb clip

- Drag the *climb* clip from the Visor to the *legs* track.

- Push it next to the *walkToClimb* clip.

- Double-click on the clip and set the following in the Channel box:

  Offset to **relative**;

  Cycle to **8**;

  Scale to **2**.

  This creates motion relative to the end of the *walkToClimb* clip and completes the animation of the legs.

- Playback the results.

  Now you have a good transition between the *walk* and the *climb*.

4 Save your work

ANIMATING THE BODY

Primitive man is made up of two sub-characters including the *legs* that you have just animated and the *body* which includes the

arms and the spine joint. You will now create clips for the swinging motion of the arms.

Create a swinging arm clip

The first swing will be designed to match the walking motion. Since the arm IK handles are parented to the body, you can create clips that work in Absolute offset mode when it is cycled. This offset mode will allow you to blend directly between body clips without having to create a transition clip.

1 Activate the body sub-character

- In the Active Character menu, next to the Range Slider, select **primitiveMan → body**.

  Now your keys will be set for this sub-character.

2 Set keys for the start position

- Go to frame 1.

- Double click on the **Move** tool and set the **Move** method to **Object**.

  This will let you move the arms in the object space of the IK handles. This means that no matter what direction the body has turned, the Move handles will be oriented to the selected handle's local rotation axis.

- **Move** the *lArm* IK handle back behind the body and low down.

- **Move** the *rArm* IK handle in front of the body and up.

  Now the arms are opposite to how the feet are set up. This makes the swinging motion work with the feet.

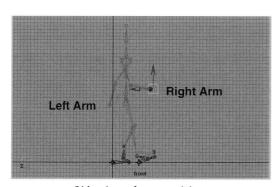

Side view of arm positions

- **Select** the *spine* joint and rotate it around the X axis by around **20** degrees.

  This has the body swinging in the opposite direction as the hips.

- Press the **s** key to set keys on the body sub-character.

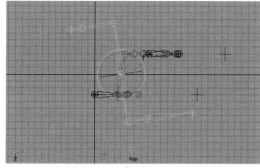

Top view of spine rotation

3 Set keys for the end position

- Go to frame **20**. This is the last frame of the *walk* clip cycle.
- Press the **s** key to set keys.

  Now the start position and the end position are the same.

4 Set keys for the middle position

- Go to frame **10**.
- **Rotate** the spine to **-20** around X.
- **Move** the *lArm* forward and up and the *rArm* back and down.
- Press the **s** key to set keys.

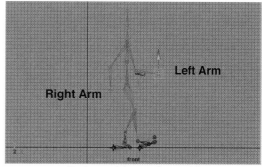

Body position at frame 10

5 Create a clip

These keys can now be used to create the first body clip.

- Go to frame **1**.
- Select **Animate → Create Clip - ❐**.
- In the option window, set the following:

  Name to *walkSwing*;

  Clip to **Put Clip in Trax Editor and Visor**.

- Click **Create Clip**.

6 Cycle the clip

- Double-click on the *walkSwing* clip in the Trax editor.
- In the Channel box, set **Cycle** to **5**.

  Playback the results.

PROJECT FOUR

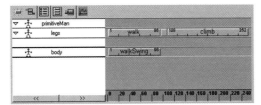

Walk swing clip in Trax editor

Create a second arm clip

When Primitive man climbs the stairs, a different arm motion is needed. In this case the arms would be both in front of the body and the swinging would not be as dramatic.

1 Set keys for the start position

- Go to frame 108 which is the start of the climbing clip.

- **Move** the *lArm* IK handle in front of the body and up and the *rArm* IK handle in front of the body and down near the hips.

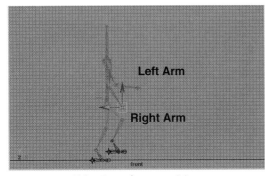

Side view of arm positions

- **Select** the *spine* joint and rotate it around the X axis by around **-5** degrees.

- Press the **s** key to set keys on the *body* sub-character.

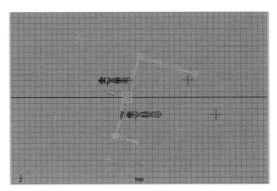

Top view of spine rotation

2 Set keys for the end position

- Go to frame **126**. This is the last frame of the *climb* clip cycle.

- Press the **s** key to set keys.

  Now the start position and the end position are the same.

3 Set keys for the middle position

- Go to frame **117**.

- **Rotate** the spine to **8** around X.

- **Move** the *lArm* down and the *rArm* and up.

- Press the **s** key to set keys.

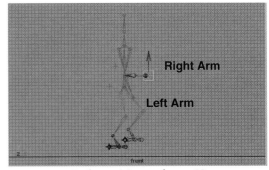

Body position at frame 10

4 Create a clip

These keys can now be used to create the second body clip.

- Select **Animate** → **Create Clip** - □.

- In the option window, set the following:

  Name to *climbSwing*;

  Clip to **Put Clip in Trax Editor and Visor**.

- Click **Create Clip**.

5 Cycle the clip

- Double-click on the *climbSwing* clip in the Trax editor.

- In the Channel box, set **Cycle** to **8**.

  Playback the results. What you find is that the swinging of the arms works great for the walking and the climbing but the area between jumps too harshly. You need to blend this area.

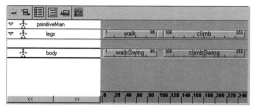

Climb swing clip in Trax editor

Blending the clips

To create a better relationship between the two swing clips, you will blend them. This will involve overlapping the clips to create a smoother blend.

1 Put the climbSwing on a new track

- Highlight the *body* track in the Trax editor.

- Select **Modify** → **Add Track**.

- Click-drag the *climbSwing* clip down to the new track. Keep its start position at frame 108.

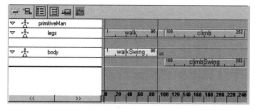

New body track

2 Blend the two clips

- Select the *walkSwing* and *climbSwing* clips.

- Select **Create** → **Blend**.

- Playback the results.

  The transition is now smoother but Primitive man switches arm swings a little to sharply. It would be good to extend and overlap the blending.

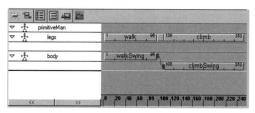

Creating a blend in Trax editor

3 Extend and overlap the clips

- Click on the lower right corner of the *walkSwing* clip and cycle the clip out to frame **116**.

- Click on the lower right corner of the *climbSwing* clip and cycle it out to frame **288**.

- Move the *climbSwing* clip back to frame **72**.
- Playback the results.

  The transition is now extended and offers a more gradual effect.

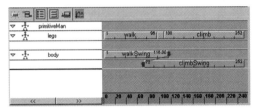

Extending the overlap

4 Edit the blend in the Graph editor

- Click on the blend icon that links the two swing clips.
- Select **View** → **Graph Anim Curves**.
- In the Graph editor, select **View** → **Frame All**.

  The curve is mapped from 0, 0 to 1, 1. You can edit the curve in-between these points but you should not reposition the points themselves.

- Select the curve then select **Curves** → **Weighted Tangents**.
- Select the two keys and click on the **Free tangent weight** button.
- Edit the tangent handles with the move tool to get the curve shown below.
- Playback the results.

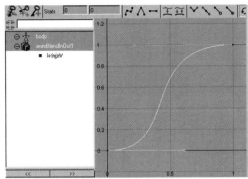

Edited blend in the Graph editor

Note: You can control the look of your blends using this method. Just don't edit the keys at 0, 0 and 1, 1.

5 Offset the clips in time

Right now the swing motion matches the motion of the feet exactly. By moving the clips forward, you can create an overlap of the motion in time which offers a more realistic result.

- Select the two swing clips and move them forward by 4 frames.
- Playback the results.

  Working in the Trax editor makes it easy to adjust large number of curves to refine your motion.

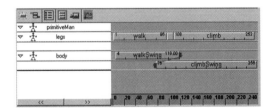

Offset clips

Non-destructive keys

You have already experienced the flexibility of working with non-linear animation clips. To further refine the motion, you will add some non-destructive keys to add some secondary animation to the walk.

1 Add a start and end key

- Go to frame **120**.

- Press the **s** key to set keys on the *body* sub-character.

- Go to frame **150**.

- Press the **s** key.

  You will notice some new keys being placed in the timeline.

2 Add a middle key

- Go to frame **135** and edit the spine joint and the arms into a new position.

- Press the **s** key.

- Playback the results.

  Now Primitive man is seen deviating from his original clip-based animation.

  These keys are not altering the clips in any way and they can in fact be deleted or moved around and the clip-based animation would be left intact. This is perfect for adding finishing touches to an animated sequence without worrying about editing your original clips.

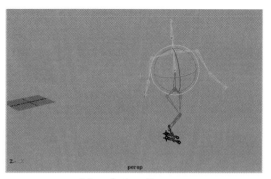

Non-destructive pose

Animating a camera and aim

You will now add a new camera to the scene and animate it so that you can follow Primitive Man as he walks.

A camera can be created on its own or with additional nodes that provide control over the *aim point* and *up direction*. Most cameras only need one node which lets you key the camera's position and rotation. You will create a camera with aim to control both the *camera point* and the *view point*. Both these nodes can be keyed individually.

1 Set up your panel display

- In the Perspective view, select **Show → Cameras** and **Show → Pivots** to add these objects to the display.

  You will need to see these in order to work with the camera.

2 Create a two-node camera

- Select **Create → Cameras → Camera and Aim**.

3 Position the camera

- Select the **Show Manipulator** tool

PROJECT FOUR

- In the Perspective view, position the *camera* and *view point* handles to set up the camera.

- In the other view panel, select **Panels → Perspective → camera1**.

- From the *camera1* view, select **View → Camera Settings → Resolution Gate**.

  You can now position the camera using both of these panels. Put the *view point* of the camera in front of the character.

- In the *camera1* view, select **Show → NURBS Surfaces** then shade the view.

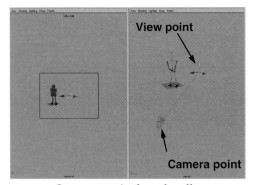

Camera manipulator handles

4 Set keys on the view point

You will now set keys on the view point to follow the character from frame 1 to 90.

- Go to frame **1**.
- **Select** *camera1_aim*.
- Press **Shift w** to keyframe the position of the view point.
- Go to frame **95**.
- **Move** *camera1_aim* so that it is again in front of the character.

- Press **Shift w** to keyframe the position of the view point.
- Go to frame **200**.
- **Move** *camera1_aim* so that it is again in front of the character.
- Press **Shift w** to keyframe the position of the view point.

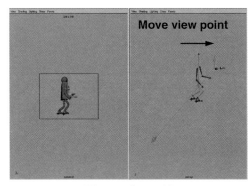

View at frame 90

5 Set keys on the camera node

The camera animation is now pointing at Primitive Man, but he is not always framed in the view as well as you'd like. You can set keys on the eye point node to fix this.

- Select the *camera1* node by clicking on the camera icon.
- Go to frame **1**.
- Press **Shift w** to set keys on the translation channels of the *camera1* node.
- Go to frame **95**.
- **Move** the *camera* node in the Perspective view to the front of the character to frame the view.
- Press **Shift w** to set keys on the translation channels of the *camera1* node.

- Go to frame **200**.

- **Move** the *camera* node in the Perspective view to the front of the character to frame the view.

- Press **Shift w** to set keys on the translation channels of the *camera1* node.

- Play back the results.

If you don't like the framing in the in-between frames, then you can reposition the camera at either frame 1 or 90 and set new keys. Repeat this until you get the camera movement you want.

Props, color and lighting

On your own, build some props, add color materials to the surfaces, and then light the scene. You will complete these steps on your own to build the set that you want, with the lighting that you feel suits Primitive Man's animation.

In the example shown below, stairs were built, as well as, several columns to help give a frame of reference for his walking. At this point, you may want to edit your camera animation to suit your new scene.

Several lights were used to illuminate the scene. These include three spot light with shadows on and an intensity of 1.0, which are placed above the path that Primitive Man's walking. An ambient light with an intensity of 0.5 further fills in dark spots and is placed near the ground. You can play with your own lighting setup to illuminate the scene.

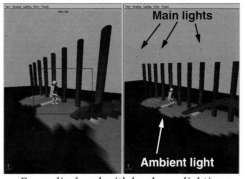

Props displayed with hardware lighting

Testing the motion

You can now Playblast the scene to test the motion. This will give you the chance to confirm the location of your props and whether or not you like the camera animation.

Playblast of the animation

Rendering the animation

You can now render the scene. To render, you should consider the various issues taught throughout this book. You need to set attributes on the surfaces themselves and in the Render Globals. Listed below is a checklist of some of the issues you should

PROJECT FOUR

consider when rendering. Test them out when you render the Primitive Man scene.

Software render test

Note:	You will have encountered most of these issues in earlier **Learning Maya** projects. This checklist offers a compiled list of those issues and some new ones.

OBJECT ISSUES

Some render attributes need to be set for your objects' *shape* nodes. You can set these attributes in the **Rendering Flags** window, in the *shape* node's **Render** section in the Attribute Editor, or in the **Attribute Spread Sheet** window. Below are some of the attributes you should consider when you render:

√ Surface Tessellation

Set a NURBS surface tessellation that is appropriate to the scene. Larger and more prominent objects will require a larger tessellation than background elements. It is very important that you don't over-tessellate.

You can also use the default tessellation settings or choose **Explicit Tessellation** and refine even further.

√ Motion blur

While you turn on motion blur in the Render Globals, you can also decide which objects will or will not use motion blur. If you have objects that are not moving or are barely moving, turn motion blur off to speed up rendering.

You must also choose between 2D and 3D motion blur. The 2D motion blur is faster.

√ Lights and shadows

Limit the number of lights casting shadows in your scene. If possible, use depth maps shadows which are a little faster. If you want to add a lot of lights to a scene then consider linking some of the lights to only those objects which need the illumination.

RENDER GLOBAL ISSUES

√ Turn animation on!

If you want to render an animation, you must choose a **Frame/Animation Ext.** in the **Render Globals** that supports animation. It is very easy to forget this and send off what you think is a long night of rendering frames, only to come in the next day to just a single frame.

√ Renderable camera

Do you have the right camera set up for rendering? It is very easy to leave the default *persp* camera as *renderable* when in fact you want to render another camera.

√ Masks and depth masks

If you plan to composite your renderings later, you may want to use these settings to create a matte layer (mask) to assist in the compositing process. You might also choose to use Maya's **Render to Layer** settings to support the compositing process.

√ Render resolution

What is the render size that you want? Be sure that if you change the pixel size, then use the *resolution gate* in your view panel to make sure that the framing of your scene is preserved.

√ Raytrace

Do you want to raytrace some of your objects? Remember that Maya has a selective raytracer and only objects that require reflections, refractions or shadows will be raytraced.

Therefore, if you limit your reflective and refractive materials to key objects, then you can raytrace them knowing that other objects in the scene are using the A-buffer.

If you are raytracing, try to limit the number of reflections set in the globals. A setting of 1 will look good in most animations unless, for example, you have a chrome character looking into a mirror.

√ Render quality

You may want to use the *Anti-Aliasing Quality presets* pop-up to suggest render quality options until you are familiar with the individual settings.

OTHER RENDERING ISSUES

Here are some other key rendering issues to consider.

√ Test render, test render, test render

Don't start a major rendering unless you have test rendered at various levels. Render the whole animation at a low resolution with low quality settings to test the motion. Render random full-size single frames to confirm that materials, lights and objects are rendering properly.

The more you test render, the less time you spend re-doing renderings that didn't work out the way you wanted.

√ Command line rendering

You have learned how to batch render from within Maya. You can also render from the MS-DOS® command line. Here is the basic workflow:

- Set up your Render Globals.
- **Save** your scene file.
- Type `Render -help` for a list of all the command line options.
- `chdir` or `cd` into the directory with your file.
- Enter the `Render` command along with any flags followed by the file name, such as the start and end frames for the rendering as shown in the following:

```
Render -s 1 - e 150
walkTest.mb
```

Conclusion

Congratulations! You have now completed your first walk cycle. Now you are going to animate Salty the seal. This final project takes you through a more complex character setup that includes the creation of special controls for Salty's eyes.

LESSON 19
Conclusion

PROJECT
FIVE

PROJECT FIVE

In this project, you are going to model, texture and animate a complete character – Salty the seal. Salty will be built out of primitive shapes that will then be bound to skeleton joints and animated. This lesson integrates modeling, rendering and animating so that the lines between them begin to blur.

1. Salty begins by bouncing a ball on her nose, two times with ease.

2. Suddenly, the ball is blown to the side of the stage and Salty loses control.

3. Concerned, Salty follows the ball as it bounces out of her reach.

4. Dejected, Salty looks back at the audience unhappy that the ball got away.

20 Building Salty

This lesson shows you how to build your first Maya character – Salty the seal. Starting with a primitive sphere, you will edit the surface's control vertices to give the sphere a more complex, organic shape. You will also build flippers out of primitive cylinders. These surfaces can then be bound to skeleton joints to begin setting up fluid character deformations when Salty is animated in Lesson 22.

Salty

In this lesson you will learn the following:

- How to create a new layer
- How to work with selection modes and selection masks
- How to model a character using CV edits
- How to build skeleton joints
- How to bind the character's skin to the skeleton
- How to develop a shading group for the seal skin

File management

In this lesson, you will be working on a single file. In order to manage the parts of this file, you will use layers to help organize your work into manageable parts.

1 Set project

A project directory is needed that contains sub-directories for different types of files that relate to your project.

- Go to the **File** menu and select **Project → Set...**

- Open the *learningMaya* directory and then click on *projectFive*

- Click on the **OK** button to make *projectFive* your current project.

  This existing project includes texture files to help you with your work.

- Select **File → New Scene**.

2 Create a new layer

To keep all of the parts of Salty the seal together, you will use a layer dedicated to this character.

- Press the **Create a new Layer** button.

- **Double-click** on *Layer1* and rename it *Salty*.

- Click **Save**.

Building Salty's body

The first step in building Salty, is to build the body and head. You will create these out of a single surface by sculpting a primitive sphere. To create the sphere, you will edit its input node using the show manipulator tool.

1 Place a primitive sphere

- Select **Create → NURBS Primitives → Sphere**.

2 Change the sphere's axis orientation

- In the Channel box, select the *makeNurbSphere1* input node.

- Select the **Show Manipulator** tool.

  Several manipulators appear that allow you to edit parts of the input node. In the case of the sphere, the manipulators control the position of the main axis of the sphere.

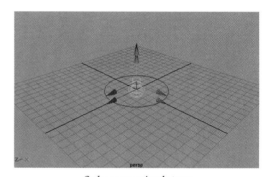

Sphere manipulators

- Press the **x** key to temporarily turn on grid snap and click-drag on the center of the top manipulator.

- Drag this manipulator down to the ground plane and place it along the X-axis with the help of grid snap.

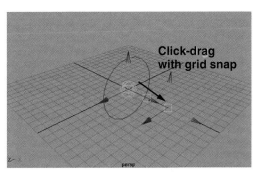

Redefined axis

Now the sphere's polar axis is pointing along the X-axis. This is the direction in which you are going to build Salty.

Note:	You could have also rotated the sphere to realign the polar axis. By using the input node, you keep the rotate values in the transform node at 0 0 0 which may be helpful when animating later.

3 Edit, then delete construction history

- In the Channel box, go to the *makeNurbSphere1* input node section and set the following:

    Radius to **4**;

    Spans to **14**.

This increases the size of the sphere and adds more isoparm spans. This will offer more flexibility when sculpting the surface into the shape of a seal.

- Select **Edit** → **Delete by Type** → **History.**

This deletes the sphere's input node. Since you are going to now pull CVs (control vertices) on the surface, the input node is no longer required.

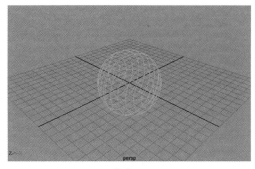

Sphere

Note:	Changing input node values after CV pulling is not recommended. Any changes to the number of spans later will negatively impact how your CV edits affect the surface.

Editing CVs

The sphere doesn't look very much like a seal at this point. You are now going to edit the positions of the surface's CVs to reshape the body.

1 Set up your view panels

While you can pull CVs using any view panel combination, it is a good idea to view the model from all four view types – Top, Front, Side and Perspective.

- Select **Panels** → **Layouts** → **Four Panes**.

Tip: Remember as you work, you can press the spacebar quickly to pop any of these panels to full screen and back for more detailed edits.

- Make the Perspective view the active panel and press the **5** key to turn on hardware shading.

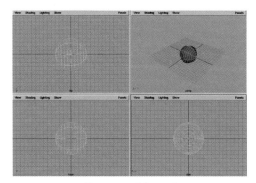

Four panel layout

2 Shape the sphere

You will now shape the sphere into a seal body by shaping the CVs.

- Pick the **Select** tool. Remember that you can use the **q** key.

- From the status line bar, click on the **Select by component** icon.

Select component mask

The sphere's surface is now highlighted in blue and its CVs are visible.

- Click-drag a selection box around all of the CVs

- Select the **Scale** tool.

- Click-drag on the X-axis handle to scale the sphere into the following shape:

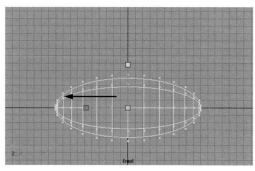

Scaled shape

3 Edit the CVs on Salty's head

When you first select a group of CVs, a special pivot is placed at the center of the selection. In some cases, you may want to move that pivot location.

- In the Front view, click-drag a selection box around the first few rows of CVs at the right end of the sphere.

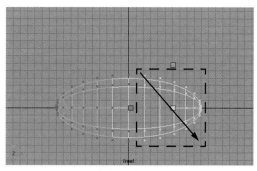

Selected CVs

The scale pivot is located at the center of the current selection.

- Press the **Insert / Home** key to make the pivot manipulator visible.

- Drag the pivot to the right edge of the surface.

  This point will now act as the reference point for the scaling.

- Press the **Insert / Home** key to return to the scale manipulator.

- Click-drag on the center scale handle to scale the head down to a smaller size.

  By dragging on the center of the manipulator, you make sure that you scale the CVs in all three axes.

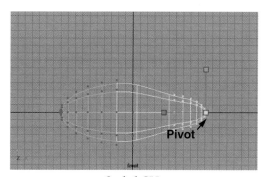

Scaled CVs

4 Edit the CVs on Salty's neck

- Click-drag a selection box around the sixth row of CVs.

- Click-drag on the center manipulator handle to scale this row down.

  This time you don't need to reposition the pivot because the center of the selection is the desired scale point.

  This creates Salty's neck.

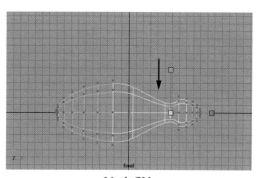

Neck CVs

5 Taper Salty's body

- In the side view panel, dolly into the view to see all of the shape.

- Click-drag a selection box around the CVs shown below. Use the **Shift** key to select both diagonal rows.

- Use the **Insert / Home** key to move the pivot point of the selection to the origin.

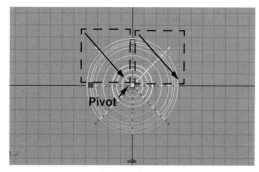

Selected CVs

- Press **Insert / Home** again to exit edit mode.

- Click-drag on the Y-axis scale handle to scale these points down.

- Click-drag on the Z-axis handle to scale these points in.

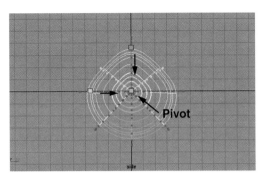

Scaled CVs

Note: In this case, you did not use the center scale handle since this would have also scaled along the X-axis. When working in one orthographic view, you must be aware of how your action may affect how the shape appears in another view.

---

6 Flatten the tail

- In the front view panel, **click-drag** a selection box around the last few rows of CVs.

- **Click-drag** on the Y-axis scale handle to scale these points down.

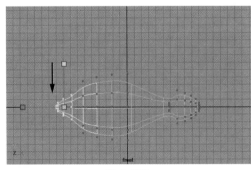

Tail CVs

Positioning the CVs

You can further position the CVs by rotating them around the Z-axis. This will further define the shape of your character and begin to create a more seal-like shape.

1 Move all of the CVs

- **Select** all of the CVs.

- Select the **Rotate** tool.

- Use the **Insert / Home** key to move the pivot point to the end of Salty's tail.

- Click-drag on the blue Z-axis handle to rotate the CVs up.

Check your other view panels to see if the rotation was successful.

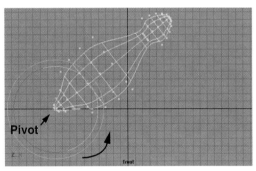

Rotated CVs

2 Rotate the neck down

- **Select** all of the CVs on Salty's head.

- Use the **Insert / Home** key to move the pivot point to the middle of Salty's neck.

- Click-drag on the blue Z-axis handle to rotate the head down.

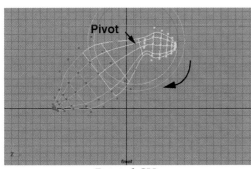

Rotated CVs

3 Adjust the surface hulls

- Click in empty space to unselect the current selection list.

- In the selection mask bar, turn the points selection mask off and turn on the hulls selection mask.

Selection masks

- Click on the cross section hull near Salty's neck. Be sure not to select any longitudinal hulls.

- **Rotate** the hull around the Z-axis.

- **Move** the hull forward as shown in the following:

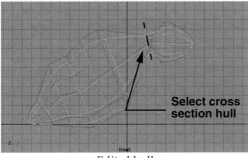

Edited hull

- Use the **left/right arrow** keys to move between the cross section hulls.

- **Rotate**, **Move** and **Scale** the cross section hulls until they create a more even distribution while creating a nice arch along the back.

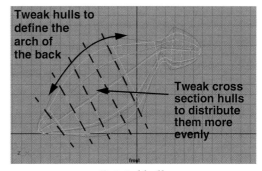

Rotated hulls

4 Save your work

- From the **File** menu, select **Save Scene As...**

- Enter the name *Salty1*.

Finishing touches

The steps taken so far have been fairly mechanical. The result is a shape that resembles a seal, but lacks those extra details to really make it look right.

Pushing and pulling CVs is like sculpting a piece of clay and the best results come from those final tweaks. Now, you can use your own sculpting skills to finish Salty's torso.

1 Tweak the CVs

- Turn off the hull selection mask and turn on the points selection mask.

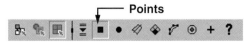

Points

Selection masks

- In the Front view panel, **Select** and **Move** CVs to refine the shape of the character.

  Try to adjust the various isoparms so that they are relatively perpendicular to the center axis of Salty's body. Also make sure that you are selecting CVs that are on both sides of Salty to keep your edits symmetrical.

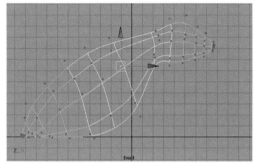

Tweaked CVs

Tip: If you don't like an edit that you make, remember that you can **Undo** and **Redo** your changes.

---

2 Increase the surface smoothness

- Press **F8** to go back to **Select by Object** mode.

  Press the **3** key to display the surface with a higher smoothness setting to evaluate the surface.

Press the **1** key when you want to go back to a low smoothness for modeling.

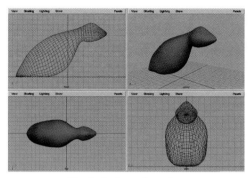

Shaded view of surface

Building skeleton joints

To animate Salty, you need to be able to deform the surface in a realistic manner. Moving and keyframing CVs would be a possibility, but would be a very time consuming process.

Skeleton joints can be used to create a structure that can be bound to your surface for more controlled deformations.

1 Draw the joints

The joints can be placed to suit the existing surface's shape.

- Go to the **Animation** menu set.
- Select **Display** → **Joint Size** → **25%**.
- Select **Skeleton** → **Joint Tool**.
- Along Salty's spine and head, click eight times to place joints as shown in the image below.
- Press **Enter** to finish drawing the skeleton.

The joints are drawn as a series of small sphere's connected by the skeleton's *bones*.

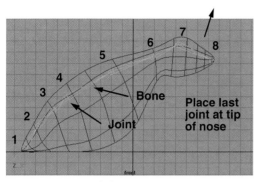

Skeleton joints

2 Change your selection mask

- From the black arrow next to the selection mode icons, select **All Objects Off**.

Selection mask pop-up

- Click on the **Select Joints** icon to activate this selection mask.

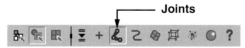

Select joints mask on

- Select the fourth joint up along the skeleton.

Tip: You can select a joint by either clicking exactly on the joint icon or by click-dragging over the next bone.

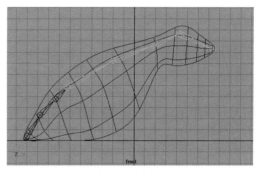

Selected joint

3 Reroot the skeleton

- Select **Skeleton → Reroot Skeleton**.

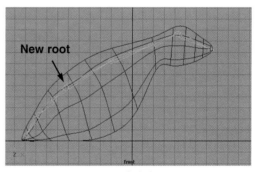

Rerooted skeleton

Bind the surface to the joints

1 Bind the skin

You must now bind the surface to the joints. Before you start, you need to change your selection masks to include surfaces.

- From the black arrow next to the selection mode icons, select **All Objects On**.

┌── **All options on** ──┐

All masks on

Tip: It is very easy to forget that you have set a particular selection mask. When you try to select a different object type, you are unable to pick anything.

The joints should already be selected.

- Press the **Shift** key and click on the surface to add it to the selection.

- Select **Skin → Bind Skin → Rigid Bind**.

2 Test the results

- Select the surface and press the **3** key to increase the surface smoothness.

- Select the first joint past the root.

- Select the **Rotate** tool.

  When you rotate a joint, you can see how the surface is set up to bend and twist with the joints.

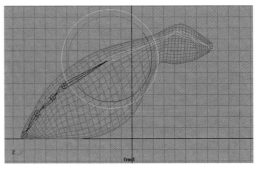

Rotating the neck joint

- In the Perspective view, click-drag the rotate manipulator to see how the bound skin moves with the joints.

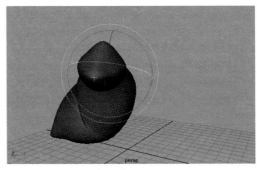

Testing the movement

3 Return to the bind pose

- Select the skeleton.

- Select **Skin → Go to Bind Pose**.

This sets the skeleton back to its bind pose.

4 Save your work

Templating objects

To build the next body part, you need the main surfaces visible, but you don't want them to interfere with your modeling. By

templating the existing surface, you can use it for reference without fear of selecting it.

1 Select the surface

- Pick the **Select** tool.
- Select the surface and the bones.

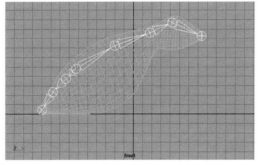

Selected pieces

2 Template the surface

- Assign the object to the *Salty* layer.
- Template the *Salty* Layer.

  Now these objects are visible but cannot be selected using the object selection mode.

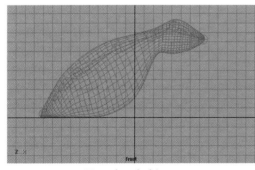

Templated objects

Building the front flipper

To build a flipper, you will now sculpt a primitive cylinder. The techniques are similar to manipulating the sphere except that now you have some extra details to model.

1 Place a primitive cylinder

- Select **Create → NURBS Primitives → Cylinder**.

2 Edit, then delete construction history

- Select the *makeNurbCylinder* input node in the Channel box.
- Set the following:

    Sections to **16**;

    Spans to **8**;

    Height Ratio to **7**.

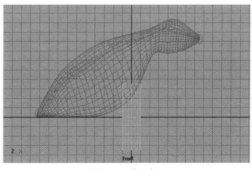

New cylinder

- Select **Edit → Delete by Type → History**.

3 Flatten and move the cylinder

- Select the **Move** tool.
- Click-drag along the Z-axis to place the cylinder just outside Salty's body.

- Select the **Scale** tool.

PROJECT FIVE

- In the Side view, click-drag on the blue Z-axis handle to scale the cylinder by a factor of about 0.25.

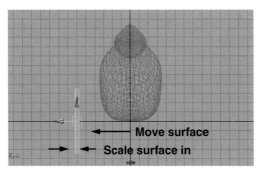

Flattened cylinder

4 Flatten the end of the cylinder

- Press **F8** to go into component select mode.
- Click-drag a selection box around the last three rows of CVs.
- Select the **Scale** tool.
- Click-drag along the Z-axis to squeeze these CVs until the end of the cylinder is flat.

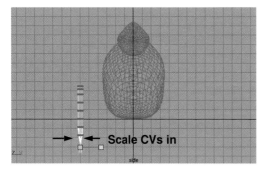

Squeezed CVs

The side shape

From the Front view panel, you can see the side of the flipper. You will now reshape this profile to make the cylinder resemble a flipper.

1 Move some CVs to add shape

- In the Front view, dolly until the cylinder fills the panel.
- Press the **Shift** key and with the left mouse button add the next two rows to the selection.
- Click-drag along the X-axis to scale the CVs out a little.

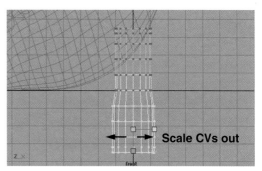

Edited CVs

2 Select the lower CVs

- Dolly in closer to the bottom five rows of CVs.
- Pick the **Select** tool.
- Click in empty space to deselect the current CVs.
- **Click-drag** a selection box around the lower middle two CVs as shown.

  You are actually selecting four CVs. Two in the front of the cylinder and two in the back.

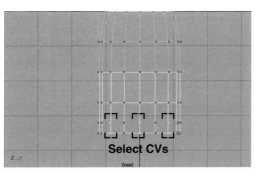

Selected CVs

3 Move the CVs

- Select the **Move** tool.
- Click-drag along the Y-axis to move the CVs up a little.

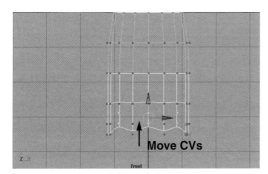

Edited CVs

4 Scale the top CVs down

- Dolly out to see the whole flipper.
- Click-drag a selection box around the top four rows of CVs

- Select the **Scale** tool.
- Click-drag along the X-axis to squeeze these CVs to tighten the top of the flipper.

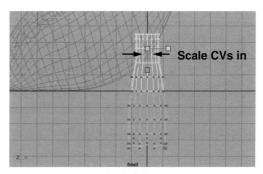

Scaled CVs

- Click-drag a selection box around the top three rows of CVs.
- Click-drag on the Y-scale handle to scale these CVs apart.

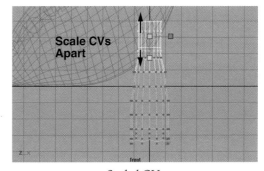

Scaled CVs

5 Rotate the top CVs down

- Select the **Rotate** tool.
- Press the **Insert / Home** key and in the Side view, move the pivot to a point in between the third and fourth rows of CVs.
- Again press the **Insert / Home** key and, in the Side view, rotate the selection around the X-axis as shown in the following:

PROJECT FIVE

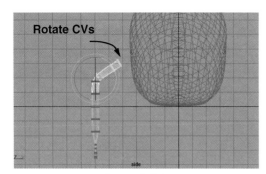

Rotated CVs

6 Rotate the bottom CVs up

- Select the bottom five rows of CVs.

- Press the **Insert / Home** key and in the Side view, move the pivot to a point in between the fourth and fifth rows of CVs.

- Again press the **Insert / Home** key and, in the Side view, **Rotate** the selection around the X-axis as shown below:

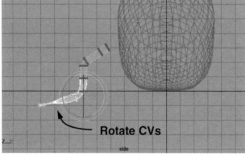

Rotated CVs

Refining the flipper

The rotations on the flipper are a little harsh. To improve the look of this profile, you can rotate and move the various rows of CVs to complete the shape.

1 Adjust the rows of CVs in the Side view

- Select the rows of CVs on the flipper one at a time.

- **Move** and **Rotate** them to create a more sculpted shape:

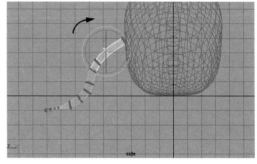

Refined CVs

Be sure to consider how the flipper is looking in other views such as the Front view or the Perspective view.

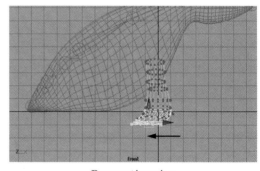

Perspective view

2 Untemplate the body surface

- Untemplate the *Salty* Layer.

  Now, these parts are available for you to work with.

3 Move the flipper up to the body surface

- Press **F8** to go to the **Object** select mode.

- Select the flipper surface.

- **Move** the flipper until its end is penetrating the side of the seal.

  Use all four views to confirm the placement.

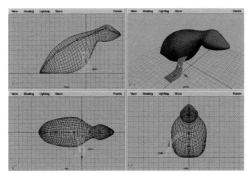

Four views of Salty

- **Rotate** the flipper around the Y-axis to angle it a little as shown in the following:

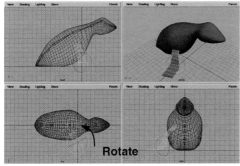

Rotate flipper

The back flipper

The back flipper will be created by editing a duplicate of the front flipper. It is useful to re-

use pieces of geometry to make your sculpting easier.

1 Build a back flipper

- Select the front flipper.

- Select **Edit** → **Duplicate**.

- Move the copy to the back of Salty.

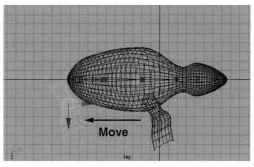

Back flipper

- **Rotate** the flipper around the Y-axis to line it up with the body.

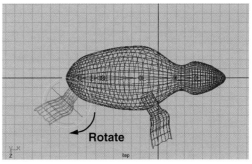

Rotated flipper

- Edit the CVs and position the flipper at the back of Salty.

PROJECT FIVE

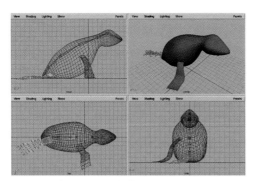

Back flipper

Mirroring the flippers

Rather than build flippers for Salty's left side from scratch, you can duplicate and mirror the existing flippers. A mirror can be achieved by scaling with a factor of -1.

1 Group, then duplicate the flippers

- Select the two flippers.
- Select **Edit** → **Group**.
- Select **Edit** → **Duplicate**.

2 Scale to -1

- In the Channel box, enter -1 in the *Scale Z* channel.

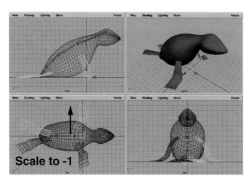

Mirrored flippers

3 Save your work

- Select **File** → **Save Scene**.

Add joints for the flippers

To connect the flippers to the rest of the body, you will build skeleton joints and then bind in the new surfaces.

1 Draw joints for the front flipper

- Select the front and back flippers and assign them to the *Salty* Layer.
- Create a new layer. Name the new layer *Bones*.
- Select the bones and assign them to the *Bones* layer.
- **Template** the *Salty* Layer.

  Now you have templated the surfaces without the bones.

- Go to the **Animation** menu set.
- Select **Skeleton** → **Joint Tool**.
- In the Side view along Salty's front right flipper, click five times to place joints as shown in the following:

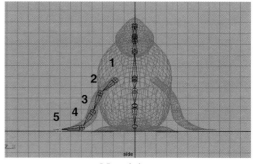

New joints

2 Move the second joint into place

- Select the second joint in the skeleton hierarchy.
- Select the **Move** tool.
- In the Front view, move the joint along the XY plane to the middle of the flipper.

  Oops! The joint and all the subsequent joints are moved at the same time. You don't want this.

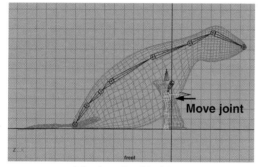

Moving the third joint

3 Set the pivot location for the joint

- **Undo** the last move.
- Press the **Insert / Home** key to invoke the joint's pivot location.
- Move the pivot to the middle of the flipper.

  Now this joint moves independent of the other joints. You can either move the joint or set the joint's pivot to relocate joints.

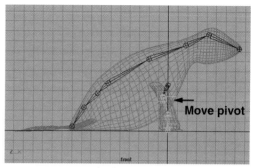

Moving the fourth joint's pivot

4 Edit the remaining joints

- Press the **up and down arrow** key to move the selection to the next joint.
- **Move** this joint's pivot into place.
- Press the **Insert / Home** key to go back to the move manipulator.

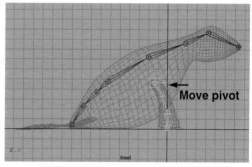

All the joints in place

5 Add joints for the back flipper

- Select **Skeleton → Joint Tool**.
- In the Top view, draw three joints for the back flipper.
- Press **Enter** to complete the joints.

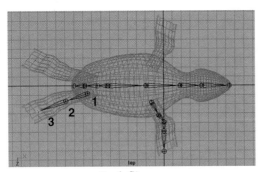

Back flippers

Joining the flippers to the body

To make sure that the new joints work with the existing skeleton, you must connect them together. The logical place to join would be the hips and the shoulders.

1 Select the joints

- Using the Select Tool, pick the root joint of the front flipper.

- Press the **Shift** key and select the shoulder joint of the main spine.

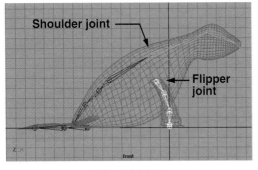

Selected joints

2 Connect the joints

- Select **Skeleton** → **Connect Joint** - ❐. In the Tool options, change the **Mode** to **Parent Joint**.

This will place a bone between the two selected joints rather than moving the flipper joint up to the shoulder.

- Click **Connect**.

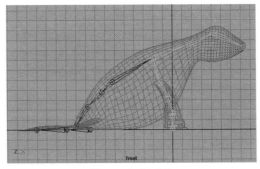

Connected joints

3 Connect the back joints

- Use the same technique outlined above to join the back flipper skeleton to the hip joint of the main skeleton.

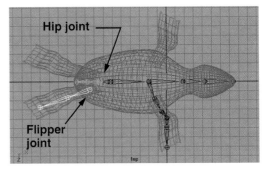

Selected joints

While you will not be animating the tail portion of Salty in this lesson, it is a good idea to complete the skeleton just in case.

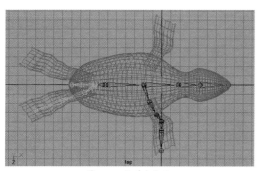

Connected joints

4 Mirror the joints

- Select the joint that used to be the root joint of the front flipper skeleton.

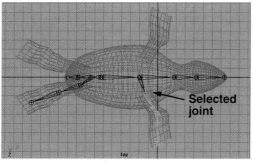

Selected joint

- Select **Skeleton → Mirror Joint.**

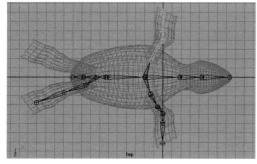

Mirrored joints

- Repeat for the back flipper.

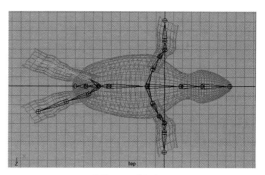

Mirrored joints

Binding the surfaces

The flipper surfaces should deform with the skeleton, and therefore must be bound.

Binding a surface is a process where the surface's CVs are separated into sets which are then bound to the appropriate joints in the skeleton. When the joints move or rotate, the sets react as part of the joint hierarchy.

1 Untemplate the Salty layer

- Untemplate the *Salty* layer.

2 Bind all the surfaces

- **Select** the four flipper surfaces.
- Press the **Shift** key and add the main skeleton root to the selection.
- Select **Skin → Bind Skin → Rigid Bind.**

3 Test the motion

- **Rotate** various joints on the skeleton to test the resulting bind.

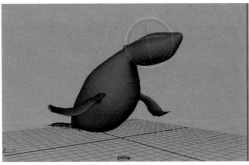

Rotated joints

4 Return to the bind pose

- Select the skeleton.

- Select **Skin → Go to Bind Pose.**

  This sets the skeleton back to its
  bind pose.

5 Assign all of the objects to a layer

- Select all of Salty's pieces and assign
  them to the *Salty* layer.

- Right-click over the *Bones* layer and
  select **Delete.**

  Since you have assigned all the
  bones to the Salty layer, you no
  longer need to use this layer.

Salty's shading group

To define the look of Salty's skin, you will
create a new shading group. The skin is to be
dark and slick with a slight shinyness. You
will set attributes on the material node to
achieve this look.

1 Set your view panels

- Select **Panels → Saved Layouts →
  Hypershade/Outliner/Persp.**

2 Create a new blinn material

You will create a new blinn material node
which is suitable for shiny, metallic or wet
surfaces.

- In the Hypershade, create a **Blinn**
  surface material.

- Rename the material node to
  skinBlinn.

3 Set the common material attributes

The general color attributes are first set to
create a basic dark color of the skin.

- Double-click on the *skinBlinn* node
  to open the Attribute Editor.

- Change the **Color** to a very dark
  brown by setting the following in
  the Color Chooser:

  (H) Hue to **24**;

  (S) Saturation to **0.3**;

  (V) Value to **0.07**.

- In the Attribute Editor, set the
  following:

  Diffuse to **0.5**.

  Reducing the diffuse value
  decreases the amount of diffuse
  color that appears on the surface.

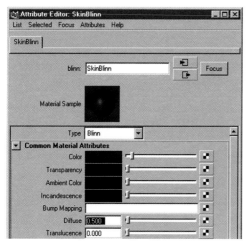

Color and diffuse settings

4 Assign the shading group

- Turn off the joint selection mask option. Now you will only pick surfaces.

Selection masks

- Assign the material to Salty's body, front flippers and back flippers.

In the shaded view, you can see the material on the surfaces.

Shaded view of Salty

5 Set the specular shading attributes

The specular shading attributes define the way that the material appears in direct and ambient lighting conditions, creating highlights and hotspots on the surfaces. The seal's skin should appear soft, with a wet, reflective quality.

- Click on the *skinBlinn* node in the Hypershade.

- Arrange this window so that you can see the shaded surfaces as you update the values.

- In the **Specular Shading** section, set the following:

    Eccentricity to **0.6**.

This creates larger areas of highlights which give a softer or more diffuse feel to the material.

    Specular Roll Off to **0.8**.

A higher value gives the impression of light being reflected at more oblique angles, making the surface appear more wet.

    Specular Color to a darker value with a slight saturation of purple.

PROJECT FIVE

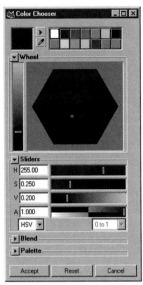

Specular shading attributes

HSV values of **255**, **0.25**, **0.2** were used. These settings darken the highlight and change its color from the warmer base color, to create a more complex surface quality.

Reflectivity to less than **0.1**.

The skin of the seal should only slightly reflect the surrounding surfaces.

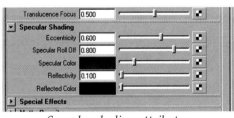

Specular shading attributes

The various attributes of the material node allow you to clearly define how a surface looks. As you become more familiar with the available settings, you will be able to create materials that clearly represent real life materials.

6 Save your work

- Select **File** → **Save Scene**.

  You will be using this scene file as the starting point for the next lesson.

Conclusion

You are now off to a great start building Salty. In the next lesson, you will add facial details with special attention to the eyes which will be set up for animation later.

21 Adding Facial Details

In this lesson, you will develop Salty's facial features. You will start by building an eye assembly that will allow you to control where Salty is looking. You will also create a control object with special attributes that will let you set where the eyes look, how the eyes blink, and how the shape of the eyes express Salty's feelings. The goal is to explore how to model using Maya's procedural capabilities to help make it easier to animate all aspects of the eyes in later lessons.

In addition, you will add whiskers and a nose. All of these elements will be texture-mapped to prepare them for rendering later on.

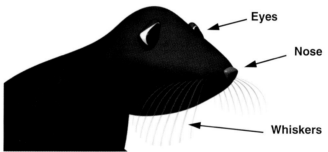

Salty's facial details

In this lesson you will learn the following:

- How to build an eyeball hierarchy
- How to use an aim constraint
- How to apply lattice and cluster deformers
- How to add an attribute to a node
- How to use Set Driven Key
- How to use transparency maps

Initial set-up

To start this lesson, will continue with your file from the last lesson as you continue to build Salty.

1 Change the panel layout

- Select **Panels** → **Saved Layouts** → **Four View**.

- Make the Perspective view panel active and press the **5** key to set smooth shading.

2 Template the existing objects

- Template the existing *Salty* layer.

Building Salty's right eyeball

To start building Salty's eye, you will build and texture an eyeball centered around the origin. Later, you will position it more closely to Salty's head.

1 Place a primitive sphere

- Select **Create** → **NURBS Primitives** → **Sphere**.

- Press the **3** key to increase the display smoothness of the sphere.

- In the Channel box, rename the node to *eyeball.*

2 Use show manipulator tool to edit axis

- Dolly in to see the sphere from a closer point of view.

- In the Channel box, select the *makeNurbSphere* input node.

- Select the **Show Manipulator** tool.

- Press the **x** key to temporarily turn on grid snap and click-drag on the center of the top manipulator.

- Drag this manipulator down to the ground plane and place it along the X-axis with the help of grid snap.

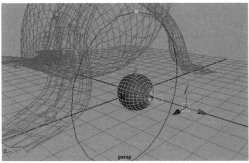
New axis location

This orientation will facilitate the mapping of a ramp texture to the sphere later.

3 Edit the input node values

- In the Channel box, change the following attributes for the *makeNurbsSphere* node:

  Radius to **0.5**.

4 Create the eye shading group

The seal's eyes will use a phong material node that is shiny with a bit of translucence.

- In the Hypershade, Create a Phong material node, and rename it to *eyePhong.*

5 Edit the material attributes

- Double-click on the *eyePhong* material node to open the Attribute Editor.

- Set the following attributes:

  Color to white;

  Diffuse value to **1.0**;

  Click on the color swatch next to **Incandescence** to set the **Value** to **0.15**.

  The illuminated and shaded regions on the material sample are now quite bright.

  This will help make Salty's eyeball shine in any lighting.

6 Assign the material node

- Assign *eyePhong* to the *eyeball* surface using the technique taught in earlier lessons.

7 Add a ramp color texture

To help differentiate the pupil from the white of the eyes, you will use a *procedural ramp texture*.

- In the Attribute Editor, click on the **Map** button next to **Color**.
- In the Create Render Node window, choose a **Ramp** texture.
- Make the Perspective view the active panel and press **6** to turn on hardware texturing.

8 Edit the ramp

- In the Attribute Editor, change the ramp attributes as follows:

  Type to **U Ramp**;

  Interpolation to **None**.

  This creates a harsh break between the first two colors on the ramp.

- Click on the square icon to the right of the blue color indicator to delete this color.

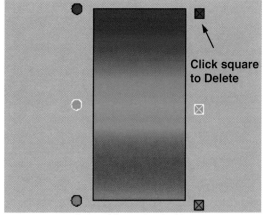

Deleting blue color indicator

- Click on the round icon to the left of the green color indicator to select it.
- Click-drag on the round icon to move the indicator up until it is set to around **0.85**.

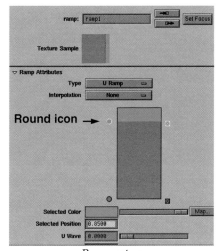

Ramp setup

PROJECT FIVE

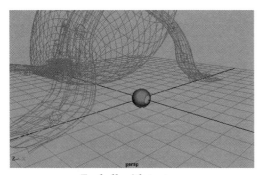

Eyeball with texture

9 Edit the ramp's colors

- In the Attribute Editor, drag the green color indicator's **Selected Color** slider all the way to the left.

This makes this color turn to black.

- Click on the round icon for the red color indicator.
- Click on the **Selected Color** swatch to open the Color Chooser.
- Change this color to white.

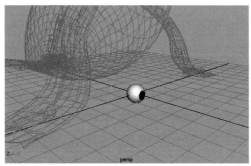

Eyeball with updated texture

- Close or minimize the Hypershade and the Attribute Editor.

Creating a target for the eyeball

To animate the eyeball later, you will want to be able to control what it is looking at. You will first create a locator object, then constrain the eyeball to aim towards it.

1 Create and position a locator object

- Select **Create → Locator**.
- **Move** the locator along the X-axis to move it in front of the eyeball.
- **Move** the locator along the Y-axis a little to place it above the ground.

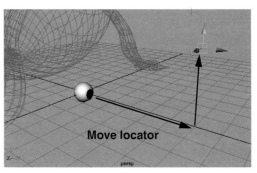

Locator object moves

2 Aim the eyeball at the locator

- Change to the **Animation** menu set.
- Press the **Shift** key and select the *eyeball* surface.

  Now the locator and the eyeball are selected. Since the eyeball was selected last, it is indicated in green. Since you are aiming the eye, it is important that it is picked last.

- Select **Constrain → Aim**.

  Now the eye is looking at the locator.

- **Move** the locator, on its own, in all axes to test the aiming of the eye.

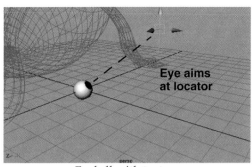

Eyeball with texture

- In the Channel box, set the following for the *locator1* node:

    Translate X to **7**;

    Translate Y to **0**;

    Translate Z to **0**.

Now the eyeball is looking straight ahead.

Creating the eyelid

You are now going to build an eyelid out of another primitive sphere. The input node will be used to set the start and end sweep of the sphere which help create the blinking action.

1 Place a second primitive sphere

- Select **Create** → **NURBS Primitives** → **Sphere**.

- In the Channel box, rename the *nurbSphere* node to *eyelid*.

- Increase the object's smoothness using the techniques taught in earlier lessons.

2 Edit the sphere's axis

- In the Channel box, select the *makeNurbSphere* input node.

 - Select the **Show Manipulator** tool.

- Press the **x** key to temporarily turn on grid snap and click-drag on the center of the top manipulator.

- Drag this manipulator down to the ground grid and place it along the Z-axis with the help of grid snap.

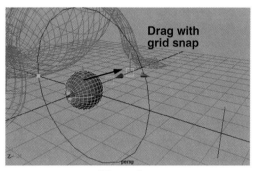

New sphere

3 Edit the input node attributes

The sphere's input node contains attributes that control the start and end sweep of the shape. You will now set these to look like a partially opened eye. You will then animate these attributes to make Salty blink.

- In the Channel box, change the following attributes for the *makeNurbsSphere* node:

    Radius to **0.55**;

    Start Sweep to **60**;

    End Sweep to **300**.

The two sweep attributes let you open and close the lid surface using the construction history built into the sphere's input node.

PROJECT FIVE

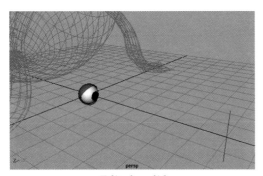

Edited eyelid

Note: When you were modeling the body surfaces, you deleted history. For the eye, you will keep history since the start and end sweep can be used to blink the eye. This will be an example of procedural animation as the keys are set on the input node to animate the sphere.

4 Assign the seal shading group

You can now assign the existing seal skin shading group to the eyelid surface.

- Change to the **Rendering** menu set.
- Select **Lighting/Shading → Assign Existing Material → skinBlinn**.

5 Group the eyelid and the eyeball

- Select both the *eyelid* and the *eyeball*.
- Select **Edit → Group**.
- In the Channel box, change the name of *group* to *rightEye*.

6 Move the parts of the eye

- Press the **Shift** key and select *locator1* to add it to the current selection list.

- **Move** these objects up and across to place the eye group on the right side of Salty's head.

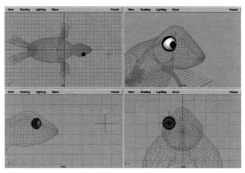

Positioned objects

7 Save your work

- From the **File** menu, select **Save Scene As...**
- Enter the name *Salty2* next to the file's path.

The Hypergraph

Whenever you create a group of objects, you create a transform hierarchy. In earlier projects, you learned how to look at these hierarchies in the Outliner. The *Hypergraph* offers a more diagrammatic view of the same information.

When working with hierarchies, you can either work with the top or *root* node, or you can work with the lower *leaf* nodes. Complex animations are possible when you combine animation at different hierarchy levels.

1 Open a Hypergraph panel

- Click in empty space to clear your selection.
- From the Top view panel, select **Panels → Panel → Hypergraph...**

- From the Hypergraph panel, select **View → Frame All**.

  This shows you all the transform node hierarchies that exist in the model now. This includes the skeleton joint hierarchy and the new eye hierarchy.

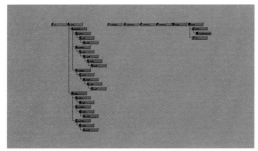
Hypergraph panel

2 Select the eye group

- In the viewport, click-drag a selection box over the *rightEye* group.

- From the Hypergraph panel, select **View → Frame Selection**.

- Use the **Alt** key and the left and middle mouse buttons to dolly out of the scene. The same view tools apply here as in other panels.

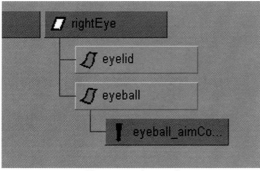
Hypergraph panel

In the Hypergraph, you can see that the two lower nodes in the hierarchy have been picked even though you may have wanted to pick the upper node.

When you are in object selection mode, you are always picking the lowest node in the hierarchy.

- Press the **up arrow** key to move up the hierarchy to the *rightEye* group node.

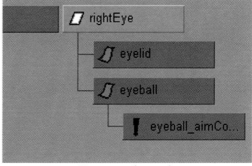
Hypergraph panel

Deforming the eye

The eye is looking good – but it needs more character. To give it a more dynamic shape, you can apply a *lattice deformer*.

Lattice deformers let you manipulate the shape of a surface using an external frame. The lattice frame has its own control points that can be edited just like CVs to let you deform both the eyeball and the eyelid as a single group.

1 Apply a lattice to the eye group

- Change to the **Animation** menu set.

  Select **Deform → Create Lattice - ❐**.

PROJECT FIVE

- In the Lattice Options window, set the following:

    Parenting to **On**.

- Click the Create button.

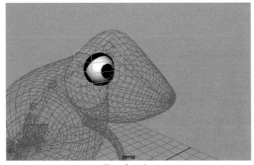

Eye lattice

In the Hypergraph, you can now see two new nodes parented under the *rightEye* group. By parenting these to the group, you can move them all together to maintain the deformations as Salty's head moves.

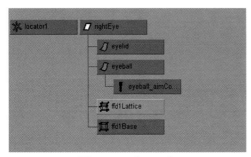

Hypergraph panel

2 Scale the lattice object

The lattice base is a special node designed to contain the geometry that is to be deformed. If your objects move out of the base, then they will no longer be deformed.

To be on the safe side, you should scale this node out to make sure it encompasses the entire eye, even when it is deformed later.

- In the Hypergraph panel, using the **Shift** key, click on the *ffd1Base* and the *ffd1Lattice* nodes.

- In the Channel box, edit the following attributes:

    Scale X to **1.5**;

    Scale Y to **1.5**;

    Scale Z to **1.5**.

This scales out the lattice and its base, allowing the eye to be encompassed more completely by the lattice. The eye group remains the same size since both parts were scaled.

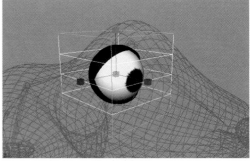

Scaled lattice

3 Reshape the eye using the lattice

You will now work with the lattice node which lets you apply the actual surface deformations.

- In the Hypergraph panel, select only the *ffd1Lattice* node.

 - **Scale** along the X and Z axes to scale the lattice into the following shape:

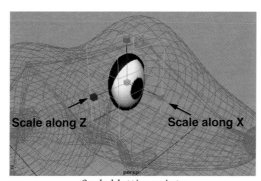

Scaled lattice points

4 Move the bottom lattice points

- Press **F8** to go into Component mode.

- Click-drag a selection box around the six points on the lower side of the lattice.

- **Move** these points along the Z-axis handle to push the points out.

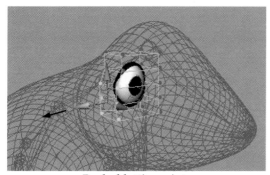

Pushed lattice points

Adding a cluster deformer

Another type of deformer is a *cluster*. Clusters let you create a set of CVs or lattice points and give these points their own special pivot point for specific scaling and rotational edits. This cluster will be used to make Salty's eyes appear to get worried.

1 Add a cluster to the top lattice points

- Click-drag a selection box around the top eight lattice points.

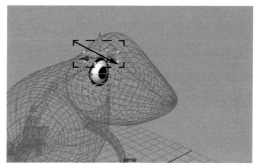

Selected Lattice points

- Select **Deform → Create Cluster**.

A cluster is now created using these points. It is indicated using a small C icon.

- In the Channel box rename the *clusterHandle* to *eyeCluster*.

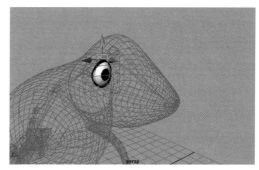

New cluster object

2 Edit the pivot location of the cluster

- Press **F8** to go back to object selection mode.

- Press the **Insert / Home** key.

- Click-drag the cluster's pivot along the Z-axis to the edge of the lattice.

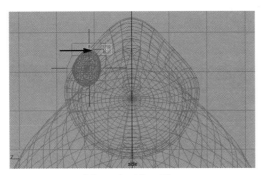

New pivot location

3 Scale the cluster

- Press the **Insert / Home** key to get out of edit mode.

- **Scale** the cluster in along the Z-axis to a value of about **0.5**.

  This gives Salty a worried look.

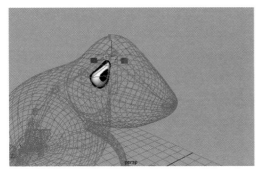

Scaled cluster

Positioning the eye

When you positioned the eye earlier, you used the templated lines for reference. You will now make sure that the eye is not intersecting the main body surface.

1 Untemplate the various surfaces

- Untemplate the *Salty* layer.

The eye may not be positioned correctly in relation to the head surface causing intersecting surfaces. You should reposition it to create a more accurate relationship between these pieces.

2 Reposition the eye group

- In the Hypergraph, select the *rightEye* group node.

- **Move** the group until it is correctly positioned in relation to the main surface.

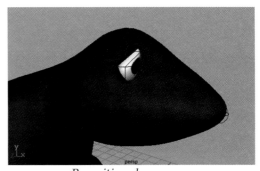

Repositioned eye group

Creating the second eye

You will create the second eye by duplicating the first. Duplicating the eye with all of its connections will make sure that the input nodes for the sphere and the constraint are included. This is important to ensure that both eyes work in the same manner.

1 Duplicate the whole hierarchy

- In the Hypergraph, select both the *rightEye* group node and the *locator1* node.

- Select **Edit → Duplicate - ❑**.

- In the Duplicate Options window, set the following:

    Duplicate Input Graph to **On**.

- Click on **Duplicate**.

2 Mirror the new eye group

- In the Channel box, change the **Scale Z** value to **-1**.

    This mirrors all of the selected parts.

Note: In some instances, the material may not be assigned to the new eye. If this is the case, simply assign eyePhong to the newly created eye.

---

3 Move the new eye group

- **Move** the selection along the Z-axis until the new eye group sits on the opposite side of the face.

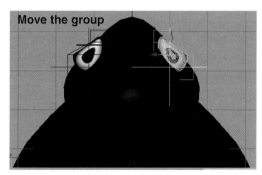

Both eyes in place

4 Rename the new eye group

- In the Hypergraph panel, press the **Ctrl** key and double-click on the *rightEye1* node.

- Type the name *leftEye* and press the **Enter** key.

Building the eye control node

You could now animate the eyes by keying the position of the locators to determine where Salty is looking, the start and end sweep of the *makeNurbSphere* nodes (to make Salty blink), or the scale of the Clusters (to give Salty a worried look).

One problem, however, is that all of these parts are buried within the eye assembly. You will now group the two locators and create an eye control node which will be linked using expressions to control all of the items mentioned above. By creating this control now, Salty will be much easier to animate in the next lesson.

1 Group the locators

- **Select** the two locators.

- Select **Edit → Group**.

- Select **Modify → Center Pivot...**

- Select **Display → Component Display → Selection Handles**.

- In the Channel box, rename the group node to *eyeControl*.

2 Restricting channels on the new group

- From the **Window** menu, select **General Editors → Channel Control...**

- In the Keyable list, press the **Ctrl / Command** key and click on the attribute names as shown in the following:

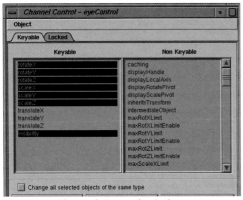

Channel Control window

- Press the **Move >>** button to move these into Non Keyable list.

  In the Channel box, you can now see only the three translate attributes.

- Close this window.

3 Add a worry attribute

So far, you have been working with attributes specific to different node types, and you have revealed hidden attributes. To control parts of Salty's eyes, you are going to add your own attribute that will be connected using expressions.

- Select **Modify → Add Attribute...**
- In the Add Attribute window, set the following:

      Attribute Name to *worry*;

      Data Type to **Float**;

      Minimum Value to **0**;

      Maximum Value to **10**;

      Default Value to **10**.

  These settings create the value range for the attribute.

- Click the **Ok** button.

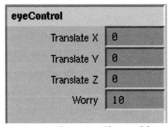

New attribute in Channel box

4 Use worry to drive the cluster

To drive the cluster's scaling along the Z-axis, you are going to use Set Driven Key. This tool lets you set up relationships between different attributes. You will set up the worry node to drive the scaling of the *eyeCluster*.

- Go to the **Animation** menu set.
- In the Hypergraph, select the *eyeCluster* node.
- Next, select **Animate → Set Driven Key → Set - □**.

  This opens a window that lets you link attributes. The *eyeCluster* node is loaded as the driven node.

- Click on the **scaleZ** attribute in the right-hand list.
- In the Perspective view, **Select** *eyeControl* using its selection handle.
- In the Set Driven Key window, click on the **Load Driver** button.
- Click on the **worry** attribute in the right-hand list.

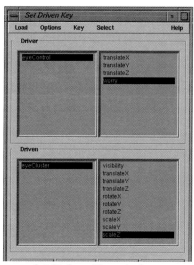

Set Driven Key window

5 Key the scale positions

- In the Set Driven Key window, click on the **Key** button.

  Now, when the **worry** attribute is set to 10, the **scale Z** attribute will be set to 0.5.

- In the Channel box, change the **Worry** attribute to **0**.

- Select the *eyeCluster* node.

Tip: You can use the Set Driven Key window to select the objects.

- In the Channel box, change the **Scale Z** attribute to **1**.

- In the Set Driven Key window, click on the **Key** button.

6 Test the results

- Select the *eyeControl* group using its selection handle.

- In the Channel box, click on the **Worry** channel name.

- In the Perspective view panel, click-drag sideways with the middle mouse button to test the attribute.

  As you click-drag from 0 to 10, Salty's eye changes its expression.

7 Edit the resulting graph curves

- Select the *eyeCluster* node.

- Select **Window → Animation Editors → Graph Editor...**

- From this window, select **View → Frame All**.

  Along one axis of the curve diagram is the cluster's *scale Z*, and along the other is the *eyeControl* node's **worry** attribute based on the keys set using Set Driven Key.

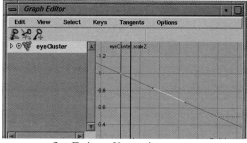

Set Driven Key anim curve

- Select the curve.

- Select **Tangents → Flat**.

  This changes the way in which the driven attribute is affected by the driver. You can edit this curve to define any relationship you desire.

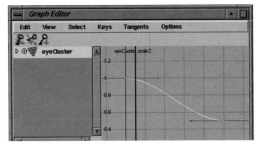

Edited anim curve

8 Repeat for the other cluster handle

- In the Hypergraph, select the *eyeCluster1* node.

- Use the Set Driven Key window to drive this node using the *eyeControl* node's **worry** attribute.

- When you are finished, set the *eyeControl* node's **worry** attribute to **7**.

  This creates a good neutral position. Later, you will animate this attribute to make Salty react to the bouncing of the ball in the next lesson.

Salty looking a little worried

9 Save your work

Adding a blink attribute

Another useful control would be a blink attribute. This would allow you to control the opening and closing of the eyes using a single attribute, instead of working with the two sweep attributes on two separate input nodes.

1 Add a new attribute

- Make sure that the *eyeControl* group is selected.

- Select **Modify → Add Attribute.**

- In the Add Attribute window, set the following:

    Attribute Name to *blink*;

    Data Type to **Float**;

    Minimum Value to **0**;

    Maximum Value to **10**;

    Default Value to **10**.

- Click on the **Ok** button.

2 Use blink to drive the sweep angles

To drive the opening and closing of the *eyeLid*, you are going to again use Set Driven Key. This time you will use the **blink** attribute to drive the start and end sweep of the eyelid's *makeNurbSphere* input node.

- Go to the **Animation** menu set.

- Move your mouse over the *eyelid* in the perspective view and with the **RMB**, select **Inputs → Make Nurb Sphere**.

  Ensure you pick the *eyeLid* node by checking the name at the top of the popup menu.

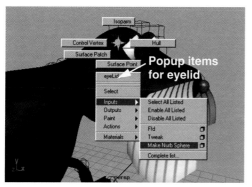

Selecting makeNurbSphere

- Select **Animate** → **Set Driven Key** →
  Set - ▢.

  In the Set Driven Key window,
  makeNurbSphere node loaded in the
  Driven section.

- Click on the **makeNurbSphere** node
  in the left-hand list, then click on
  both the **startSweep** and **endSweep**
  attributes in the right-hand list.

- In the Perspective view, **Select**
  eyeControl using its selection handle.

- In the Set Driven Key window, click
  on the **Load Driver** button.

  This updates the list to contain the
  blink attribute.

- Click on the **blink** attribute in the
  right-hand list.

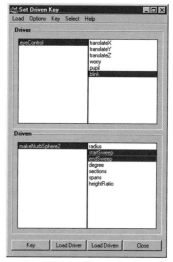

Set Driven Key window

3 Key the scale positions

- In the Set Driven Key window, click
  on the **Key** button.

  Now when the **blink** attribute is set
  to 10, the two sweep angles will be
  set to their open position.

- In the Channel box, change the **Blink**
  attribute to **0**.

- Click on *makeNurbSphere* in the
  Driven section.

  You can also make the inputs active
  through the Attribute Editor.

- Change the Channel Box set the
  following:

    Start Sweep to **0**;

    End Sweep to **360**.

- In the Set Driven Key window,
  press the **Key** button.

4 Test the results

- Select the *eyeControl* group using its selection handle.
- In the Channel box, click on the *Blink* channel name.
- In the Perspective panel, click-drag with the middle mouse button to test the attribute.

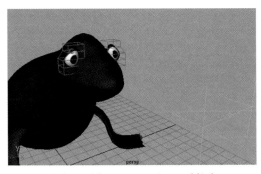
Salty with eyes starting to blink

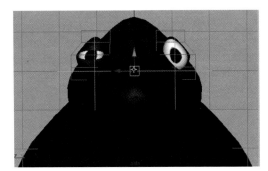
Salty blinking

5 Use Set Driven Key on the left eye

- Set the **Blink** attribute back to **10**.
- Select the *eyeLid1* node belonging to the *leftEye* group.
- Load it as **Driven** in the Set Driven Key window then key the relationship between the *blink* and the *eyeLid* node's *startSweep* and *endSweep* angles. This eye should work just like the first eye.
- In the Channel box, test the *Blink* attribute to make sure that both eyes are working properly.
- In the Channel box, set the following:

    Blink to **8**.

Building the whiskers

For Salty's whiskers, a primitive plane will be used. You will then create and assign a shader that uses a transparency map to create the effect of the whiskers.

Using CV editing techniques which you learned in the last lesson, you will shape the whisker surface.

1 Place a half cylinder

- Go to the **Modeling** menu set.
- Select **Create → NURBS Primitives → Cylinder -** ❑.
- In the Option window, set the following:

    Axis to **X**;

    End Sweep to **-180**;

    Radius to **2**;

    Height to **1**;

    Number of Sections to **8**;

    Number of Spans to **1**.

- Click on **Create**.
- Press the **3** key to increase the display smoothness of the shape.

- In the Channel box, rename the *nurbsCylinder* node to *whisker*.

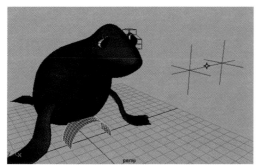

Half cylinder

2 Move the whiskers into place

- **Scale** the surface down in Y a little.

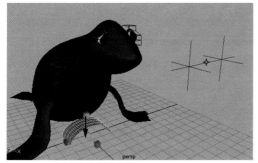

Scaled whisker surface

- **Move** the surface until it sits in the proper position on Salty's face.

Moved whisker surface

3 Edit CVs on the shape

- Press **F8** to go into component selection mode.

- In the Top view, click-drag a selection box around the middle three rows of CVs and scale them along X.

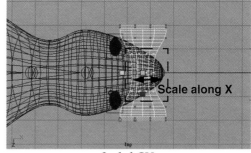

Scaled CVs

- Repeat this for the next two rows of CVs to scale them in a little.

  This creates a more gentle curve at the edge of the whiskers.

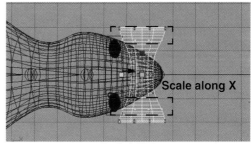

Scaled CVs

4 Scale out the middle CVs

- Click-drag a selection box around the middle two CVs at both ends of the surface.

- **Scale** these out from the center.

PROJECT FIVE

This will add some curvature to the end of the whiskers.

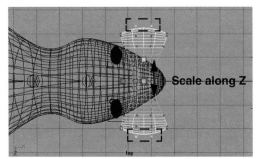

Scaled CVs

- **Move** these down along the Y-axis.

Now the center of the whiskers droops down a little further than the edges.

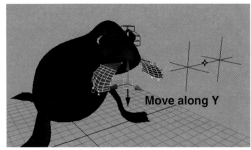

Scaled and positioned CVs

- Press **F8** to return to object selection.

Texturing the whiskers

The whiskers have been created with one surface and a texture will be used as a transparency map on the material node to create the lines of the whiskers.

1 Create whisker material

Because a transparency map will be used, it is important that the highlights do not appear on the surface. A lambert material node will be used because it does not produce any specular shading qualities.

- Select **Window** → **Rendering Editors** → **Hypershade**...
- Create a new **Lambert** material node.
- Rename the node to *lambertWhisker*.

2 Map grid texture onto material color

Although the whiskers will eventually be created with just a transparency map, a grid texture will first be mapped onto the color attribute. This means that the adjustments to the texture and placement can be seen in the context of the model view by those who can use hardware texturing.

- Open the *lambertWhisker* material node's Attribute Editor.
- Click on the **Map** button for the **Color** attribute.
- Click on the **Textures** tab of the Create Render Node window.
- Make sure **With New Texture Placement** is checked on.
- In the **2D Textures** section, click on the **Grid** button.
- **Assign** the *lambertWhisker* node to the *whisker* surface.

Texture on whisker surface

Whisker texture qualities

3 Edit the grid texture's attributes

The grid texture is adjusted to produce black lines on a white surface. The lines in the direction of the whiskers are thickened to become more visible and the cross lines are set to be invisible, transforming the grid into a series of parallel lines.

- Open the *grid1* texture node in the Attribute Editor and set the following:

  Name to *whiskerTexture*;

  Line Color to black;

  Filler Color to white;

  U Width to **0.2**;

  V Width to **0**.

If the lines of the grid texture do not flow as shown, switch the **U Width** and **V Width** settings.

4 Edit the grid texture placement

The number of lines in the grid texture is not set in the texture node itself. Instead the number of lines, or whiskers, is set in the *place2dTexture* node.

- Click on the *place2dTexture* node tab in the Attribute Editor.

- Change the following:

  Repeat U V to **8** and **4**.

  Because the thickness of the grid lines for V has been set to be invisible, the grid lines along V will be invisible.

Edited placement attributes

PROJECT FIVE

5 Remap grid texture onto transparency

Now that the texture for the whiskers has been developed as a color map, the same texture can be mapped onto the transparency attribute of the same material node. The white areas of the texture will be transparent and the black areas opaque.

- Open the *lambertWhisker* material node's Attribute Editor.

- With the middle mouse button, click-drag the *whiskerTexture* node from the Hypershade onto the **Transparency** attribute in the Attribute Editor.

Click-drag with MMB

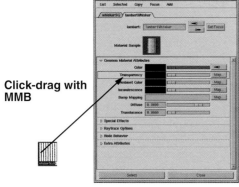

Assigning texture to tranparency

The one texture node is now mapped onto both the color and transparency attributes of the material node.

Note: Transparency maps cannot be seen by default with hardware rendering. Since the color map and the transparency map share the same placement node, you can use the color map's position to determine the position of the transparency map.

6 View the shading group dependencies

- In the Hypershade, highlight *lambertWhisker*.

- Press the **Input and Output Connections** button.

The material now contains several nodes — the shading group node, the material node, the texture node and the texture placement node.

The structure of the shading group nodes appear in the Work Area of the Hypershade panel. There are two connections between the texture node and the material node which is, in turn, connected to the shading group node itself.

- Move the cursor over each of the connection lines.

The connected attributes of both the up and downstream nodes are indicated.

Move cursor over connection lines

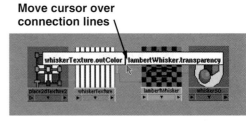

Hypershade view of connections

7 Add a ramp texture to grid texture

In order to add some more detail to the whiskers, another texture map can be

added to the material. In this case, an embedded texture node can be used. This is when one texture node is connected to an attribute of another texture node. This overlays the effects of the two textures.

- Open the *whiskerTexture* node's Attribute Editor.

- Click on **Map** next to the **Line Color** attribute.

- In the Create Render Node window, go to the 2D Texture section and click on the **Ramp** button.

  A new texture node and 2D placement node is added to the shading group and connected to the existing texture node, not to the material node.

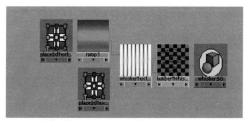

Shading group with new ramp

The lines of the whiskers now take on the color of the ramp texture.

Texture with ramp

8 Edit the ramp texture parameters

The ramp texture can be adjusted so that the whiskers are light at the ends, and dark and heavy closer to the face. Because the whisker surface is one surface that goes through the body of the seal, the ramp should be symmetrical about the center.

- Open the ramp texture node's Attribute Editor.

- Click on the round selector at the center of the ramp.

  The **Selected Position** should be **0.5**.

- Change the **Selected Color** to black.

- The other two selectors should be light gray and positioned as shown.

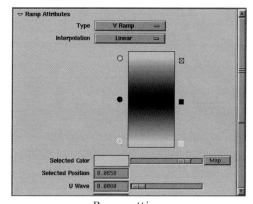

Ramp settings

9 Save your work

Building Salty's nose

You will now build Salty's nose using the techniques learned so far. You will CV pull the surface into shape shown below:

Front view of Salty's nose

1 Place a primitive sphere

- Create a primitive sphere and rename it *nose*.

- **Move** the sphere up to the tip of Salty's face.

2 Manipulate CVs on the shape

- Go to component selection mode.

- Use techniques taught in the last lesson to reshape the sphere into the desired shape as shown below:

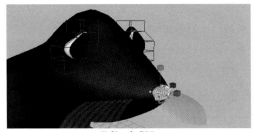

Edited CVs

3 Create the nose material

The material for the seal's nose will be similar to that of the seal's body, but with sharper or harder specular shading qualities to produce the effect of a nose that is hard, wet material and slightly reflective.

- **Create** a new **Blinn** material in the Hypershade.

- Rename the node to *noseBlinn*

- Open the *noseBlinn* node in the Attribute Editor.

- Change the **Color** to a pale purple.

- In the **Specular Shading** section set the following:

  Eccentricity to below **0.15**;

  Specular Roll Off to about **0.8**;

  Specular Color to almost white;

  Reflectivity to **0**.

The specular highlight on the surface becomes small and sharp, with high contrast against the base diffuse color. Reflectivity has been turned off since this piece is too small to create any useful reflections in the final animation.

- **Assign** the *noseBlinn* to the *nose* surface.

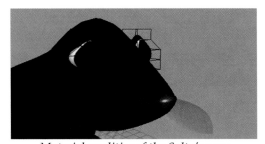

Material qualities of the Salty's nose

4 Save your work

Parenting to the skeleton

It seems like Salty is built and ready to animate. But since you will want all these pieces to move when Salty's head moves, you will need to parent them into the skeleton.

Parenting can be used to add nodes into existing hierarchies. To help you visualize the

results, you will use the Hypergraph panel's freeform layout where you can move nodes wherever you need them.

1 Hide the main surface

- Select Salty's main body surface.

- Select **Display** → **Hide** → **Hide Selection**.

  Now you can more easily see the joints and the other surfaces.

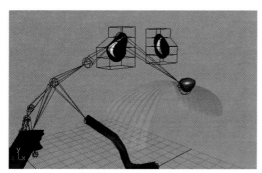

Hidden body surface

2 Rename joints in the Hypergraph view

- In the Hypergraph view, click on the **Scene Hierarchy** button.

- Dolly and track until you see the joints that belong to the head.

- Press the **Ctrl** key and double click on joints to rename them. Rename the head joints as shown below:

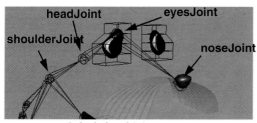

Salty's head joint names

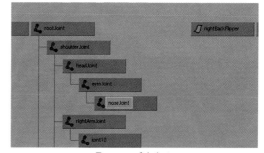

Renamed joints

3 Move the nodes using Freeform mode

- Make the Hypergraph panel full screen.

- Click on the **Toggle Freeform/ Automatic Layout Mode** button.

- Dolly out until you can see all of the nodes.

- With the left mouse button, drag the left and right eyes groups, the *nose* node, and the *whisker* node next to the head joints.

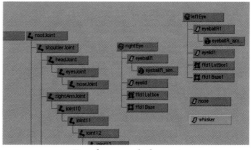

Freeform node layout

- Double-click on the top nodes of the left and right eye groups.

- This collapses the hierarchies into a single node.

  This makes it easier to work with these two nodes.

PROJECT FIVE

- Click-drag on the nodes with the left mouse button to move them close to the head nodes.

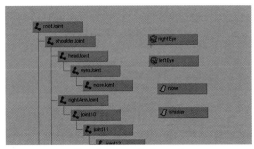

Freeform node layout

4 Parent the whisker to the head

- Click-drag with the middle mouse button on the *whisker* node and drag it onto the *noseJoint* node.

- Click-drag with the middle mouse button on the *nose* node and drag it onto the *noseJoint* node.

This parents this node to the *noseJoint*.

Now the whisker will move when the skeleton is animated.

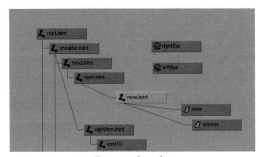

Parented nodes

5 Parent the eye groups to the head

- Click-drag with the middle mouse button on the *rightEye* node and drag it onto the *eyesJoint* node.

- Click-drag with the middle mouse button on the *leftEye* node and drag it onto the *eyesJoint* node.

This parents these nodes to the *eyesJoint*.

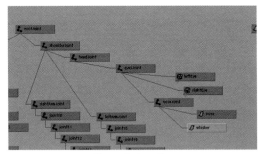

Parented nodes

6 Test the results

- Select the *headJoint*.

- **Rotate** it to test the new hierarchy.

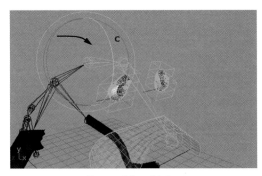

Rotated head joint

- Select **Display → Show → Show Last Hidden**.

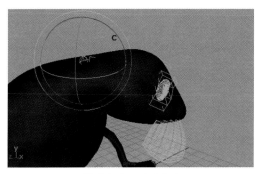

Rotated neck joint

- Test the rotation with all of the surfaces.

7 Return to the bind pose

- Select the skeleton.

- Go to the **Animation** menu set.

- Select **Skin → Go to Bind Pose.**

  This sets the skeleton is back to its bind pose.

8 Save your work

Conclusion

Salty is now built and ready to animate. In the next lesson, you will add IK chains to Salty's bones, and then you can animate the bouncing ball. You will also begin to take advantage of the extra work used in this lesson to build the eye controls, since keying these features using the new attributes is a straightforward process.

PROJECT FIVE

22 Animating Salty

In this lesson, you will make Salty bounce a ball on her nose. At first you will set up *Inverse Kinematic* (IK) chains that offer you control over the motion of Salty's bones. You will also animate the movement of the eyes so that they follow the ball around the scene.

Salty on the move

In this lesson you will learn the following:

- How to set up IK chains
- How to animate the IK chains
- How to constrain a bouncing ball to Salty's nose
- How to animate the eyeControl group
- Soft body dynamics to animate whiskers

Initial set-up

To start this lesson, you will continue with
the file from the last lesson.

1 Change the panel layout

- Select **Panels** → **Layouts** → **3 Panes Split Left**.

- Set the top left window to a Front view, the bottom left window to a Side view, and the right view to a shaded Perspective view.

- Make the Perspective view the active panel and press the **6** key to set smooth shading.

2 Use the Show menu to set up views

- In the Front view panel's **Show** menu, turn **NURBS Surfaces** to **Off**.

- Repeat this step for the Side view.

  This lets you focus on the skeleton in these views while still seeing the surfaces in the Perspective view.

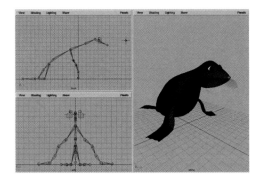

Recommended panel layout

Adding IK single chain handles

To help control Salty's flippers, you need to build *inverse kinematic* (IK) chains. These will

let you control the flippers while Salty bounces the ball with her nose.

To animate a joint hierarchy, you could rotate each joint individually to set poses for the character. But, this can be time-consuming if you were to set keys for all of the joints.

Instead, you will use an *IK chain*. With an IK chain, you define a start joint and an end joint. The start joint is known as the *root* of the chain while the end joint has a corresponding *end effector*. You define the end effector by placing an *IK handle* that is then used to control all the bones within the chain.

1 Set the IK handle options

Maya offers you several types of IK chains. For the flippers, you will use an IK single chain solver which is the simplest IK solver.

- Go to the **Animation** menu set.

- Select **Skeleton** → **IK Handle Tool** - ❐.

- In the option box, set the following:

  Current Solver to **ikSCsolver**.

- This tool is now active.

2 Add IK handles to the right flipper

IK chains are defined by a root joint where the chain starts, and an IK handle where the chain ends. This handle can then be used to control the chain.

- Click on Salty's right shoulder joint to set the root of the IK chain.

- Click on the second-last joint on Salty's flipper to place the IK handle.

The chain is drawn between these two joints.

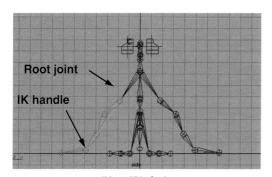

First IK chain

3   Add a second IK handle to the flipper

- Press the **y** key to reinvoke the **IK Handle Tool**.
- Click again on the second-last joint to start another IK chain.
- Click on the last joint on Salty's flipper to place the IK handle.

  This IK chain will be used to help keep Salty's flipper on the ground as Salty strains to bounce the ball.

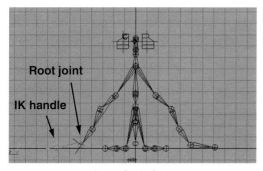

Second IK chain

4   Add similar IK chains to the left flipper

- Use the same technique to add two similar IK chains to the left flipper.

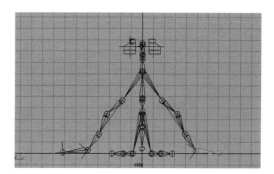

Left flipper IK chains

5   Test the IK chains on the right arm

- Select the two IK handles on the right flipper, making sure that you mask everything except the handles.
- **Move** the flipper in the Side view and watch the results in the Perspective view.
- All the joints in the flipper hierarchy are moved as one. As you move the IK handles, the interior joints bend.

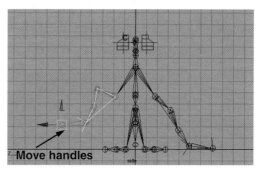

Translated IK handles

- Press the **z** key to **Undo** this move.

Rather than moving the legs during this lesson, you want them to stay on the ground. Later, you will lock them down so that they don't accidentally move on you.

Add an IK spline handle

The *IK Spline* solver is another type of IK solver that lets you use a curve to control the joint rotations. You can then animate the skeleton by either moving the joints along the curve, or by animating the position or shape of the curve.

This kind of IK chain is a good choice for Salty's neck where most of the animation in this lesson will take place.

1 Set the spline IK options

- Select **Skeleton → IK Spline Handle Tool** - ❑.

- In the option box, make sure that the following options are set:

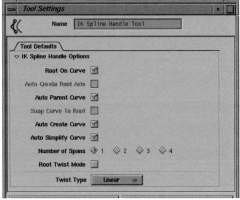

IK handle tool options

- Click **Close**. This tool is still active.

2 Add an IK spline handle

- Click on the joint at the nape of Salty's neck as the root joint.

- Click on Salty's nose joint as the end joint.

An IK chain is drawn between these joints. At the same time, a curve has been placed along the joints. You can use the panel's **Show** menu to see this curve.

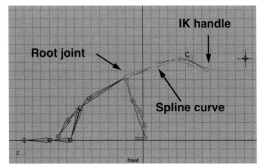

IK spline chain

3 Show the curve in the Front view

- Change the Side view to another Front view panel.

- In the new Front view panel's **Show** menu, turn **Joints** and **IK Handles** to **Off**.

Now you can use this window to select and transform the curve itself, while viewing the effect on the joints in the other views.

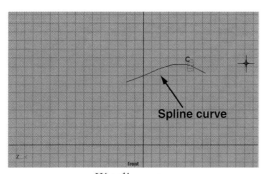

IK spline curve

4 Test the effect of the new chain

- **Select** the new curve.

- **Move** the new curve up in the Front view.

  The whole head and neck moves as one, bringing the flippers along.

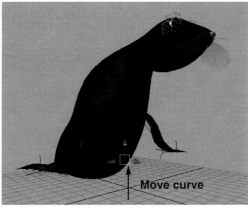

Moving the spline curve

- **Undo** this move.

5 Set a key on the flippers

- In the Perspective window, **Select** all four of the IK handles belonging to the flippers.

- **Move** the IK handles along the Y-axis to raise the flippers above the ground level just a little.

- Set the **Time slider** to frame **1**.

- Press **Shift w** to set keys on only the translation channels belonging to the IK handles.

  Setting keys helps to lock down the flippers, which helps when you move Salty's neck later.

Tip:	To set keys for only translation, rotation or scaling remember the following hotkey combinations: **Shift w** - Translation **Shift e** - Rotation **Shift r** - Scaling

6 Re-test the chain

- **Select** the new curve.

- **Move** the new curve down in the Front view.

  As the head and neck moves down, the flippers stay planted on the ground.

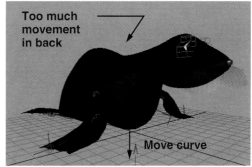

Curve moved with flippers keyed

- **Move** the curve up.

PROJECT FIVE

The flippers try to stay planted until Salty goes beyond their reach. Now, you can focus on the fact that Salty's back is deforming in an uncomfortable manner.

- **Undo** these two moves.

Cluster the spline curve

In order to get more control over Salty's motion, you will place a *cluster deformer* onto the curve, then adjust the cluster weights of the CVs to refine how they will animate.

You could now animate the joints by setting keys for the CVs of the new spline curve, but a cluster will offer better control because of the ability to weight the cluster points.

1 Cluster the curve

By adding a cluster to the new curve, you will be placing the curve's CVs into a special cluster set.

- Select the spline curve.

- Select **Deform → Create Cluster**.

  A cluster is now created using the spline's CVs. The cluster is indicated using a small 'c' icon. This represents a cluster handle node.

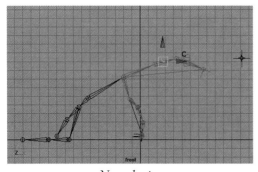

New cluster

2 Edit the cluster weights

One key feature of a cluster is the ability to set weights for each CV in the cluster. For Salty, you will use a lighter weight for the CVs near Salty's neck and a heavier weight at her nose. This means that her head will move more than her neck, thereby giving you more subtle control as to how the head moves.

- Select the spline curve.

- Press **F8** to enter Component mode.

- Select the four CVs for the curve beginning from the neck.

- Select **Window → General Editors → Component Editor...** and click on the *Weighted Deformers* tab.

- Press **Load Components** in the Editor.

  The four CVs are now listed with their current weight setting of 1.0.

- Enter the following values for the CVs:

  cv[0] to **0.25;**

  cv[1] to **0.5;**

  cv[2] to **0.75;**

  cv[3] to **1.0;**

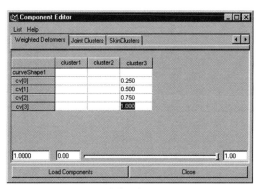

Weighted CVs

- Close the Component Editor.
- Press **F8** to go back to Object mode.

3 Test the results

Now that the CVs cluster weights have been set, you can move the cluster to see the advantage of using the weights.

- Since one of the CVs is now the current selection, once again **Select** the cluster handle using the small 'c' icon.
- **Move** the cluster down along the Y-axis.

The head and the flippers move.

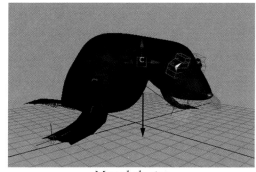

Moved cluster

- **Move** the cluster out along the Z-axis using the manipulator in the Perspective view.

The cluster is helping the head move in a more graceful manner. The cluster makes sure that the neck remains fairly stationary while the head moves more freely.

As the head moves, you may notice that a little bit of motion is placed on the neck because the first CV in the IK spline curve has been given a weight of 0.25. Generally, it is a good idea to *not move* the first CV of an IK spline curve. For Salty, a little bit of motion is used because of Salty's more limited range of motion.

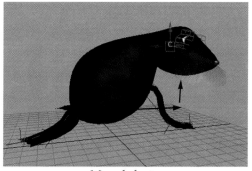

Moved cluster

- **Undo** these moves until you return to Salty's start position.

4 Display the cluster's selection handle

- With the cluster handle selected, select **Display → Component Display → Selection Handles**.

PROJECT FIVE

This toggles on the cluster node's selection handle. Every node in Maya has a selection handle that can be revealed to simplify selection later.

5 Move the selection handle

- Press **F8** to go into component selection mode.

- Turn off the points selection mask and turn on the handles mask.

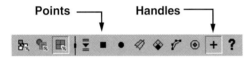

Points ——→   Handles ——→

Selection masks

- Click-drag a selection box around the cluster's selection handle to pick this component.

- **Move** the handle along the Y-axis to place it above Salty's head.

It will now be easier to find later.

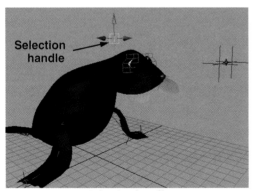

Selection handle

- Turn off the handles selection mask and turn on the points mask.

- Press **F8** to go back to object selection mode.

Create a ball

To animate Salty bouncing a ball, you need to create the ball itself. This ball will use a simple hierarchy of grouped nodes. One node will be used to animate the bounce of the ball while the top node will be used to constrain the ball to Salty's nose.

1 Create a sphere

- Select **Create → NURBS Primitives → Sphere**.

- Name this node *ball*.

- Press **3** to increase the surface smoothness.

- Click on the input node in the Channel box and set the following:

    Radius to **1.5**.

- **Move** the sphere up until it sits just above the ground plane.

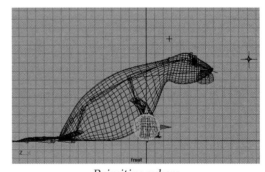

Primitive sphere

2 Delete history

- Select **Edit → Delete by Type → History**.

3 Group the sphere to itself

This will create a node hierarchy for your animation. One node will be used to animate the ball's bounce while the top node will be constrained to Salty's nose.

- Select **Edit → Group**.

- Name this node *ballConstrain*.

4 Create a ball material

- In the Hypershade, create a Phong material node.

- In the Channel box, rename this node *ballPhong*.

5 Map a texture to the color

- Press **Ctrl-a** to open the Attribute Editor.

- Click on the **Map** button next to **Color**.

- Choose a checker texture from the Create Render Node window.

- In the *checker1* node tab of the Attribute editor, change the two colors to red and white.

- Click on the *place2DTexture* node and set the following attribute:

    RepeatU to **0.5**.

6 Assign the material

- With your middle mouse button, click-drag the *ballPhong* node onto the new sphere.

Ball with checker texture

7 Add Ball to Salty Layer

- Select the *ballConstrain* node and add it to the *Salty* layer.

8 Save your work

Connect the ball to Salty's nose

You now want the ball to move with Salty's nose as she gets ready to start bouncing it. A point constraint will be applied to the top node of the ball group.

1 Constrain the ball to Salty's nose joint

- Go to the **Animation** menu set.

- In the Front view panel, select **Show → None,** then **Show → Joints**.

- **Select** the nose joint of the skeleton.

    Only the round joint icon at the end of the skeleton should be highlighted. The first bone should *not* be highlighted.

- Click on the **Select by hierarchy** button.

PROJECT FIVE

Select by hierarchy

Pick masks

- Press the **Shift** key then **Select** the ball.

  The select by hierarchy mode forces your selection to the top node of the ball hierarchy. The *ballConstrain* node is the node that you will use to constrain to the nose.

- Select **Constrain → Point**.

  Now the ball is constrained to Salty's nose.

Ball constrained to Salty's nose

2 Move the cluster to balance the ball

- Press **F8** to go back to object selection mode.

- **Select** the cluster handle using its selection handle.

- **Move** the cluster up until Salty appears to be balancing the ball.

Moving the cluster handle

3 Put a selection handle on ball node

You will now place a selection handle on the *ball* node to make it easier to select.

- **Select** the *ball* node.

  Use the Channel box to confirm that the correct node is selected.

- Select **Display → Component Display → Selection Handles**.

- Press **F8** to go into component selection mode.

- Turn off the **Points** selection mask and turn on the **Handles** selection mask.

- Click-drag a selection box around the ball's selection handle to pick this component.

- **Move** the handle along the Y-axis to place it above the ball.

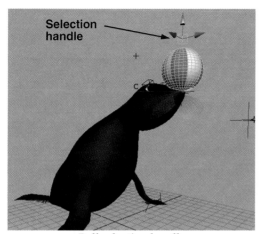

Ball selection handle

- Turn off the **Handles** selection mask and turn on the **Points** mask.

- Press **F8** to go back to object selection mode.

Setting up for the animation

To get ready to animate the scene, you will set up the animation preferences, refine the display of Salty in the Perspective view, and use the channel control to make it easier to set keys on the *clusterHandle* and *ball* nodes.

1 Set the length of the animation

In the animation preferences, you can set the frames per second to 30 and the length of the animation to 450 frames. This will give you a 15-second animation.

- At the right end of the Time slider, click on the preferences button.

- Click on **Settings** in the Categories section and set the following:

  Time to **NTSC (30 fps)**.

- Now click on **Timeline** and set the following:

  Playback Start/End to **1** and **450**;

  Animation Start/End to **1** and **450**;

  Playback Speed to **Real-Time**.

  The length of your animation is now 450 frames long and play back will be at 30 frames per second.

- Click on **Save**.

2 Prepare the Perspective view

It is a good idea to focus on how the surfaces look when animated.

- In the Perspective view panel, select **Show** → **Deformers**, and **Show** → **IK Handles** to turn these object types off for this window.

  You can now use the three selection handles to quickly select and key the various parts of Salty.

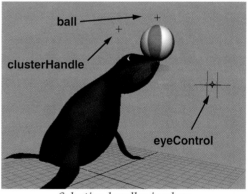

Selection handles in place

PROJECT FIVE

Note: By turning off deformers, you have hidden Salty's cluster handle. This is not a problem because you can use the selection handles to pick and animate this node.

3 Restrict the cluster handle channels

To make sure that you are keying the correct channels, you will make some of the attributes non-keyable on the *clusterHandle* and *ball* nodes.

- **Select** the cluster handle for Salty's neck using its selection handle.

- Select **Window** → **General Editors** → **Channel Control**.

- Press the **Ctrl / Command** key and click on all the *rotate* and *scale* channels, and then the *visibility* channel.

- Press the **Move >>** button to make these channels non-keyable.

Keyable channels

4 Restrict the ball channels

- **Select** the *ball* node using its selection handle.

- In the Channel Control window, make the *translate X*, *translate Z*, the *rotate* and *scale* channels, and the *visibility* channel all non-keyable.

This leaves only the *translate Y* channel. This is the only channel you will be keying on the *ball* node.

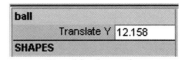

Keyable channels

Animating Salty

It is now time to get Salty moving. You will start by keying Salty's neck using the cluster handle and then you will animate the ball bouncing. You will start with a single bounce, then you will copy and paste these keys to extend the animation.

1 Set initial keys

- Set the **Time slider** to frame **20**.

- **Select** both the *ball* node and the *clusterHandle* node using the two selection handles.

- Press the **s** key to set keys for the keyable channels.

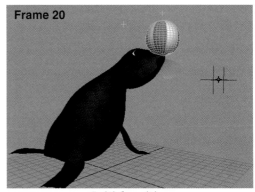

Initial position

2 Set keys on Salty's cluster handle

- Set the **Time slider** to frame **40**.

- **Select** only the *clusterHandle* node using its selection handle.
- **Move** Salty's neck down along the Y-axis.
- Press the **s** key to set keys for the keyable channels.

  This drop is where Salty builds the momentum to start bouncing the ball. This action is designed to give the audience a clear indication that Salty is going to bounce the ball. In traditional animation, this is called *anticipation*.

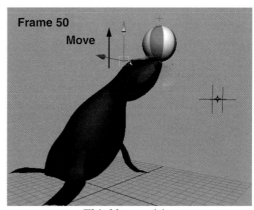
Third key position

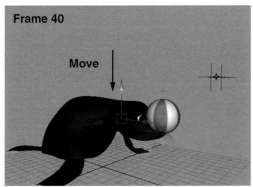
Second key position

- Set the **Time slider** to frame **50.**
- **Move** Salty's *clusterHandle* up along the Y-axis.
- Press the **s** key to set keys for the keyable channels.

  Salty is now pushing the ball up to project it into the air.

3 Set keys on the ball

Salty has been pushing the ball up to project it into the air. You will now key the ball's motion in the air.

- **Select** only the *ball* node using its selection handle.
- Press the **s** key to set keys for the keyable channels at the current frame.

  This key makes sure that the ball is touching Salty's nose as it is being pushed off.

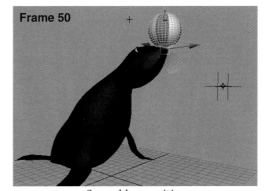
Second key position

PROJECT FIVE

- Set the **Time slider** to frame **70**.
- **Move** the *ball* node up along the Y-axis.
- Press the **s** key to set keys for the keyable channels.

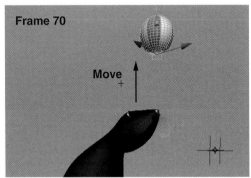
Frame 70
Move
Third key position

- Click-drag on the Time slider to scrub through the roughed out sequence.

4 Copy a range of keys

To make Salty bounce the ball three times, you will copy and paste the existing keys to extend the animation.

- **Select** both the *ball* node and the *clusterHandle* using the two selection handles.
- Set the **Time slider** to frame **20**.
- Press the **Shift** key and in the **Time slider,** drag to frame **71**.

  A red selection bar appears to indicate the selected time range. The start and end frames of the selection are displayed in white. Make sure that the Start frame is **20** and the End frame is **71**.

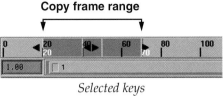
Copy frame range
Selected keys

- Click in the Time slider with your right mouse button and select **Copy** from the pop-up menu.

5 Paste the keys

- Set the **Time slider** to frame **90**.
- Click in the Time slider with your right mouse button and select **Paste** → **Paste** from the pop-up menu.

  New keys have been placed starting from frame 90.

- Set the **Time slider** to frame **160**.
- **Paste** → **Paste** the frames again at this frame.
- Play back the results.

6 Select the animation curve for the neck

- Open the Graph Editor.

Note: You can open the Graph Editor either in one of the existing view panels using its **Panels** menu or as a floating window using the **Window** menu. In earlier lessons, you learned both methods. Now you can begin using the method that you like the best.

- From the Graph Editor, select **View** → **Frame All**.
- Click on the name *Translate Y* belonging to the *clusterHandle*.

This isolates this curve from the others.

7 Edit the curve tangents

- Select the bottom three keys on the curve.
- From the Graph Editor, select **Tangents → Flat**.

Free tangent weights

Break tangents

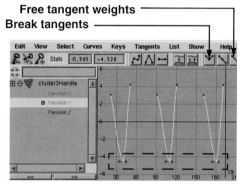

New tangent setting

- Select **Curves → Weighted Tangents**.
- Click on the **Break tangents** button and then on the **Free tangent weight** button.

  The first button lets you break the tangents to create a sharp reaction. The second button lets you refine your curves to make them extra steep.

- Press the **Shift** key and select the tangent handles to the left of each of the selected keys.
- Select the **Move** tool.
- Click-drag with the middle mouse button to drag the tangents out to increase their weight.

This curve indicates that Salty will slow down to a stop as she drops her neck down.

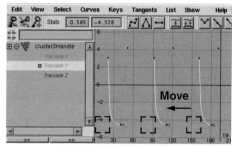

Tangent handle edits

- Press the **Shift** key and drag a selection box over the three keys to deselect the tangent handles.
- Press the **Shift** key and select the tangent handles to the right of each of the selected keys.
- Click-drag with the middle mouse button to drag the tangents up to a vertical position.

  This curve indicates that Salty will quickly snap her neck up to project the ball into the air.

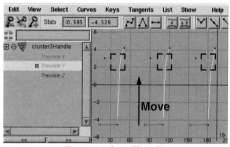

Tangent handle edits

- Play back the results.

PROJECT FIVE

As the curves suggest, Salty slows down as her head drops then speeds up in order to toss the ball.

Always remember the importance of using the animation curve tangents to refine your motion. The tangent controls help define what happens before and after your keys.

8 Edit the animation curve for the ball

- Click on the name *Translate Y* belonging to the *ball*.

- Select all of the keys at the bottom of the curve.

- Click on the **Linear Tangents** button.

- Select all the keys at the top of the curve.

- From the Graph Editor, select **Curves → Weighted Tangents**.

- From the Graph Editor, select **Tangents → Flat**.

- Click on the **Free tangent weight** button.

- Press the **Shift** key and select the tangent handles on the left side of the keys.

- **Move** the handles to the left to change the weight at this point.

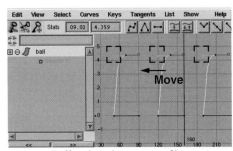

Ball animation curve edits

- Playback the results.

9 Delete the last key on the ball

Since the new locator will be controlling the animation as the ball leaves Salty's nose, the key on *ball* after frame 190 can be removed.

- Select the *ball* node.

- In the Graph Editor or Timeline, delete the key at frame 210.

10 Save your work

Bounce the ball off the floor

For Salty's last bounce of the ball off the nose, you will be constraining the ball to another locator. You will then animate the new locator going off screen.

1 Create a new Locator

- Go to frame **190**.

- Select **Create → Locator.**

- Use the Channel Control editor to have only the Translation channels keyable.

- Place the Locator in front of the ball.

New Locator in front of ball

2 Constrain the ball to the locator

- Select the new Locator.

- **Shift-Select** the *ball* node.

- Press the up arrow to move up the ball's hierarchy to the *ballConstrain* node.

- Select **Constrain → Point.**

  The ball is floating half way between Salty's nose and the locator. This is because both the constrains have equal weighting.

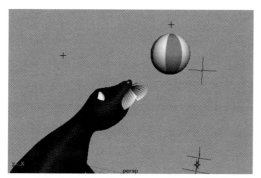

The ball with two constrains applied

3 Key the Constraint weights

- Select the *ballConstrain* node.

- Select *ballConstrain_pointConstraint* input node and set the following:

    Nose Joint W0 to **1;**

    Locator3 W3 to **0;**

    The ball is now favoring the nose.

- Go to frame 189

- In the Channel Box highlight *Nose Joint W0* and the *Locator3 W3* attributes.

- Select **Key Selected** from the right mouse button popup menu in the Channel Box.

4 Move the new Locator

- Select the new Locator.

- While holding the **v** key, point snap the new locator to the end joint at salty's nose.

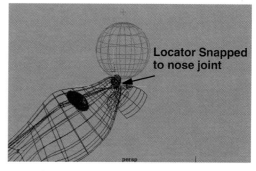

The locator point snapped to end joint

5 Key the Constraint weights

- Go to frame 190.

- Select the *ballConstrain* node.

- Select*BallConstrain_pointConstrain1* input node and set the following:

    Nose Joint W0 to **0;**

    Locator3 W3 to **1;**

- Click on the Channel box with your right mouse button and select **Key Selected**.

Animate the Locator

You will now animate the locator exiting the scene. Since the weight of the constraint is fully on the locator and not the joint, the ball will follow the locator. You will also be adding a floor under Salty.

PROJECT FIVE

1 Create a floor

You will create a flat polygon surface for the platform which Salty will perform on.

- Select **Create** → **Polygons Primitives** → **Plane**.

- Rename the surface *deck*.

- Click on the *polyPlane* input node and set the floor as follows:

    Width to **25**;

    Height to **75**.

- **Move** the surface along the negative X-axis so that it is positioned with Salty at its front edge.

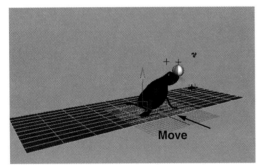

Polygon plane moved to position

2 Set a key on the locator

- Go to frame **190**.

- Select the new locator.

- Press **s** to set a key on the translation channels.

- Go to frame **305**.

- Move the locator to the floor and beside salty.

- Set a key for the locator at this position.

The ball on the floor at frame 305

The ball is going straight from the nose to the floor. You will need a key in between where the ball is in the air.

- Go to frame **240**.

- Translate the locator in **Y** higher than Salty's head.

- Set a key.

The ball on in the air at frame 240

3 Refine the motion

- Use the techniques taught earlier to refine the motion of the ball in the Graph Editor.

- Add further keyframes to make the ball bounce a few more times.

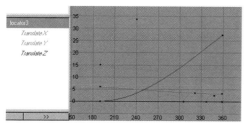

Refining curves in Graph Editor

4 Add roll to the ball

To add some rotation to the ball you will add the Rotation Channels back to the *ball* node.

- Select the *ball* node.
- With the Channel Control editor, make the rotation channels keyable.
- Go to frame **305**.
- Key rotations on the ball as it bounces off screen.

5 Save your work

Finishing Salty's motion

Salty is sure to be upset that the ball is bouncing away out of her control. You will now set more keys to animate Salty's reaction.

1 Key Salty's cluster handle node

- Select the *clusterHandle* node using its selection handle.
- Go to frame **240**.
- **Move** the *clusterHandle* along the Z-axis to begin following the ball.
- Press the **s** key to set keys for the keyable channels.

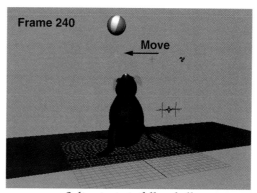

Salty starts to follow ball

- Go to frame **305**.
- **Move** Salty's cluster handle along the Z-axis then down along the Y-axis so that Salty is looking at the ball.
- Press the **s** key to set keys for the keyable channels.

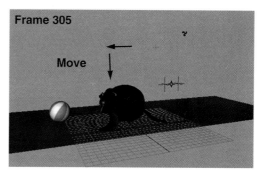

Salty watching ball bounce

- Go to frame **340**.
- Press the **s** key to set keys for the keyable channels.

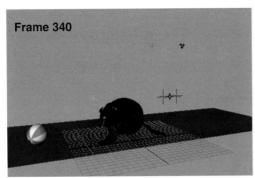

Frame 340

Salty continues to watch ball bounce away

- Go to frame **385**.

- **Move** Salty's cluster handle back along the Z-axis then down a little further along the Y-axis so that Salty is looking out at the audience in a dejected pose.

- Press the **s** key to set keys for the keyable channels.

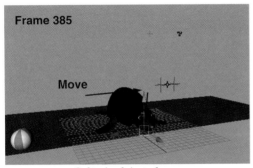

Frame 385

Move

Salty in dejected pose

- Play back the results.

Animating Salty's eyes

Earlier, you built a special *eyeControl* node that is designed to control where Salty is looking and other important eye features. Now you will animate this node to make use of this control.

1 Animate the eyeControl position

- Go to frame **5**.

- Select the *eyeControl* group using its selection handle.

- **Move** it to be in the same position as the ball.

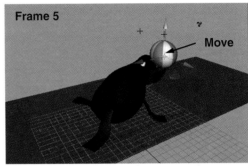

Frame 5

Move

Eye control node positioned

- Press **Shift w** to key the translation channels of this node.

- Go to frame **190**.

- Press **Shift w** to key the translation channels of this node.

- Go to frame **300**.

- **Move** the *eyeControl* node to Salty's right close to where the ball is landing.

- Press **Shift w** to key the translation channels of this node.

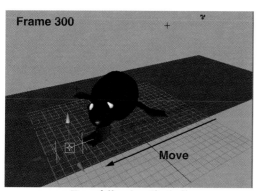

Eyes following the ball

- Go to frame **440**.
- Select the *eyeControl* group using its selection handle.
- **Move** the *eyeControl* node out in front of Salty near the ground since Salty doesn't want to make eye contact with the audience.
- Press **Shift w** to key the translation channels of this node.

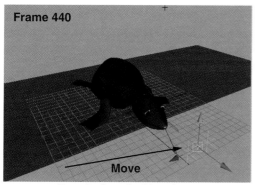

Eyes in front looking down

- Play back the results.

2 Animate the worry channel

You will now animate the worry channel to control the shape of Salty's eyes over time.

- Go to frame **5**.
- In the Channel box, change the **Worry** channel to **0**.
- Click on this channel and use the right mouse button to select **Key Selected** from the pop-up menu.
- Go to frame **190**.
- Again select **Key Selected** to keep the **Worry** set to **0**.
- Go to frame **300**.
- Set **Worry** to **5**.
- Select **Key Selected**.
- Go to frame **440**.
- Set **Worry** to **10**.
- Select **Key Selected**.

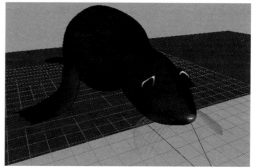

Salty worried about dropping the ball

Note: The other two eye attributes will not be animated right now. Blinking will be animated in Lesson 23.

3 Save your work

Making the whiskers flop

With Maya, you can use soft body dynamics to animate Salty's whiskers. Soft body dynamics lets you use forces on an actual surface to get realistic secondary motion.

A soft body is actually a surface that is defined by particles. These particles can then be animated using dynamic forces, and the surface deforms as required.

Note: After creating the softbody, it is advised not to scrub back and forth until a Particle Disk Cache File is created in step 7.

---

1 Create the soft body

The whisker surface will be turned into a soft body. The original surface will be hidden and used as a *goal* for the particles. This means that as the whiskers move around using dynamics, they always try to maintain their original shape.

- Go to frame **1**.
- Go to the **Dynamics** menu set.
- Select the *whiskers* surface.
- Select **Soft/Rigid Bodies** → **Create Soft Body** - ❐ and set the following options:

    Creation Options to **Duplicate, Make Copy Soft**

    Hide Non-Soft Object to **On**;

    Make Non-Soft a Goal to **On**;

    Weight to **1**.

By setting a weight of 1, the soft body will always attempt to match the original whisker surface.

- Click **Create**.

2 Open the Component Editor

You will now edit the individual particle weights to make the edges of the whisker more free.

- In the Outliner or Hypergraph select the *copyOfwhiskerParticle* node.

- Open the Attribute Editor and click on the *copyOfwhiskerParticleShape* tab.

- Open the **Per Particle (Array) Attributes** section.

- With the right mouse button, click on the **goalPP** field and select **Component Editor...** from the pop-up menu.

    This window lets you set the weights for the particles on a per particle basis.

3 Go into select particles mode

To edit the particles, you have to be able to pick them. They can be picked using component mode.

- Press **F8** to go into component mode.

- Click on the **Points** mask button to turn it off.

- Click on the **Points** mask button with the right mouse button and choose **Particles**.

Selection masks

4 Set goal weights for the points

- Set up a Side view panel and dolly in to see the whiskers.
- **Click-drag** a selection box around the three middle rows of particles.
- In the Component Editor, press **Load Components**.
- Click on the *Particles* tab.
- Set the **goalPP** to **1.0** for the selected particles.

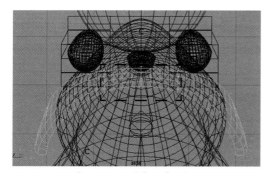

Center particle selection

- Select the next two rows of particles on both sides of the whiskers.
- In the Component Editor, press **Load Components**.
- Set the **goalPP** to **0.8**.

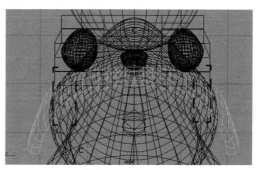

Middle particle selection

- Select the outside rows of particles on both sides of the whiskers.
- In the Component Editor, press **Load Components**.
- Set the **goalPP** to **0.7**.
- Close the Component Editor.

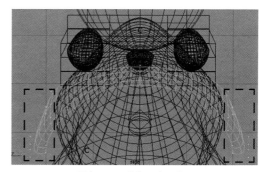

Edge particle selection

5 Link gravity to the whisker soft body

To achieve a realistic effect with the soft body, it is important that it is affected by gravity.

- Press **F8** to go back to object mode.
- Select the *copyOfWhiskers* node.
- Select **Fields → Gravity**.

PROJECT FIVE

The whiskers are now connected to the gravity field. You can verify this by opening the Dynamics Relationship Editor.

6 Add a spring to the soft body

To make the whiskers bounce, the soft body needs the help of some springs.

- Select *copyOfWhiskers*.

- Select **Soft/Rigid Bodies → Create Springs** - ❑ and set the following options:

    Under **Spring Methods** set:

    > **Creation Method** to **MinMax**;

    > **Min Distance** to **0**;

    > **Max Distance** to **1**.

- Under **Spring Attributes** set:

    > **Stiffness** to **30.00**.

- Click **Create**.

7 Set up cache for whiskers

This step is important for when using particles or softbodies. Since particles are evaluated every frame and need to played back from the beginning of the simulation, it is advised not to scrub back and forth in the timeline until a Particle Disk Cache File is created.

- Select **Solvers → Create Particle Disk Cache** - ❑.

- Read through the description.

- Press **Create**.

    All dynamics information in the scene is being written to a cache file.

- Play back the results

This will create a cache file so that you can scrub in the time slider and playback more quickly in subsequent playbacks.

Note:	If you change any attributes for the softbody, springs or gravity, you will need to regenerate the cache file. You can also disable the cache file from **Solvers → Edit Oversampling or Cache Settings**.

8 Save your work

You will use this scene in your next lesson.

Playblasting the animation

You will now Playblast the scene to test the results. Playblast gives you fast access to your animated sequence and lets you quickly evaluate the results using a Movie Player movie.

1 Set up the Perspective view

- From the Perspective panel, select **Show → None** to turn all object types off. Next, select **Show → NURBS Surfaces** and **Show → Polygons** to turn these types on.

    This gets rid of any icons that may be cluttering up the view.

2 Playblast the animation

- Select **Window → Playblast** - ❑ and set the following:

    > **View** to **On**;

    > **Show Ornaments** to **Off**;

    > **Display size** to **From Render Globals**;

- Click the **Playblast** button.

3 Play back the movie

- Use the Movie Player controls to play back the sequence.

Conclusion

In this lesson you have taken advantage of the set-up time you put into preparing Salty. The cluster handle helped simplify the animation of Salty's neck and the eye control node made it much easier to control various aspects of these important parts of your character.

In the next lesson, you will build a stage for Salty to perform on and then set up the scene's lighting.

You may be wondering why you didn't set keys on Salty's blinking – you will do this by building a special command in Lesson 25, using Maya's scripting language.

PROJECT FIVE

23 Building the Set

In this lesson, you will build Salty's stage which is sitting at the edge of a swimming pool. This stage will be created using: a back surface as a wall, the polygonal deck surface created earlier, two polygonal surfaces which will act as the side and bottom of a pool, and a NURBS surface that will act as the water's surface.

Afterwards, you will place lights into the scene to create some mood and atmosphere. Several lights will be used to give the stage the look of a performance.

These surfaces will be built using very simple geometry that will be enhanced in later lessons when you build and assign materials to the various parts.

Salty's stage

In this lesson you will learn the following:

- How to draw a spline curve
- How to create a lofted surface
- How to use curve snapping
- How to place multiple lights into a scene
- How to add color to the lights

Initial set-up

To start this lesson, you will continue with
the file from the last lesson.

1 Create a layer for the set

To help manage the scene, you will set up
a second layer for the new objects and the
deck surface.

- Create a new layer and call it *stage*.

2 Template the Salty layer

- Template the *Salty* layer.

3 Set up your view panels

- Select **Panels → Saved Layouts →
  Four View**.

  Make sure that all of the view
  panels are in wireframe mode. This
  will make it easier to see the wire
  lines as you build the stage.

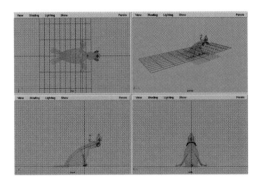

Four view panels

Creating the pool

The first part of the set is the pool which will
be built using polygonal surfaces that are the
same size as the deck surface.

1 Create a new polygonal surface

You will create the side and bottom of the
pool using a polygonal surface that has the
same size as the deck surface.

- Select **Create → Polygon Primitives
  → Plane**.

- Rename the surface *poolSide*.

- Click on the *polyPlane* input node
  and set the floor as follows:

  Width to **25**;

  Height to **75**.

- **Move** the surface along the X-axis so
  that it is positioned in front of the
  deck surface.

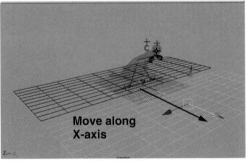

**Move along
X-axis**

New surface

2 Position the pivot point

You will now move the surface's pivot
point from the center to one of the corners.
This will make it easier to allow the side of
the *poolSide* surface to share a common
edge with the *deck* surface.

- Press the **Insert / Home** key on the
  keyboard.

- Hold down the **v** key to activate the
  Snap to points function. This will let
  you snap to the edge of the surface.

- Drag the center of the pivot manipulator to the far corner of the poly surface.

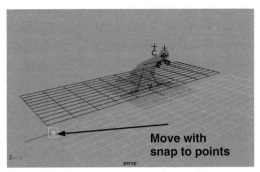

Relocated pivot point for surface

3 Position the pool surfaces

The pivot point's new position allows you to snap the two surface edges together.

- Press the **Insert / Home** key again to return to the move manipulator.
- Hold down the **v** key.
- **Move** the *poolSide* surface to the front edge of the *deck* surface.

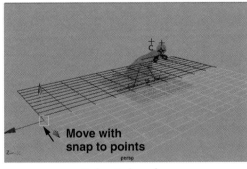

Relocated surface

4 Duplicate and rotate the surfaces

The third surface is created by duplicating the second surface. This will maintain the

repositioned pivot point. The new surface is then rotated about the common edge.

- Select **Edit → Duplicate - ❏** to open the option window and set the following:

    Duplicate Input Graph to **On**.

- Click **Duplicate**.

    The third surface is created with a duplicated *polyPlane* input node.

- Rename the surface *poolBottom*.
- **Move** the duplicate surface down to form the pool bottom.

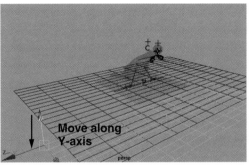

Moved surface

- **Select** the *poolSide* surface.
- **Rotate** the surface -90 degrees around the Z-axis.

The pool and deck are now complete.

PROJECT FIVE

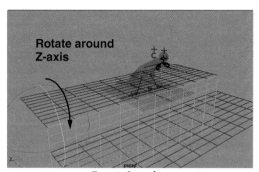
Rotated surface

Tip: By keeping the surfaces the same size and proportion, one shading group can later be applied to all three surfaces without affecting the detail of the texture maps. In this case, you should let the surfaces overlap to maintain the same size and proportion.

5 Create the water surface

To simulate the effect of a pool filled with water, the surface of the water will be created as a NURBS surface which will later be textured to appear wavy.

- Select **Create → NURBS Primitives → Plane**.
- Rename the surface *water*.
- Click on the *makeNurbsPlane* input node and set the floor as follows:

    Width to **25**;

    Length Ratio to **3**;

    U Patches to **1**;

    V Patches to **1**.

- **Move** the surface about 1 unit below the *deck* surface.

- **Move** it in front of the *poolSide* surface as shown below.

It is not necessary for the edge of the water surface to be snapped to the side of the pool. If the surfaces intersect each other, the rendering process will define the line of intersection.

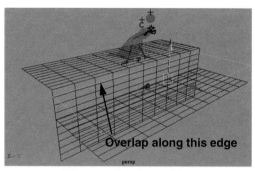
Water surface in position

Note: A displacement map will be assigned to this surface to create the waves and, by intersecting them, it ensures that the water remains tight to the side of the pool – instead of creating a gap.

Creating the back wall

You will now create a curved vertical wall as the backdrop to the scene. This wall will be created by lofting two curves to create a NURBS surface.

In the last lesson, you learned how to sculpt a NURBS surface by editing the control vertices. In this situation, you will focus on creating a curve with the desired shape which you can then use to create the surface.

1 Draw a curve

To form the base line of the wall, a straight single span curve is positioned to stretch between the opposite edges of the deck surface. For this purpose, an edit point curve will be used.

- Select **Create → EP Curve Tool**.
- Hold down the **v** key to point snap.
- Snap the first edit point to one of the *deck* surface's isoparm grid points as in the figure below.
- Snap the second point to the opposite side of the surface.

  Because the curve is coincident with the center line of the surface, it cannot be seen while it is being created.

- Press the **Enter** key to finish the curve construction.

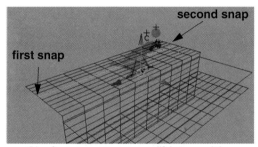

Single span curve snapped into position

Note: It is important that you only click once at each location, or else two edit points will be placed at the same location; the curve will extend beyond the points and double back on itself.

2 Select and move the center CVs

By moving the curve's two middle CVs, you create a symmetrical and uniform curve that stretches between the edges of the deck surface. To do this, the curve's CVs must first be displayed.

- Press **F8** to change the selection mask to **Select by component type**.
- **Select** the two CVs close to the middle of the curve.
- **Move** the CVs back away from the seal.

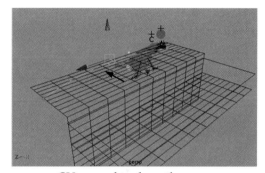

CVs moved to shape the curve

3 Duplicate and move the curve

The top of the wall is defined by a copy of the curve.

- Press **F8** to change the selection mask back to **Select by object type**.
- **Select** the curve.
- Select **Edit → Duplicate - ❑** to open the option window and set the following:

  Duplicate Input Graph to **Off**.

- Click **Duplicate**.
- **Move** the duplicate up along the Y-axis.

The curve should be positioned at the desired location for the top edge of the back wall.

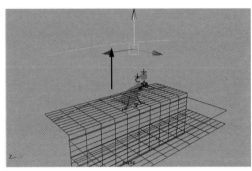

New position of second curve

4 Create a loft surface

A single span NURBS surface is created that connects between the two curves.

- **Select** the bottom curve then **shift-select** the top curve.

- Select **Surfaces → Loft**.

  A surface is created between the two curves.

- Press the **3** key to increase the surface smoothness and the **5** key to turn on smooth shading.

- Rename the surface *wall*.

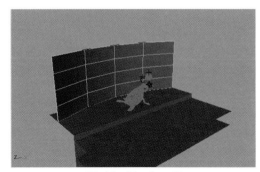

Finished back wall

LIGHTING THE SET

Now that the set is ready, you will add lights. Lighting is an important part of any scene since it adds mood and atmosphere.

Creating spot lights

In this scene, you will illuminate Salty with three main spot lights that will be colored red, green and blue. When all these lights combine you will get white light with fringes of color at the edge.

1 Create and position a spot light

You will create a spot light in the scene then reposition it using the show manipulator tool. You will then use the *look through* function to more accurately position the light.

- Select **Create → Lights → Spot Light**.

- Select the **Show Manipulator** tool.

- Position the *look at* and *eye* points of the light so that the light is pointing down at Salty from the upper left.

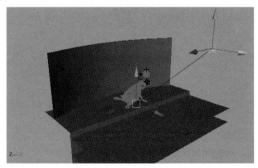

New position of second curve

- From one of the orthographic view's **Panel** menu, select **Look Through Selected**.

The panel view changes to a Perspective view that looks through the spot light.

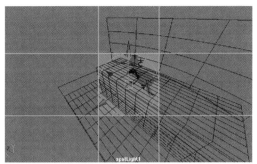

View looking through the spot light

- Dolly, tumble, and track the view in the spot light view panel.

  The position and direction of the spot light changes to that of the changed view.

- Change the position of the view so that it is centered on the seal from above.

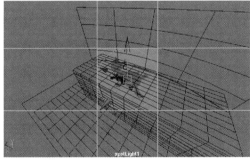

View through the repositioned spot light

2 Change the angle of the spot light

The cone angle of the spot light is changed using the light's multilayered manipulators.

- Click twice on the small blue manipulator button or select **Display → Camera/Light Manipulator → Cone Angle**.

- The circular outline in the spot light view represents the outside extent of the spot light's cone.

- Click-drag on the blue dot of the manipulator to change the cone angle.

  The circular outline of the manipulator should slightly overlap both the *wall* and the *water* surfaces.

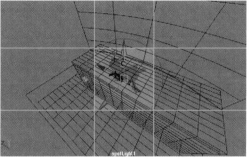

Modified cone angle of the spot light

3 Change the penumbra of the spot light

The spot light is created with a hard outside edge to the cone of light. The light can be given a softer edge by adjusting the penumbra.

- Click once on the small blue manipulator button or select **Display → Camera/Light Manipulator → Penumbra**.

- Click-drag the manipulator in the spot light view to increase the angle of the penumbra slightly.

  This softens the edge of the spot light.

4 Change the spot light color

You will now give the spot light a color to create more dramatic lighting, and to differentiate it from the other light sources that will be added later to the scene.

- Press **Ctrl a** to open the Attribute Editor.
- Change the **Color** to a full, saturated red.

5 Use smooth shading and default lighting

In order to see the approximate affect of the spot light, you can use Maya's smooth shading and lighting in the hardware rendering of the views.

- Press the **7** key to turn on **Use All Lights** in the Perspective view panel.
- Press the **5** key then the **7** key in the spot light view panel to turn on smooth shading and the lights.

  You can now see the lighting, but it seems a little bit broken and fuzzy.

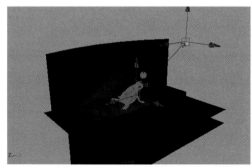

Smooth shading and default lighting

6 Increase the NURBS smoothing

The curved wall is displayed as a flat plane and the lighting is not rendering the effect of the spot light very well. This is because of the low display subdivisions of the NURBS surface.

- **Select** the *wall* surface.
- Select **Display → NURBS Smoothness → Custom - ❏**.
- In the **Shaded** section of the option window:

  Set **Surface Div per Span** to **32**.

- Click **Apply** and **Close**.

  The light areas of the surface are now more defined.

- **Select** the *water* surface.
- Select **Display → NURBS Smoothness → Custom.**

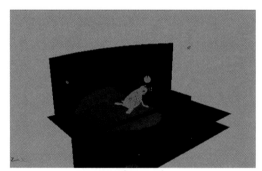

Increased smoothness

Tip:	The higher the surface shading divisions are set, the smoother the hardware lighting will appear – but increased division settings will slow down the interaction of the model views.

7 Increase the polygon smoothing

The detail of the hardware lighting conditions for polygon surfaces is determined by the size of the polygons – the smaller the polygons, the more detailed the lighting conditions.

In this case, the size of the polygons is determined by the number of polygon subdivisions which is set in the input shape node.

- **Select** the *deck, poolSide* and *poolBottom* polygon surfaces.

- In the Channel box, click on the *polyPlane* node under the **Inputs** section.

- Click into the *Subdivision Width* field then press the **Shift** key and click into the *Subdivision Height* field.

  The first value highlights in black while the second highlights in white, allowing both to be changed at once.

- Enter a value of **32**.

INPUTS	
dynController1	
polyPlane3	
Width	25
Height	75
Subdivisions X	32
Subdivisions Y	32

Entering values in the Channel box

The subdivisions of all three surfaces are increased. When a series of objects or nodes are selected, the changes that are made in the Channel box affect the particular attribute on all of the selected nodes.

- Deselect the surfaces to see the increased detail of the lighting.

Increased polygon subdivisions

By increasing the smoothness of the surface display, you can see the lighting more accurately.

8 Duplicate and position the spot lights

- **Select** and **Duplicate** the spot light.

- In the spot light view panel, select **Panel → Look Through Selected**.

- Tumble the spot light view to a position looking from the right side.

- Change the spot light **Color** to full saturated blue.

PROJECT FIVE

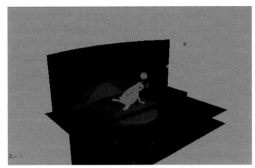

Three different colored spot lights

- Repeat the procedures above to create a green spot light positioned in the middle.

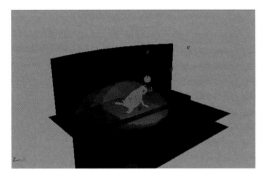

Three different colored spot lights

9 Test render the scene

- In one of the orthographic panels, select **Panels → Panel → Render View**.

- From this panel, select **Render → Render → persp**.

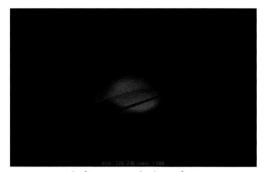

Software rendering of set

Note: Salty does not render because she is templated.

Creating background lighting

With the main spot lights established, it is necessary to light the background wall of the stage. You will also create additional ambient lighting.

1 Create and position a spot light

A series of spot lights will be used to illuminate the back wall. The lights should focus on a centralized area of the wall where a logo will be later assigned.

- Select **Create → Lights → Spot Light**.

  The light is positioned at the origin.

- Select **Show Manipulators**.

- Position the manipulators so that the light is shining down on the center of the back wall as shown.

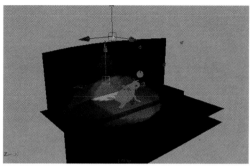

Hardware rendering of the light position

- If you cannot see the lights with hardware rendering, use the **Look Through Selected** to position the light.

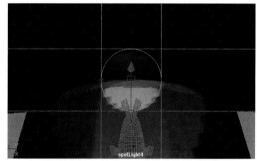

View looking through the spot light

Note: If hardware rendering is on, you may notice a slowing of the interactivity while positioning the lights, due to the increased display smoothness.

2 Set spot light parameters

To contrast the dynamic colored spot lights that focus on the seal, several identical spot lights illuminate the background with a warm soft light that washes the wall.

- In the Channel box, select the new light's *spotLightShape* node and set the following:

  RGB to **1 1 0.75**;

  Intensity to **0.5**;

  Cone Angle to **60**;

  Penumbra Angle to **20**;

  Dropoff to **5**.

The Dropoff setting causes the light to lose intensity as the distance from the source increases. The RGB settings define a pale yellow color for the light.

3 Duplicate and position the lights

Once the settings are established for the first light, it can be duplicated to create an even pattern of lights across the back wall.

- **Move** the spot light to one side of the Z-axis.

- **Duplicate** the spot light.

- **Move** the new light to the other side of the axis.

- **Duplicate** and **Move** two more spot lights.

The four spot lights should be equally spaced and centered around the axis line.

PROJECT FIVE

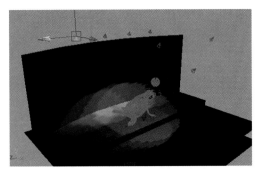

Hardware rendering of four lights

4   Adjust all of the spot lights

In situations where you have multiple lights which you want to stay the same, the Channel box can be used to modify any of the attributes.

- Select all four of the background spot lights.

   In the Channel box, you can see that more than one node is selected because the node name is followed by three dots.

- In the Channel box, click on the top light's *spotLightShape* node.

- Change the **Cone Angle** to **70**.

   The cone angles are now set for all four of the selected lights.

Tip: The attributes for the node that was selected last will be displayed in the Channel box. If different node types are selected, the changes that are made to the attributes will only affect those nodes that have the attributes.

---

5   Add an ambient light

Ambient lighting is needed to fill in the shadows and areas of the scene that are not directly lit with the spot lights. Even though there are a lot of lights in the scene, the light from a spot light will not "bounce" but will only illuminate what it is directly shining on. Ambient light is good for filling in the dark areas.

- Select **Create** → **Lights** → **Ambient Light**.

   If you have hardware lighting turned on, you will see that this light significantly increases the illumination in the scene.

- **Move** the light behind Salty and slightly above the deck surface.

   The light in this location will approximate the light that is expected to bounce off the deck.

Ambient light in position

- In the Channel box set:

   Intensity to **0.2**.

- In the Attribute Editor set:

   Color to a pale turquoise;

   Ambient Shade to **0.75**.

The Ambient Shade attribute affects the amount that the ambient light illuminates surfaces that are facing away from the source.

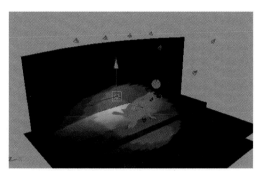

Position of the ambient light source

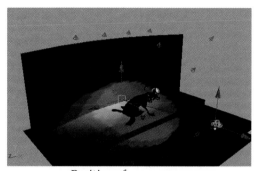

Position of new camera

Animating the camera

To preview the animation, you will now add a new camera and animate its position. When working in 3D space, an animated camera can help accentuate the depth of a scene.

1 Untemplate Salty

- Untemplate the *Salty* layer.

2 Create a new camera

It is a good idea to always create a new camera for your animations. The default Perspective view should be saved for modeling, and set up while the new camera is used for the final take.

- Select **Create → Cameras → Camera**.
- Select the **Show Manipulator** tool.

    Position the look at point of the camera just behind Salty and the eye point of the camera in front.

- From the Perspective view panel, select **Panels → Perspective → camera1**.

    Don't worry if you don't like the resulting view. It's difficult to properly position a camera using the manipulators. You can now fix the view using the normal view tools.

3 Set focal length

- In the Channel box, set the **Focal Length** to **30**.

    This widens the view angle to show more of the scene.

4 Position the camera

- From the Camera 1panel, select **View → Camera Settings → Resolution Gate**.

    The view expands and a line is drawn around the area that will be rendered. This allows you to see the scene and animation outside of the rendered area.

- Dolly, track and tumble in this view to get a good view of Salty.

PROJECT FIVE

You should see the water surface in the foreground and the illuminated area of the back wall.

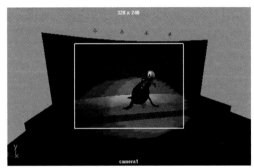

Scene with resolution gate on

5 Keyframe the camera position

- Go to frame **340**.

  This should be the point where Salty is just finished watching the ball bounce away.

- From the Camera 1 panel, select **View → Select Camera**.

- Press the **s** key to set a key at this position.

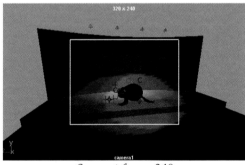

Scene at frame 340

6 Keyframe a second position

- Go to frame **400**.

This should be the point where Salty is just finished watching the ball bounce away.

- Dolly in for a close-up of Salty and press the **s** key to set a key at this position.

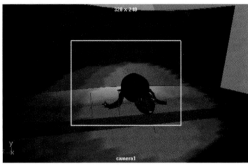

Scene at frame 400

Playblasting the animation

You will again Playblast the scene to test the results. It is always good to do rough tests to make sure that everything is working properly.

1 Set up the Perspective view

To Playblast you do not need to see the resolution gate outline.

- From the Camera 1 panel, select **View → Camera Settings → No Gate**.

- From the Camera 1 view, select **Show → None** to turn all object types off then select **Show → NURBS Surfaces** and **Show → Polygons** to turn these types on.

2 Playblast the animation

- Select **Window** → **Playblast...** - ❑ and set the following:

  View to **On**;

  Show Ornaments to **Off**;

  Display size to **From Render Globals**;

  Save to File to **Off**.

- Click the **Playblast** button.

3 Playback the movie

- Use the Movie Player controls to play back the sequence.

MoviePlayer view of Salty

4 Save your work

- Select **File** → **Save Scene As...** and save your work as *Salty5*.

Conclusion

Your scene is now built and lighting has been applied. Now you can build materials for the various surfaces to create a more interesting environment for Salty to bounce her ball.

24 Texture Mapping

In this lesson, you will add different kinds of texture maps to the stage, then prepare the file for rendering. The stage's simple surfaces will become more visually complex using textured materials.

The tiled deck and pool surfaces will be textured using a grid *bump map*, giving an appearance of being raised. The water surface will be created using a *displacement map* that actually raises the surface. The water's texture will include animated attributes to give the water a more realistic appearance.

The textured set

In this lesson you will learn the following:

- How to use a bump map texture
- How to build and animate a displacement shader
- How to build a layered texture
- How to set up a textured light
- How to set up a raytrace rendering
- How to render the final animation

Initial set-up

To start this lesson, you will continue with the scene file from the last lesson.

1 Set up your panel arrangement

- Select **Panels** → **Saved Layouts** → **Hypershade/Render/Persp.**

- In the Perspective view panel, select **Panels** → **Perspective** → **camera1**.

Creating the deck shading

The floor and the side of the pool will be textured using a series of grid textures that give it color and material qualities.

1 Create and assign a phong material

To produce a shiny, reflective surface for the floor and side of the pool, a phong material node will be used.

- In the Hypershade panel, **Create** a new **Phong** material.

- Rename the node *tilesPhong*.

- **Assign** *tilesPhong* to the *deck*, *poolSide* and *poolBottom* geometry.

2 Map a grid texture to the color

Instead of using a simple color for the material, a grid texture is used to produce a colored tile pattern on the floor.

- Open the *tilesPhong* node's **Attribute Editor**.

- Click on the **Map** button next to **Color**.

- In the Create Render Node window, click the **Textures** tab.

- From the 2D texture section, select the **Grid** texture.

3 Set the grid color

Once the texture is assigned, the parameters of the texture node can be adjusted. The overall fill color of the tiles is set to one color, while the joints between the tiles is set to be a different color.

In the **Attribute Editor**:

- Rename the node *gridColor* and set the following:

    Line Color to a pale yellow;

    Filler Color to a dark turquoise;

    U Width and **V Width** to **0.02**.

    A turquoise grid with thin yellow lines is produced.

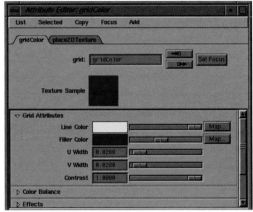

Settings in Attribute Editor

- Next open the **Effects** section and set the following:

    Filter to **0.5**.

4 Set grid placement

- Click on the *place2dTexture* tab in the Attribute Editor.

- Rename the node *sharedGrid*.

This node will be shared by other textures later.

- Increase the **Repeat UV** to **8** and **24**.

This changes the number of grid squares across the entire surface.

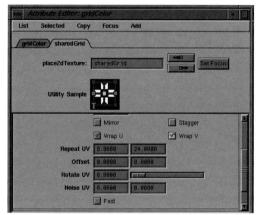

Attributes of the texture placement

5 Set your Render Globals

Even if you are able to display the scene with hardware texturing, the quality of the texture does not display very well on the surfaces. It is necessary to create a software rendering of the surfaces in order to evaluate the tile pattern.

- In the **Render View** panel, select **Options** → **Render Globals...**
- Click the **Maya Software** tab.
- Open the **Anti-Alias Quality** section.
- Set the **Quality** to **Intermediate Quality**.

Notice that the anti-aliasing attributes change.

- Click the **Common** tab.
- Open the **Resolution** section.
- Set the **Presets** to **320x240**.

6 Test render the scene

- In the **Render View** panel, select **Render** → **Render** → **camera1**.
- Once the rendering is finished, press the **Keep Image** button.

This allows you to keep a series of renderings for comparison purposes so that you can watch the development of the shading group.

Test rendering of the color texture

Note: A scroll bar is placed at the bottom of the panel which you can use to scroll between the different test renderings. Renderings that are kept are not saved onto the hard drive and are only maintained while Maya is running.

Adding a bump map

A *bump map* is a special map type that lets you render a surface as if it has some surface relief. The areas of black, gray and white on the bump map create the effect of a raised surface when rendered.

Bump texture node —

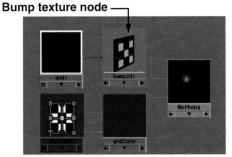

Hypershade view of the shading group

1 Map grid to bump node

A second grid texture is used to produce a bump map that will produce the appearance that the lines between the tiles are recessed. A second texture node is used so that the thickness of the lines can be different than the *gridColor*.

- In the Hypershade, double-click on the *tilesPhong* node.

- Click on the **Map** button next to **Bump Mapping**.

- In the **Textures** section of the **Create Render Node** window, turn **With New Texture Placement** to **Off**.

- From the 2D texture section, select **Grid**.

  In the Hypergraph, if you press **Input and Output Connections**, you will see a *bump2d* node is placed between the texture and material nodes, but no texture placement node is produced.

2 Set bump and texture attributes

The depth of the bump is set in the bump node, and the areas that are to be recessed are set in the grid texture node. Any color that is used in the texture will be ignored, because the bump map only deals with the grayscale or *alpha channel* values.

- In the **Attribute Editor** for the *bump2d* node, set the following:

  Bump Depth to **-0.2**.

  The dark areas of the texture will appear slightly recessed.

- Click on the new *grid* tab to bring this node forward and set the following:

  Name to *gridBump;*

  Line Color to black;

  Filler Color to white;

  U Width and **V Width** to **0.025**.

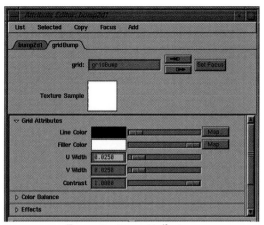

Bump texture attributes

- Next open the **Effects** section and set the following:

    Filter to **0.5**.

    This blurs the texture less than the default setting of 1.0. For most textures, you will generally want a lower filter setting.

Tip: The line thickness for the bump map is set to be thicker than the color texture so that the bump will occur within the tile color instead of the fill color.

---

3 Share the texture placement node

Because the color map and bump map need to be positioned identically on the surface, the same texture placement node for the color map will be used for the grid map.

- With the middle mouse button, click-drag the *sharedGrid* swatch onto the *gridBump* swatch. From the pop-up window select **Default**.

The 2D texture placement node for the first grid is connected to the second grid.

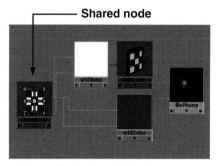

Hypershade view of shading group

Tip: You could use separate texture placement nodes but you would have to make sure that they both had identical attribute settings. Using the one node simplifies changes that you could make to the number of tiles on the surface.

---

4 Test render the scene

To see the effect of the bump map, the scene must be rendered.

- Dolly into the Perspective view to get closer to the tiles.

- In the **Render View** panel, select **Render → Redo Previous Render**.

- Once the rendering is finished, use the scroll bars at the bottom of the panel to compare this rendering with the previous one.

    If the view or lighting conditions have not been modified, it is easy to evaluate the material before and after the change.

- Press the **Keep Image** button to keep this rendering.

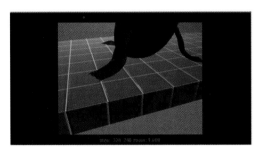

Rendering of bump texture

Note: If you do not select to keep the latest rendering, it will be replaced the next time the scene is rendered.

Refining the floor material

You will now reassign the bump map as a specularity map. You will then preview the results using a *raytrace* rendering. Raytracing lets you see reflections and refractions.

1 Connect node to shading group

You will now connect the *gridBump* node to the material node as a specularity map. This texture can now play two roles.

- In the Hypershade, click-drag with middle mouse button the *gridBump* swatch onto *tilePhong*.
- Select **Specular Color** from the pop-up menu.

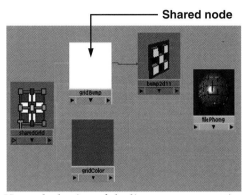

Shared node

Hypershade view of shading group connections

2 Test render the scene

In order to see the subtleties of the bump texture and added effects of the shading group, you can produce a test rendering that uses raytracing.

- From the Render View panel, select **Options → Render Globals...**
- Select the **Maya Software** tab.
- Open the **Raytracing Quality** section and set the following:

  Raytracing to **On**;

  Reflections to **1**;

  Refractions to **1**;

  These settings only allow 1 level of reflections, and refractions. This will keep rendering times faster for your tests.

- In the Render View panel, select **Render → Redo Previous Render**.

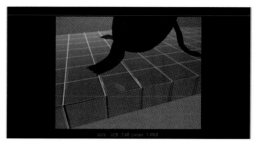

Rendered floor with raytracing

The water material

The water is going to be textured using a color texture that is also mapped as a displacement map. This means that the surface will raise and lower based on the value of the map texture. Compared to bump mapping, a displacement map is slower but achieves more realistic results.

1   Create and assign a Blinn material

- **Create** a new **Blinn** material node.
- Rename the node *waterBlinn.*
- Assign *waterBlinn* to the *water* surface.

2   Edit transparency, specular and raytrace attributes

- Open the *waterBlinn* node in the Attribute Editor and set the following:

  Transparency to about **0.3.**

Tip: Open the color swatch and set **Value** to about **0.3.**

In the **Specular Shading** section:

  Eccentricity to about **0.06;**

  Specular Roll Off to over **0.9;**

  Specular Color Value to **0.7;**

  Reflectivity to **0.4.**

- In the **Raytrace Options** section:

  Refractions to **On;**

  Refractive Index to **1.33;**

  Refraction Limit to **1;**

  Reflection Limit to **1.**

3   Create a water color map

- In the Hypershade, select **Create → Create Render Node...**
- In the **Textures** section of the Create Render Node window, turn on **With New Texture Placement.**
- In the 2D texture section click on the **Water** texture.
- Rename this node *waterColor.*
- In the **Water Attributes** section of the Attribute Editor, set the following:

  Number of Waves to **20;**

  Wave Amplitude to **0.075;**

  Smoothness to **1.0.**

- In the **Color Balance** section, set:

  Color Gain to a bright turquoise-blue;

  Color Offset to a dark saturated blue;

4   Connect the map to the material

- Using the Hypershade, click-drag with middle mouse button the *waterColor* texture node onto the

PROJECT FIVE

waterBlinn material node. Select
Color from the pop-up menu.

5 Create a displacement node

- Click **Input and Output Connections**
  in the Hypershade.

- Open the *BlinnSG* node's Attribute
  Editor.

- Rename this node to *waterSG*.

- Drag the *waterColor* texture node
  onto the **Displacement Material**
  attribute.

Displacement in shading group

- View the shading group in the
  Hypershade.

  Notice that the shared texture node
  is connected to the material node
  and to a new displacement shader
  node. This node is similar to a
  bump node except that it connects
  directly to the shading group node
  and not to the material node.

Note:	A displacement map moves the actual geometry when rendering, whereas a bump map only gives the rendered appearance of bumps in the material surface.

6 Animate the waves

Since texture nodes are just like other
nodes in Maya, their attributes can be
keyed. You are now going to key some of
the wave attributes so that the water
moves during the animation.

- Set the Time slider to frame **1**.

- Open the *waterColor* node's
  Attribute Editor.

- With the right mouse button, click
  and hold on the **Wave Time**
  attribute.

- From the pop-up menu select **Set
  Key**.

Setting a key on a texture node attribute

- Change the **Wave Frequency** to **5.0**.

- Select **Set Key** from the pop-up
  menu for the **Wave Frequency**
  attribute.

  The attribute fields are colored to
  indicate that keys have been set for
  these attributes.

- Change the current frame to the last
  frame of the animation.

- Change the **Wave Time** to **2**.
- Select **Set Key**.
- Change the **Wave Frequency** to **6.0**.
- Select **Set Key**.

7 Change the direction of the waves

- Open the texture placement node for the *waterColor* node from the Hypershade and set the following:

   Rotate Frame to **90**.

8 Test render the water material

- Go to first frame button in the Time slider.

   This should pop your camera back to its initial position.

- In the Render View panel, select **Render → Render → Camera1**.

Raytraced rendering of the water

LAYERED TEXTURES

A unique material node type in Maya is the *layered texture node*. This material node lets you layer texture nodes together to create more sophisticated effects. After layering a number of textures together you can then map the final layered texture into any channel on a material node.

The back wall material

The back wall is going to be designed to look like a peeling plaster wall revealing a wood surface below. To achieve this you will create two separate textures and then layer them into one node which will then be assigned to the back wall surface.

1 Create the first layer of the texture

You will first create the background layer of the texture that will make up the peeling painted wall background behind Salty.

- Create a **Marble** and a **Wood** 3D texture in the Hypershade.

- Rename the Marble texture *paintedWall*.

- Open the Attribute Editor for the *paintedWall* texture.

- With the **MMB**, drag the *Wood* texture onto the **Vein Color** attribute of *paintedWall*.

   This texture will act as your background wall.

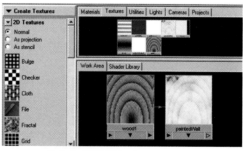

Painted Wall texture

2 Create the second layer of the texture

You will now create a separate file texture node containing the WaterWorld logo. In this case you will use a file texture with an embedded alpha channel which will be used to stencil out the lettering on the logo.

- In the Hypershade create a **File texture** node.
- **Rename** this node *logo*.
- Assign the image called *logoMap* found in your *sourceimages* directory.

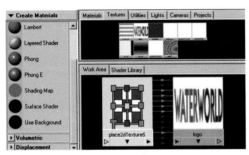

Logo node

3 Layer the separate textures into one node

You will now take your two separate textures and layer them into one using the layered texture node.

- In the Hypershade, create a **Layered Texture** node. You can find it by scrolling to the bottom of the Create Textures section.
- Open the Attribute Editor for the Layered texture.
- From the Work area, **MMB** drag the *logo* node from the Hypershade, next to the green swatch in the Attribute Editor.
- From the Work area of the Hypershade **MMB** drag the *paintedWall* texture next to the *logo* node in the Attribute Editor.

- Click on the **x** below the green swatch to delete it.

Note: If you examine the connections made in the Hypershade, you will see that there are two connections between the file texture and the layered texture. One is for the color channel while the other connects the alpha channel to the alpha attribute of the layered texture.

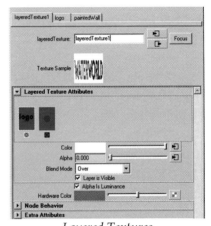

Layered Textures

4 Create a Lambert material

You are now ready to connect your layered texture into the color channel of a material node which will then be assigned to the back wall surface.

- In the Hypershade create a **Lambert** material. Rename this node to *backWallM*.
- With the **MMB**, drag the layered texture node onto the *backWallM* material.
- From the pop-up option menu, select **Color**.

- Assign *backWallM* to the back wall surface.
- Open the Render View window and create an IPR render of the scene.

You should now see the rendered WaterWorld logo placed on top of the *paintedWall* material.

Rendered Back Wall

Depending on the way the surface was built, the logo on the back wall may be rotated, inverted or upside down. If this is the case proceed to **step 5** below. If the logo is properly positioned skip to **step 6**.

Note:	If you find you get an error when rendering in IPR view, open the Render Globals and turn off Raytracing.

5 Adjust surface direction if necessary

The reason for an incorrectly placed logo is because the UVs of the surface are facing the wrong direction. You will need to adjust the direction of the UVs.

- Select the back wall surface.
- Select **Display** → **NURBS Components** → **Surface Origins**.

This will display the surface origin of the back wall with the direction of the U,V, and the normal coordinates. To have the logo placed correctly you will want the origin to be in the lower left corner.

- Select **Edit NURBS** → **Reverse Surface Direction** - ❑. Set the options to achieve the origin placed as shown in the figure below:

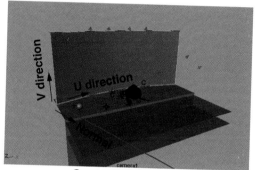

Correct UV direction

Note:	If after correcting the surface direction, your logo is still not properly aligned you may need to adjust the **Rotate UV** attribute found in the *place2Dtexture* node of the *logo*.

6 Position the image

- Open the Attribute Editor for the 2D placement node for the *logo* node. Click on **Interactive Placement**.

The wall is outlined with a red interactive placement manipulator.

- In the side panel, using the middle mouse button, click-drag the sides of the manipulator until the texture is positioned as shown:

PROJECT FIVE

Logo texture positioned

The IPR window will render the update to the *logo* texture placement. However you will notice that the area outside of the actual file placement is greyed out. This is because the *Default Color* value of the logo node is adding a grey value to the overall texture.

- In the Attribute Editor, select the *logo* tab. Open the Color Balance section and set the **Default Color** to **Black**.

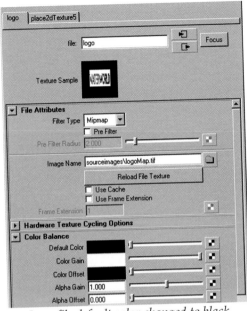

Logo file default color changed to black

7 Tweak the look of the final texture in the IPR window

By using IPR you can interactively manipulate the texture attributes or 3D placement nodes to create the final look of the background wall.

- **Click-drag** over an area of the background wall in the IPR window.

- Open the Attribute Editor for *paintedWall*. Experiment with different settings for *Vein Width*, *Diffusion* and *Contrast*.

- In the Hypershade, select the *paintedWall* node's *place3Dtexture* node. Click on the **Interactive Placement** button.

A combined move, scale and rotate manipulator is displayed in the view panel.

- In the perspective view, experiment with the scale, rotate, and move of the manipulator.

- Continue experimenting with different values for the *wood* and *paintedWall* texture while viewing the results in the IPR window until you are satisfied with the results.

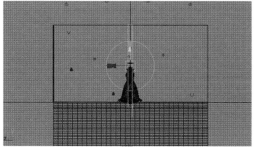

3D placement node for paintedWall

Final background wall material

Tip: You can also scale, rotate and move the placement icon for the marble texture to fine tune the look and position of the peeling paint.

8 Save your work

REFINING THE LIGHTING

To refine the lighting in the scene, you will add a new light that represents light reflecting off of the deck and then you will add shadows to some of the other lights.

Adding reflected lighting

The light in a computer generated scene cannot reflect off surfaces. You can see the reflection of images but light serves only to illuminate the scene.

To simulate the reflection of light off of the water, you will use a new light, then map the animated water texture to the light's color.

1 Add a new spot light

- Select **Create → Lights → Spot Light**.

- Position the light so that it is looking up at the seal from just below the surface of the water.

  Use *look through selected* to verify the position. The spot radius should cover the seal and the ball at its highest point.

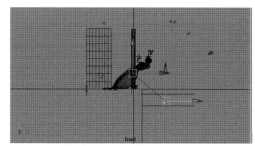

Spot light view looking up at Salty

2 Add water map as filter to light

- Open the attributes for the new spot light.

- Drag the *waterColor* texture swatch from the Hypershade onto the **Color** attribute.

  The animated texture node is now connected to the spot light and will be projected up onto Salty.

- Set the **Intensity** to **0.5**.

3 Link light to seal and ball

Since this light is not needed on all of the surfaces, you are going to link it to the ball and Salty. This will later make your rendering more efficient because this light is only rendered in relation to the linked shading groups.

- In the Attribute Editor, click on the **Illuminates by Default** button to turn it **Off**.

  The light is no longer linked to any of the objects, and must be specifically linked to the objects that you want the light to shine on.

- Select all of Salty's surfaces and the ball's surface.

- **Shift-Select** the new spotlight.

- Select **Lighting/Shading → Make Light Links**.

Lights linked to shaders

Turning on shadows

To achieve realistic lighting, shadows become very important. At the same time, they take longer to render and, therefore, must be set with caution. By default, lights do not cast shadows. You can then turn shadows on for lights that are key to the scene.

For Salty, you will use the three main lights for casting shadows while the other lights are used only for illumination.

1 Turn shadows on for the lights

You will use depth map shadows for the three main lights. This shadow type is fast and offers a soft look.

- Select the three colored spot lights.

- In the Channel box, set the **Depth Map Shadows** to **On**.

- Test render the scene.

Rendering with depth map shadows

You will notice that the lights are casting colored shadows. This is a natural phenomenon that is mimicked by colored lights in Maya.

You may want to leave these different shadows or edit the way the scene is lit to achieve a different result. If you increase the value setting for the three lights, then their color will be less prominent and the shadows will be darker.

You could also choose to only cast shadows from the light that produces the best shadow. In this case, the green light is producing the strongest shadow. Another option would be to change the color of the tiled deck which also affects the look of the shadow.

These are the kinds of decisions you need to make during the test rendering of a scene. You'll find that you will have to evaluate the look of the rendering, and tweak and adjust your settings until you are happy with the results.

2 Save your work

RENDERING

You are now going to batch render the scene. Rendering an animation offers you the chance to see the fruits of your labor. Before proceeding, you should prepare your surfaces and set the Render Globals.

Preparing the surfaces

To render as quickly as possible with the best quality possible, you should look at how to subdivide your polygonal and NURBS surfaces.

1 Reduce the polygon subdivisions

- **Select** the deck surface.

- Click on the *polyPlane* input node, and set the following:

    Subdivisions Width to **1**;

    Subdivisions Height to **1**.

    The higher settings made it possible to preview the lighting on the surface; however, rendering only one subdivision in each direction is better because less geometry will render faster.

- Repeat the same edit for the input nodes of the other polygonal surfaces.

2 Set the NURBS tessellation

You should now set the tessellation for your NURBS surfaces.

Tessellation is the method by which your NURBS surfaces are broken down, or subdivided, into triangles for rendering. If you use a higher tessellation, the results are better but the rendering is slower.

Maya offers you a *Best Guess* option that lets the renderer choose the appropriate tessellation.

- **Select** the surfaces that make up Salty, the ball surface and the back wall.

- Select **Window** → **General Editors** → **Attribute Spread Sheet...**

- Click on the tabs at the far right and choose **Tessellation** from the pop-up.

- Under the **Mode U** column, click-drag over all the entries.

  By selecting all of this column, you can edit one value to update them all.

- Type **4** to enter the mode option then press the **Enter** key.

  This value sets the tessellation to **Best Guess Based on Screen Size**. This means that the renderer will tessellate your scene based on the size that the object fills the screen. This offers you an optimized tessellation solution.

- Repeat for the *Mode V* column.

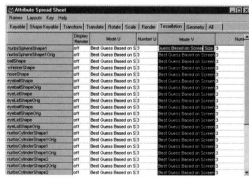

Attribute Spread Sheet window

Note:	The number 4 represents the fourth option if you were to look up Mode U in the tessellation control section of the Attribute Editor.

Setting the Render Globals

You have already used the Render Globals window to set up some test renderings. This window is where you make your final decisions before sending a rendered animation off to the batch renderer.

1 Open the Render Globals window

- Select **Window** → **Rendering Editors** → **Render Globals...**

2 Set the Camera's render status

- In the **Image File Output** section set **Camera** to **camera1**.

- Make sure **Channels** to **RGB Channel (Color)** is set to **On**.

- Turn **Off** the **Alpha Channel**.

  These settings mean that this camera will be considered by the renderer. If you were compositing, you might also turn on the mask layer but, for now, only the image is required.

3 Turn on animation and motion blur

  By default, the Render Globals are set up to render the current frame. If you want to render an animation, then you have to turn animation on.

- Set **Frame/Animation Ext** to the following:

  name.ext.# for **IRIX;**

  name.#.ext for **Windows, Mac**

- Set the following:

  Start frame to **1;**

  End frame to **450.**

4 Set the quality

- Under the **Maya Software** tab, click on the **Anti-alias Quality** section.

- Set **Quality** to **Production Quality**.

5 Set the size

- In the Resolution Section, set **Resolution** to **320x240.**

6 Turn on motion blur

- In the Motion Blur section, click turn **Motion Blur** to **On.**

- Set **Motion Blur Type** to **2D.**

7 Save your work

- Select **File** → **Save Scene As**... Enter the name *Salty6* and press **Save**.

8 Batch render the scene

- Select **Render** → **Batch Render.**

Look at the Feedback line in the lower right to follow the rendering progress.

Tip: At this point, you could exit Maya and the rendering would continue. This is because the renderer is a separate application. If you do this, then you will lose the feedback on the renderings

progress but you will free up RAM for the renderer. You can then use *fcheck* to check the progress of each frame.

---

9 Preview a frame

- Select **Render** → **Show Batch Render.**

This shows you the progress on the frame being rendered right now.

10 Preview the animation

Once you have completed the animation, you can use Playblast or *fcheck* to view the movie.

Conclusion

Congratulations, you now have a fully animated and articulated character. You have learned how to work with a wide range of Maya's feature set in an integrated project.

In the last lesson, you will explore Maya's scripting language, MEL as you set up custom controls for blinking Salty's eyes.

25 Blinking using MEL

In this lesson, you will set keys on the blink attribute that you created on the *eyeControl* node in Lesson 21. To help with this task, you will create a MEL (Maya Embedded Language) script that will help you animate the blink.

MEL is a powerful scripting language that can be used by both technical directors and animators to add to what Maya can do. Animators will be able to take advantage of simple *macro-like* scripts to enhance their workflows, while technical directors can use more advanced MEL commands to rig up characters, add special visual effects, or set up customized controls.

If you know nothing about programming and scripts, this lesson will, at first, seem foreign to your world of graphics and animation. While you can certainly be successful with Maya without relying on the use of MEL, this lesson offers a good chance to get your feet wet and see the possibilities. If you do learn how to use MEL, you will be quite surprised how a simple script can be used to enhance your work.

In this lesson you will learn the following:

- How to recognize and enter MEL commands
- How to create a MEL script procedure
- How to use this procedure within Maya's existing UI
- How to build a custom UI element for the procedure
- How to animate Salty's blinking using the procedure

Starting a new file

Rather than working in the Salty scene file, you will practice using MEL in a new file. Once your scripts have been written and saved, you will return to the Salty scene and use the custom user interface tools in context.

1 Start a new file

- Select **File** → **New Scene**.
- Set up a single Perspective view panel.
- Make sure that the Command line, the Help line and the Channel box are all visible.

WHAT IS MEL?

MEL stands for Maya Embedded Language. MEL is built on top of Maya's base architecture and is used to execute commands that you use to build scenes and create user interface elements. In fact, every time you click on a tool, you are executing one or more MEL commands.

Typing commands

A MEL command is a text string that tells Maya to complete a particular action. As a user, it is possible to skip the graphical user interface and use these commands directly. Generally, animators will choose the user interface instead – but it is still a good idea to know what MEL can do at a command level.

The Command line

You will now use Maya's Command line to create and edit some primitive objects. The goal at this point is to explore how simple commands work.

1 Create a cone using the Command line

- Click in the Command line or press the ` key to set your *focus*.

  The Command line can be found at the bottom left, just above the Help line.

- Enter the following:

Entering a MEL command

- After you finish, press the **Enter** key on the numeric keypad section of your keyboard.

Tip: The keyboard has two **Enter** keys that each work a little differently with the Command line. The **Enter** key associated with the numeric keypad will keep your focus on the Command line, while the **Enter** key associated with the alpha-numeric keyboard switches your focus back to the view panels.

---

2 Rotate and move the cone with commands

The next step is to transform the cone using MEL commands.

- Enter the following:

```
rotate 0 0 90 < Enter >
move 5 0 0 < Enter >
```

You now have a cone sitting on the ground surface, five units along the X-axis. You entered the commands by first entering the command then adding the desired values.

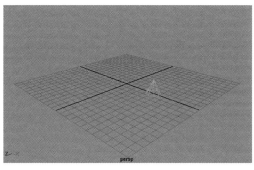

Perspective view of cone

3 Rename the cone

You can also rename objects from the command line.

- Enter the following:

```
rename "nurbsCone1" myCone < Enter >
```

You can look in the Channel box to confirm that the object has been renamed.

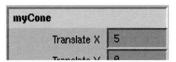

Channel box with cone's name

4 Execute two commands at once

If you quickly want to enter more than one command without pressing the enter key along the way, then you can place a semicolon between the commands.

- Enter the following:

  sphere; move 0 0 6; scale 4 1 1 **< Enter >**

  Using the semi-colon(;), you executed three commands in a row. First, you created a sphere, then you moved it, then you scaled it. The semi-colon will become important later when you write scripts.

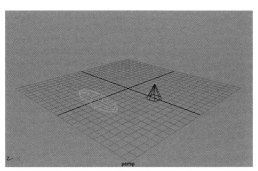

Perspective view of new sphere

5 Execute a command on an unselected object

If you want to execute a command on an object that is not selected, then you simply have to add the name of the node that you want to affect. The node will follow the command without requiring the cone to be selected.

- Enter the following:

  move -5 0 0 mycone **< Enter >**

Oops! You get an error message saying that Maya cannot find the `mycone` object. This is because the object name has a capital C for the word 'Cone'. MEL is case sensitive which means you should be especially aware of how you spell and capitalize any names or commands.

- Enter the following:

  move -5 0 0 myCone **< Enter >**

  `scale 5 1 1 myCone` **< Enter >**

Always remember the importance of getting the spelling of commands correct. Later, when you write scripts, this spelling will be very important.

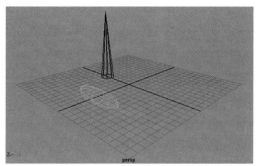

Perspective view of edited cone

6 Use command flags

Another important MEL capability is the command flag. You can use these flags to be more specific about how you want the commands to be executed. The command flags can have short or long names. Flags are indicated with a hyphen in your script. Shown below are examples of both kinds of flags.

- Enter the following using long names for flags:

  cylinder -name bar -axis 0 1 0 -pivot 0 0 -3 **< Enter >**

- Enter the following using short names for flags:

  cylinder -n bar2 -ax 0 1 0 -p 0 0 -6 -hr 10 **< Enter >**

PROJECT FIVE

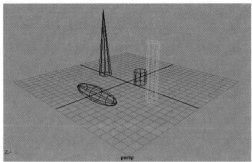

Perspective view of cylinders

The short flag names represent the following:

`-n` name

`-ax` axis

`-p` pivot

`-hr` height ratio

Tip: You will notice that long flag names can create a command that is easy to read but hard to type in – the short names are harder to decipher but easy to type. Generally, entering in the command line is a good place for short flags while long flags should be used in scripts to aid in readability.

---

7 Delete all objects

- Enter the following:

    ```
    select -all; delete  < Enter >
    ```

The Script Editor window

You may have noticed that the Command line is a small space to work in and only one line of feedback. The Script Editor is a special user interface element that will make entering commands easier.

Up until now, you have been entering random commands in order to learn a little about their syntax and how they work. You will now use the script editor to build a sphere and a locator which will mimic the *eyeLid/eyeControl* relationship that you set in Lesson 21. The ultimate goal is to set up a blink attribute that will control the blinking of the eyelid.

1 Open the Script Editor window

- Click on the Script Editor button in the lower right of the workspace or select **Window** → **General Editors** → **Script Editor**.

  The window opens to show all of the commands you just entered.

- From the Script Editor, select **Edit** → **Clear History**.

2 Create a primitive sphere using the Primitives menu

In the earlier lessons, you have been using MEL without having to type a single command. Most Maya tools and windows have been designed and implemented using MEL.

- Select **Create** → **NURBS Primitives**→ **Sphere**.

  In the Script Editor, you can see the MEL command that was used to create the sphere. Also included are the flags with default settings presented in their short form.

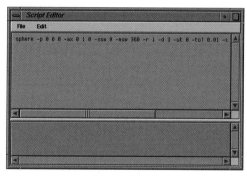

Script Editor

- In the lower portion of the Script Editor, type the following:

  ```
  delete
  ```

- Press the numeric keypad **Enter** key to execute the command.

Tip: In the Script Editor, the numeric keypad's **Enter** key executes an action while the alpha-numeric keypad's **Enter** key returns to the next line.

PROJECT FIVE

3 Copy and edit the sphere commands

Now that the sphere command is in the Script Editor's history, you can use this command as a start point to write your own command.

- In the Script Editor, select the parts of the Command line up to the `-r 1` flag.

- Copy the text into the lower portion of the script editor.

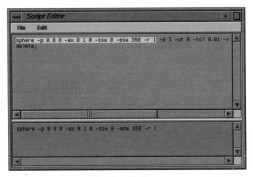

Script Editor

- Edit the first part of the command to read as follows:

```
sphere -name eyeLid -p 0 0 0 -ax 0 0 1 -ssw 60 -esw
300 -r 2
```

Edited commands

- Press the **Enter** key on your numeric keypad.

4 Create a locator

- Select **Create**→ **Locator**.

  In the Script Editor, you will see a corresponding MEL command.

- Enter undo to go back one step.

5 Echo all commands

- In the Script Editor, select **Script** → **Echo All Commands**.

- Select **Create** → **Locator**.

  In the Script Editor, you can now see a MEL command that you can use to create a locator – `createPrimitive nullObject;`

Note: This command is surrounded by other commands that belong to Maya. You only need to focus on the locator command.

- In the Script Editor, select **Script** → **Echo All Commands** to turn this option off.

6 Rename and move the locator

You will now name the locator as *eyeControl*. This object will be used as a substitute for the control node you built earlier in the Salty scene.

- Enter the following:

```
rename "locator1" eyeControl;
move 10 0 0 eyeControl < Enter >
```

7 Add an attribute to the locator

You will now add a blink attribute. This command is the same as using **Modify** → **Add Attribute** from the UI.

- Enter the following:

```
addAttr -ln blink -at "float"
-min 0 -max 10 -dv 10 eyeControl < Enter >
```

The short flag names represent the following;

  `-ln` long name of the new attribute

  `-at` attribute type

  `-min/max` minimum/maximum values for the attribute

  `-dv` default value for the attribute

8 Make the attribute keyable on the blink attribute

- Enter the following:

```
setAttr -keyable true eyeControl.blink < Enter >
```

9 Set up your Perspective view panel

- Set up your view panel so that you can see the eyelid object and the locator.
- Select the eyelid and press **3** to increase the smoothness and **5** to turn on hardware shading.
- Select **Display** → **Grid** to turn off the grid.

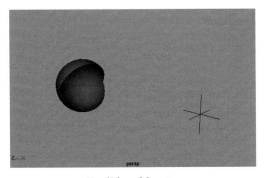

Eyelid and locator

Learning more about commands

You now know how to use a few of the many Maya commands. To learn more about the commands, refer to the online documentation where you will find a complete list of all the commands available in MEL. Each command is listed with descriptions of the various flags.

Expressions

When you write an expression in the Expression Editor, it can be written as a MEL script. You can also use MEL to create the expressions from within the Script Editor.

You will create two expressions to control the *start* and *endSweep* of the eyeLid's *makeNurbSphere* input node. In Lesson 21, you used Set Driven Key. Now you can compare the use of expressions to that earlier approach.

1 Add an expression to the eyelid's startSweep

This expression is designed to make sure that as the blink attribute goes from 0 to 10, the eyelid rotates 60 degrees. Therefore, the blink attribute is multiplied by 6.

- Enter the following:

```
expression -n toplid -o makeNurbSphere1
-s "ssw = eyeControl.blink * 6" < Enter >
```

2 Add an expression to the eyelid's endSweep

This expression is similar to the last one except now you want the eyelid to rotate from 360 to 300 degrees. Therefore the blink attribute is multiplied by 6 then subtracted from 360.

- Enter the following:

```
expression -n bottomlid -o makeNurbSphere1
-s "esw = (360 - eyeControl.blink * 6)" < Enter >
```

3 Test the blink attribute

- Enter the following:

```
setAttr "eyeControl.blink" 5 < Enter >
```

4 Set keys on the blink attribute

- Enter the following:

```
setKeyframe -at blink -t 1 -v 10 eyeControl;
setKeyframe -at blink -t 5 -v 0 eyeControl;
setKeyframe -at blink -t 10 -v 10 eyeControl < Enter >
```

The short flag names represent the following:

-at attribute that is being keyed

-t time at which you want the key set

-v value of the attribute that you want to key

- Play back the results.

PROJECT FIVE

Keys have been set at several frames with the eye opening and closing to match.

Building a blink procedure

You are now going to create a blink procedure that you will save as a MEL script. The next few steps outline all of the parts of the MEL script with some tips for how to enter it and how to execute it. At the end of this lesson, you will find the script without descriptive text. You can enter the script later, in case you want to read over this section first.

Writing the script

You will write the blink procedure not in the Script Editor but in a text editor. A text editor is an application that lets you quickly work with text then save in a generic text format.

1 Open a text editor

- Open a text editor such as *Notepad, WordPad or TextEdit*.

2 Type comments to create header information

Every script should start with a header that contains important information for other people who might read your script later. Below is an example header. The // that is placed in front of these lines indicate that these lines are comments and therefore will be ignored when you later execute the script.

- Type the following:

```
//
// Creation Date:    Today's date
// Author:           Your name here
//
// Description:
//      Learning Maya tutorial script
//      This script builds a procedure for animating
//      Salty the seal's eyeControl.blink attribute
//
```

Tip: Please don't underestimate the importance of commenting your scripts. Down the line, someone will need to read what you have done and the comments are much easier to follow than the actual script.

---

3 Declare the procedure

The first thing you will enter is designed to declare the procedure. This line loads the procedure into Maya's memory so that it can be executed later.

- Type the following:

```
global proc blink (float $blinkDelay){
```

This line defines a procedure named *blink*. The required argument is within the round brackets. This tells Maya what the script requires to execute. In this case, the length of the blink action is required. This is defined as a floating value called $blinkDelay. Because this value is not yet determined, it is known as a variable. The $ sign defines it as a variable. The open bracket – the { symbol – is added to the end of the declaration to let you start inputting MEL statements.

4 Set up variables

Within your script, you will use variables to represent values that may need to change later. At the beginning of the script, you need to set up the variables and set their value. In some cases, you may set their value with an actual number. But for this script, you will use attribute names and values instead.

- Type the following:

```
// Set up variables that will be used in the script

    string $blink = "eyeControl.blink";
    float $time = `currentTime -query`;
    float $blinkCurrent = `getAttr $blink`;
```

The first variable set defines *$blink* as the blink attribute found on the *eyeControl* node. The second variable queries Maya for the current time.

PROJECT FIVE

The third attribute gets the actual value of the *eyeControl.blink* at the queried time.

Note: The quotation marks for the float $time and float $blinkCurrent in the above lines use the ' quotation mark which is located to the left of the number 1 key on most keyboards.

---

5 Set keys on the blinking

Next, you want to set keys on the blink attribute at the beginning, middle and end of the blink. The length of the blink will be defined by the *blinkDelay* variable that was set out as the main argument of the procedure. Notice that, while other variables were set at the beginning of the script, the *blinkDelay* is used as an argument so that you can set it when the script is executed later. As you enter the keyframe commands, notice how you use the normal setup of command/flag/node name.

- Type the following:

```
// set key for the blink attribute
// at the current time

   setKeyframe -value $blinkCurrent
        -time $time
        -attribute $blink
        $blink;


// set key for a blink of 0
// half way through the blink

   setKeyframe -value 0
        -time ($time + $blinkDelay/2)
        -attribute $blink
        $blink;


// set key for the original blink value
// at the end of the blink
```

```
setKeyframe -value $blinkCurrent
      -time ($time + $blinkDelay)
      -attribute $blink
      $blink;


}
```

In this part of the script, you have set keys using the *setKeyframe* command. The keys set at the beginning and end of the blink use the queried value of the blink attribute, while the key set in the middle uses a value of zero. At the end, a closed bracket – the } symbol – is used to declare the statement complete.

6 Save your script

You can now save your script into your Maya scripts directory. This will make sure that the procedure is easily available within Maya any time you need it.

- In your text editor, save the script using the following path:

```
\[drive]:\maya\scripts\blink.mel
```

Note: Because the procedure is named *blink*, it is important to save the file as *blink.mel*. This helps make it easier for Maya to find the function.

7 Testing the script

Because you named the file *blink.mel* and placed it in your *maya/scripts* directory, you can execute the command in Maya without having to load the script. If you enter `blink` with a value for the blink delay, then Maya will look in the scripts directory for a procedure called *blink.mel*.

- Set the **Time slider** to frame **40**.
- Enter the following:

```
blink 10 < Enter >
```

- Scrub in the Time slider to test the results.

If this works, then you can congratulate yourself on completing your first MEL script and you can move on to the next section.

If it doesn't, then you typed something incorrectly and MEL is finding your mistake.

8 Debugging your script

To debug your script, you need to find out which line is causing the error, and then you need to go back and check your spelling and syntax. Did you use the correct symbols? Did you name your nodes correctly? Is your capitalization correct? These and similar questions are what you need to ask yourself.

- To display line numbers in the Script Editor, select **Script** → **Show Line Numbers.**

Adding the function to the UI

Now that you have created your own function, you will want to have easy access to it. Below are three methods for adding your function to the default UI, which you can easily set up using interactive methods.

1 Creating a shelf button

- In the Script Editor, select the text `blink 10`.
- Click on the selected text with the middle mouse button and drag up to the shelf.

  It is placed on the shelf with a MEL icon. You can now move the Time slider to a new position and test it. You could also drag up different *blinkDelay* settings to offer different blink settings. Or you could set up a marking menu as outlined below.

2 Creating a blink marking menu set

- Select **Window** → **Settings/Preferences** → **Marking Menus...**
- Click on the **Create Marking Menu** button.
- Click on the top middle square with your right mouse button and select **Edit Menu item...** from the pop-up menu.
- In the Edit North window, type *Blink 10* in the **Label** field.
- In the **Command(s):** field, type `blink 10`.
- Click **Save** and **Close**.
- Repeat for the other quadrants to set up blink commands that use a *blinkDelay* of 20, 30 and 40.

- In the **Menu Name** field, enter: `blinking`.
- Click the **Save** button, then **Close**.

3 Prepare the blink marking menu for a hotkey

The blink marking menu now needs to be set up.

- In the marking menu customize window, set the following:

   Use Marking Menu in to **Hotkey Editor.**

   Now the marking menu can be set up in the Hotkey Editor so that it can be evoked using a hotkey.

- Click the **Apply Settings** button then **Close**.

4 Assign the blink marking menu to a hotkey

- Select **Window** → **Settings/Preferences** → **Hotkeys...** and set:
- Scroll to the bottom of the Categories list and click on the **User Marking Menus.** In the Commands window, click on the **blinking_Press** listing.
- In the **Assign New HotKey** section, set the following;

   Key to **F6**;

   Direction to **Press**.

Note: Use the pulldown menu next to the key field when assigning a function key as a HotKey.

A message will appear stating whether or not a particular key has been assigned or not. In this case F6 is not assigned.

- Press the **Assign** key.

   A message should appear stating that the hotkey will not work properly unless the release is also set. Maya will ask if you want the release key set for you.

- Click **Yes**.
- Click on **Save** in the Hotkey Editor Window and then **Close**.

5 Use the new marking menu

- Go to frame **80**.
- Press and hold **F6**, **LMB** click, then pick one of the blinking options from the marking menu.

PROJECT FIVE

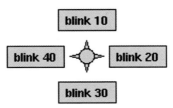

Blink marking menu

Building a custom UI script

In the next section, you will write a second script that will build a custom user interface window that includes a slider for the *blinkDelay* variable and a button that executes the blink procedure you scripted earlier. In Maya, you have the ability to use MEL to build custom user interface elements.

Custom user interface window

1 Start a new text file

2 Adding the opening comments

Start the script with a commented header that helps others read your work. While this was taught earlier, it can never be emphasized enough.

- Type the following:

```
//
// Creation Date:    Today's date
// Author:           Your name here
//
// Description:
//      Learning Maya tutorial script
//      This script builds a custom user interface
//      for executing the blink procedure
//      and for setting the blink delay
```

```
//
```

3 Declare a get info procedure

You are now going to create a procedure called *blinkGetInfo* that will be
used to get the *blinkDelay* value from a slider, which you will build later
in the script. Since the value set in the slider is meant to be the chosen
value for the blink, this procedure queries the slider to set the
blinkDelay, and then adds that value next to the blink command.

- Type the following:

```
global proc blinkGetInfo() {

    // get necessary information from Maya

    float $blinkDelay = 'intSliderGrp
    -query -value
blinkWindow|columnLayout|delaySlider';

    blink $blinkDelay;

}
```

4 Declare a second user interface procedure

You are now going to declare a procedure that will build a floating
window. This window will look and act like any other window in Maya
but will be designed to help you put a blink to Salty's eyes.

- Type the following:
```
global proc blinkWindow() {
```

5 Remove any existing blink windows

As you start a user interface script, it is a good idea to check if the same
UI element already exists in the scene and, if so, then to delete it. This
makes sure that your new element is the only one recognized by Maya
at any one time.

- Type the following:

```
// clean up any existing blinkWindows
if ( (`window -ex blinkWindow`) == true ) deleteUI
blinkWindow;
```

6 Build the window called blinkWindow

The next part of the script is designed to build a window that is 400 pixels wide and 75 pixels tall. You will call it Blink Control in its title bar but Maya will know of it as *blinkWindow*.

- Type the following:

```
window
    -width 400
    -height 100
    -title "Blink Control"
blinkWindow;
```

7 Form a column layout

Within the window, you need to organize your user interface elements. One method of organization is a *columnLayout*. This sets up a column with a particular spacing in relation to the window.

- Type the following:

```
columnLayout
    -columnAttach "right" 5
    -rowSpacing 10
    -columnWidth 375
columnLayout;
```

8 Create a slider group

Within the layout, you want to build a slider that lets you set the *blinkDelay* value. MEL offers you preset *kits* using special group commands that build several UI types in one go. The *intSliderGrp* builds a slider along with a field for seeing the resulting value and for entering the value yourself. This slider is set to integer values since frames are generally set in whole numbers. The flags let you set the various values for the minimum and maximum settings of the slider.

- Type the following:

```
intSliderGrp
    -label "Blink Delay"
    -field true
    -minValue 2
    -maxValue 30
    -fieldMinValue 0
    -fieldMaxValue 100
    -value 10
delaySlider;
```

9 Create a button

The next part of the script builds a button that you will be used to execute the *blinkGetInfo* procedure, which in turn uses the *blinkDelay* value from the slider to execute the *blink* command. At the end, you will enter *setparent* to link the button to the *columnlayout*.

- Type the following:

```
button
    -label "Blink"
    -width 70
    -command "blinkGetInfo"
button;

    setParent ..;
```

10 Show the window

You are almost finished, except that you must tell Maya to show the window.

- Type the following:

```
showWindow blinkWindow;
```

11 Finish the script

Finally, you must complete the procedure then make one final declaration of the *blinkWindow* procedure name.

- Type the following:

```
}


blinkWindow;
```

12 Saving the script

You can now save your script into your Maya scripts directory.

- In your text editor, save the script using the following path:

```
\[drive]:\maya\scripts\blinkWindow.mel
```

13 Test your script

- In the Command line or the Script Editor, type the following:

```
blinkWindow < Enter >
```

The window should open. You can now set the Time slider to a new time, and then set the blink delay using the slider; pressing the button will key the blink.

Keyframing Salty's blink

Congratulations! You now have your own custom user interface element built and ready to go. You can now open your Salty file from the last lesson and use this script to make her blink. Note that this will only work if you named your `eyeControl` node correctly and created a `blink` attribute as taught.

THE SCRIPTS

Here are the two scripts listed in their entirety for you to review.

blink.mel

```
//
// Creation Date:    Today's date
// Author:           Your name here
//
// Description:
//       Learning Maya tutorial script
//       This script builds a procedure for animating
//       Salty the seal's eyeControl.blink attribute
//

global proc blink (float $blinkDelay){

// Set up variables that will be used in the script

    string $blink = "eyeControl.blink";
    float $time = `currentTime -query`;
    float $blinkCurrent = `getAttr $blink`;

// set keys for the blink attribute

    setKeyframe -value $blinkCurrent
        -time $time
        -attribute $blink
        $blink;

    setKeyframe -value 0
        -time ($time + $blinkDelay/2)
        -attribute $blink
        $blink;

    setKeyframe -value $blinkCurrent
        -time ($time + $blinkDelay)
```

PROJECT FIVE

```
              -attribute $blink
              $blink;


          }
```

blinkWindow.mel

```
      //
      //Creation Date:Today's date
      //Author:Your name here
      //
      //Description:Learning Maya tutorial script
      //      This script builds a custom user interface
      //      for executing the blink procedure
      //      and for setting the blink delay
      //

      global proc blinkGetInfo() {

            // get necessary information from Maya

            float $blinkDelay = `intSliderGrp
        -query -value blinkWindow|columnLayout|delaySlider`;

        blink $blinkDelay;


      }

      global proc blinkWindow() {
        if ( (`window -ex blinkWindow`) == true ) deleteUI
      blinkWindow;

        window
          -width 400
          -height 100
```

```
        -title "Blink Control"
    blinkWindow;

    columnLayout
        -columnAttach "right" 5
        -rowSpacing 10
        -columnWidth 375
    columnLayout;

    intSliderGrp
        -label "Blink Delay"
        -field true
          -minValue 2
        -maxValue 30
        -fieldMinValue 0 -fieldMaxValue 100
        -value 10
    delaySlider;

    button
        -label "Blink"
        -width 70
        -command "blinkGetInfo"
    button;

        setParent ..;

    showWindow blinkWindow;

}

blinkWindow;
```

PROJECT FIVE

NUMERICS

3D Paint 166

A

absolute values 96
action curves, see animation curves
Action Window, see Graph Editor
actions 103, 104
Add Attribute window 172, 416
aim constraints 408
alpha channel, see masks
anim curves, see animation curves
animation curves 117, 417
  breaking tangents 44
  cleaning up 44
  deleting static channels 44
  editing curve shapes 43, 417
  Graph Editor 87, 417, 445
  Hypergraph 117
  keys 45, 116
  motion 446
  smoothing 43
  static channels 44
  tangent handles 44, 445
  tangent weights 445
  tangents 43, 116, 348, 445, 446
  walk cycle 348
animation paths
  orientation markers 298
  position markers 298
animation tests 279, 280, 470
anti-aliasing 68
anticipation 443
Artisan Paint Textures 166
ASBD Window, see Hypergraph
attach
  curves 135
  surfaces 141
attach to path 191
Attribute Editor 32, 99, 113, 117
  connections 112
  effects 474
  light effects 291, 295
  nodes 112
  placement 286

  tabs 113
Attribute Spread Sheet 488
attributes 33
  Add Attribute window 416
  animating channels 116, 451
  animation curves 42
  Channel box 111
  connections 109, 114
  coordinate input 96
  Dependency graph 111
  Graph Editor 42
  grayscale channels 80
  keyable channels 113
  linked attributes 416
  nodes 468
  particles 300, 303
  procedural texture attributes 116
  reflectivity 403
  relationships 416
  scene hierarchy 111
  shading groups 403
  specularity 403
  spring attributes 454
  testing in view panel 417
  transform attributes 265
  transparency 424
  twist attributes 297
Auto Key, see keys

B

background images
  animating 278
  importing 278
  rendering 276
batch rendering 70, 82, 209, 305
bend deformer 50
bind skin 321, 392, 401
  bind pose 392, 402
  lattices 326
  soft 172
  testing 326
  to joints 321, 391
  to skeletons 311
binding surfaces, see bind skin
birail 242, 245
bones 391
bound surfaces, see bind skin

C

D

E

I

J

K

L

P

NOTES

NOTES

NOTES

NOTES

NOTES

Alias SketchBook PRO™

Express your visual ideas with Alias SketchBook Pro™, the first pen-driven application designed specifically for use with the Tablet PC and Wacom™ tablets. The high-quality pencils, pens, markers, paintbrushes and airbrushes feel and respond just like the real thing.

Easy to use, but brimming with a rich collection of tools, Alias SketchBook Pro is the perfect companion to Maya® as a front end to your 3D digital workflow.

Alias SketchBook Pro Features:
- Fast, high-quality, customizable brushes
- A user interface designed for artistic flow
- Canvas size up to 8,000 x 8,000 pixels
- A flexible layer system

Image courtesy of Dale Keown - Full Bleed Studios

To download a free trial version and for more information, visit:

www.aliassketchbook.com